A Classic Automobiles

for Profit and Capital Gain

BY Richard H. Rush

To Paul, Rodney, Nick and Nancy

---

10 9 8 7 6 5 4 3 2 1

Library of Congress Cataloging in Publication Data
Rush, Richard H.
    Investing in classic automobiles for profit and capital gain.

    Bibliography: p.
    Includes index.
    1. Automobiles—Collectors and collecting.
I. Title.
TL7.A1R875   1984   332.63   84-3862
ISBN 0-671-47324-7

All color photographs, unless otherwise credited, were taken by Julia Rush.

Contents

Automobiles: The Emerging Investment

IN AREAS OF investment, collector automobiles included, 1970 was "year one" of recent economic cycles. From the price level of that recession bottom year until the early 1980s, the value of almost every investment—from residential real estate to Impressionist paintings, from Tiffany lamps and Georgian silver to classic and antique cars—has risen dramatically. Here is how collector cars compare with some major categories of collectibles in degree of value appreciation:

Nineteenth- and twentieth-century paintings	Up to 12 times
Vintage wines	Up to 8½ times
Collector cars	*Up to 8¼ times*
English antique furniture	Up to 8 times
Tiffany lamps	Up to 7 times
Middle Eastern carpets	Up to 6 times
Drawings	Up to 5 times
American antique furniture	Up to 5 times
Jewelry	Up to 4 times
American folk art	Up to 4 times
American silver	Up to 3½ times

As can be seen, classic and antique cars multiplied in value during this period about 8¼ times. The car that sold for $1,000 in 1970 was worth about $7,000 in 1980 and $8,000 today. Of course, some cars increased much more in value, while some increased less; but many good buys are still available in antique and classic cars, and values are, in general, continuing their upward trend.

For example, in 1970, a Mercedes-Benz 300S cabriolet with chrome cabriole bars was offered for sale in Washington, D.C., for $1,900. The seller advertised the car in the local newspaper. He probably would have accepted an offer of somewhat less than $1,900. The car was in good mechanical condition. The chrome was good. There was no rust on the body. The paint was in fairly good condition and the leather upholstery was in fair shape. Overall, the car was in reasonably good condition. In precisely this condition the car would sell today for at least $50,000. In excellent condition it would sell for about $65,000, possibly more. In January 1982, a car of this make and model in fine condition sold at auction for $100,000, and another sold for $100,000 in 1983.

Automobile Values over Long Periods of Time

There is little point in indicating the rise in price of a car between 1909 and the present. That stretch is too long to represent an "investment period." An investor would grow old and probably die before he could realize the gain on his investment.

The period of from, say, 1940 to the present is also probably too long to be considered an investment period from the point of view of most people. Still, there are those who bought cars as investments in that early period and are still buying for investment in the 1980s. Even a person on a modest salary, such as this writer on his annual salary of $1,620 in 1938, had the chance and the funds to collect enough cars to have realized a fortune by the 1980s.

In 1938, I bought a Mercedes-Benz SS touring car for $550, about market value at that time for such a car in reasonably good condition. The clutch and brakes were gone, however, but were replaced by an expert for a total cost of $50, so my total investment in the car was $600. In early 1979, Christie's held a car auction in California where an absolutely comparable Mercedes-Benz SS brought $320,000.

In the era before World War II there were many fish that got away. One of the most notable I can remember was a Duesenberg SJ supercharged convertible coupe in mint condition owned by a racing driver. The asking price was $750. Today the car would bring about $300,000 or a little more.

Another significant car offered in 1941 was a Bugatti Royale cabriolet— for $600. There were no more than seven of these enormous Bugatti cars ever built. Today this car would bring over $2,000,000. But at that time it was unwanted and was to be broken up! Tastes change.

What About the Investment Outlook Today?

Good buys are still available. Classic and antique cars are still not "investment media" for strict investors or investment funds. A great amount of publicity accompanied the cooperative agreement between Sotheby Parke Bernet, the big auction house, and Citibank, in which the Citibank trust department became interested in investing some portion of the trust funds it administers in art—with the cooperation of Sotheby Parke Bernet. So far as I have been able to ascertain, few or no trust funds are presently being invested in antique and classic cars. Nor do strict "collectible investors" seem to be putting much money into cars. For that reason, prices for most cars have not been driven up as have prices of Impressionist paintings, Tiffany lamps, and Paul de Lamerie Georgian silver.

There is still no organized marketplace other than auctions for classic and antique cars, so prices are below what they might otherwise be. Art gravitates more and more to the big auction houses, where few car sales are held. Sotheby Parke Bernet handles practically no cars at auction. Phillips has handled a few car auctions with success. Only Christie's in England has been a major international auction outlet for cars. There are, however, special auctions for cars, and we will discuss those in this book.

There are practically no large and important dealers in cars comparable to Wildenstein or Newhouse in paintings. Thus there are a limited number of dealers from whom car investors can buy—and prices are lower than they would be with a well-organized dealer setup.

The individual who wants to sell his classic or antique car often sells at a very "reasonable" price because it is difficult to reach the market for the car he has for sale, and he often ends up selling to a dealer, who, in turn, marks the price of the car up and finds a buyer from among those who come to his showroom.

The dealer can reach buyers much more easily than can the individual seller; and the individual sellers are often numerous and are willing to compromise on price rather sharply. I once offered a Ferrari for sale for $12,000. I ended up selling it to a dealer, after numerous advertisements, for $7,700. Quite a buy for someone! The Ferrari was a 1960 250GT convertible with 35,000 miles on it (in seventeen years) and in near-mint condition. It had a ten-coat lacquer paint job and new red leather seats put in by a top car upholsterer. All the chrome had been replaced. There were brand-new Pirelli Cinturato tires on the chrome-plated Borrani wire wheels. Everything under the hood looked almost as finished and sparkling as the outside of the car. Mechanically it was as perfect as it could be made.

This car would sell today for about $30,000. No car is more in demand than Ferrari, and particularly Ferrari convertibles. While many Ferraris are temperamental and require almost constant attention, this 250GT was reliable, and for a time it was the only car I had to go anywhere in. It had to be reliable.

I sold the car in 1977—too soon. Still, in 1967 I had paid $2,500 for it, so I didn't lose money.

It is possible to buy a car for transportation that at the same time is a good investment. The early Ford Mustangs are one example of such cars. These cars are reliable, trouble-free, easy and cheap to repair, and a good investment. Also, many collector cars are low-priced compared with many new cars and even recent used cars. At one extreme is the Chevrolet Corvair, which can be bought for a little over $1,000. At the other extreme is the 1973 Mercedes-Benz 450SL convertible, which may possibly be bought for $12,000, while a new 450SL, essentially the same car, sells for about $30,000! One can buy a good Chevrolet rear-engine Corvair for $1,500 or a Duesenberg J or SJ for $200,000 up. Cars of all prices are on today's market, so there is something for everybody's pocketbook.

Many collector cars are low-maintenance, even compared with new and relatively new cars. The classic Mercedes-Benz 300S of the mid-1950s is a low-maintenance car. I make this pronouncement after having owned four of them over a period of twenty-five years.

The Mercedes-Benz 300S is not simply a top-quality automobile; it is a highly reliable automobile. The other three cars of this make and model that I owned were, at the time I owned them, my only car, the car I used every day for trips to and from the office, for visits to the market and for trips from Washington to New York and back—in the same day. Repairs never ran as high as $500 a year, even when the cars were my sole means of transportation and were used constantly. By contrast, the new Mercedes-Benz 450SE and 450SEL are high-maintenance cars, with fuel-injection systems and other mechanical refinements. An annual repair bill of $5,000 for such a car is not unknown.

If a person learns something about classic and antique cars and can locate inexpensive sources of parts and competent but reasonably priced repair shops, classic and antique cars can be a sound investment. You may be able to restore a car to mint condition for a reasonable outlay, resulting in a total cost below market value of the car. Reselling at a profit is then possible without holding the car for a long period of time.

When you're investing in a classic automobile, it is important to keep restoration costs within limits, or else you can end up spending much, if not all, of your expected profits. A good illustration is a 1960 Rolls-Royce Silver Cloud II sedan that I own. This car had been owned by a Washington real estate developer. He sold the car to me in late 1977 for $7,000.

The entire restoration job on the Rolls, including bodywork, paint, and upholstery, came to over $16,000, making my total investment in the car $23,000 plus. This cost was well above the market price for an average-condition Rolls-Royce Silver Cloud II, but today it is under market for one in fine condition. Still, the car is mint and upholstered better than when it was originally made by Rolls-Royce.

The $16,000 I spent restoring the Rolls might have been spent on another car that is in my collection—a 1974 Cadillac Eldorado convertible. If I had added a restoration cost of $16,000 to the $5,200 I paid for this car in 1978, the total cost of $21,200 could never have been recouped. Admittedly the leather, paint, and chrome would have produced a better car than General Motors had turned out in 1974, but how much better in dollars and cents? With luck I might sell such a finely restored 1974 Eldorado convertible today for an absolute maximum of $15,000.

This brings us to the point that there are many collector cars that actually have a *negative* value to the collector-investor. There are many Ford Mustangs of the vintage years 1965 and 1966 for sale that are no more than jalopies with bodies rusted away, dented and missing chrome, worn-out upholstery, top and carpets, engines that need overhauling or complete replacement, and, in the case of many Mustangs, steel floors front and back that are completely rusted out and need replacement. In fact, today this is the condition of the average Mustang. To put such a car in condition equal to the present market value of a Mustang I own—about $6,000—would cost at least $5,000, and this sum would have to be added to the $600 to $1,200 purchase price of such a jalopy. The completely renewed jalopy would probably represent a total investment above the present market on this make and model car.

Collector cars today can provide ultimate luxury, luxury at least comparable to the highest-priced new luxury cars. Today the top luxury car is almost certainly the Rolls-Royce. The new standard Silver Spirit sedan sells for as much as $100,000, and the price did not seem to come down very much as the pound sterling declined. The new Rolls-Royce Corniche convertible sells for about $155,000 and still seems to be rising.

The Bentley Continental of 1963 to 1965 (the SIII) is certainly the equal of these new Rolls cars. The 1959–1962 Bentleys are also excellent in every way. The Rolls-Royce Silver Cloud III convertible, the Chinese Eye coupe, and the Flying Spur (the equivalent of the Bentley Continental Flying Spur) are at least the equal of the new Rolls-Royce and Bentley cars. I wonder how much Rolls-Royce would have to charge for one of these 1960s cars if they turned out an identical car today. It would certainly have to be more than for the new sedan and possibly more than for the new Corniche convertible.

In June 1980, the *New York Times* carried an advertisement for a Bentley Continental SIII coupe. The owner was a car collector who wanted to raise cash to complete the restoration on a classic Rolls-Royce that he owned. His asking price was $16,000, a sum that represented what he had paid for the car a few years earlier. Many classic cars for sale are not only super-luxury cars but can often be bought for less than comparable new cars. They are also good "transportation cars" that can be run every day with great reliability.

When you get into a postwar Rolls-Royce or Bentley and turn the key it generally goes—and keeps on going!

In art and antiques, one of the criteria for selecting suitable items for investment is: "Does the collectible have an international market?" If the art is Renoir or Picasso or Canaletto, the market is international. Then, whatever happens to the American economy, the market may still be there—in England, Holland, Italy, France, Germany, or Japan. The same is true for antique and classic cars. A four-cylinder Rolls-Royce will sell just as well in England or Geneva as it will in New York. An SSK Mercedes-Benz will sell just as well in England or in America as it will in its native Germany. A Lamborghini Miura is regarded just as highly in Germany as it is in America or in its native Italy. There are many such internationally traded antique and classic cars, and such cars provide a kind of insulation of one's investments against the vagaries of the American economy. In a sense, these cars represent a kind of international currency. If they will not sell here, then they may be shipped to London or Geneva for sale. In the present car market, many foreign buyers are coming to America to make their car purchases and shipping them to their native countries.

So classic and antique cars offer the possibility of profitable investment. And while a collector-investor is waiting for his investment car to appreciate in value, he knows that in his garage there may be a superb piece of machinery, possibly a beautifully designed car or simply a relatively rare and sought-after car, that provides satisfaction just in being owned and driven, whether occasionally or quite steadily.

The past ten years or so have seen an almost constant rise in the value of classic and antique automobiles. In the second half of the decade of the 1970s, the rate accelerated, and to date there has been little fall-off in the price of investment automobiles. If demand and price level falter in recession, prices should again strengthen in the recovery phase of the cycle.

At almost any time it is possible to make a good buy in classic and antique cars—to make a wise investment. This is done simply by buying intelligently. I will indicate strategies for "buying right" and estimating restoration accurately in the pages that follow.

1

Investment Automobiles—What They Are

AN INVESTMENT AUTOMOBILE is one that can be expected to go up in price sufficiently over a reasonable period of time to provide a fairly substantial gain for the investor—a gain comparable to expected gains over the same period of other investments, such as stocks, bonds, real estate, art, antiques, and other collectibles. If a car was purchased in 1970 for $1,000 and in 1980 was worth $2,000, it rose 10% per year (ignoring the compound interest factor), a rate of growth that might just allow the car to squeak by as an investment, not too out of line with growth over the period in an investment in stocks or bonds.

Whether an investment automobile is a *successful* investment can be determined only in retrospect, of course. But like any investment it can be judged relatively good or relatively bad right from the start, at least by the knowledgeable.

It might be of some use to point out the cars that are *not* investments, and these are the majority of all automobiles that are on the road today or were produced in the past. There are a few "limited-edition" cars produced currently or recently that may turn out to be investments and some that definitely are investments. The Clenet is the most glamorized of all of the recent "elite cars" or "throwbacks." It has appeared in ads and TV commercials as a background prop, as well as in TV shows and movies as the car driven by the hero or the heroine or the rich parents. This car dropped in value when it was sold initially, but it did not drop very far. It rode along on a price plateau, and then rose. Now the factory is out of business and the car will almost certainly increase in value over the years. The same for the De Lorean, which is definitely out of business. The same for the Bricklin, produced several years ago.

These are just some of the new and recently produced cars that did not follow the crowd down in value as the new cars became old, but they are certainly the exceptions. Ford, Chrysler, and General Motors cars, no matter how good and how beautiful they are, all decline in value once they leave the showrooms.

After an ordinary automobile gets to a certain age, it too may become a collectible and an investment—even a very ordinary car. There is hardly any pre–World War II car that is not up in value as against its low point. The 1934 Ford V-8 two-door sedan that I bought for $50 during the war and drove for several years, a car in average condition and certainly no great standout, today would bring $4,000 in the condition that it was in at the time I drove it.

In the same way, many very ordinary cars of the 1950s and 1960s are today becoming investment automobiles, including many Chevrolets, particularly the Chevrolet convertibles of the 1950s. (A later chapter is devoted to these "ordinary cars" that have turned into investments and are now called "special-interest cars.")

The Classification of Collector Cars

The classification of collector cars is a little technical. The oldest cars are, as might be expected, called antiques, and different organizations define antiques somewhat differently. One way is to define them as all cars made before 1925. The *Old Car Value Guide* defines "Authentic Antique Cars" as all cars built from 1895 to 1942 "except Classic Cars." The same publication defines "Authentic Classic Cars" as certain cars made from 1925 through 1948.

The Fédération Internationale des Véhicules Anciens (FIVA) is the world sanctioning body for all veteran car rallies. This organization makes these definitions:

Antiques: Those vehicles built through 1904. This is Class A.
Veteran: Those vehicles built between 1905 and 1918. This is Class B.
Veteran Class C: Vehicles built between 1919 and 1930.
Post-Vintage Class D: Vehicles built between 1931 and 1945.

As a general rule, we use the year 1925 as the cutoff date between antiques and prewar classics.

Prewar classics are those cars, in our definition, produced as a general rule after the year 1925 and up to the war—1942 in the case of the United States.

Postwar classics are those cars produced from the war years to the present.

All classics are those cars which have attracted collector interest and whose value depends on collector demand, not simply on demand in the "used-car market." The values of classics tend to be based on collector or investor demand and are higher than the cars would achieve simply on the used-car market.

"Special-interest cars" are cars of both the prewar era and the postwar era that are not definitely classics but whose value seems to be rising because of collector or investor interest. The 1934 Ford roadster and the 1955 Chevrolet Bel Air hardtop may well turn out to be great collector and investor cars. They seem to be moving in that direction, but they are, generally, classified as special-interest cars, by the *Old Car Value Guide* and by other organizations.

Replicas and throwbacks, or the so-called elite cars, are cars of recent manufacture whose design is more or less based on prewar luxury cars like the Cord 810 and 812 and the Mercedes-Benz S, SS, and SSK. Some cars are very careful copies (replicas), like the Duesenberg II and the many replicas of the Auburn 851 and 852 speedsters of 1935 and 1936. These replicas and throwbacks are in a very distinct market, different from the other categories of collector or investment cars.

The Importance of Critical Opinion

The preeminent authority on Italian art, Bernard Berenson, once said, "Great art is that art which is considered great by the authoritative opinion of the time." That is, of course, begging the question. What he said, in effect, was that if a substantial amount of expert critical opinion in the area of fine art says a particular master or painting is fine, then it is fine. But actual opinion can change. An authority on Genoese art once told us definitely that the Baroque Genoese artist Piancha was a poor artist and should hardly be collected. In 1959 we found an altar panel by this artist in Genoa for an asking price of $15, a price that reflected her opinion and probably the opinion of other authorities on Genoese art. Today that panel would bring several thousand dollars. Critical opinion changed and the market changed—probably both.

In the early 1950s I spotted a prewar Mercedes-Benz convertible for sale in a car lot. I thought it might be a 500K or a 540K of the mid-1930s, and I stopped to examine and price it. It turned out to be a 380K, a smaller-engined car than the ones I liked, and the price was $750. I didn't want it and neither did any of the car collectors who were with me. Today that car would bring at least $200,000. Opinion, both expert automobile opinion and buyer opinion, has changed markedly.

The Importance of Excellence

An investor car is one that in some way is unique, in some way particularly excellent. The Duesenberg, built in the 1920s and 1930s, is one such car, and almost everything about this car was and is excellent—the appearance, the quality of craftsmanship of the body, the precision with which the engine was built, the advanced design of the engine with double overhead camshafts. Don Vorderman sums up this critical opinion in *Automobile Quarterly's Great Cars and Grand Marques*, edited by Beverly Rae Kimes:

"Blatantly put, the Model J [Duesenberg] was the most superlative automobile ever built. During its prime years, it surpassed the finest cars of Europe—Hispano-Suiza, Isotta Fraschini, Rolls-Royce, Mercedes-Benz—not to mention everything else built in the United States. There was simply nothing on wheels that could equal its combination of technical sophistication, power output, performance, smoothness and superlative road manners, all dressed in a bewildering array of coachwork which ranged from blisteringly fast two-seaters to sedans, touring and town cars of awesome opulence and elegance. The Duesenberg was, in a word, stupendous."

A bit extreme, perhaps, but this is just about the general critical opinion today as regards the Duesenberg. A lot of Duesenbergs are offered on the market, probably more than any other "great" make of car, and they never go cheap or even at a reasonable figure. The Duesenberg was the first car that I know of to top $100,000 at auction. If you have made an absolute killing in the bull stock market and you want the most distinguished car that is fairly readily available, your best choice is probably Duesenberg.

Critical opinion of the time! In 1940 two superb Duesenbergs were offered to me, one a convertible coupe, an SJ, for $750, and the other a dual-cowl phaeton, for $600. I passed them both up, as did most other car collectors at the time. Many Duesenbergs were junked then. Still one had to admit, even in the prewar years, that the car was of absolutely top quality and beauty.

To move from the sublime to the more ordinary, the Ford Mustang convertible of 1965 and 1966 is also a standout. Robert Wieder and George Hall have this to say about it in *The Great American Convertible*: "This was the Mustang's first model year and also the hottest collector's car in the series. It's one of the few really 'bulletproof' cars; meaning almost nothing bad can be said of one...."

The Mustang is a standout in many ways. It is a performer, and it certainly was in those years in which it was produced. In race trim one important driver called it the poor man's Ferrari, and in race trim it was not so far behind the Ferrari. It was, and is, a good road-holding car—not like a Ferrari, but compared with most other American cars of the period. It was and is extremely economical to maintain. Parts cost little and labor is at standard, not Ferrari, rates. It is absolutely reliable; I did not hesitate to drive from Connecticut to Washington, D.C., and back again in the same day, 600 miles, with a six-cylinder 1966 Mustang. It was, and is, a masterpiece of style, simplicity, and reliability.

The Lamborghini Countach is most certainly a standout—in performance and particularly in its "space capsule" appearance. There has never been a more ultramodern-looking production car. It is not likely to go down much in value from its present level, unless we go into a deep depression.

The Lamborghini Miura of 1967 to 1972 was, and is, a standout, unique, in demand. There is, however, a special feature of the most recent models of the Miura, the SV models of 1972. In the Miura the transmission and crankcase are combined in the rear-transverse-engine, rear-drive layout of the car. The earlier models (before the last SV's) have the oil circulating through crankcase and transmission—that is, the same oil services both crankcase and transmission. If a tooth is picked off a gear or a small piece is chipped off some part in the transmission, it might well find its way into the bearings floating in oil in the crankcase. The resulting damage might be so great as to require a whole new engine. The SV models of 1972 have a transmission and crankcase that are entirely separate and the oil in the transmission never mingles with the oil of the crankcase, so this potential danger is eliminated.

Maybe in many cases such damage never took place. It never has taken place in my earlier-model Miura. But critical collector-investor opinion vastly favors the last few models of the SV that have this separate construction. Translated into dollars in the collector car market, the earlier models can be bought for about $35,000, whereas the later ones can easily cost $85,000 to $90,000, more than twice as much.

The Ferrari 275GTB can be bought for about $40,000. But the 275GTB-4 with four overhead camshafts (the meaning of the 4) sells for about $65,000. Certain features are value-adding, and their absence means a vastly lower price for some makes and models of car.

The Rarity Factor

In indicating that an antique is really a good investment, the big auction houses and the dealers often point out that eighteenth-century antiques (as well as other eras of antiques) are absolutely limited in supply. No more are being produced and no more can be produced. As the market gobbles up the limited supply, so they point out, fewer will be on the market, and in the face of the same demand, prices must rise. True, up to a point.

In any event, the car that has many of the value elements that we have pointed out so far is worth more if the supply on the market, or potentially on the market, is limited.

Let's take the extreme—the Bugatti Royale of the late 1920s, the behemoth that probably represented the greatest production of the supreme automobile builder Ettore Bugatti. No more than seven of these great machines were ever produced. None is on the market, and it is unlikely that any will ever come onto the market. It is great and at the same time it is rare in the extreme. Its price today? Probably well over $2,000,000.

Glamorizing and Public Exposure

One reason California wines go over so well in the United States compared with French, Italian, and Spanish wines is that the American wines are glamorized. The vineyards and vineyard owners appear again and again in movies and TV shows, and as backdrops in advertisements of things other than wines, with the result that California wines are now "comparably" priced with their European competitors.

One very nice sports car is the Ferrari 308, the coupe that Magnum drives on the TV series. It is a good-looking car, a fairly good performer, and it sells at a "reasonably" priced $55,000. A large number of Ferrari 308's are produced, but the cars sell well both on the new market and on the secondhand market. They are "glamour wagons."

In the same way, the Rolls-Royce is a glamorized car, particularly the Silver Cloud III with its four prestigious headlights. These Silver Clouds were last produced in 1965, when they might have been bought for as little as $12,000 new. Today, such a car easily sells for $35,000 and even more in mint condition. Ten years ago, $7,500 would buy a good Silver Cloud III.

Automobiles become prized because they *look* glamorous. One of the most glamorous American cars ever built is the streamlined Auburn 851 and 852 boattail speedster of 1935 and 1936, respectively. These cars cost about $2,500 new. The 1931 model, the predecessor of these ultimates, sold new for about $1,150. In 1945, I bought a very good 851 boattail for $800. Today the same car would sell for about $60,000, and mint-condition boattails can bring over $100,000.

In the same way that this car was the ultimate in glamour in its day, the Ferrari 308 is glamorous today, and the car is most likely to cost more in the future. The Auburn boattail, it might be added, is glamorous even today. In fact, it is the most-copied car of any of those serving as models for the many replicas being turned out right now. More companies make Auburn boattail replicas than any other car, replica Cords and Duesenbergs included.

A fine-condition prewar Packard or Cadillac makes a stunning appearance, whether at auto meets and shows or on the highways. If the buying public gets to know the car as a beauty, its value is built up.

The Isotta Fraschini Monterosa is one of the really unique cars produced by one of the great car manufacturers of the world, but the Monterosa is all but unknown to the public, even the sophisticated collector car public. Produced in the fairly early postwar years, it had a V-8 engine behind the rear axle. Possibly not as many as twenty of these uniquely designed cars were produced. What one would bring on the market is unknown, because the cars themselves are unknown on the market.

The same for the great pioneering Cisitalia produced in the late 1940s, a car with unique style and phenomenal road-holding abilities. I can speak from experience, because I drove one almost every day for about a year and made many mechanical changes to the car in order to increase its performance. But today, if the car should be offered for sale, its price would be questionable. Some car aficionados of today haven't even heard of this great pioneering automobile. Rich Taylor, the authority on modern classic cars, says in his *Modern Classics*: "[The coupe] was shown at the Coppa d'Oro show in September 1947, held in Como. And it won the grand prize. Mama mia. Dusio knew he had something special. In October he sent the new Pininfarina coupe to the Paris Auto Show, where it was the undisputed star." Rich Taylor calls the Cisitalia coupe "the most important body design of all."

Occasionally one of these cars comes up for sale. Taylor feels one should bring between $30,000 and $40,000. I have never seen one bring anywhere near this sum, and to achieve it, a real Cisitalia collector would have to know about the sale.

On the other hand, let a Duesenberg roll down the street. Many people will recognize it. Many will inquire of others on the street what it is. When they find out the name of the car they are not likely to forget it. In many ways, the public has been made aware of the Duesenberg, again through the media. The car is fairly widely known as the ultimate even by those who have never even seen one in the flesh.

I will never forget the auction several years ago when a Duesenberg was purchased for the then enormous auction price of $159,000. The sale made headlines. It meant that Duesenberg was the ultimate in the marketplace. In the years thereafter, no Duesenberg went cheap, and today $200,000 seems to be the *low* price for one of these classics.

If a particular make and model of collector car brings a certain price at auction or in a publicized private sale, then the price, to a large extent, is established, and future prices may well be in line with the publicized figure. This principle holds true for *all* collectibles.

The more important or significant a car is, the better investment it has been. A curved-dash Olds of 1903 is a well-known car and a collector car. It is, however, not the most important car on the collectible car market. It is small, primitive, and one-cylinder, and has not risen high in value. If anything, it is undervalued.

At the other end of the "important" scale is the massive sixteen-cylinder Cadillac, especially the 1931 convertible model, a car that may very well stand at the very top in price. It can sell for as much as $350,000.

Multicylinder cars *tend* to be worth more than cars with few cylinders— four, two, or one. The multicylinder cars are big, significant, and they tend to bring prices very much higher than the simple oldies. Driving them and riding in them are real experiences.

Style, Year, and Condition

Body Style

Any dealer in collector cars hears this question dozens of times every year, sometimes every month: "I have a Packard and I understand that Packards are investment cars. What do you think my car is worth?" Three years ago, I visited a company in New Jersey that specializes in parts for Packards, the Packard now being extinct. In the yard was a Packard sedan of the early 1950s, a car in average or just above average condition. I asked the price of the car and was told it was $600. This firm was in the Packard parts and used-car business and certainly had an idea of market price. I would say $600 for the sedan was about right.

On the other hand, I owned a Packard convertible of about the same year, called the Packard Caribbean. The prices new of the sedan and the convertible were not far different, but my Packard convertible, or any Packard convertible in average or above-average condition, is worth about $8,000, more or less, and this is quite a distance from the $600 value of the sedan.

Body style is extremely important in most cars, the convertible being the vastly preferred body style. The Ferrari Daytona coupe of the late 1960s and early 1970s sells for about $65,000. The open Daytona, the Spyder, sells for about $125,000.

The Rolls-Royce town car of the late 1920s for a long time was not a preferred automobile. The back seat was enclosed and the front seat was open to the elements. This body style had to be driven by a chauffeur, and it was often called the "chauffeur killer." This was the correct appellation. I know. I drove a Rolls-Royce Phantom I Riviera town car, which I had just purchased, from New York to Washington in a downpour. The rain even filled my eyes so that I could hardly see. Today the town car and the limousine are worth just about as much as the convertible, at least in this model car. Times change and market demand changes.

Or take the Model A Ford of 1928 to 1932. Everybody wants the convertible, and prices are around $15,000 for a fine-condition 1928 or 1929 convertible. The two-door sedan can be bought for about $7,000.

There are a number of body styles, and these styles have definite terms applied to them.

A four-door sedan (or a sedan) is just that—a closed car with four doors. In England the car is called a saloon.

If the closed car has two doors and seats five, it is a two-door sedan or simply a coach.

If the closed car has only one seat for two or three people, it is called a coupe.

A hardtop is generally a two-door closed car of sporty design that has a back seat and seats four or five people.

A four-door convertible is a four-door car with front and back seats, but with a soft top that can be folded down. This car may very well have some chrome cabriole bars on the top behind the back seat to help the top fold down and for ornamentation. There are windup windows.

A roadster is a one-seat car for two or three people with no windup windows—or *usually* with no windup windows, but the term is now getting to include such cars with fold-down tops but *with* windup windows. With windup windows, it is a convertible or drophead.

A cabriolet is like a roadster except that it *definitely* has windup windows and has cabriole bars, almost always chrome-plated, for ornamentation and to help fold down the soft top.

A limousine is very like a four-door sedan except there is a glass divider between the front and rear seats. This divider might be designed so that it can be cranked down and more or less disappears. The divider was made to separate the chauffeur from the passengers.

A Berline is a car designed to have a glass partition between the front and the back seat.

A town car is a car to be driven by a chauffeur and only by a chauffeur. The car has a front and back seat like a limousine, but the front seat, occupied by the chauffeur, generally has a fabric top that can be removed. Sometimes there is a detachable hard top over the front seat. These cars are also called sedanca de villes, broughams, and chauffeur killers.

A landaulet (or landaulette) is a four-door sedan with the back seat convertible. The top over the back seat is fabric and it folds back.

A torpedo is, generally, a touring car with a somewhat pointed tail and presumably superior performance to the standard model. A touring car is a two- or four-door car with soft top that folds back and generally no windup windows. It was a standard body type of the era before the war. It is also called a phaeton.

A boattail speedster is a roadster with a pointed tail and generally superior speed. It can be called a boattail *or* a speedster. The "speedster" designation does not necessarily mean "boattail."

The Weymann body was developed by Charles T. Weymann in 1922 and was used on some of the finest cars of the 1920s, particularly the Stutz. The frame was wood, with the various strips of wood fastened together by strips of a light metal. Over this frame was stretched leatherette (leathercloths). The body was unique and very light. Relatively few collector cars today have Weymann bodies.

Body style is important, not only to describe what the car is but to establish value. A fine-condition 1932 Cadillac V-16 seven-passenger sedan will sell for about $50,000. A 1932 Cadillac V-16 phaeton will sell for $200,000.

Model Year

If a person owns a Cadillac V-16 convertible coupe or convertible sedan he may have pretty much the ultimate in a prestige collector car. The ultimate V-16 is, however, the model put out in 1930 and 1931 and continued for a few years thereafter, a carefully designed and carefully built super-luxury car that, to some extent at least, was influenced by the Rolls-Royce of the period. The General Motors engineers who were designing the Cadillac V-16 studied the Rolls-Royce of the time very thoroughly. The convertible sedan and convertible coupe in very good condition might bring $200,000. The Cadillac V-16 was also produced in 1938. This later car in very good condition might sell for under $75,000. The earlier car is worth over twice what the later car is. One reason for the lower current selling price of the later car is that it retrogressed from an overhead-valve engine to a flathead engine, probably as the company tried to economize during the Depression. Both models were, and are, excellent, but the earlier cars are the "value cars."

Similarly, the Lamborghini Countach of earlier years is probably worth more than the later cars. The later cars often used the spoiler or foil as a kind of ornament but mainly to provide some downward air thrust when the car moved along at high speed.

On the other hand, as I have already pointed out, the later-model Lamborghini Miura is worth twice what the earlier car is, although the bodies are almost identical and one has about the same performance as the other, because the later car has the improved feature of the separate crankcase and transmission.

Condition

Not so long ago the professional car buyer (who was mostly the dealer in used cars) went to the auto auction and looked over the cars that were to be put up for sale. The professional buyer usually didn't bother to drive the car before bidding on it. The reason was that the big repair costs were involved in the body, paint, and chrome. These were the parts of the car that it would cost real money to repair and restore, and he could see the condition of these elements. If he didn't start up the motor and drive the car, he couldn't tell much about the condition of the engine, the transmission, the clutch, and the differential; but he didn't need to know much about these mechanical features. They didn't cost much to repair or replace. The Cadillac overhead-valve V-8 engine, essentially the same engine put out in today's Cadillac, cost $525 *new*. But it was quite possible that a new engine was not required. Maybe only a ring job was needed, or possibly a rebore and the fitting of new pistons— maybe a $250 job. Just before World War II, I had a complete valve and ring job done on my Mercedes-Benz SS supercharged touring car for $100. New brakes and a new clutch on this same car cost $50 in total.

Today cars are vastly more complicated than they were even ten years ago. To overhaul a Ferrari engine or a Lamborghini engine costs about $10,000 in a speed shop in Phoenix. And that's just where my Lamborghini engine goes to be overhauled when it needs it! The engine is twelve-cylinder with twin overhead camshafts on each bank of cylinders. There are six carburetors. The engine and transmission are, essentially, one unit made out of a most complicated casting. Many new cars use fuel injection and an electronic ignition system and computer carburetion. A professional buyer would have to be out of his mind to buy one of these complicated new cars, even a standard mass-produced American or Japanese car, without testing it thoroughly on the road. To summarize, a rather good-condition Lamborghini Miura was bought by a dealer in Italian sports cars who had his own repair shop. To put this car in first-class condition cost him, with his wholesale labor and parts costs, over $14,000 in actual cash outlay.

As a general principle, it pays to buy a car in top condition mechanically and in appearance. I would buy a car in excellent condition—a step down from mint—in body and mechanical components, but with present labor and parts costs, unless the car was a great rarity, I would not want to buy an average-condition car or a poor-condition car. I have restored two poor-condition cars, and the costs were frightful and far above what I anticipated.

Restored or Unrestored

Many Rolls-Royce Silver Ghosts (manufactured between 1906 and 1926) are advertised for sale. It is imperative when considering such an automobile to know whether it is a restored or an unrestored car. No unrestored Silver Ghost is likely to be in show condition or probably even in usable condition. Few have been kept "under glass" for all the years since they were first produced. A poor-condition Silver Ghost can easily cost $50,000, and perhaps as much as $100,000, to restore, depending on the number and kinds of parts that are needed and the hours of labor to restore a rusted chassis and body— among other things.

For older collector cars, it is usual to have the for-sale advertisement state "unrestored" or "recently restored" or "just restored" or "older restoration." If it was recently restored or just restored, the implication is that everything necessary has been done to the car to put it into original condition. Probably so, but maybe not!

"Unrestored" means that it is probably in pretty poor, if not deplorable, condition. "Older restoration" probably means that the paint is cracked, the engine has things wrong with it, and the upholstery, top, and carpeting are ready for instant replacement.

I recently saw offered for $12,500 an unrestored Rolls-Royce Silver Cloud II of 1960–1962 that was simply an average-condition car—in need of some mechanical work and upholstery and a paint job. No rust was visible. A restored Rolls-Royce of the same year and model was for sale by the same New York dealer for $45,000.

Mileage

A low-mileage car—any kind of car, collector car or ordinary transportation car—always sells at a premium over the car with average miles on it. If we figure 10,000 miles of average driving per year for the average car, then 5,000 miles per year represents "premium mileage." If the low mileage is "extreme," like 8,000 miles on a five-year-old Ferrari, then the premium is very great. I saw a 1967 Ferrari 275GTB-4, one of the greatest Ferraris ever built, at Motor Classic Corporation. This car was in absolutely mint condition and had 5,700 miles on the odometer. There was little question in my mind that this was the correct mileage because it belonged to Nick Soprano, the owner, whom I knew very well. He once advertised it for sale and the phone rang all day with inquiries. The more it rang the more of a treasure he realized he had. Although he certainly could have sold it, he decided that he wanted to own it himself and perhaps never part with it.

The value of a 1967 275GTB-4 Ferrari with average miles on it—say, 50,000—would be about $60,000. This low-mileage car would sell above $70,000.

On the other hand, about two years ago Nick Soprano had a black 1968 Ferrari 330GTC coupe with 78,000 kilometers on it, not low mileage for this classic car. The mechanical condition was pretty good, but the interior needed replacement and the body really needed a new paint job. The car might also have needed a new clutch. In fine condition the market value on this car would have been about $30,000, perhaps a little less. Nick sold this car for a figure in the high teens.

One often hears a car owner inquire whether his "classic" isn't a very valuable collector's item. He may have, say, a Bentley SIII sedan, 1965, with right-hand drive, in average condition, neither mint nor poor. He saw that a Bentley of the same year just sold for a big sum. His car may have upholstery in fair condition. The paint may be poor and there may be some rust on the car in various places. The chrome may in general be poor. He may point out that he has a brand-new set of tires, new brakes, and a new exhaust system, but that the engine is a little noisy and uses "some" oil. To me, on the present market, this car is worth about $10,000.

On the other hand, a Bentley Continental Flying Spur with left-hand drive of the same year—1965—in excellent or mint condition all around can easily have a market value of $50,000.

Automobile value is by no means fortuitous. It is fairly definite but it is very technical. A Ferrari 250GT coupe of 1960 may sell for $12,000 on today's market. The same year convertible in the same condition, which we will assume is very good, will sell for $25,000 to $30,000, and in mint condition for even more.

To go to extremes in value, a 1965 Bentley Continental coupe with left-hand drive in mint condition will bring $50,000 or more. The same car with right-hand drive and in very poor condition I would pass up for even $12,000. In fact, a Rolls-Royce dealer offered $1,500 for a 1960 Silver Cloud II on which $4,200 had just been spent on the mechanics. But the dealer's offer was reasonable, for the restoration on this car ran to over $16,000!

2

What Determines the Price of an Investment Car

IN 1931 A luxury car, the Hispano-Suiza V-12, Type 68, appeared in the Paris salon. It was produced well into the 1930s. On today's market the Type 68 V-12 convertible in the finest condition will sell for over $300,000. In 1982 a Hispano V-12 auctioned for $350,000, in 1984 for $400,000.

In the 1930s, there was another outstanding V-12, the Lagonda, and for decades I have admired the cabriolet. The car is certainly not distinctly inferior to the Hispano V-12 in mechanics or body but can probably be bought for a maximum of $50,000, possibly less. Why is the Hispano worth six times what the Lagonda is worth, or more?

Or take another great V-12, the German Horch, produced in 1931 and 1932. In 1933 Horch produced a V-8, also a standout car. Both convertible coupes were super-luxurious, beautiful, fine pieces of machinery. The Horch was certainly a competitor of the Mercedes-Benz of the period and, I believe, more prestigious than the Mercedes. Today, the Horch may be worth somewhere near the Hispano-Suiza, possibly a little less.

In March 1974, Christie's auction in Geneva sold a magnificent Horch two-passenger convertible for £7,746—then about $18,126. At about this time a Hispano-Suiza cabriolet in top condition was worth about $50,000, possibly a little more.

In 1970 the Hispano was selling for about $35,000, the Horch for less than $6,000.

Why did the Horch rise in value over a period of a little over a decade from one-sixth the value of the Hispano-Suiza to roughly the same value?

In March 1975, Christie's in Geneva sold a very fine Delahaye Type 135 cabriolet, 1939, for the equivalent of $6,400. In the Barrett-Jackson sale of

January 1983, another very fine Delahaye Type 135, 1939, sold for $110,000. What was the reason for this incredible price difference just seven years later?

The Demand Factor

One can track demand quite accurately, but one cannot always explain it. The Ford Mustang appeared in April 1964, and Lee Iacocca, then president of Ford (and now of Chrysler), planned for first-year sales of 100,000. It took only four months to sell 100,000 Mustangs, not a year. These were of two body styles: coupe and convertible. From April 1964 through December 1965, 680,992 Mustangs were produced and sold, an industry record for sales of any new-model car in the first year. By March 1966, in essentially two years of production, 1,000,000 Mustangs were produced, but now a fastback was added to the coupe and convertible.

Today, even with many Mustangs on the road, a seller can command over $12,000 for a mint-condition convertible with low mileage, because demand is there, and demand that apparently is never satisfied. The Kruse auction in Arizona in January 1983 offered no fewer than thirteen Mustangs of the years 1964–1966. One 1966 convertible brought $9,750; a 1965 model brought $8,400; a hardtop of the same year brought $7,000. One owner of a 1964½ (came out in midyear) convertible refused $10,250.

In 1978 there was no enormous demand for Mustangs. Even as late as 1979, demand for this make and model car was moderate. By 1982, less than four years later, demand had burgeoned and prices rose by at least two and a half times. Then demand increased tremendously, particularly at the automobile auctions.

As far as the most expensive collector cars went, Duesenberg was the big name, the car in the greatest demand by 1975. The price level of a mint J or SJ convertible or roadster, speedster, or touring car was about $200,000. A 1929 Model J phaeton was recorded sold at $207,000 and an SJ phaeton at $210,000. Two 1937 cars were recorded sold at prices of $195,000 and $192,500.

Then interest and demand shifted. This did not mean that the Duesenberg owners now sold their Duesenbergs and bought something else. A fact of significance was that certain collectors wanted to own Duesenbergs, and when they had bought, and thus owned, a Duesenberg—that was it! Those who wanted to own Duesenbergs now owned them, and demand for this make died down after the mid-1970s.

In the late 1970s, Ferrari was the focus of demand. Ferraris never reached the price level of Duesenbergs, but by 1981 prices rose at a tremendous clip. Over a two-year period, prices at least doubled for most models of Ferrari.

After 1981, demand for Ferraris slackened off. Demand for Mercedes-Benz cars increased in 1980–1981 and kept on increasing through 1982. The real Mercedes classics were the ones in the greatest demand at the highest prices, and particularly the large supercharged cars of the mid-1930s and the 300 series of cars, turned out in the early to late 1950s.

In 1975 it was a rare thing for a Ferrari, any Ferrari, to sell for as much as $10,000, and very good Ferraris could be bought for $7,500 and even $5,000 to $6,000. By 1980 this same convertible was selling for almost $25,000 and Ferraris were being sold almost as fast as they arrived at the automobile showroom.

Then demand shifted at about the turn of the 1980s. Ferraris leveled out in demand and in price by 1982, and there was no great demand and prices were flat in the last half of 1982 and in 1983.

By then interest had already shifted to the Mercedes-Benz, particularly the later and smaller Mercedes cars, rather than the most expensive classics. The 190SL, the 230SL, and the 280SL, small two-seaters, all boomed in price.

One of the most obvious shifts in demand was the shift first to the Rolls-Royce and then later away from it. This demand shift was felt most in the standard sedans of the Silver Cloud series made from 1955 through 1965, the Silver Cloud I, II, and III.

In early 1974, the price of a Silver Cloud III sedan in America was as low as $16,000, a Cloud II $12,000, and the six-cylinder Cloud I $9,000. In 1981 these respective prices, at the bottom of the price range, were $35,000, $28,000, and $25,000. At the top the prices were $50,000, $35,000, and $30,000.

In England the prices at the top end of the range in 1974 were $11,500, $10,350, and $9,000 respectively for the Silver Cloud III, II, and I.

Although prices were high in 1981, they had been on a plateau for about two years. After 1981, demand turned away from the Rolls-Royce standard sedan, partly because it was a big gas user in a time of gasoline austerity and the prospect of a gas shortage (and unlike many collector cars, Rolls-Royce sedans are often used for transportation).

In America the price of a Cloud III in very fine condition is about $32,000, and of a Cloud II or Cloud I about $25,000. In England, slack demand drove prices almost back to their level in 1974, when a Cloud III sold for $9,650 to $11,500.

Price Differentials Abroad

The price of a Rolls-Royce standard Silver Cloud sedan has gone down in England more noticeably than in the United States. One reason is very poor business conditions, but just as important is the decline of the pound sterling. In early 1981 the pound was about $2.25. In early 1983 it was $1.55 and even less. Theoretically, the car that two years ago sold for $22,500 would now be worth $15,500 (all other factors but the rate of exchange being equal). This is just about the amount by which the Rolls-Royce sedan dropped in price in two years in England.

In 1980 in Florence, Italy, I located two classic cars for sale by a well-known dealer. The first was a Pantera for $6,000 and the second was a Maserati Ghibli for $6,500. At the time, the Pantera was worth more than twice this figure in America, and now it is worth three to four times this figure, particularly for a 25,000-mile car as the Florence car was. The Ghibli was worth about $11,000 in America at the time.

It is possible to buy a Ferrari Boxer 512 in Italy for about $30,000. In America it is worth twice this figure. Of course, the car must be modified for emissions control if it is imported into the United States, but a private collector or private buyer can purchase *one* car made five or more years ago and, with a minimum of modification, import it into the U.S.

The decline in value of the Italian lira in this period from about 850 per dollar to over 1,600 is one reason for the price differential, but try to buy a Lamborghini Miura in Italy or a 1960 Ferrari Super America! Prices are higher than they are in the United States, and still emissions modifications have to be made before the cars can be brought in. Italians want the Miura and the Super America and have the money to back up their preferences.

The Investment Automobile as a "Collectible"

Business conditions have a direct effect on the demand for collector automobiles. As business grew worse in 1982, demand for collector cars fell off. Prices stopped their rise and moved onto a plateau. Some prices dropped, if not greatly, even for the popular Ferrari. Inventories accumulated in the showrooms of classic car dealers. By January 1983, auction business was very nearly at the disaster level, as seen in some of the Arizona auctions.

Business conditions seemed to be a far more important factor in collector car demand than the level of the stock market. In January and February 1983, the stock market was on a new high level, with the Dow Jones Average hovering between 1000 and 1100 and pushing toward 1250; but car demand did not correlate directly with this new stock market prosperity. People did not seem to cash in on their stock market earnings and go and buy Ferraris, although many of the newly prosperous brokers talked about buying one.

To date, one can only conclude that there is a direct relationship between the economic health of the country and demand for collector cars, even though those cars may well be investments, not simply fancy transportation and prestige builders at the country club!

In the public mind there is a group of investments simply known as "collectibles," and these are alternative methods of investing one's money (instead of in the stock market and various funds). Also in the public mind, this is a homogeneous group, moving up and down together—art, antiques, Georgian silver, coins, stamps, vintage wines, etc., and collector automobiles. More than one stockbroker pointed out to me in late 1982 and early 1983 that collectibles were now "out" as investments and the stock market was the thing. They were certainly right about the stock market being *the* investment in this period, but they were wrong in lumping collectibles—with Old Master paintings, the vintage wines of France, and collector cars all moving together— down in demand and down in price.

The less-than-top paintings moved down in demand and down in price, but not the finest. The finest American furniture moved up in price; the lesser pieces moved down in price and demand. The vintage wines of France moved up in price and in demand, and Christie's had a banner year in its Wine Department in 1982.

But most buyers secured their knowledge of "the collectible market" from the newspaper journalists, not from analysts intimately familiar with the market. They put all Old Master paintings together and stated that they had moved down in price—too broad a generalization. With the press stating that collectibles were down in demand and in price, people turned away from collector cars, and demand was off in 1982 and 1983.

Brand-New Areas of Automobile Investments

In 1970, "special-interest cars" were not an important segment of the collector car market. Over the years, special-interest cars have been something of a transition category for a car moving from simply "secondhand" to collectible or classic. In 1970, what was a Mercedes-Benz 300S cabriolet? It was certainly not considered to be an investment car. A good car of this make and model could be bought for $2,500—and bought very easily. A mint-condition restored car of this make and model was offered for sale as of 1970 for $4,500, a high price at the time.

Let's take one of the most popular of all special-interest automobiles today, the Chevrolet Bel Air of 1955 and 1957, and trace its price and demand in the very recent past. This is one of the greatest and highest-priced of all of the new investment cars, those that have moved into the investment car category in recent years.

In 1970 these cars may have been special-interest cars, but they were, to a large extent, only secondhand cars. A 1955 Bel Air convertible (and convertibles are the most valuable of the cars) sold for $700 if in top condition. If in average condition, it could well sell for under $500. These are secondhand car prices, not collector car prices. The 1957 Nomad station wagon followed up the Bel Air in interest in the decade of the 1970s, and this car in mint condition would have sold for under $1,000 in 1970. The Corvette, on the other hand, was selling as high as $2,600. It was a collector car even in 1970.

By 1975, the *Old Car Value Guide* recorded a 1955 Bel Air convertible in fine condition selling for $3,250 and a 1957 model selling for $3,750. Nomad station wagons were selling for $2,250 to $3,400. All of these prices at the time were collector car prices, not secondhand car prices.

In the Grand Old Cars Museum auction in January 1983, a 1957 Bel Air convertible sold for $9,750, a car in fine, but not mint, condition. At the Barrett-Jackson auction in January 1983, a 1955 Bel Air convertible sold for $16,750, a car in class 2 condition, not class 1. For this price at this auction, one could buy a very fine Corvette convertible or coupe of the mid-1960s or a 1935 to 1938 La Salle convertible—certainly a collector car.

We have only barely touched on hot rods, but they are a segment of the collector car market of some importance. In 1970 a mint hot rod, with all sorts of special equipment in it, might cost its owner $25,000 to modify and equip. I know one that sold for about $5,000, and many good hot rods sold for $2,500 and even less. Nobody seemed to want one of these "grease machines" on the secondhand market. Today the same car that sold for $5,000 might very well sell for $25,000. This is a brand-new area of collector cars, at least new in the last decade.

The March 1983 issue of *Car Exchange* carried an advertisement with picture of a "1932 FORD 5 window coupe, 350 hp, 327 Chevy, Muncie 4 speed, Corvette rear, Super Bell front, paint black lacquer, received two achievement awards '76 Tulsa Nationals, $19,500."

A decade ago it might have taken a long time to sell this car—at one tenth the present price. As time goes on, these grease machines are going to be of greater importance in the specialized and collector car market.

Supply in Relation to Demand

In January 1982, a Mercedes-Benz 300S roadster sold at the Barrett-Jackson auction in Phoenix for a new auction high for this car—$100,000. This model car had been rising in price fairly steadily since 1970. Few of them were made; in the year my 300S roadster was built, I believe Mercedes-Benz turned out only fifty. As demand increased in the decade of the 1970s, supply did not keep up in the marketplace. Prices rose steadily from $4,000 or thereabouts for a mint 300S roadster in 1970 to $100,000 in 1982.

When the Barrett-Jackson car sold for $100,000, a huge price for this make and model car at the time, a number of 300S roadsters and cabriolets came onto the market. One firm, a dealership, offered four of them for sale at prices ranging from $115,000 to $135,000. On the other hand, they were selling at auction, at dealers' establishments, and privately for as low as $40,000, but it must be remembered that the $100,000 car and the dealers' cars priced at $115,000 and up were absolutely mint.

The high price of $100,000 in January 1982 brought this make and model car onto the market. Had the car not sold, or not sold at such a high price, certainly fewer cars would have come out of the woodwork.

Publicity and High-Priced Glamorous Cars

The fact that in January 1982 the Mercedes-Benz 300S brought $100,000 did not go unnoticed. Six-figure prices for cars attract the attention of the press. The car became recognized as a high-priced car and as a glamour car.

Years ago a Duesenberg sold for $159,000. This was a new auction high for any car. It started the Duesenberg craze that lasted for a number of years.

Every once in a while some newspaper or magazine—a general-interest magazine, not simply a car magazine—asks some connoisseur to name the finest and most prestigious car, and the response is often the Bugatti Royale. In fact, a few years ago a journalist came to interview me on some of the things that I was doing, things totally unrelated to cars. He said that he was going to start an article on the Bugatti car that day after he finished the interview with me. I asked him whether he had ever driven or ridden in a Bugatti. He replied that not only had he never driven or ridden in a Bugatti—any Bugatti— but he had never even seen one!

So great has been the publicity surrounding the fabulous and huge Bugatti Royale that one can only guess what one of these very rare machines would fetch at auction. Tom Barrett of the Barrett-Jackson auction estimates $2,500,000 for the Bugatti Royale in the Harrah Collection.

Here, in this book, we are not talking about prestige transportation cars but about collector cars of prestige. I believe one ultimate collector prestige car of today is the Ferrari. The publicity that this car has received has been great, with such advertising slogans as "What Man Can Conceive Man Can Create"—under the picture of a Ferrari 308. In other words, when you buy a Ferrari you enter a new world, the world of the unique and elite.

But how about the Lamborghini Miura and Lamborghini Countach? The fact of the matter is that these cars are almost unknown to the general public and are certainly not advertised. They are not recognized as being ultimate prestige cars—or any prestige cars, for that matter. Very few Lamborghinis are produced, and even fewer are in the U.S.

The Spread of the Concept of "Investment"

If the concept of an automobile as an investment had not developed, it is highly unlikely that cars would be selling for sums in six figures. The Mercedes-Benz roadster that Christie's sold in California in early 1979 for $400,000 stunned the collector car market watchers. The car was later sold to a European buyer for a reported $620,000, an even more unbelievable sum.

How much better is this car than the Barrett Mercedes-Benz convertible of essentially the same series that failed to go over $190,000 in the Scottsdale January 1983 auction, the Graber-bodied two-seater convertible? For his other fantastic 540K convertible, Tom Barrett certainly would have taken $400,000. The $620,000 price may be justified on the basis that the car is unique, beautiful, rare in its roadster form, and in mint condition. But $620,000?

It is hard to dispute that these high values result from buying for investment rather than for mere ownership of a great automobile. In a valuation case in the U.S. Court of Claims, I made a survey of twenty-three European art dealers and asked them what the motive of their customers in buying was. Twenty-two dealers answered right away, "Investment," and the twenty-third stated, "Investment in the long run," merely qualifying the motive slightly.

Does the Car-Buying Public Know the Car?

The 1929 Windsor White Prince roadster that was offered for sale at the January 1983 Barrett-Jackson auction was in class 1 condition, about mint. It was a rare and very good car. Very few people knew about it. Even fewer knew the car from actually having seen it. In 1929 when I was in high school and visited car salesrooms almost every afternoon, I never saw a Windsor car, let alone the White Prince. I never saw a Windsor showroom. Anyone who wanted a Windsor White Prince might have to look for years before finding a trace of one.

This Windsor White Prince roadster brought just $22,000 at the auction, about the price today of a mint 1957 Chevy Bel Air convertible.

For a car to have value, the collecting and investing public has to know the car. Let us cite an analogy in the art field. Certainly Vermeer is one of the few greats of seventeenth-century Dutch art, along with Rembrandt and Hals. Still, one of his paintings rarely comes onto the market. Right after the war, exactly five paintings by Vermeer were in private hands out of a total of thirty-six known still in existence. The remaining thirty-one are in museums. In this period a painting by Vermeer came onto the market, and sold for approximately $320,000. Yet it is fine enough to have hung since its purchase in the Metropolitan Museum of Art. For this rare a painting by this great a master, $320,000 would seem to be a small price; but until this century the artist was not known on the market. His works had no market price. What a Vermeer would bring today (now that the artist is well known and highly valued) is also uncertain—maybe $3,000,000, maybe as much as $10,000,000.

The public knows the Packard V-12 convertible. It knows the Duesenberg J and SJ. It knows the Ferrari Daytona. It does not know certain cars that are rarely on the market or on the road either—like the Windsor White Prince.

If the Windsor White Prince is at the unknown end of the recognition scale, the Ford Mustang convertible of 1964–1966 is at the other end of the scale. There is hardly a gas station attendant who does not recognize this car, now at least eighteen years old—and recognize it as a valuable item to own. Not only is the car popular and loved, but its rising value is recognized; and, to repeat, since I have owned one I have had, over the past four years, at least fifty inquiries as to whether I would be interested in selling it, and at least a dozen offers.

Price Trend of the Car

In 1979 and 1980 the Lamborghini Miura began showing a strong uptrend. Its price had skyrocketed in a period of two years from about $12,000 for the 1967 P-400 to over $25,000.

A car with a strong up price trend has a plus added to the market price. At least, the liquidity of the car is great. Of course, behind price trend is price, and price is determined by scanning advertisements, visiting collector car dealers, and noting auction results. One of the best and most up-to-date auction price records is *Ray's Auction Record* (Route 6, Box 732, Shawnee, OK 74801). Each year Ray's puts out an auction record of cars sold and at what price, with a rating of each car according to condition. The main and largest auctions are covered. For $5 one can get a quick record of the price received at each auction, and the price booklet is mailed soon after each auction. *Old Cars Weekly* (Iola, WI 54990) also reports all prices of cars sold at major auctions as they occur. A year's subscription to this car newspaper is $17.

In addition to auction prices, the highest bid prices are recorded for those cars that were not actually sold. One can follow a particular make and model car from auction to auction during the year and determine price trend. One can also often follow the same car from auction to auction, from a "no sale" to finally an actual "sale." Sometimes cars are actually sold several times over a period of a year or two, and the price at each sale can be seen.

Condition of the Car

Ten years ago, condition was less important in a collector car than it is today. It was possible to get expert work done on a complicated foreign car for about $10 an hour, and services like chrome plating were reasonably priced. Today, a restoration bill of $38,000 on a complicated car like a Lamborghini Miura is not unusual, even at today's reasonable rate of $35 an hour. Many repair and restoration shops charge well over that.

As I mentioned earlier in the book, and keep repeating, the big question today in buying a car is not simply the price of the car and the probable cost of restoration, but the *condition* of the car. Some of the cars offered at auction as well as by dealers are in such fantastically perfect condition that it is virtually impossible to duplicate them starting with an average-condition car. How much would it cost to get an average car into such perfect condition? Where could the various restoration jobs be done? How long would it take?

Where do you get a Ferrari 275GTB-4 in mint condition and with 5,700 miles on the odometer? What is this car worth as compared with the market on this make and model car?

In other chapters I will indicate how to examine a car to determine its condition and how much the restoration and repair of the car would cost. The thing to emphasize is that today no one except an expert should buy a car that he has not paid a mechanical and body firm of experts to examine.

One big advantage of buying from a reputable dealer is that usually he has bought the best cars for resale and turned down the rest. He has checked over and restored these "best" cars, and he will very likely tell the truth about the condition of the car and what he has done to it before offering it for sale.

The auctions do have their advantages for the car collector-investor. The important auctions grade the car after examining it, and the auction officials generally know the condition of the cars they are auctioning. Maybe they do not know the cars as well as dealers selling collector cars, but they do have a knowledge of cars, having sold many over the years.

Some auctions, such as Barrett-Jackson, use the system of grading cars to 100 points—the best—"new, as new, 98-100 points. Concours." A perfect car scores 100 or 100%, and few cars are graded 100 by any auction house.

The Kruse auctions rate cars on the basis of F, G, and E. F stands for fair—running and drivable but needing some repair to be either mechanically dependable or cosmetically presentable. G stands for good—average condition, serviceable, and attractive. Suitable for everyday fun and use. E stands for excellent—car restored to top condition, or an unrestored car needing no restoration work. A potential prizewinner.

Values depend tremendously on condition. Dean V. Kruse explains his grading of cars offered by the firm at auction:

"For a Cadillac 370 Phaeton, which lists in excellent condition at $85,000, a dealer might pay $45,000 for a specimen in that grade of condition, or slightly better than 50%. For the same car in good condition, which lists at $45,000, he would probably give around $20,000, or less than 50%. For a specimen in fair condition, listing for $25,000, his offer is not likely to be above $10,000, which represents an even smaller percentage of the book value."

This sliding scale of value according to condition is what the auctioneer has learned prevails as a general rule; the top-condition car sells for $85,000, the good-condition car for $45,000, and the fair-condition car for $25,000. If the $85,000 car represents 100%, then the good-condition car at $45,000 represents 53% of the value of a top-condition car. The fair-condition car at $25,000 represents a value of 29% of a top-condition car.

These comparative values according to condition are recorded all through the Kruse record of collector cars sold at auction. Value does depend tremendously on the condition of the car.

Not all cars, however, step down from 100% to 53% to 29% according to condition. The Kruse directory of cars sold at auction gives, for instance, values of a 1956 Ford Thunderbird in various states. For a top-condition car the value is given as $29,000, for the grade next down $12,500, and for the bottom grade $4,200—maybe a little extreme, but this grading of the Thunderbird on condition does indicate that condition is of paramount importance in the determination of value and market price.

Price guides both in the United States and in Europe quote market prices on collector cars by condition of the car. The *Old Car Value Guide* has five grades of car:

> Restored—Excellent—Grade 1
> Restored—Fair—Grade 2
> Unrestored—Good—Grade 3
> Unrestored—Fair—Grade 4
> Unrestored—Poor—Grade 5

The Grade 1 Cadillac V-16 phaeton of 1932 is worth $200,000. The Grade 5 Cadillac V-16 phaeton of 1932 is worth $50,000.

Old Cars Weekly, which reports most major collector car sales, grades the cars from 1 (the best) to 5 (the worst). This newspaper reported the North Dakota Junkyard Sale with very few cars above Grade 4 and most Grade 5— junkers.

"Mint" cars or mint-condition cars are absolutely perfect cars, perfect either because never used since new (or little used and well maintained) or because restored to new condition. At about this quality level or just under it is the car called a "creampuff"; dealers all seem to love creampuffs and will almost always pay premium prices for them—often far over market value for the same make and model in average condition.

Grades are flexible. The top grade I sometimes call "mint" or "creampuff," the latter being a common dealer's term. The next term is "fine" or "excellent." The next is "good." These terms are also used in numismatics and mean the same thing.

It is apparent that condition classifications are not simple, with some auctions employing a system of six categories, the Kruse auctions a system of three categories, the *Old Car Value Guide* a system of five categories, etc. Furthermore, the same car may be put in a higher category in one auction than at another even if both auctions use essentially the same grading system, because grading is inevitably somewhat subjective. Terms such as "mint," "excellent," and "fine" are perhaps even less exact. There simply is no Moody's or Standard & Poor's in the collector car market.

For simplicity throughout the book, I have used "mint" and similar terms with some vagueness, as they are used by collectors—sometimes with quotation marks to indicate that a car was so represented but I cannot personally vouch for it. I have used "class 1," "class 2," etc., to represent the number gradings actually applied at given auctions, without attempting to impose a system that would be valid for all cars at all auctions—an impossible goal.

The Probable Cost of Restoration

One has to know the condition of a car to know the probable cost of restoration, and a determination must be made as to *what kind* of restoration. In the early 1980s I went to Mobile, Alabama, to look at a Rolls-Royce Silver Cloud III sedan that was represented to me by its owner as being "nearly perfect." As is so often the case, the car was far from perfect. I could not take the engine and transmission apart and examine them, but I could make estimates on the cost of cosmetic restoration. I knew that the restoration should be good, but not mint, as I wanted to use the car, at least occasionally. We took it from shop to shop and I explained what I wanted done. From each shop I secured a written estimate of the cost. After I finished making the rounds of the shops, I added up the estimates, added probable mechanical restoration, assuming certain things had to be done after driving the car and examining it mechanically, at least superficially. At a price of $17,000 I turned down the car. At that price, it was only a fair buy, not a good buy, and at least $10,000 in restoration costs would have had to go into it.

A prime car sold at the Barrett-Jackson auction in January 1983 was a 1954 Mercedes-Benz 300S roadster "with perfect restoration including luggage, tools, and original handbooks. Winner AACA President's Cup." The car sold for $100,000. From my best information, the car cost the seller something over $25,000 a year before the auction, and he spent a year doing a top-notch restoration job, possibly costing him $25,000. I feel sure the car turned out to be a good investment. This was like a similar car that he had sold a year earlier, in January 1982, for exactly the same price—$100,000 less the commission to the auction house.

How Desirable Is the Particular Car?

I once owned a 1927 Mercedes-Benz cabriolet with cabriole bars. It sounds like a "dream machine," only it wasn't quite. It was in excellent condition and had a new lacquer paint job and white fabric top, both paint and top done by one of Washington's finest shops. The leather was perfect, and so was the mahogany trim.

Today I wouldn't expect the car to sell for over $60,000, and perhaps not over $50,000. However, the "usual" S cabriolet in the same condition that mine was in when I owned it might well go for $100,000 or even $140,000, and one was recorded as selling at auction for $140,000 a year ago.

But mine was one of the ugliest Mercedes I have ever seen. It was like a box, and there was absolutely no slant to the windshield. I bought the car prewar from Zumbach's Mercedes-Benz Company in New York, the leading Mercedes dealer in the city and probably in the United States at the time. I paid $350 for it—at an important retail dealer. The dealer hadn't been able to sell it for some time because of the lack of appeal of the body.

That same year, 1927, Mercedes made some beautiful small convertibles and cabriolets, and I would expect that it was one of these beautiful cars that Kruse reports as having brought $140,000 recently.

So when we talk about the value of an automobile, we are talking not strictly generically but about the value of a particular automobile.

In 1982 I saw a Lamborghini Miura SV, one of the later 1972 models, in a showroom. Had the dealer called me to say he had just secured an SV Miura and did I want to come over to look at it, I would have come over immediately, dropping whatever it was I was doing. I'm glad he didn't call me about the car. It was hardly worth coming over to see. The paint was no more than "pretty fair." It was charcoal gray—not too attractive. The interior had been chewed up by the owner's dog before he sold the car to the dealer. The engine may have been good, but it didn't sound like any standout, and it was not particularly clean. For the car as it was, I might have gone as high as $28,000 and possibly $30,000.

I looked at the same car after $14,000 had been spent on restoration. The paint was an Italian racing red, a magnificent lacquer. The chrome was like new. The interior was the best Connolly English leather. There was chrome under the hood and the engine compartment looked even better than new. The car did not stay around long, and was sold for $65,000.

The same dealer could have called me about a Rolls-Royce Silver Cloud III that he took in. Had he called me and stated that he had taken in a Cloud III, I might have thought the car was in average condition and possibly with right-hand drive and a limousine, and I might have guessed the price at $25,000 to $30,000.

When I looked at this Rolls-Royce, I realized that this was probably one of the finest Rolls-Royces of the model in the world. The black paint was absolutely perfect. The chrome was perfect. So were the leather, fabric, and wood trim. There were wide whitewalls—like new. The car had gone very few miles. It seems to me that this car would be worth $65,000 to $75,000.

When you buy a collector car you are buying an individual car, something of a unique investment, not one share of IBM common—which you may never even see. The car can be in perfect condition and absolutely beautiful in line and in finish, a car that many people would want and want fairly quickly. Or it can be ugly, in poor mechanical condition, in mediocre cosmetic condition, a car that essentially nobody would want except at a real bargain price. If you like a car, probably some other buyer will too. If you don't like it, it may be hard to find anybody else who likes it either. The Rolls-Royce Silver Cloud III can be worth as little as $25,000 and possibly as much as $75,000, depending on the overall appeal of the car. That includes many things, from body style to mechanics to cosmetics, including color combination and quality of paint and interior.

3

Quality and Its Importance

EXCELLENCE OF OVERALL design, detail, finish, and performance is important. Collector cars of value have quality in two areas. The first is the quality of the make and model car—whether a Packard 734 boattail speedster or a 1936 Ford V-8 Tudor sedan. Both cars may be well made, and in its way perhaps the Ford is a beautiful car, but prevailing opinion in the collector car market is that the Packard 734 is top-quality. The second area where quality is important is in the condition of the car. During the later years of World War II one of the members of the Sports Car Club of America bought a Mercer Raceabout in a junkyard for $25. The *model* car was top-quality. The condition of the car, this particular car, was bottom-quality. After rehabilitating the car, this same Mercer had a value of about $7,000, which seemed a lot of money at the time. Of course, here we are talking about the same car before and after restoration. We could, however, be talking about different cars. The first, the junker, was worth no more than $25. The second, the restored Raceabout, was worth $7,000.

Or take a Cadillac Eldorado convertible made between 1971 and 1976, the last year of the Eldorado convertibles. A mint-condition 1976 Eldorado convertible with, say, 3,000 miles on the odometer can bring approximately $18,000. One that has been run 15,000 miles a year will have over 100,000 miles on it. It will look run-down and will be severely rusted in many cases. The mechanical condition of the car may be just fair, not terrible but far from good. This car can sell for $2,500. In fact, in 1982, one that had a good paint job and very little rust, ran well and had about 30,000 miles on the odometer went for $3,800.

Quality of the Make and Model

As I have said, quality automobiles are what people *think* are quality. If everyone whose opinion is important in antique and classic car circles says a particular make and model car is good, other people are likely to think so too. Currently, the prevailing automotive opinion is that the Renault Alliance is one of the best inexpensive utility cars on the road today. Before I even drove the Alliance (priced at about $5,500) I was convinced that this was exactly the car I wanted for around-town use. As a matter of fact, the experts were right, and after I tried it, I was still convinced.

After a car has been on the collector car scene for a number of years, opinion of the experts becomes less important and the actual quality of the car—the quality that the car itself commands—becomes more and more important. When the car is so old and so well respected that it is in effect a "museum car" and seldom used, then expert opinion regains importance.

The "gilt-edged collector cars" listed later in this book represent the opinion of other experts in the field of collector cars as well as my own, and the cars, to a considerable extent, are the highest-priced on today's market. The *buyers* have "voted" on which cars are the best.

1. The "big-name" cars are usually top-quality cars. The big names are makes like Ferrari, Mercedes-Benz, Rolls-Royce, Duesenberg, Bugatti. These are sought-after in automobile collecting today, and they have been the big names in the automobile industry in the past. The list also includes makes that are less seen on the market, but are still great names: Isotta Fraschini, Hispano-Suiza, Stutz, Packard.

2. The important models are usually the collector cars, not the less important models. In Rolls-Royce the V-12 prewar Phantom III was a tremendously important model, and it is more important on today's market than it ever was. So are the Phantom V and Phantom VI—big, luxurious postwar Rolls-Royces— and the Rolls-Royce Corniche convertible. The Silver Shadow sedans of the same period as the Corniche are not as important as collector cars and therefore do not bring the same high prices. At one time, about the mid-1970s, the Corniche may have been the most-sought-after late-model automobile of any make.

The Ferrari Daytona, which appeared in 1968, is one of the most sought-after collector cars. It is luxurious, quiet, and dependable, and it probably performs as well as the latest-model big Ferrari, the Berlinetta Boxer. The Ferrari 275GTB-4 is possibly the most desired of all of the fairly recent Ferraris.

Going on back to important Ferrari models, there is the Ferrari America and the Ferrari Super America, the latter car possibly the most-sought-after of all classic cars in present-day Italy.

In Mercedes-Benz, the most important collector car models are the SSK and the SSKL (an almost nonexistent car on the market), both cars of the late 1920s and early 1930s, and the 500K and the 540K of the mid-1930s. In postwar Mercedes-Benz cars, the most-sought-after models are the 300S and the 300SL Gullwing—without much doubt the most-sought-after Mercedes cars of the postwar period.

3. The top-of-the-line cars are the most desirable. The Chryslers that are the most sought-after cars, those that bring the very highest prices in the whole area of collector cars, are the custom Imperial Eights of the early 1930s. This model car is far and away the most expensive collector car in the entire Chrysler series. It rose from under $1,000 twenty-five years ago to about $200,000, or a little less, in the market of the early 1980s. It was Chrysler's most expensive car when it first came out, and it is still the most expensive Chrysler in today's collector market.

The top-of-the-line Rolls-Royce cars in the postwar period are the Phantom V and Phantom VI, the cars that cost the most when new and still cost the most on the collector car market. The prewar Packards that bring the most are the Super Eight and the V-12. In Cadillac, the top of the line is represented by the Cadillac V-16 of the early 1930s. No other Cadillac approaches the value of these giants, certainly not the V-12's and V-8's of the same era.

4. The convertibles are the favored collectibles. The Ferrari 250GT of the late 1950s and early 1960s is an excellent piece of machinery and road car. There is no difference in quality between the coupe and the convertible. On the present market, however, the 1960 coupe can easily be purchased for $18,000 and sometimes less. The convertible of 1960 or thereabouts will cost at least $25,000 if in any condition and possibly as much as $30,000.

The Maserati Ghibli of 1967 to 1972 is no rarity on the market. It is possibly the most beautiful sports coupe ever designed at any time in automotive history, and it is sophisticated from an engineering point of view. It is a top road holder and luxurious from paint to upholstery and instrument panel. It can easily be bought for $18,000 to $20,000.

The Ghibli convertible is a beautiful car, but no more beautiful than the coupe. The convertible can almost never be bought for under $32,000, and it can range as high as $42,000. True, it is rarer than the coupe, but it can still be bought, especially on the West Coast. It was selling in 1980 for over $30,000 when a Ghibli coupe could have been bought for $15,000.

Among less exotic cars, the Cadillac Eldorado convertible of 1976 in fine condition will bring at least $12,000. The Eldorado coupe of the same year, also in fine condition, will not bring half that figure.

To go to a very important late collectible car, the Ferrari Daytona coupe brings about $65,000 on today's market. The Daytona Spyder (convertible) of the same period will bring at least $110,000, and $125,000 is not an unreasonable figure.

5. The special models are usually the premium investor cars. There is little difference in constuction between the prewar Mercedes-Benz S and SS and the SSK and SSKL. The SSK is shorter than the S and SS and the engine puts out more horsepower. The SSKL is a lightened version of the SSK with a frame in which holes have been drilled. The car also uses a supercharger with more pressure. A Model S roadster might bring $250,000. The SS might bring $300,000 or a little more. The SSK might bring close to $500,000, and the ultra-rare SSKL is priceless. No one has one for sale, and I have never seen one for sale ever. All the cars are constructed similarly, in general, and they look more or less alike, but the SSK and SSKL are rare special models (super models with higher preformance) and they command enormous price premiums.

The Aston Martin is a collector car, but it is not greatly sought after and it has always seemed to drag behind in price rise while the other collector cars rose in value. The Aston Martins that are in better demand and at higher prices are the Vantage models, those with the special Vantage high-performance engine.

The 1970s "Boss" Mustang brings a tremendous premium, selling for close to $10,000, while the ordinary Mustang for the same year sells for less than $5,000.

The Chevrolet Corvair is a plentiful collector car and not in the greatest demand at the highest prices. It is not hard to find a Corvair for $2,500, a good one. On the other hand, a "special" was put out from 1966 to 1969 by a Corvair modifier named Don Yenko. It was a high-performance Corvair, often used for racing, called the Stinger. I would not expect to find any Stinger for sale, in any condition, for a price as low as $5,000, and fine Stingers might go at astronomical prices.

6. The special-body cars often go at premiums. In 1939, Jacques Schaerly, general manager of Zumbach's in New York, located what he thought was a suitable Mercedes-Benz for me. He had previously sold me a 1928 Model S, and I was looking for an SS. He sent me to see a Mercedes-Benz SS convertible coupe. Mr. Schaerly pointed out that the price of this car was high—$750— but the car had a Castagna body. My Model S had a body by Erdmann and Rossi, not one of the most beautiful Mercedes bodies by any means. The Castagna body on the Model SS was beautiful and very well constructed. This was one of the great bodies put on the Mercedes-Benz S and SS models.

The Talbot Lago was a very good automobile, but the "street car" was not the greatest performer among sports cars of the late prewar period. The "real" collector Talbot Lago was, however, the car with the streamlined body by Figoni and Falaschi. When one talked about the Collector Talbot, he meant the Talbot with the Figoni and Falaschi body. Today, that car can bring over $150,000.

While the Aston Martin is not the most sought-after of collector cars, one model is very much in demand, and this is the coupe with body by Super-leggera. This body transforms the whole car from a somewhat heavy sports car to a beautiful and desirable sports car, something any collector of postwar coupes might well consider, even Ferrari collectors. There is nothing the matter with Aston Martin mechanically. It is a well-made, rugged automobile (the "James Bond" car with the "special features"). Sometimes we are slow in acting on our investments—too slow. In 1982 I passed up not one but two Aston Martins of the early 1960s, with Superleggera bodies and with left-hand drive, and both of these cars were priced at about $7,000! In mint condition, they should bring at least $15,000 each. The ordinary-body coupe in the same condition would possibly not bring as much as $10,000.

7. Special features sometimes *make* the car a collectible at a top price. The Lamborghini Miura of 1967 can be bought for $30,000; the 1972 SV model for about $60,000. But the last few SV models with the separate transmission and crankcase that keep the oil from circulating between engine and trans-mission can bring $85,000 or even as much as $100,000. As time went on in this innovative automobile, the bugs were ironed out and the car became a better car, the separate crankcase and engine being the ultimate development and an extremely important one from the point of view of the longevity and reliability of the engine.

In the mid-1960s the Ford Mustang appeared, an instant success in the area of "sporty cars." The Mustang convertible of 1964–1966 is very popular and rising in price, and in fine condition one of these cars will sell for $5,000 and up. If, however, the Mustang convertible has the GT engine, which is not really much of an innovation, and it has what is called the Pony interior (special upholstery), it will bring at least $1,000 more.

For different cars there are other value-giving features. If a Ferrari has Borrani wire wheels, that is a plus. If the Borrani wheels are chrome-plated, that is a plus-plus. In the same way, wire wheels on the Maserati Ghibli are a plus; they might add as much as $1,000 to the value of the car.

The Qualities of the Particular Car

In the next chapter we discuss inspections and tests to make—whether the car is a Corvair two-door sedan or a Duesenberg SJ speedster. Here we are concerned with the outstanding *qualities* of a particular example of a collectible car that give that particular car a high value.

What characteristics of the particular car give that car extraordinary, or above-average, value?

1. The appearance of the car is extremely important. Most Ford Mustangs have an enamel paint job on them, such as they had originally when they came from the factory. The paint job on most Mustangs is just "satisfactory." A lacquer job is unusual on a Mustang, and a superb job is almost unknown, although more fine lacquer jobs are going onto Mustangs each year as the value of this make and model collector car goes up. A superb lacquer job gives great value to a car. A Mustang convertible with an average enamel paint job will be worth, say, $4,000. With a superb paint job it may well be worth $6,000.

Chrome is important. There isn't a great deal of chrome on a Mustang, but good chrome adds value and it says a good deal about the owner of the car. It says that he has put on new chrome parts or else had the old parts replated. In the case of most Mustangs, the chrome has been worn off or pitted. The man who paints his car well and has good chrome has probably done other things to maintain or restore his car.

Then there is upholstery. My own Mustang has the original upholstery, and it is in very good condition even though it is not real leather. In my closet there is top-grain leather of a color to match the paint on my Mustang. Eventually I will install this genuine leather; but the imitation leather on the Mustang is original and characteristic of the Mustang, and the real-leather job might be considered something like putting in an engine from another make of car. Certainly the new engine might be good, but then the car would no longer be a Mustang.

In a Rolls-Royce, new fine leather does nothing but increase the value of the car, particularly Connolly English leather.

Next, if the rest of the car is in keeping with the paint, chrome, and leather, not only is value added by good carpets, top, tires, etc., but the attitude of the owner toward his car is clarified. If carpets, top, tires, etc. are all perfect, then I am inclined to think the mechanics of the car may be in similar fine shape.

But if we stop at paint, chrome, upholstery, and the other externals, what about the value of a car that has all these things perfect as compared with an average car? Recently I saw, as I indicated elsewhere, two Rolls-Royce Silver Cloud II sedans. The first looked superb. The second looked to be in average condition, no more. The price of the first car was $45,000. The price of the second car was $12,500. Maybe this disparity was too great. Maybe the superb car should have been priced at $35,000 and the average-condition car at $14,000 or $15,000. These prices seemed more in line with the market. In this case, I may have been right on the price of the superb car. It was on consignment from a fastidious owner who may have had an inflated idea of his car's worth.

In the case of these two cars, I assumed that the mechanics of the superb-looking car were in keeping with the car's appearance and that the average-looking car had average mechanics. One often judges by appearance, and mechanical condition often goes along with appearance.

2. The owner of the car can be very important. Early in the game of inspecting a car that I am considering buying, I ask what the background of the car is. Generally the private owner and the dealer will tell me. Sometimes the dealer will state that the car is a one-owner car, or that the owner is the second in the line and he has owned the car for, say, fifteen years.

One of the finest cars I have seen in recent years was a Rolls-Royce Silver Cloud III long-wheelbase with left-hand drive. Everything about the car was superb. When I asked the dealer where he had gotten it, he said from a major collector who traded the car in on a highly unusual Lamborghini Miura SV whose appearance could not be faulted in any way. The Miura SV was expensive and the collector felt he did not want to pass it by, so he traded his superb Rolls. Needless to say, the Rolls did not remain in the dealer's show-room for long.

Tires are sometimes telltales. The Rolls had special very wide whitewalls in perfect condition, expensive tires that showed no wear. In Italian cars the tires may often be telltales. If the car has P7 Pirelli tires, that says a lot about the owner and probably about the car too, since these are the very best that $250 a tire will buy! A dealer may buy new tires for a car to pretty it up, but he will hardly put on P7 Pirellis.

In summary, the appearance says a lot about the owner and how he cared for the car, and it also says a lot about how he *probably* kept the mechanics, which can cost a great deal to put right.

3. Mileage can be of the essence in buying a collector car. A 1976 Eldorado with 1,500 miles on the odometer can bring $18,000, perhaps more. A 1976 Eldorado with 110,000 miles on it and in above-average condition can bring $4,000, a very fair price, and I have seen 1974 Eldorados in very good condition sell for prices of $3,000 to $3,500.

Not so long ago, mileages on odometers were turned back and the car that read 8,000 miles could have really had 80,000 miles on it. Today cheating takes other forms, and in some states dealers who turn back odometers face severe penalties as well as very unfavorable publicity.

Originality is important in many cars, including the important and older collector cars like Duesenberg, prewar Mercedes-Benzes, and many high-priced classics and antiques. The classic car restorer Rodney Bostian, asked what he looks for in any car he buys to restore, whether a classic or a modern utility car, says, "I want to see whether it is original or whether it has been fooled with." Mileage is *one* indication of original condition. On the other hand, repairs and restorations can be made to a "bad shell" and there may well be little originality left in the car.

Low mileage allows a car to be bought with some confidence, even though a higher price has to be paid for it. On the other hand, Bob Wallace, a Ferrari and Lamborghini restorer in Phoenix, Arizona, showed me the interior of the engine of a Ferrari Berlinetta Boxer that had about 5,000 miles on it. This car was apparently in a damp climate and in a damp garage or other storage space. The cylinders were "pockmarked," and the entire engine had to be rebuilt and possibly the entire block replaced.

Paul Longo, another car restorer, "opens up" every engine he buys from a used-parts company to see what the interior looks like, even if the company says the engine came from an almost new car that had been wrecked. Once he found the entire interior of the engine rusted beyond repair.

An older car, like a Ferrari Daytona, with few miles on it may be just as represented, near new. At the same time, the interior of the engine may be severely damaged by moisture. It will probably pay to have any one of these older cars examined with the cylinder head or heads removed before paying a big purchase price. Pay the selling garage to remove the heads to let you look at the cylinders before you shell out $65,000 for the car.

Valuing a Restored Car

Appearance and actual condition of a car are "value elements" in two ways. The first is a clear indication of the overall condition of the car. A car, classic or antique, in perfect restored condition, perfect outwardly at least, is a premium car, and the appearance tends to say a good deal about the mechanics of the car. The car that is perfectly restored on the outside may well be restored inside too. The Rolls-Royce Silver Cloud II that was offered for $12,500 was a fairly priced car, for a Cloud II in average condition or slightly above average condition. The perfect appearing Cloud II that was selling at the same time for $45,000 was perhaps a little overpriced, but possibly not much.

To elevate the condition of the average car to that of the fine car would probably cost no more than $22,500. No prudent man could spend $32,500 turning the $12,500 car into the $45,000 car. The restoration bills simply would not run that high.

Perfect condition *creates* value, and the value is usually more than the cash outlay.

On the other hand, perfect condition may well be an indication of originality, original perfect condition, and originally perfect cars go at a premium, such as the 1940 Buick sedan, no great collector car, that brought $11,750 at auction in Arizona in 1982.

Old Cars Weekly described this auction on the first page of the April 8, 1982, edition in this way:

"Total sales for the day were at 48% (52% of the cars offered did not sell). Hard rain began again at 3 p.m. in the afternoon and everything, including the bidding, cooled off. Two (2) world records were set during the auction. The first record toppler was an original 1940 Buick Super 50 Series 4-door sedan with factory fender skirts and an immaculate original interior including dash. The car was in superb condition. The underside on this 21,000-original-miles auto showed no wear, and its maroon finish was flawless."

Still another element of value is created by perfect exterior condition. I looked at a Maserati Ghibli offered for sale. The paint caught my eye first because of its superb quality. It was far better than original paint, and I asked the car dealer how much the paint job had cost. The answer: $4,500. The paint alone created value for this particular car, maybe not a full $4,500 but substantial value nevertheless.

To go back to condition of a car, my 1966 Ford Mustang convertible had to have all the paint removed and the body repaired where it had been damaged by rust. I put in an entire new Ford six-cylinder engine, the type the car had originally. The top, floormats, exhaust system, and brakes were restored to new.

My Mustang, now completely restored, is worth about $6,000. The dealer who sold me the car had bought it for $100, but restored it and sold it to me for $1,600. Literally everything had to be done to it. In just average 1966 Mustang condition the car might be worth $2,500.

Had the car been in the condition it is in now *but original* and with, say, 10,000 original miles it should bring at least $10,000 and might even rival the record price of $21,500 paid for such an original car at auction.

So prime condition is an indication of the whole car through and through—mechanically as well as appearancewise. In addition, restoration creates a kind of premium value. Finally, restoration costs money, and one can add up in his mind what rechroming must have cost, what the paint job cost, what the leather cost, the top, the carpets, the tires. If the car didn't have these elements of restoration, you, the buyer, would have to pay for them yourself.

As a kind of summary on the subject of quality and its importance, let's go back to the 1940 Buick sedan that auctioned for $11,750. A car buff about a year ago purchased a Buick convertible of about the same year, and a convertible is certainly worth more in the market than a sedan in the same condition. The Buick convertible was in excellent external condition—body, chrome, paint, upholstery, top. The price was $3,500. It was not original, although it was almost an "excellent car" in appearance. The engine was not an original Buick engine. It was a recent Buick V-6 engine, and this substitution destroyed the car's originality and made it almost useless as a collector car.

4

What to Look for in Buying a Collector Car

THE FIRST QUESTION one must answer in deciding to buy (or not to buy) a collector car is: "Why do I want to buy a collector car at all?" If a stock market investor thinks an investment car might be a good alternative to investing further funds in the stock market he measures the possible appreciation of his investment in the collector car against the possible appreciation in his stock (plus his dividends on the stock).

If he compared the "growth potential" of his collector car with the actual growth of his stock investment in the months following August 1982, he would almost certainly have to turn down all cars as an alternative investment. Almost no car will show the rapid appreciation that the stock market did in just a few months following August 1982. He might have bought the car opportunistically and equaled the rise of the stock market. I purchased my Lamborghini Miura in early 1980 for $20,500 and I probably could have sold it even before I took delivery for $32,000—50% appreciation in a few days. At least this was the offer made on the car while it was sitting in the paint shop waiting to have the final touches put on the new paint job.

This is, however, the great exception to the rule, and almost no car can show such appreciation in so short a time. Almost all collector cars are beaten in the short run by a short bull market in stocks.

The expert buyer can sometimes make such an investment—one that will realize a quick and very high appreciation—but the buyer must be *very* expert, or very lucky.

But over the long pull, automobiles can show a respectable appreciation as compared with investment in the stock market.

Automobiles as Pure Investment

From the point of view of actual facility of an investment, facility of buying, holding, and selling, stocks and bonds rate at the top of the list. One calls up his broker and tells him to buy 200 shares of IBM at market or at 150 or whatever. The broker then calls back and says, "I got your 200 IBM at 149." A short time later the brokerage firm sends the buyer a bill for the purchase. The buyer mails in a check to the brokerage firm for the purchase price and then forgets about the stock—at least taking care of this IBM investment. It can stay right with the brokerage firm.

Three months later, the owner of the 200 shares of IBM stock sees it quoted at 160. He calls up his broker and instructs him to sell at 162 or market or whatever price he would like. Subsequently, the seller of the 200 shares receives a check for the proceeds of the sale of the stock, which check he deposits with his bank. That's the end of the purchase, ownership, and sale of 200 shares of IBM.

An automobile is at the opposite end of the facility-of-investment scale. The purchase, ownership, and sale of a collector car is anything but simple and easy.

In the first place, one share of stock or one bond is just like another share of stock or another bond of the same series in the same company. A Ferrari 275GTB-4 is most certainly not like another Ferrari 275GTB-4. The first may be mint and the second average or worse.

If you propose to buy 200 shares of IBM, you can ascertain the market price simply by looking it up in the newspaper. If the close of the stock in the newspaper is 150, then the price on the day you purchase might be 152 or 149 or 147, but at least not far from 150.

Not so with an automobile. You may have a target purchase price for a Ferrari 275GTB-4 of, say, $65,000. You find that a dealer has one for $75,000 and will not take $65,000. So you go out looking elsewhere, and now you find one for $59,000; only this one has plenty of miles on it, the engine is noisy, the paint could be better, and much of the body is rusted. Is it worth $59,000, or is it worth $55,000?

There is no repair and restoration problem in many investments—stocks and bonds included. Repair and restoration are the essence of the ownership of a collector car, and these things do not come cheap.

If you have $60,000 worth of IBM stock, you can put it in a safe deposit box. Fire insurance is not a problem. Nor is liability insurance or collision insurance. Insurance is a major problem in the ownership of a collector car— all kinds of insurance, and expensive insurance.

There is no problem of storage for stocks and bonds. The brokerage firm will store them free of charge, or you can place the stocks and bonds in your safe deposit box and forget about them. Storage for a collector car, on the other hand, can be both expensive and a major problem. A fine car needs special storage away from the risk of fire, theft, and vandalism, and such safe storage can be difficult to find and costly.

There are two theories about storage of collector cars. The first is that such cars should be run fairly regularly, otherwise things will deteriorate. This can happen, certainly, under some poor storage conditions. The other theory is that if you run a collector car, you will have troubles, costly troubles. This has been more or less my theory over the past twenty-five years, and my cars have deteriorated, but very little.

Whether a car is used occasionally or not used, the paint and upholstery deteriorate, and at least one new paint job is required every ten years. Fine leather upholstery might last fifteen years if taken care of. If the car is not used for a year, the brake cylinders (wheel cylinders) might very well rust in one position, and various diaphragms will probably deteriorate beyond usefulness, like the diaphragm in the fuel pump. The rubber around doors, windows, and windshield will certainly deteriorate, just as the tires will deteriorate.

Licensing may not be a major problem, but in many states licensing means an annual personal property tax based on the value of the car, and this tax may well run to four figures annually on an expensive car. Now tax assessors are aware of the value of "old cars," and they have raised the annual property tax on one of my cars several thousand percent in just one year.

One savvy investor from Massachusetts once told me that he shifted into paintings from automobiles because, he said, every time he went out to his garage to look at his investment cars, there were flat tires and dead batteries, and he could not stand these burdens anymore.

One car that I bought was practically given to me. But it was worth very little to me, or to anyone else, because of the ownership problems, mainly storage problems; and yet it was a classic investment car—a Mercedes-Benz 300S. Apparently the car had been stored in a leaky garage or barn. It was eleven years old and should still have been in reasonably good condition. Only it wasn't!

The top was rotted out, as were the leather upholstery and carpets. The paint was gone, and large parts of the body and metal under both doors were rusted out. Most of the chrome was gone. The headlight reflectors were rusted. The body required hundreds of hours for restoration. Of course the tires were completely rotted, and some blew out—before I could get the car to the garage.

The fellow who sold the car to me knew that it was a desirable model, that it was an investor car, and that it should have had some investment value. Maybe it did if it had been stored properly and cared for—even a bit. But this car wasn't far from being a parts car. We won't go into the mechanical deterioration, as part of this deterioration was caused by improper storage and part by improper use and maintenance.

One might conclude that not only is it difficult to handle a car as an investment but it is almost impossible to consider a car as a pure investment at all.

But to move from the gloomy side of the ownership of a strictly investment car to the more positive side, I bought a 1955 Mercedes-Benz 300S in 1966 and restored it completely, bringing my total investment in the car to about $4,800. I now have $6,500 in the car in total capital outlay and have had only storage bills plus a few license fees and taxes that until a year ago were nominal. This is a strict investment car that I have run 3,000 miles in sixteen years, and my "ownership expenses" have been most reasonable. Four years ago I was offered $35,000 for the car and turned it down.

Defining Your Objectives

An automobile can be a pure investment, although certainly it can be difficult to buy it correctly, keep it correctly, keep it in condition at moderate expense, and sell it profitably. It can under a few circumstances be a passive investment, one that does not perform but stays put in the garage or warehouse. A Mercedes-Benz SSK or 540K roadster or a Bugatti Royale might be treated as a "museum exhibit" and stored carefully with only very occasional use. It is also possible to secure an "oldie," a very old, turn-of-the-century one- or two-cylinder car, and place it on display in your drawing room, provided you have a mansion.

Enough of a car as a pure investment to be compared dollar for dollar with stocks and bonds! The original purpose of an automobile was to take somebody somewhere, and this is possibly still a purpose of an automobile that is desirable enough to be considered an investment.

One legitimate purpose of a collector car is use. My 1966 Ford Mustang was bought as a use car—with an eye to appreciation. It was not bought the other way around—as an investment that might be used. As time went on and the value of this model car went up, then gradually it became more and more of an investment and less and less of a use car.

The goal of the car collector must be carefully defined or decided in advance of purchase. A Corvette or Sting Ray can probably be used for transportation, although when a car is used regularly, it will decline in quality and will require not only repairs but periodic restoration, perhaps very expensive periodic restoration.

Recently I looked at a Ferrari 365 two-plus-two (four-passenger) coupe that was used for transportation. It needed a major engine overhaul, and this work was performed for about $7,500—not a huge sum for overhauling a quality car, and probably low for the overhaul of a Ferrari engine. After the overhaul job was completed, the owner then put the car in regular service again. I wouldn't like a $7,500 bill for overhaul regularly. On the other hand, I was quite prepared to pay $1,433.15 to repaint my Mustang and put in a completely new engine.

I would not expect anyone to buy a Duesenberg J or SJ for a use car. At most one might run such a car 100 miles on a weekend once in a while or drive it a few miles each weekend. Repairs and restoration are expensive, and parts can run to an enormous sum and require time to locate or have made new for the car as required.

The objective in buying and owning a collector car may be a kind of advertising—prestige-building. A collector may very well buy a Mercedes-Benz 500K roadster just to drive to the country club, letting his family out in plain view of the other members of the club, then roaring off. He and the car will create something of a sensation. If the owner is single, the impression may be even more important!

It can be ego-building, certainly, to ask your dinner guests to come out to look at the Rolls-Royce Phantom III V-12 convertible sedan that resides in your garage. Emulation and conspicuous consumption are, no doubt, major motives of buyers of collector cars today.

Nostalgia can be a motive in buying collector cars, but I believe that it used to be more important as a buying motive than it is today, although it is still a motive, particularly for new collectors. When I was a boy, I used to be tremendously impressed with Mercedes-Benz cars, and at that time they were the big supercharged S, SS, and SSK models that outran almost everything on the road, certainly most American cars. When I could I purchased one such car—eleven years after it was new and in vogue. In a sense, one brings back the past by the purchase of a collector car. My first Mercedes cost me $350. The less affluent collector today can buy a Corvair for $1,500.

There are collateral benefits to owning a collector car. There is a camaraderie among collector car owners. Through my early collector car ownership, I made friends that remained close to me for over forty years, and we got together for meets and races many times over the decades, starting with the first Watkins Glen race.

How Much to Invest

An early decision for the car collector is how much to invest. It is well to start out rather modestly, not risking too much capital, getting into repair and restoration gradually so as to get used to the sums required for this purpose, and getting the feel of a collector car. The car will not be like the American car with a twelve-month 12,000-mile guarantee with an extended guarantee for $150 a year. It will very likely be costly and a good deal of trouble, and it is well to experience both expense and trouble modestly before plunging heavily into automobiles as an investment.

Review of advertisements for cars in newspapers and visits to classic and sports car dealers will give an idea of what is available and at what price.

If one is considering investing, say, $50,000, is it better to buy just one car or several cars? New collectors would do well to stick to inexpensive cars, since repairs will probably not be costly—the Ford Mustang, the Chevrolet Corvette and Corvair, and the semiclassic cars of the 1950s.

On the other hand, a very solid investment can be made in a fairly recent sports car, with Ferrari probably in the lead, and if the $50,000 is stretched a bit then one might buy a Ferrari Daytona coupe or a 275GTB-4 or a Lamborghini Miura, among many other cars.

Price Trends

If one considers a collector car as primarily an investment, then there is a considerable resemblance between the collector car market and the stock market. One looks for uptrends in both as one means of forecasting future movements. If Ferraris have been moving up, then the chances are that they will continue to move up. Two years ago, Ferraris were in a rather steep uptrend in price. Duesenbergs, after having risen tremendously in price over a five-year period, were not just on a plateau, they were settling back in price. It seemed that everyone who wanted to own a Duesenberg owned a Duesenberg and there were not many very active and wealthy seekers of Duesenbergs.

In 1982, Rolls-Royce cars were settling back in price after having risen tremendously over a ten-year period—particularly the Silver Clouds of 1955–1965. As of late 1982, the Silver Clouds and corresponding Bentleys in England were certainly off in price, particularly so when one considers the very strong dollar in relation to the pound sterling. In America, on the other hand, in late 1982 prices of the same model Rolls-Royces were starting upward again.

One could, of course, look for sleepers, cars that have not risen much in price but seem to be good candidates for a price rise. The Maserati Ghibli is probably the most beautiful sports coupe ever built. In 1982 prices seemed low for the quality of the car—under $20,000 even for the best Ghiblis of 1972. Perhaps the Ghibli will rise. The Mustang was a sleeper until about 1979; then it took off, but it still is not extremely high in price. It is still in the process of working out an upward price trend, particularly the convertibles of 1964–1966.

Individual Taste

This heading might also read: "What Kind of Collector Car Do You Like—If Any?" In collecting cars you should buy what you like, or else go in for collecting coins or postage stamps or something else you do like. No matter how fine the car and what a fine investment it may be, I will never buy a car that I do not like, and I will almost never consider a car that I do not like a good deal. I must get satisfaction out of owning the car, driving it occasionally, and knowing that a beautiful vehicle is in my garage. Otherwise the car is not worth the trouble, and there is plenty of trouble connected with the ownership of exotic cars.

Some people like huge classic cars like the Locomobile and the Cadillac V-16. Others, but rather few, like the really old antiques, like the curved-dash Olds of 1903, the single-cylinder Brush, and other "oldies." At the other extreme in time are those who like the Ferrari 275GTB-4 and the Lamborghini Miura.

There is another group, possibly distinct from these two groups, that likes the enormous Rolls-Royce Phantom III V-12 and the Phantom V, big, opulent automobiles.

On the other hand, the man who likes the single-cylinder Olds just might like the Phantom III Rolls too.

Many years ago, someone writing about sports cars said, "If you are on the fence about purchasing a particular car, don't buy it, because if you do you will get to hate it after a while." How right he was—at least as far as I am concerned. Every car that I was on the fence about buying and purchased I got to dislike intensely after a time. Conversely, the irresistible cars remained that way for as long as I owned them—irresistible. So it is a good policy to invest in only those cars that you like and that give you satisfaction; and if no cars give you satisfaction, then don't buy any collector car.

To end this section on a more businesslike and investor-oriented note, one might lean in the direction of buying a car that people want, that the market seeks out, provided it is one's objective to sell the car after a time for a gain. The car should be one that dealers and auctions will reach for, if possible. Some of these cars are the Ferrari Daytona and 275GTB-4, the Duesenberg J and SJ, the Cadillac V-16, all prewar sports Alfa Romeos, and all Rolls-Royce two-, three-, and four-cylinder cars, if any of these are available. This is only a sampling of the cars in demand. The market will not reach so hard for a Bentley right-hand-drive SII sedan, an early Corvair, or a medium-condition Mustang convertible—to name just a few of the cars that are more difficult to sell today.

Condition of the Car Before and After Purchase

At this point, it might be well to backtrack to the cost of maintaining a collector car and emphasize one aspect of ownership—maintenance. For example, I like a late-1920s Bugatti, and also a late-1920s Packard Straight Eight. The Bugatti, I feel, would cause me a great deal of trouble and expense just to own it, and if I ran it very much I would expect repair costs to be enormous. On the other hand, the Packard Straight Eight of the same period is a vastly simpler car and anything but a troublemaker. If the two cars were equal in my preference (in other words, all other things being equal), I would choose the Packard, since it is far easier to maintain than a Bugatti.

A water pump went on my Maserati Ghibli recently. I priced a new one—the best price I could get in my area—at $850. For my Mustang of about the same year, the price of a water pump was $41.40.

My Rolls-Royce Silver Cloud II required an oil pump. I found an advertisement in an auto magazine of "bargain price oil pumps" for the Silver Cloud series—$700. For my Mustang of about the same vintage, the price was $38.15.

Of course, we may be comparing champagne with beer in comparing a Ghibli or a Rolls-Royce with a Mustang. On the other hand, to compare two champagnes, a new windshield for a Ghibli costs $699—down from $980 a few years ago—and a new windshield for my Rolls-Royce cost me $250. Quite a difference, and the two cars are comparable luxury automobiles.

Some parts are extremely hard to come by. Maserati parts are not the easiest to find. On the other hand, Rolls-Royce parts are not at all hard to find, especially parts for the Silver Clouds of 1955–1965.

New parts may cost a good deal. Used parts in many cases are about as good as new parts—for instance, a door handle, a windshield, a shift lever, a hubcap. An auto parts firm in New York sold me, among many other Rolls-Royce parts, an oil pump for my Cloud II for $125—very much less than the "bargain price" of $700. The Rolls-Royce radiator ornament, the figure of a lady, may be bought for $350 to $450. A firm in California sold me one of these, an original and not a later copy, for $150.

So while you are deciding whether a Bugatti Type 55 or a Rolls-Royce Flying Spur will suit you, remember repair costs and parts costs as well as parts availability—and, of course, costs of skilled labor to repair the make of car you have collected.

Over the years I have owned four Mercedes-Benz 300S roadsters and cabriolets. This is one of the highest-quality cars made in the entire postwar period. It sold new for about $13,250, in the region of the Rolls-Royce Silver

Clouds of the same era. My first 300S I bought rather quickly. It was a near-new top-quality car. The second Mercedes-Benz 300S I thought a long time before purchasing—not the particular car I purchased but whether I wanted a 300S or some other kind of car. I had just sold a sizable financial interest in my corporation and I felt I could afford a fine car. After thinking it over for a month I decided on another Mercedes-Benz 300S.

After only brief searching I found in a New York showroom a 1953 300S convertible that looked fine. The paint was perfect, the chrome was bright, the leather upholstery was in excellent condition. Carpets and top were very good, and even the tires were very good. I told the dealer I liked the car, but that the price, $4,800, was too much. Perhaps it was a little too much for that time—early 1958. The dealer asked me to go for a drive to try out the car, but I declined his offer and said that no, I was willing to offer $4,000 and forgo a test drive, a drive that might turn up mechanical faults. Whether this was correct buying technique I am not sure. I thought it might be. In any event he took my offer of $4,000 and I drove off with the car.

Today I wouldn't think of buying a 300S Mercedes without giving it a thorough road test and probably other tests besides; but in 1958 the things one could see (such as the body, chrome, top, and interior) were important, not the things one didn't see. A rusted body could cost a good deal to repair. Chrome plating did cost, even in 1958. A fine leather interior job could be done for $500. A top could be put on for $100 and another $100 would buy four excellent tires. Finally, a very good lacquer paint job could be put on for probably a maximum of $250.

I did have to buy a radiator cap with the Mercedes-Benz circular star, and this cost me $7.50. Today one can't be secured. If anyone wants to sell one, I am sure he can get $500 for it.

Labor in 1958 cost me $3 an hour, the best labor by mechanics who knew the 300S and had worked on it. I could have secured all the motor parts I wanted either new or secondhand.

Professional buyers, dealers, often just looked at the cars they were going to bid on. Perhaps they started them up and listened to them, but generally they bought on sight, recognizing that what was seen could cost the most, not the mechanics, which were not seen. Today someone told me that his V-8 diesel engine had conked out and had to be replaced. He was quoted a price for replacement of his engine with a new one from the factory—$8,000 for engine plus installation. I have referred several times to my Rolls-Royce Silver Cloud II of 1960 that I bought in 1977 for $7,000, a car in need of considerable restoration. Times changed very rapidly in the decade of the 1970s, and now one should look at a proposed purchase very carefully before going through with the deal.

Exterior of the Car

The first thing to consider in deciding whether a particular make, model, and year of a car is for you is to look at the exterior of the car, just as buyers have always done. A rusted-out body can cost a fortune to put right. The last Mercedes-Benz 300S convertible I bought required about 1,000 hours on the body and paint. It would have taken less if I'd been willing to have the rust holes filled with fiberglass, but I wanted steel plates welded in so that the body would be as near to what it was originally as possible. At the $3 an hour that was standard at the garage I used in 1966, this amounted to $3,000. Today one is lucky to get a rate of $15 an hour—or $15,000 for the job, charged today by this same garage with the same men doing the work.

When I bought my first Mercedes-Benz in 1938, a first-class paint and body shop in Washington, D.C., painted and striped the car for $25 and put on a new top for another $25. The same firm in 1960 painted my 1951 Bentley with Graber body in two-tone silver on white and charged $125 for an excellent job.

The last paint job I had on a Rolls-Royce sedan cost about $6,000. Chrome can usually be done for under $1,000. On the same Rolls-Royce the labor alone on the leather interior cost $5,350—in 1977. This figure was too high, but today a leather upholstery job on the same car would probably cost in the region of $5,000, so the times have caught up with the price.

On the other hand, a very respectable leather upholstery job might be secured, even today, for $1,500—not a superb job, but a satisfactory job. Top and carpets aren't major factors. A fine top was recently put on my Cadillac Eldorado convertible for $225, and for the same figure the finest carpets can be secured.

There are all grades of bodywork, paintwork, and upholstery. To get a top price for a car, the exterior of the car must be absolutely top in today's market.

The Engine

Not so long ago, one could buy a brand-new Cadillac engine from the factory for $525. Today the cost is staggering, by comparison. The owner of an Oldsmobile diesel had a crankshaft break while he was driving along the road. The cost of repairs to the engine was $3,500.

On the other hand, I just installed a factory-rebuilt engine in my 1966 Ford Mustang. It cost about $600 plus $19 freight from the factory to my repair shop. I did locate a Mustang engine for my car that had a reported 2,000 miles on it after complete rebuild. The price was only $150 plus $100 installation.

A complicated sports car engine today might very well require $10,000 for overhaul. When I bought my Lamborghini Miura, the seller had just spent $13,000 on the body and engine. I had to spend another $4,500 on it before I felt the car was in top condition.

In the "old days," as I've indicated, many professional buyers didn't bother to try out a car they were considering buying because the things they *saw* were the costly things, not the internal parts. Today no one would think of buying a car, except at a giveaway price, without starting it up and driving it.

The sound of the engine is highly important. What kinds of noises do you hear? Piston slaps and bearing noises should generally disqualify any car you are considering buying. Valve noises are something else. They can generally be cured and at not too great cost. The Eldorado Cadillac that I bought had very noisy valves. I pointed out this valve noise to the dealer and immediately improved my bargaining position. He agreed to lower the price $800 and repair the valve system at cost—$8 an hour plus parts at his cost instead of $25 an hour plus parts at retail. It seemed to me that the trouble was with worn hydraulic valve lifters, and I asked that all of these valve lifters be replaced. He did this job, but there was still noise. Next, at his cost, he replaced some worn rocker arms, and this did the job. The car's engine then sounded perfect and quiet.

Soon after starting up the engine, any prospective buyer should look at the oil pressure gauge. It should read normal, probably halfway up the dial. The Lamborghini Miura that I was considering buying showed absolutely no oil pressure on the gauge when the engine was started. I indicated to the seller that unless the gauge showed satisfactory pressure I wouldn't be interested in the car. In this case, the problem was merely a disconnected wire.

Once I bought a car that smoked from the exhaust. A lot of blue smoke, after the car has warmed up, usually means worn piston rings and probably worn cylinders. The car I was considering showed white smoke out of the exhaust pipe. I should have turned down the car, a Ferrari 250GT coupe, immediately, since white smoke probably means water leaking from the water jacket into the combustion chamber. I took the car anyway, and thereafter began a series of repairs to try to stop the water leak into the combustion chamber. I never did quite solve this problem.

A complicated and expensive car should not be bought without a compression test—a tester for cylinder compression placed in the hole of each spark plug. Low compression in one cylinder *may* mean a leaking exhaust valve, possibly a leaking intake valve, and a valve-grinding job may be required— not so expensive on most cars but it can cost $1,000 or thereabouts on an Italian super car like a Maserati. On the other hand, low compression may mean worn rings and even worn cylinders, and possibly an entirely new engine.

A few years ago, a firm in New Jersey charged a "bargain rate" of $3,500 for the rebuilding of a Rolls-Royce Silver Cloud eight-cylinder engine. I would expect the cost today to be higher. I would turn down a car with much dropoff in the compression reading of even one cylinder.

Next, I would look for cracks in the engine. In the first place, a cracked head can be seen. It can be welded, but it is not original. A cracked head on a Mustang is not so serious. A cracked head on a Rolls-Royce Phantom I or II may be replaced—I have seen used Phantom I and II heads advertised at $2,000 and above.

Next, the car must be put on a lift and the crankcase examined in the same way—for cracks. Oil seepages sometimes lead to cracks. Oil leaking from the crankcase gasket is not serious in most cases; all that is required is a new gasket. On the other hand, I would turn down most cars, certainly the complicated cars, with a cracked crankcase. Again, a Ford Mustang is another matter.

Transmission and Differential

From the engine inspection with the car on a lift, you move to the transmission and to the rear end (or differential), examining for leaks in the same way. Oil may be leaking out of the front or back of the transmission from worn seals. While seals cost little, putting them in can cost a good deal, several hundred dollars on the more complicated cars. A leak from the differential might possibly mean that the differential has been running with low lubricant or running dry, in which event you are in real trouble with an expensive car.

The car should now be driven to test the transmission and differential. Noise from these parts means expense. The noise in the differential of my Mercedes-Benz 300S meant that the differential had to be taken out of the car and disassembled three times—to get out the hum. Today it is probably necessary to send such a "humming rear end" to Germany for repairs, which repairs will cost at least $1,000. A replacement rear end is almost impossible to find for this model car. In fact, for rare cars trouble in the transmission or rear end probably is an indication that you should pass up the car.

Automatic transmissions are a different proposition and must be assessed differently. Most automatic transmissions are American adaptations, like the Borg-Warner transmission in my Maserati Ghibli. If the car has an American transmission, the transmission can probably be repaired quickly and relatively inexpensively by a transmission shop, of which there are now some responsible and skilled ones. On many American postwar classics, the overhaul of an automatic transmission can be accomplished quickly and at minimum cost, like $400. This was what it cost to overhaul my Mustang automatic transmission two years ago. A Cadillac transmission might cost a little more, but not much. Many Rolls-Royce cars use a modified GM automatic transmission.

Chassis and Suspension

Ten years ago, and certainly twenty years ago, the chassis was not generally any problem in buying a car. The traditional type of chassis was a steel frame made out of heavy-alloy metal. In sports cars, tubular or other special chassis members were sometimes used. One rarely had to examine the chassis to see its condition. It was sometimes twisted because of an accident, but it could usually be jacked straight. Even a twisted frame (chassis) was the exception. I never found one in the cars I bought over a period of forty years—not until 1980. The chassis was a rugged element of the automobile, and rust or other deterioration was rarely a problem. In the mid-1950s, chemicals began to be used to melt snow and ice on highways, and from that time on, car frames began to be attacked—and they deteriorated, even truck frames.

A visual examination must be made of the chassis with the car on the lift to determine the degree of deterioration. A deteriorated chassis may or may not be a determining factor. If the chassis is detachable, like the A.O. Smith chassis that was used on many of the older GM cars, a new chassis can be installed, and a chassis is not costly to buy. Of course, the removal of the car body to install a new chassis can be costly.

The new super sports cars are something quite different, however. The chassis of a Lamborghini Miura looks somewhat like the frame of a space vehicle, with twists, turns, and holes to lighten it. If it is damaged, it might be best to reject the car. It can be pulled into shape only to a degree—even with specialized chassis equipment. It can be welded, but the weld never looks like the original, and therefore could affect the value of the car. A perfectionist would probably turn down the car.

Installing a new chassis on a Lamborghini Miura is a major piece of work, provided a new chassis can even be bought—one may not be available, not even from the factory in Italy. And one trouble with the chassis on these super sports cars is that the chassis often seems to be damaged. Too many of these cars have been hit, and even a small hit can seriously damage the delicate and lightweight chassis. In fact, many such super cars are advertised as "never hit."

If the chassis has been bent, many of the suspension parts may be bent and twisted out of shape, and it may be next to impossible to get them back in shape. Certain parts of my own Miura were twisted. New parts were bought in Italy at the factory, but even when the chassis had been straightened (and it could not be straightened completely) the new parts would not fit. For them to fit, the chassis would have had to be straightened completely.

One of the difficulties with front-wheel drive is the universal joints located at each of the front wheels. For the Cadillac Eldorado, each of these universals complete costs about $650, so that the two cost $1,300, a sum large enough to give a prospective buyer second thoughts about purchasing an Eldorado with bad joints. The same for any front-wheel-drive car, like the Cord. These units on my Cord 810 had to be replaced regularly.

Sometimes the entire steering mechanism and suspension members are worn out and must be replaced. On a lift, it is not hard to see the amount of wear, and worn members sometimes even rattle because they are so worn and dry from improper lubrication. For the Ford Mustang the entire steering and suspension system can be replaced for $300 or $400. On older and limited-production cars, including expensive sports cars, the total cost of such replacements can be staggering.

Wiring System

Inspection with a flashlight along the chassis and under the dash may give an idea of the condition of the wiring system. Old, greasy, and drooping wires may mean an entire rewiring job. Of course, all electrical elements must be tested to see that they work, and that if they do not work the trouble is minor. A complete rewiring job can cost as much as $1,000, possibly more. On the other hand, my Lamborghini Miura was rewired almost completely for $550. For some fairly modern cars, it may be possible to get entire wiring systems from junkyards, systems that are not old and worn-out. Yet for some older cars and some custom cars, it may be next to impossible to trace out the wires and replace them as they were originally. One of the most complicated wiring systems is found on the XJ-S twelve-cylinder Jaguar. Straightening out the wiring system on this car may take days.

Brakes and Exhaust System

It may be wise to pull off the wheels in order to inspect the brakes and the wheel cylinders. The drums may be worn out, and on an older car it may be next to impossible to locate drums. It might seem difficult to locate wheel cylinders for older classics like the Mercedes-Benz 300S, but a brake specialist to whom I talked stated to me, "I have all sizes, every size, and I can replace whatever you need." And he did. Linings are, of course, nothing to replace. Discs for brakes can cost as much as $400 a disc, and there are two to four.

The exhaust system may or may not be an important factor. Several years ago I needed a resonator and tailpipe for a Rolls-Royce Silver Cloud I that I owned. The Rolls-Royce shop had the part I needed, all right—for $475. A complete system, a replacement system, but done well, might cost $2,200. On the other hand, the entire system for a Mustang might cost $150. For the Italian exotics, the cost of replacement parts may be almost prohibitive, even more than for a Rolls-Royce; and I will have to confess that the cost of a resonator and tailpipe for my first Maserati Ghibli was so high ($475 five years ago) that I replaced them with Midas parts. An exhaust system is little more than a pipe with parts for muffling the sound of the exhaust; and while there is talk of "engineering balance" and the like, if the pipe is large enough so that there is no back pressure, then it does the job and cannot damage the engine. Of course, original parts are better than substitute and bargain parts, and on some exotics, like the Maserati, excellent replacement parts can be secured from special sources. The Maserati Information Exchange in Washington State supplies the front section for the Ghibli for $189 and the rear section for $152. I bought both sections for my own Ghibli from this source.

Know the Car's Peculiarities

The Mercedes-Benz 300S is a masterpiece of engineering, construction, and materials. It has peculiarities, however, and one of these is a differential that has a tendency to hum, sometimes loudly. This hum is almost impossible to repair without sending both differential and axles to Germany. My differential was out of the car and in expert hands three times. I will not say that I won't buy a Mercedes-Benz 300S with a humming differential, but such a fault would be a deterrent. I would not buy any 300S without first hearing whether the car had a rear-end hum.

In the Maserati Ghibli I would want to make sure that the radiator cooled the car in hot weather, and I would let the car stand and idle for an hour and note the heat rise. The car has a tendency to overheat. The compressor for the air-conditioning system on this car does not seem to last long, and it might be worn on the car you are thinking of buying. A compression test is a must to see that pistons and cylinders are not worn. Sometimes the valves hit the top of the piston, causing damage that in some cases is almost beyond repair. A Ghibli must be very carefully studied before purchase.

All cars have certain weaknesses, some more than others. The Cord 810 and 812 had a transmission with electric shift that gave trouble periodically. I had to send my old transmission to the Auburn-Cord-Duesenberg Company in Auburn, Indiana, on occasion, for a replacement.

By talking with owners of cars of the type you are thinking of buying, you can get an idea of the difficulties with the car, and almost all cars have certain difficulties. The car clubs are often frank about the difficulties of certain models of the car owned by their members. The Maserati Information Exchange supplies in its newsletter enough information to indicate exactly what the weaknesses are in many Maserati models. The repair shops for Mercedes-Benz, Ferrari, etc., will often supply similar information. One might think the long-block Ferrari engine is better than the short-block engine simply because there is more engine to do the job; however, the predominant expert opinion is in favor of the smaller short-block engine.

How Original Is the Car?

The originality of a collector car can often be of the essence. If it is totally original, perhaps a true antique such as say, a Thomas Flyer with its enormous engine, the car has a distinct plus for it as a collector car. On the other hand, a number of Maserati Ghiblis are advertised with Chevrolet engines substituted for the original engine. In fact, one owner of such a Ghibli wrote an article in the *Maserati Market Letter* showing exactly how the Chevy engine could be substituted for the Maserati engine. Of course, the substitution reduced the value of the car by at least half, and maybe more. I have seen such a Ghibli advertised for sale for $4,000 when the market was about $11,000 for an average-condition car with an original Maserati engine.

One big trouble with the Briggs Cunningham Stutz Super Bearcat that Christie's auctioned off in early 1981 in Los Angeles was the substitute transmission. An official of Christie's said that he was quite sure an original transmission could be purchased from one or two sources, and he indicated the names and addresses of these sources. The substitute transmission, if it could not be replaced with an original Stutz transmission, might cut the value of this great car by 25% to 35%, perhaps even more.

When I bought my Rolls-Royce Silver Cloud II sedan, one of the troubles with the car was that it had no original tools and no box of accessories, including light bulb, small wrenches, etc. The absence of these accessories is a great deterrent to the sale of any Rolls-Royce, and the missing items are hard to find and costly. Over a period of time I replaced everything—secondhand, of course. The jack cost $75, the tire iron $50, the air pump $75. An air pump of similar quality, simply a hand air pump, could be bought for $12.50 or thereabouts new, but it wouldn't be an original Rolls-Royce pump. The parts kit cost $250, and the peculiar wrench for removing a part of the transmission cost $50. And so it went.

It is not by any means easy to determine the original condition of a car. I once bought a convertible in deplorable condition, from differential to transmission and clutch to engine. I concentrated first on its appearance, putting on all new chrome, including hubcaps and new tires, new leather upholstery, a fine lacquer paint job, new fine fabric top and carpets. The car looked as good as it ever did when it was brand-new. But mechanically? That was something else, and it took years to straighten out the car. Had a person bought it with all of these cosmetics done, he would not have secured what he thought he was buying—a car in perfect condition all through.

Classic cars are like antique furniture—only sometimes better! A slant-top desk with replaced feet (and there are many of these) is a far different thing from a slant-top desk with original feet, particular ogee feet, or ogee bracket feet (curved and very much in demand). Replacement feet can cut the price of a desk in half. An exchange engine of the same type will, however, usually not cut the value of a collector car, but originality of a collector car is very important. Putting in a different kind of engine will tremendously lower value in a collector car.

What Is the Car's History?

In visiting antique dealers and looking at their wares, I very often ask, "Where did you buy this table? At auction?" The auctions produce some fine pieces, but I would rather have the dealer tell me he bought the piece privately or from an estate. The antique should not be a tired (unwanted) piece of merchandise that a dealer decided to unload to auction—either because it was not of top quality or because it had been around too long, unsold.

If the classic car dealer tells me that he bought the car he is offering for sale at auction, then unless it was an estate auction or there was a good reason for the sale, I lose at least a little interest. One dealer had a Maserati Ghibli that he said he was going to sell in Atlantic City in the next auction. Why didn't he keep it and sell it at retail? Because everything was wrong with the car and the more parts and labor he put into fixing up this car, the more he had to do, until his patience with the car ran out and he felt he had put enough money into fixing it up.

Now I would certainly not want to buy this car at auction or buy it from a dealer who had bought it at auction. This is "tired" merchandise, like the antiques and paintings that dealers dump at auction because they are not of sufficient quality to be offered in their showrooms.

If the car dealer tells me that the car he is selling is a one-owner car and that he knows the mileage is a genuine 23,000 because he has known the owner for a long time, that background is a definite plus for the car.

If the car comes from a known fine collection, that is a plus. "Collection cars," from the best collections, do not often come onto the market. Their owners want to hold on to them, and these collector cars that are not generally offered for sale are premium automobiles. If the background of a car is known, and if it is a good background of few owners and a high level of maintenance and few miles, that is the kind of collector car to go after.

The Maserati Information Exchange offers a unique service to its members and one that can prove very valuable to prospective Maserati buyers. This organization, located in Mercer Island, Washington, keeps detailed records on a number of Maserati cars—who the owners have been, when the car changed hands, what work was done to the car and when. Such a record also helps in avoiding buying a stolen car, since one can check prior ownership by contacting this organization. I would feel a lot safer buying a car if I knew its whole history. I would also get an idea of total mileage on the car, a fact that is very important, since whatever way you look at it, the more miles on the car the less good it is overall.

It should be noted that almost all collector cars require some restoration. Top-grade dealers often do fine restoration jobs, which they can do, at their out-of-pocket costs, for much less than a collector can. Probably 75% of dealer cars are in such good condition as to require little restoration, but only 25% of cars offered for sale by private owners are in this fine condition.

Caveat Emptor

Here is an actual example of the purchase of an automobile as an investment that didn't turn out to be an investment after all. A young man in college felt that he might well buy a 1970 Chevrolet Camaro, since it would very likely turn out to be a good investment. He purchased the car in October 1978 for $1,200, with the knowledge that it would require work. In 1981 he bought a new engine for $1,500, and he also had had many minor items of expense totaling $430.

When I talked to him in late 1982, he was getting ready to do the bodywork. Four fenders had to be purchased for $2,500, and all the bodywork necessary, including the fenders, would come to $4,000, the best estimate he had been able to secure. He also felt he must buy a rebuilt transmission for $400.

He apparently had $3,130 in the car and faced future costs of $4,400, a total of $7,530.

The day after I talked with him I called Paul Anthony Longo, an excellent restorer, and one who, I know, has restored Camaros. He told me that he had sold a 1971 Camaro in very good condition but not by any means mint for $2,000.

I would estimate that when this other Camaro is complete at a cost of

$7,530 it may well be in better condition than the $2,000 Longo car, but not enough to make a difference this great.

To me this is a perfect example of buying a car that is hardly a collector or investment car. Maybe it will be one day, but it is hardly a good investment as of today. This is also a perfect example of buying a car that has *no value at all* to the investor. To have made the car an investment in any sense of the word, he would have had to be given his Camaro free. The next question is how much the man who sold the Camaro should have given the new owner along with the Camaro to make the whole "investment" make sense.

Many people think they are buying investment cars that will be worth a fortune when they are really buying cars that have little or no investment aspect. In addition, *the car* is the important thing for them to buy—so they think—and not the *condition* of the car. So they get stuck with a tremendous potential cash outlay which will result in a total investment so high that they cannot get a material part of it back in the foreseeable future.

5

The Gilt-Edged Investment Cars

THE TERM "GILT-EDGED" applied to collector cars has approximately the same meaning as in stocks and bonds. Gilt-edged stocks are the most solid, risk-free, conservative stocks, the stocks that the big mutual funds, pension funds, and other institutions buy—and buy in some quantity. They are not necessarily the "get-rich-quick" stocks. They are the stocks issued by the largest and soundest corporations, those with a long history and with a fairly continuous uptrend in earnings as well as in price. Such stocks can be expected to rise in an up market and go down most moderately in a bear market.

"Gilt-edged" in art may well mean the paintings of Rembrandt, Rubens, Titian, Velasquez, and the like, top artists in the museums of the world.

The term "gilt-edged" is synonymous with "blue-chip." If a bank administering a trust fund decided it would like to include some collector cars in one or more of its trust funds, the gilt-edged cars that we describe in this chapter are what the bank might include. As far as I know, no trust fund manager has included any collector cars in any portfolio and the mutual funds do not invest in cars. Citibank, however, has shown a definite interest in placing some of the assets of its trust funds in art, the program developed in conjunction with Sotheby Parke Bernet, the big art and antique auction house.

Webster's dictionary defines "gilt-edged" as "of the highest quality, grade or value: said of bonds, securities, etc." And that is our use of the term in connection with collector cars.

The Great Classic Cars

Bugatti Royale

When the Bugatti Royale is mentioned, most people think of a chariot for the Deity to ride in. It wasn't always so. Just before the onset of World War II, the sports or classic car in the greatest demand and at high prices was probably the Alfa Romeo, and of all of the Alfas probably the most wanted was the Model 1750, a small, very sporty-appearing car that looked something like a racer. It had a six-cylinder engine with twin overhead camshafts. Some cars were supercharged. The New York firm of Whalan and Gilhooly, both ex-racing drivers, had one of these cars for sale in 1939 for $3,000. This was about market at the time. What collectors wanted then were small, compact, very sporty cars.

At the other extreme was the Bugatti Royale, a massive machine with a 14-foot wheelbase and an enormous 12.7-liter engine (the largest Cadillac Eldorado had an 8.2-liter engine).

No one was even remotely interested in this mammoth car in the immediate prewar days. Nor was anyone much interested in any other of these "oversize" cars, including the Duesenberg J and SJ, the Grosser Mercedes-Benz 770K, and the Cadillac V-16.

Now all that has changed, and probably at the very pinnacle of collector and investor interest is the Bugatti Royale, the Type 41 of the late 1920s. None is on the market or is likely to be on the market, at least in the near future.

The designer of the Bugatti was Ettore Bugatti, who was almost certainly the greatest automobile innovator in the entire prewar period. He came up with more new ideas on automobile design, particularly on engine design, than anyone else. His specialty was super-luxury sports, semi-sports, and competition cars.

The Bugatti Royale was designed in 1926 and was listed in the Bugatti sales catalogue from 1926 to 1933, although no more than seven cars were ever actually constructed. It was meant to be the greatest car in the world, greater than Rolls-Royce, Isotta Fraschini, Hispano-Suiza, Duesenberg, and Cadillac. Whether this objective was realized is a matter of engineering and design opinion—expert opinion. In any event, the car was probably the most impressive production car ever manufactured. The engine, a straight eight with three valves per cylinder and an overhead camshaft, is so large that one has to turn his head to take it all in. It turns out 300 horsepower and may well drive the car at 130 mph.

The bodies were different, some open and some closed, but with the very long hood the effect is more than significant. When I first saw the Bugatti Royale, I was impressed, but not enough to buy it at the time, although I could have afforded the $600. The car is massive, and I could visualize a great deal of mechanical trouble if I wanted to drive it regularly. Now it is so valuable and so expensive to repair that no one would want to drive it except very occasionally and on very short trips.

It is highly unlikely that if one of these cars came onto the market it would sell for less than $2,000,000, although $2,000,000 would be a record price for a classic or antique car. The Harrah Automobile Collection of Reno, Nevada, is probably the world's largest collector car museum. Recently, forty cars from the museum were sent on tour around the country. One was a Bugatti Royale. The tour manager, Howard J. Cohen, said that the Bugatti Royale was worth "close to $5,000,000." Maybe so; the value is certainly very high. The Bugatti Royale is an absolutely unique car.

Duesenberg J and SJ

The Duesenberg J and SJ were produced in very limited numbers. The J was introduced in 1928 and the SJ in 1936, and everything ground to a halt in 1937. Only 470 of these great cars were produced in all. In the eighteen-year production life of *all* models of Duesenberg, only about 1,000 cars were produced.

On the market there is not a great deal of difference in price between the Model J and the Model SJ, the S standing for supercharged. Surprisingly, it is not at all hard to buy a Duesenberg J or SJ today. Certainly, prices are high, but not sky-high, considering the quality of the car, what it cost new, and the interest of collectors in owning one of these all-time greats. Currently, prices are on a plateau after having risen greatly in the past five years, and $200,000 should purchase a very fine Model J or SJ convertible coupe or convertible sedan, some of the most wanted models.

The Duesenberg is placed right after the Bugatti Royale because the cars are in many ways similar. Ettore Bugatti produced the Royale as the finest car in the world. E.L. Cord, the head of the Auburn-Cord-Duesenberg Company, wanted to "produce a new car which, in terms of style, engineering and sheer panache, should rival the best the world has to offer."

The car was and is that. The company advertised it as "the world's finest car." The bodies were big and impressive, like those on the Bugatti Royale, and made by the greatest body builders in the United States and Europe. The engine of the Bugatti Royale was a straight eight with single overhead camshaft and three valves per cylinder. The Duesenberg engine, also a straight eight, had twin overhead camshafts and four valves per cylinder. The J produced 265 horsepower and the supercharged SJ a reported 320 horsepower, which drove the car at a reported 130 mph—as compared with 55 mph for the Ford of the same era!

In the late prewar period and in the war years, the Duesenberg was a drug on the market. The dual-cowl phaeton was too big, too long, too heavy. Today, the same dual-cowl phaeton that was offered for $600 in 1940 would bring $200,000 plus. The car is actually a thing of beautiful workmanship, engineering, and style. Today, it could not possibly be manufactured for anything like its market price. The price would have to be so high that few or no cars could be sold.

Cadillac V-16

A third car in the ultra-luxury class is the Cadillac V-16. It is also a car in the ultra-high-priced class on today's market. A good case can be made for the Cadillac V-16 as the most expensive car on the classic car market today. The Bugatti Royale is never on the market, and the Duesenberg hardly tops the most desired years and body models of the Cadillac V-16.

The Cadillac V-16 was introduced by General Motors in 1930 at the onset of the Depression. It was priced very high for the time—$5,350 to $8,750. Prices were, however, below those of Duesenbergs of the period, because more Cadillac V-16's were built and sold, and all bodies were in effect factory-made, by Fleetwood, exclusive body builders to General Motors.

In the 1980s we are still talking about GM, Ford, and Chrysler, all of whom, so it is said, turned out whatever they wanted to dump on the public with no thought of quality construction. Such is, and was, not quite the case, however. The Cadillac V-16 was a thoroughly studied project, under the direction of Cadillac's chief engineer, Ernest Seaholm.

To aid in the design of a super-luxury car, General Motors purchased England's finest—a Rolls-Royce—and tore it to pieces to see what made it tick. Maurice Olley, a Rolls-Royce engineer, worked on the suspension method of the Cadillac V-16 and developed new testing methods. The "roadability" of the car was very carefully developed.

The engine, for the era of the car, was extremely smooth, having sixteen cylinders, the largest number of cylinders of any production car in the world. It was silent, one reason being that it used hydraulic valve lifters, common in all standard nonsport cars today, but something of an innovation in 1930, when the V-16 first appeared. The engine put out a good 165 horsepower with its overhead-valve design, and its top speed was a healthy 90 mph.

In the two Depression years of 1930 and 1931 a total of 3,250 Cadillac V-16's were produced, vastly more than all of the Duesenbergs produced in eighteen years of production; but from 1933 on, Cadillac never produced more than 300 V-16's in any year. In 1938, a less complicated and less modern engine was introduced into the V-16—a flat or L-head V-16 engine. It was smaller and lighter than the overhead-valve V-16, but it produced more horsepower—185 as against 165 for the overhead-valve engine. In the final year of production of the V-16, only sixty-one cars were built.

Perhaps the Cadillac V-16 was, and is, not in the same league with the Bugatti Royale and the Duesenberg J and SJ, but the impression is the same. All are large, beautiful, well-designed luxury automobiles, and the V-16 is the equal of the Duesenberg in price on the collector market of today.

The great V-16's, the value cars, are those built from 1930 to 1932. The particular body models that create the greatest values are the convertible coupe and the convertible sedan. The 1930–1932 convertibles can easily be worth three times what the 1938–1940 convertibles are, and $350,000 is not an unusual price as of the mid-1980s for a 1930–1932 convertible coupe.

Chrysler Imperial 8

The Chrysler Imperial of the early 1930s is in the same super-luxury class as the Bugatti Royale, the Duesenberg, and the Cadillac V-16. There is a vast difference in quality of construction and engineering between the Chrysler and the Duesenberg and Bugatti. In fact, in terms of engineering, Bugatti and Duesenberg stand at the top, Cadillac V-16 in the middle, and Chrysler Imperial "comes next." The Chrysler is not the equal of the top two—Royale and Duesenberg—in quality of materials and workmanship on the body. But in appearance the Chrysler Imperial is certainly the equal of the Royale, the Duesenberg, and the Cadillac V-16.

Impressions are important in determining demand and price of collector cars, and of all of the cars on the market, new and used, in the early 1930s, the car that I dreamed of owning and driving up to McKinley Technical High School in Washington, D.C., where I was living at the time, was the Chrysler Imperial.

From the time it was first built in 1924, the Chrysler was a prestige car. It was, first of all, a good car, reliable, low-priced, and inexpensive to maintain. It was also of advanced design, with a high-revving engine, a high top speed, and the latest amenities. Four-wheel brakes were something of a pioneering feature, as was the hydraulic braking mechanism.

Through the years, Chrysler put out its Imperial 80, a six-cylinder top-of-the-line car, but it was just that—top of the line but not an ultimate prestige car. Chrysler's ultimate prestige car came out in 1930, as did the Cadillac V-16, Cadillac's ultimate prestige car. The styling of the 1930 Imperial was every bit as good as that of the other American prestige cars, and the Imperial was possibly aimed at the Packard market, the top prestige American *volume* car.

The wheelbase was a very long 145 inches, 21 inches longer than the Packard wheelbase. The Chrysler Custom Imperial roadster, a stunner, was priced at an amazingly low $3,220. The car was long and low with sweeping lines. The fenders were beautifully curved, and the grille was even more impressive than on the other Chryslers of the period. The hood was enormous. Bodies could be secured by such coachbuilders as Murphy, LeBaron, Derham, Locke, and Waterhouse, so that in appearance, the Chrysler Imperial seemed to be the equal even of Duesenberg.

The engine was a flat or L-head straight eight that drove the car at a top speed of perhaps 96 mph.

The Chrysler Imperial convertible sedans and roadsters of 1931 and 1932 are among the highest-priced collector cars on the market in the early 1980s. Today they are easily selling in the $200,000 range. By way of contrast, the closed Imperials of the same years are selling for one fourth as much. The last of these great and high-priced Imperials was produced in 1933. The Imperial was produced even up to the 1980s, but it is a far different and far less prestigious car, not a great standout.

Packard

In the late 1920s and 1930s, one never saw a Bugatti Royale, the Duesenberg was confined to the big cities, and there were few enough Cadillac V-16's and Chrysler Imperials anywhere. The Packard was *the* big prestige car, known as such probably because those with money were buying them and there were a lot of Packards around, and at that time Packard made nothing but prestige cars. The cheaper models were introduced late in the 1930s. Karl Ludvigsen in the series of books entitled *The World of Automobiles*, had this to say: "Packard, now with a new plant behind its spotless reputation, consolidated its position as the number one luxury car in the United States." One didn't simply refer to a Packard. It was almost always "a Packard Straight Eight."

There are, essentially, two great and valuable collector Packards—the eight-cylinder made in the years 1930 and 1931 and the V-12 of 1932 and 1933, all Depression cars. Eight-cylinder cars were made in the 1920s, but the most-wanted eights are those produced in the two years 1930 and 1931. The eight-cylinder model 740 and model 745 and the V-12's, the model 840's, and the various "900 numbers" are favorites in the car auctions and always bring high prices—generally in six figures. The convertible sedans and convertible coupes are the cars most in demand at the highest prices.

Packard put out a beautiful speedster in 1930—the Model 734, and, apparently, only six boattail speedsters of this model were produced. In the Leake sale of 1980, one of these rare cars brought $125,000, a low price for the time and certainly a low price for today.

In the December 1981 Christie's sale of the cars belonging to the Wings and Wheels Museum of Orlando, Florida, a fabulous Packard V-12 of 1934 brought $350,000, the highest auction price ever paid for an American car. The car was a dual-cowl phaeton with an extremely rakish body by the coachbuilder Rollston. In the Wings and Wheels sale, a number of Duesenbergs were offered, but this Packard topped them all. It was at least the equal in appearance of most Duesenbergs.

A custom-bodied eight or a V-12 of this era, convertible or touring car,

1930 Isotta Fraschini Type 8A convertible cabriolet with Castagna body, sold at Christie's in 1979 for $100,000. In 1970 this same car might have brought only $20,000; today it would be valued at about $125,000. (Christie's, New York)

would be one of my choices for inclusion in a target collection of great cars. A car of this rarity and beauty is not likely to appear again in the near future, but one auction contained two Packard 734 boattail speedsters, and it would be my objective at some time to secure one of these 734's for a collection of prime cars.

Hispano-Suiza

In 1940, I asked the German mechanic in New York who worked on my Mercedes-Benz supercharged SS what car he would choose for himself if he could have any car of any type and any year. He replied, "Hispano-Suiza. I feel that is the finest car made."

There are two models of Hispano-Suiza that in many ways stand at the apex of the cars produced by this firm.

Almost certainly, the most celebrated is the H6C model, also known as the 46CV. This was an overhead-camshaft car with a big (8-liter) engine. This model was also known as the Boulogne. One such chassis fitted with an exotic tulipwood body was raced in the Targa Florio competition in 1924 by André Dubonnet. This car has a market price of about $400,000. Production Boulogne model Hispanos do come onto the market, and the cars on which to concentrate are the open cars. They can cost up to $200,000.

In 1931, the enormous V-12 model S4-220CV appeared. This car was known as the Type 68. This car "went backward" in design from the previous model in that it had overhead valves operated by pushrods, not by an overhead camshaft.

One has personal preferences, and I would want, of all the Hispanos, a mid-1930s convertible coupe, a V-12. The earlier models were straight sixes, and this one had twice the number of cylinders. Very important, most bodies were fantastically beautiful. I would expect to have to pay $250,000 for such a car, less for the more "normal" cars of the V-12 model. Production of this model, and of all Hispano-Suizas, stopped in 1938 during the Spanish Civil War. In the 1984 Barrett-Jackson auction a 1935 V-12 sold for $400,000. This price is a "breakthrough."

The previous model, the 46CV, was produced from 1923 to 1934. A convertible might be purchased for, say, $150,000 as of the early 1980s.

A third collector's model is the 32CV, a six-cylinder car like the 46CV, but with smaller engine capacity—6.2 liters. It was produced from 1919 to 1934. This would be my third choice for a Hispano. An open car of this model will probably cost as much as the later 46CV, into six figures.

Rolls-Royce Phantom III

The twelve-cylinder Rolls-Royce Phantom III of 1936 to 1939 was one of the most finely constructed cars ever to appear on the road. It also was, and is, one of the most complicated cars ever to come out commercially. If it could be made to function better, then complication was allowed in this car— number of cylinders, brakes, whatever.

The PIII is one of the most regal-looking cars ever built anywhere at any time. The English magazine *Autocar* reviewed the PIII in its October 2, 1936, issue as follows: "Some cars have to fight their way to fame; others are born to it, because of the reputation of their predecessors and the vast store of knowledge and experience possessed by their builders. Of this noble order is the 12-cylinder Rolls-Royce Phantom III. . . . Somewhere is an ultimate in the highest expression of road travel, comfort and performance, and the Phantom III is beyond question the nearest approach to it as yet."

On April 15, 1938, after the car had been in production for two years, the same magazine reviewed the Phantom III again and said, "No car attains quite the same impressiveness of appearance. The Rolls-Royce radiator is masterly in its dignity and sets off the whole machine, almost irrespective of the particular style of body it may carry. It is a custom to bestow bouquets upon this car, and sincerity may even be doubted by some; but it does unquestionably deserve them."

This was the prevailing expert opinion on this car when it appeared and during its production life. Its reputation today isn't quite so extravagant, and the PIII is not priced as high on the collector market as might be thought.

The body style on which to concentrate is the convertible sedan, a big open car about as impressive as the Mercedes-Benz 770K that Hitler and the other Nazi bigwigs rode in, but in many ways, the Rolls-Royce PIII is preferred to the Mercedes-Benz 770K. It might, on the present market, be possible to secure a PIII convertible sedan in excellent condition for $100,000.

The car is strictly a show car. It is complicated and is in constant need of maintenance if it is used to any great extent. In 1952 I advised a close friend of mine to buy one for his only car. The cost of repairs at Rolls-Royce of New York in one year exceeded the price my friend paid for the car.

The car was a bit hard to drive and hard-riding, but maybe I was comparing it with cars of much later and more advanced design. In any event, for $100,000 one could hardly go wrong on a PIII convertible. It is probably one of the underpriced great collectibles today.

Isotta Fraschini

One of the most impressive-looking cars I have ever seen for sale was an Isotta Fraschini Type 8A sport phaeton, offered for sale just before World War II by Whalan and Gilhooly at the Liberty Warehouse in New York. I was told it had been owned by Preston van Wyck. The car was tremendous and had a flathead straight-eight engine. The paint job was the unusual feature of the car—twenty-seven different colors (I counted them), achieved by striping in one color, and then placing another thin stripe of color alongside the first stripe. This paint job was a thing to behold.

Any auction that includes an important Isotta Fraschini has a real drawing card, an automobile that will attract people who just want to see the car and watch it being auctioned.

The Type 8 was introduced in 1921, and in 1924, the 8A was introduced, a more powerful car than the Type 8 but with essentially the same flathead straight eight. A still more powerful car was produced in 1931, the 8B, but only about thirty were made before production came to an end in 1935.

The chassis of these cars and their engines were no great innovations, but the cars were big and powerful, and what made them particularly attractive was that the bodies were installed by such leading Italian body builders as Castagna, Sala, Farina, and Touring. A prime 8A was sold at auction in Los Angeles in March 1980, a four-passenger sport phaeton with Castagna body. It brought $110,000 and might bring as much as $150,000 today.

A price "breakthrough" occurred at the 1984 Barrett-Jackson auction when a 1935 two-door dual cowl phaeton was sold for the unprecedented price of $410,000.

The Sports Cars

So far we have made selections of collector cars of the luxury variety to include in an ideal collection. The cars were the very finest "transportation cars" produced that constitute investment quality on today's market. They are big cars, most with elaborate bodies which seat four or more persons in comfort. They were the most prestigious cars of their era, and they are prestigious today.

A second general category of car is the sports car, generally a performance car that seats two people, or two in comfort and another two in discomfort on an inadequate rear seat. In my first category, I listed luxury big cars from what I considered the most desirable on down, but, of course, any such classification of "best to least best" must be, to a considerable extent, subjective. In my selection of sports cars, I also list in order of my own preference. Still, the cars at the top of the list are those that everybody seems to want, and at a huge price, whenever they appear on the market.

Mercedes-Benz 500K and 540K

One of the most breathtakingly beautiful sports cars ever built was, and still is, the Mercedes-Benz supercharged roadster of the mid-1930s—the model 500K produced in 1934 and the 540K produced the following year. There is some overlap in production years of these two models. The bodies of the two cars are essentially the same. The 500K has a 5-liter engine and the 540K a 5.4-liter engine. Perhaps the 540K is the preferred model, since it has a bigger engine, but the performance is not much different. I owned a 500K and a 540K at the same time, and, if anything, the 500K was a better performer than the 540K.

The engines of both cars are straight eights. Both are supercharged, and the supercharger is engaged by pressing the accelerator down as far as it will go. The supercharger was meant to be used only for accelerating and for short bursts.

Mechanically, the 500K and the 540K are top, but they are not trouble-free. Still, for a long period during World War II my only cars were these supercharged Mercedes. I drove to and from the office every day with one or the other and drove from my home in Wilmington, Delaware, to New York and Washington regularly on business.

The bodies on these cars are everything. The streamlined 500K roadster that was sold by Christie's in early 1979 for $400,000 was the ultimate in body design. My 500K convertible had an English body by Corsica. Had my car

The world auction record established in 1979 at Christie's in Los Angeles was the $400,000 ($440,000 with the 10-percent buyer's premium added) reached for this superbly designed 1936 Mercedes-Benz 500K roadster. The auction record stood for several years, but there were higher private sales, and this same car reportedly was resold for just over $600,000.

been sold in the same sale with the $400,000 Christie's Mercedes, I would have expected to get a maximum of $125,000. My recommendation would be to settle for only the streamlined roadster-bodied 500K or 540K.

Mercedes-Benz SSK

Up until a decade ago, the SSK Mercedes of 1928 was the ultimate sports car. The 500K and 540K were certainly not; many sports car purists considered them to be bulbous attention-getters put out by Hitler's Nazis. The SSK is one of my two favorite automobiles of all time, the other being the 540K roadster. (I dearly love the SSKL, described below, but that automobile and the SSK, for that matter, rarely come on the market.)

The SSK has a six-cylinder supercharged overhead-cam engine with a short chassis (the K stands for *kurz*, which means "short"). It puts out about 225 horsepower and might well turn 150 mph, quite a speed in 1928. This car was a prizewinner in 1930 at the hands of the great Mercedes driver Rudolf Caracciola.

It is possible to buy an SSK roadster, but prices are sometimes quoted at about $250,000—or more. Sometimes some of these cars come up at auction, and one might be bought in the neighborhood of $250,000.

A very special SSK was built in 1931, designated SSKL—a "light" SSK. It also had an "elephant blower," a large supercharger, that increased the horsepower to 300. What this car would do is anybody's guess—but certainly in excess of 150 mph.

There are very few SSKL's in existence. They can be recognized by the holes drilled in the frame (which is exposed on the SSK) to make the car lighter. The chief engineer of one of the big American car companies a few years back had his picture taken with his own SSKL from his collection. Otherwise I have seen no SSKL's at all—for sale or privately owned.

Bentley Eight Liter

In early 1981, Christie's auctioned in Los Angeles a Bentley Eight Liter sedan owned by Anthony Thompson, president of Rolls-Royce of Beverly Hills, California. Since the head of the Rolls-Royce agency owned this car and restored it, I presume it was in top condition. It certainly looked it. It brought $90,000, a good price considering it was not an open car, nor was it the best-looking closed car. In fact, it had a replacement body.

Bentley owners and Bentley enthusiasts are divided into two groups. Those in the first group prefer Bentleys made before Rolls-Royce took over Bentley in the early 1930s. Those in the second group like the Rolls-Royce-produced Bentleys, or at least do not feel the Rolls-Royce Bentleys are inferior to the old original Bentleys made by W.O. Bentley.

The last important Bentley put out before the Rolls-Royce takeover was the enormous Bentley Eight Liter of 1930 and 1931, and this car is probably the most desired of any of the old original Bentleys. It is a real firesnorter (besides being an excellent car). It is noisy and a little hard-riding, as it is a sports car, and absolutely reliable. It is also a tremendously impressive-looking automobile.

The open car is the one on which to concentrate. A good-looking touring car, close-coupled (rear seat and front seat close together), can probably be purchased on the present market for about $150,000 or less.

Alfa Romeo 2.9

In my opinion the 2.9 Alfa Romeo is one of the greatest sports cars ever produced, and in my own theoretical collection of great cars I would include a 2.9 Alfa Romeo roadster. I have felt this way ever since I saw a 2.9, in 1938. It was a very low, long roadster and it was in the shop of Charles Zumbach, the Mercedes-Benz dealer in New York. When the engine started you knew it, and there was no peace and quiet until it was turned off. It was a straight eight with overhead cam and two superchargers—one for the first four cylinders and the other for the last four cylinders, a unique arrangement.

The body was an absolute stunner. I believe this is the same car that became part of the Huguely collection in Washington, D.C., where I saw it about fifteen years later—still as impressive as it was when I first saw it.

This is a strict sports car and can hardly be used regularly. Of course, one would not want to use such a valuable car regularly, even if it were not temperamental.

All of the 2.9 Alfas are impressive, but some bodies are vastly more beautiful than others, and in this make and model car, the body contributes greatly to the value of the car as well as to the pride of ownership. When such cars do occasionally come onto the market, there is a wide range of possible prices. They are not in as tremendous demand as the Mercedes-Benz 500K, 540K, and SSK. The 2.9 Alfa might, on occasion, be bought for under $100,000.

Very near the end of 1982, a very famous Alfa Romeo 2.9 came onto the market, not the roadster that we have recommended buying but a very famous sports coupe. It was the car that won the 1947 Mille Miglia race, driven by Biondetti against Nuvolari. The car was a 1938 model and almost ten years old when it won the race. It was priced at $210,000 in 1982—probably a fair price for a celebrated car. This same model Alfa won the very first Watkins Glen race, where it was driven by Frank Griswold.

Stutz Super Bearcat

In early 1981, I journeyed to Los Angeles to bid at auction on one of the greatest sports car classics ever built—the Stutz Super Bearcat. I missed it by only a small amount, and it sold for about $70,000. To put it into fine condition would, however, have cost about $25,000. Even a transmission had to be located, as this car had in it a substitute transmission from a Marmon.

In the early years of the Depression, Stutz, the prestige American automobile manufacturer, introduced a car that was to be fully competitive with the Cadillac and Packard, particularly the sports models. It was a new Bearcat. David Burgess Wise, in his book *Classic American Automobiles*, describes the new Stutz Bearcat in this way: "It was perhaps the finest of all the luxury cars of the Depression, combining superlative engineering with elegant styling.... The DV32 [Bearcat] seems even more remarkable when you consider that the only comparable American car, the Model J Duesenberg, cost $9,500 in chassis form against $4,995 for a complete five-passenger DV32 sedan."

The engine design was the latest and best and very like the Duesenberg J— a straight eight with double overhead camshafts, and this car had four valves per cylinder for the best possible aspiration. The car would exceed 100 mph.

The 1932 Super Bearcat is a short-chassis version of the Bearcat with higher performance than the Bearcat. The 1932 Super Bearcat that went for about $70,000 in 1981 in California is the most famous of all of these cars. Tom Barrett of Scottsdale, Arizona, bought the car. A mint car today might bring $250,000.

Only seventeen of these cars were built, and only five are thought to have survived. Still, one comes up for auction from time to time. One came on the market a few years ago, and the price was under $100,000. If one cannot buy one of these rarities, he might buy a DV32 open car of the same era for a little less money, even a boattail speedster; but the Super Bearcat is a super car to add to a collection of prime automobiles.

The Auburn Boattail Speedsters—851 and 852

Auburn had made the famous speedster model roadster as early as the late 1920s. In 1931 a more streamlined and beautiful body was designed, and in that same year I saw this car in the Washington, D.C., Motor Show priced at $1,150. It was the sensation of the show.

In 1935, however, Auburn developed the speedster into its ultimate form in the Model 851. I recall seeing two of these boattail speedsters displayed in a dealer's showroom in East Hartford, Connecticut, priced at $2,500, which seemed a high price at the time, but the car was a sensation.

The 851 and 852 models (1935 and 1936) used a Lycoming straight eight with a centrifugal supercharger. The cars had a two-speed Columbia differential, so that while there were the normal three speeds ahead, the changeable rear-axle ratio doubled the actual number of forward speeds to six. Although the engine was a flat, or L-head, straight eight, still it propelled every car that was sold at over 100 mph. The exact top speed of each car was engraved on a metal plate attached to the dashboard of each car and "signed" by the tester, Ab Jenkins, the famous racing driver.

The main feature of these cars is not the mechanics but the body, designed by Gordon Buehrig, who also designed the greatest of all of the Duesenbergs—the J and the SJ models.

The price of these Auburn boattail speedsters has risen from the $800 I paid for mine in 1940 to about $70,000 on today's market for a completely restored mint-condition example of this landmark car.

The True Antiques

There are two absolutely prime American antiques that might well be included in any balanced collection of American collector cars.

Mercer Raceabout

One of the most pioneering and glamorous cars of the early days of motoring is the Mercer Raceabout. First produced in 1911, it is one of the most desirable of all antiques from any country, England included, with its great early Rolls-Royces. By the late teens, a new car had come onto the market with the same name and put out by the same firm, but it was a much different car and far less desirable then and far less desirable on today's collector car market.

The 1911–1912 Mercer Raceabout was a rudimentary automobile. It had four cylinders and had to be cranked by hand. It had no top, no doors, and no windshield, only a kind of "monocle," a round piece of glass in front of the driver. The Mercer weighed about a ton and it had 55 horsepower, which may have driven the car as fast as 75 mph, an enormous speed in 1912, and a high enough speed even today. On today's market, the Mercer Raceabout is not hard to find, and it should cost somewhere around $125,000 to $160,000.

Stutz Bearcat

Of these early great sports cars, the next in importance as a pioneering machine and a collector's item is the Stutz Bearcat of 1914. This car too is stark, with no top, no doors, and no windshield; like the Mercer Raceabout, it used a monocle glass in front of the driver. David Burgess Wise in his write-up of the Stutz in *The World of Automobiles* says, "In 1914 . . . the archetypal Stutz, and one of motoring history's most legendary models, was born. The original Bearcat aped the Mercer Raceabout formula of massive engine, minimal coachwork—bonnet, wings, two seats and a bolster fuel tank were deemed adequate—and proved remarkably popular with sales rising from 759 cars in 1913 to 2,207 in 1917."

The Mercer Raceabout is slightly preferred by the market and slightly higher in price than the Bearcat, but the cars are very similar, and if I could not find one of them then the other would do fine. If the Mercer Raceabout is priced at $150,000 then the early Stutz Bearcat might be priced at $125,000.

Rolls-Royce Silver Ghost

Any fine collection of classic and antique cars should include a Rolls-Royce, not simply because of the prestige of the name Rolls-Royce for most of the present century, but because Rolls-Royce has turned out to be a good investment. Finally, a Rolls-Royce is a "good car." It is well made, fine-looking, and reliable; and it has been reliable for practically all of its existence—which is more than can be said about a lot of exotics.

The car I would pick to include in an elite collection of antique automobiles would be a six-cylinder L-head Silver Ghost produced between 1906 and 1909, with a 7,036-cubic-centimeter engine. The later cars produced up to 1926, while still Silver Ghosts, are less desirable as collector cars, although they are still fine cars. I would select a touring car and expect to pay about $250,000. If I had to, I would go on to Silver Ghosts produced up until World War I, and I would expect to pay slightly less.

The Postwar Classics

It is not so hard to pick out a number of the great collector cars from those produced in the era before World War II. There were many such cars produced, and I have exercised my judgment in selecting those that I consider to be the best as well as the most suitable to collect—to create a fine collection that it is both possible to accumulate and possible to sell at some time in the future with some anticipation of a capital gain.

It is a great deal harder to pick out the great collectibles from the crop after World War II. The cars have not yet "settled down"; it is not yet obvious that car A is definitely a good investment and car B is probably not such a good investment. Still, certain cars are beginning to emerge as greats of all time.

Mercedes-Benz 300S

One of the greatest classics of all time is probably the Mercedes-Benz 300S roadster and cabriolet made from 1951 to 1957. I say "probably" because time is still required for the market to sort out the most preferred cars of the postwar era. The 300S was, however, one of the finest-constructed cars of any era. It was very carefully designed from an engineering point of view and its styling was conservatively elegant.

The 300S has a 3-liter engine with six cylinders, one overhead camshaft, and three Solex carburetors. It is not tremendously innovative in either engineering or stylistic design. The engine is very much like the engine of the prewar Mercedes-Benz six-cylinder overhead-cam S, SS, and SSK series, except that the 300S is not supercharged.

The 300S body is a throwback to the design of the 1930s. It is not so rakish or streamlined as the 500K and 540K, both powered by straight eights with supercharger. It is more conservative in engineering and body design but is as good a performer as the 500K and 540K, and vastly more reliable than the cars of the 500 series or S series.

Aside from advanced engineering design and body style, is the 300S a good car? I can answer that over the past twenty-five years I have rarely been without my own 300S, and I have owned four of them. It is one of the lowest-maintenance-cost cars that I have ever owned, Mercury and Opel included, both of which required constant expensive repairs.

As repair costs become ever greater, a collector is inclined to give more and more thought to the reliability of his collectible car and the amount of repairs required, even though he may use it only occasionally. Some collector cars seem to require constant repairs even though they are almost never used.

The two preferred body models are the roadster and the cabriolet with cabriole bars. On the roadster the top folds down flat. On the cabriolet it goes down only partway, and in that position the car is not so attractive.

The car came out first in 1951, and each year the horsepower was increased. In 1956, a fuel-injection system was installed, and this sytem was continued through 1957, the last year the 300S was made. This fuel-injected car is probably the preferred model. On the present market, this model in good condition can probably not be bought for under $100,000. The non-fuel-injected model can be bought possibly as low as $60,000, although in absolutely mint condition it can also bring $100,000.

In mid-1982, four Mercedes-Benz 300S cabriolets and roadsters came to my attention. They were for sale by one firm, appeared to be in absolutely mint condition, and were priced at $115,000 to $135,000. They were worth the asking price, provided they were in the condition they appeared to be in and in the condition represented by the selling firm. So why don't we use these figures as target prices for the purchase of a 300S open car? Because these are the exceptions. They appear to be better than a 300S in "excellent" condition. They are great rarities. Besides, when one is shown, say, the $115,000 car he might pull out a check for $98,000 and say, "This is all I can pay for the car, if you would like to accept this offer. If not, then I will have to look elsewhere." The purchase might well be made at this price of $98,000.

Mercedes-Benz 300SL Gullwing

The Mercedes-Benz Gullwing coupe with the doors that open upward instead of outward was, and still is, one of the most popular and sought-after cars put out in the entire postwar period. The engine is a straight six with one

A 1956 Mercedes-Benz Gullwing, restored, sold at auction in 1981, at the peak of interest for this car, for $95,000. (Kruse International)

overhead camshaft, and about 3-liter displacement. Between 1954 and 1957, 1,400 of the cars were produced. They exceeded 150 mph and at the time seemed to be in command of almost all road-racing events. The 300SLR, a somewhat similar car, but made for racing only, had a straight eight. It was retired from road racing in 1955. In fact, the Mercedes-Benz factory stopped racing its cars in 1955. There was little competition.

There are 300SL Gullwings for sale. They are not hard to find, but they are not low in price, certainly not low compared with the later 300SL roadster. The roadster on the present market is not the preferred car and it is not at this time one of the great cars of all time. The 300SL Gullwing is. One in near mint condition can probably be bought for $75,000.

Ferrari

The most popular collector car in the sports car category as of the early 1980s is almost certainly the Ferrari. Which model of Ferrari? Every model of Ferrari.

To put it another way, if Ferrari had made only one model in the postwar period, there is a good chance that this one car would turn into *the* great collector car after all the postwar cars were sorted out by collector-investors over a long period of time. In other words, Mr. Ferrari turned out practically no "dogs."

It is hard to pick out one model of Ferrari and say, "This of all Ferraris is the great Ferrari, the ultimate Ferrari for collectors."

My selection of great Ferraris would be three cars, and there will be little argument from Ferrari aficionados as to the collectibility of these three cars.

To start with, I'd want a Ferrari Daytona Spyder. The Ferrari Daytona first appeared in Italy in 1968 and was first exported to the U.S. in 1970, with a price tag of $19,500. In 1973 it was discontinued as far as the American market was concerned.

The Daytona is a beautiful and docile coupe in its usual form, of traditional design with engine in the front, and rear drive. It will go about 175 mph and has fierce acceleration. It will probably beat the latest Ferrari, the 512 Berlinetta Boxer, from zero to 150 mph. It is the traditional V-12 with the large 365 engine of about 350 horsepower. The real value of this particular car is that while it is a top performer, it is the kind of car one can drive anywhere at any time. It will cruise at over 100 mph and can also be operated in city traffic. The suspension is not over-hard. In fact, the suspension could well be used in any luxury car, Rolls-Royce included.

The ultimate Daytona is probably the Spyder, the open car. There are more and more Daytona open cars, but these are conversions from the coupe, and these are not the true collector cars that we are talking about. The true collector Spyders are the original Ferrari-built Daytona Spyders, and these are extremely popular, prestige collector cars. They are selling for $125,000 and more at present, not in the $65,000-to-$75,000 range of the Daytona coupes.

After the Daytona Spyder I'd select a Ferrari 275GTB-4. If I say, "The 275GTB-4 coupe is the finest street Ferrari ever built," there are few Ferrari dealers, mechanics, or simply Ferrari enthusiasts who will take issue with me. It is the favorite car of many of these people.

The 275GTB-4 first appeared in 1966 and was continued until 1968, when it was replaced by the Daytona. It is the traditional design of engine and engine layout—front engine and rear drive—but each bank of cylinders has two camshafts, and the engine produces 300 horsepower. The body is by Pininfarina, a traditional coupe, not quite as good-looking as the later Daytona, but beautiful in a traditional way. The suspension is harsher than in the later Daytona and the car is probably better as a road-racing machine. As for top speed, the car will probably do an easy 160 mph.

To indicate the capabilities of this automobile, I was sitting in a 275GTB-4 with Nick Soprano, competition driver and owner of Motor Classic Corporation of North White Plains, New York, waiting for a traffic light to turn green. Suddenly the driver of a Mercedes-Benz 450SL started blowing his horn, trying to attract our attention. He pulled alongside of us and indicated that he would like to try out his car against the one we were in.

When the light changed to green we both started off. It was as if his car had been going in reverse. We were up to 110 mph on the speedometer very quickly, even around fairly sharp corners. In two miles we lost the Mercedes, and we never saw it again.

There are 275GTB-4's for sale, and $65,000 should buy a near-mint one. I am not sure how these cars will stand the test of time. They are the best Ferraris mechanically right now, and they drive the best right now.

For my third Ferrari, I'd want either a Super America or a Superfast. The Ferrari Super America (second series put out from the early 1960s on for a few years) is the favorite Ferrari in Italy today, and the car is sky-high in price. No Italian owner of a Ferrari Super America seems to want to part with the car at any price. The car is a powerful, big-block automobile but still not up to the Daytona and 275GTB-4 in performance. When the dust settles, this model may well come out on top or, at least, near the top of all collector Ferraris.

Alternatively, the 500 Superfast may well emerge as a top collector Ferrari. The last model Super America was produced from 1961 to 1964, when it was replaced by another big-engine car, the Superfast. This car was produced for two years, during which time thirty-six were turned out. The car has a powerful 400-horsepower engine coming out of 4.9 liters.

On the present U.S. market, the Super America second series might be purchased for about $45,000 and the Superfast for perhaps $10,000 more. It may well be that these two cars will turn out to be the major collectible Ferraris of the future.

Lamborghini Miura

The Lamborghini Miura of 1967 to 1972 is one of the most innovative, radically styled, and best performers in the sports car category put out in the entire postwar period. Tractor maker Ferruccio Lamborghini developed the Miura without regard to monetary outlay, and the Miura developed into "the shape of things to come." Gianpaolo Dallara was the chief engineer on the Miura project. Bob Wallace, now in Phoenix, Arizona, was both engineer and racing driver. The body was built by Bertone and designed by the most celebrated auto body designer obtainable.

The car is a rear-engine rear-drive model with the transverse engine behind the driver's head. It has a 4-liter V-12 with twin overhead camshafts for each bank of cylinders and six Weber carburetors. Its 350 horsepower drives the car close to 180 mph.

The 1967 Lamborghini Miura P-400. (*Stan Zagorski*)

All Miuras are of the same general mechanical layout, from 1967 to 1972, but the last models, the SV models, are vastly preferred in the market.

The car has a firm suspension and the gears whine a bit, so that the car seems to be a cross between a street car and a road-racing car. Still, it is docile in traffic, does not heat up, and does not overload the carburetors with gasoline.

The Miura is an ultramodern sports car that seats two people. On the present market the SV model, the last model, just a few of which cars had separate crankcase and transmission, will cost up to $100,000. For $100,000 one should be able to buy a mint-condition Miura, and such a car can possibly be secured for as little as $85,000. As of late 1983, these were the prices on two late-model Miuras in mint condition.

This car was followed by the "space capsule" Lamborghini—at least this is my own private designation of the Lamborghini Countach put out from 1973 to the present. The engineering layout of this car is the same, essentially, as the Miura. It too is low, about 41 inches high, like the Miura; but here the similarity ends. The Countach has a short, rather stubby, body. The doors slide upward, not outward in the traditional way, nor do they angle outward like those of the Mercedes-Benz 300SL. The power is upped from essentially the same engine used in the Miura and the car will *possibly* do 190 mph. With spoiler in the back and certain other changes it is possible that the car will do 205 mph.

Unlike the Miura, the early Countach cars are the more wanted ones on today's market. One can get a mint-condition early Countach for about $85,000. Whether this car will turn out to be one of the great collector cars is a guess, but it looks right now as though it will.

This represents a selection of the great collector cars, the "gilt-edged" cars. Few people will argue that these are not the greatest collector cars. They will point out, however, that important collector cars have been omitted from the list. To prepare such a list, a list of workable size and one that represents a reasonable investment, involves opinion and simply picking out cars from a host of fine automobiles. One can well point out that there is no Pierce-Arrow. There is no Thomas Flyer with pistons the size of coffee cans. Where is the little curved-dash Olds of 1903? How about the Maserati Ghibli, a highly significant postwar sports car and possibly the most beautiful sports coupe ever built? Why is there no Porsche at all on the list? And how about a postwar Rolls-Royce like the Silver Cloud III Flying Spur and the enormous Phantom V?

Let me say that I am fairly sure of all of the cars on the list. They are great collector cars and they are likely to remain great collector cars in the indefinite future.

It might next be pointed out that the purchase of these cars for a collection

SUMMARY

Great Classic Cars

Bugatti Royale	$2,000,000 +

Great American Classic Cars

Duesenberg J or SJ open	$200,000
Cadillac V-16 (early)	250,000
Chrysler Imperial Eight	200,000
Packard Super Eight or V-12 or 734	125,000
	$775,000

Great Foreign Classic Cars

Hispano-Suiza	$250,000
Rolls-Royce Phantom III	100,000
Isotta Fraschini	150,000
	$500,000

Prewar Sports Cars

Mercedes-Benz 500K and 540K	$400,000
Mercedes-Benz SSK	250,000
Bentley Eight Liter	150,000
Alfa Romeo 2.9 (roadster)	100,000
Stutz Super Bearcat	250,000
Auburn boattail (851 or 852)	70,000
	$1,220,000

True Antiques

Mercer Raceabout	$150,000
Stutz Bearcat	125,000
Rolls-Royce Silver Ghost (early)	250,000
	$525,000

Postwar Classics and Sports Cars

Mercedes-Benz 300S	$75,000
Mercedes-Benz 300SL Gullwing	75,000
Ferrari Daytona Spyder	150,000
Ferrari 275GTB-4	65,000
Ferrari Super America	60,000
Lamborghini Miura SV	85,000
	$510,000

TOTAL OUTLAY	$5,530,000
WITHOUT BUGATTI ROYALE	$3,530,000

involves an enormous outlay of funds—$5,530,000. True, very few people can afford an outlay of this magnitude. It represents the price of one fine Gauguin painting, or a fine Van Gogh, or a great Renoir, or a first-class Titian, and this is not much more than the price that J. Paul Getty paid for the Titian he bought about a decade ago, *The Death of Actaeon*.

There are twenty-three cars on the list in total. We can start to pare this list by eliminating just one car, the first car, the Bugatti Royale. Probably no one will be able to purchase one of these rarities, at least in the next several years. The elimination of this one car from the list cuts the total investment by $2,000,000 and makes the new total investment in twenty-two cars $3,530,000.

We are, of course, indicating the greatest possible cash outlay—for all cars on the list that might reasonably come onto the market for purchase in the near future. But the cars are divided as to categories, and for some categories the total outlay becomes much less.

Bugatti Royale	$2,000,000
Great American classics	775,000
Great foreign classics	500,000
Prewar sports cars	1,220,000
Antiques	525,000
Postwar classics	510,000

Still, one starts a journey with but a single step, and one might start out collecting with the Auburn boattail for $70,000 or the Ferrari 275GTB-4 for $65,000. I would be happy to step out and buy either one of these cars if I had no collector car. Then I would be prepared to wait some time before I made another purchase for my collection.

In any event, I have set out a list of super collectible cars that are from time to time available for purchase, some of them available right now.

6

The Top Postwar Classics

IT IS FAIRLY firmly established what the top prewar classics are—cars like the S, SS, SSK, 500K, and 540K Mercedes-Benz, and the Cadillac V-16 convertible, Packard V-12 convertible, and Chrysler Imperial of the early 1930s. These cars are classic collector cars as well as investor cars. Maybe a strict investor would go wrong in investing in one of them, but not likely. The prewar classics have been sorted out and values established for them— not completely, but pretty well.

But what about the Rolls-Royce Silver Cloud III sedan of 1963–1965? This car hit a peak in about 1980. Today it can be bought in London for about 50% of the peak price. Is it finished as a classic? Will it come back? Will it rise to new value levels? In retrospect, is it a classic at all or just a big, important-looking, but out-of-date sedan?

Today the Ferrari 275GTB-4 and the Ferrari Daytona are tops. The Ferrari Daytona Spyder (convertible) is one of the very few postwar classics selling for sums in six figures.

Rich Taylor, postwar classic car critic and author of *Modern Classics*, says this about the Ferrari 275GTB-4:

"The GTB isn't a styling milestone like the Cisitalia 1100 or the Maserati Ghibli, it doesn't have earth-shattering performance like a 427 Cobra, it doesn't handle like a Lotus Eleven or cradle you in the luxury of a Rolls-Royce. No single component dominates the others, no one factor stands out to make you pine for a GTB for that and that alone. In fact, the 275GTB is kind of the swan song of Pininfarina's bulbous postwar oeuvre. . . ."

Critical thinking shies away from the Boxer as being the very latest, the very finest, and the most sought-after. And that leaves the 275GTB-4 and the Daytona as the best to date.

I have ridden in the 275GTB-4 when it trimmed the pants off a Mercedes-Benz 450SL—as indeed it should. I have ridden in the Daytona when it could have done the same thing, not just to the 450SL but probably even to the Berlinetta Boxer, at least up to 150 mph.

So that doesn't leave us much that outperforms the 275GTB-4 and the Ferrari Daytona in the postwar period as far as sheer performance goes.

Now suppose Ferrari comes out with a transverse engine (or a rear longways engine) of 5 liters and 500 horsepower but incorporating the latest racing technology that the Berlinetta Boxer (and the 275GTB-4 and the Daytona) does not incorporate. Suppose it way outperforms all three of these Ferraris. What then?

Is demand going to shift to the new 5 liter car of 500 horsepower? Maybe. In other words, I think a great deal of the popularity of the 275GTB-4 is due to its superior performance today, to the fact that it can outperform almost anything on the road today for top speed, acceleration, and road holding.

Today there are dealers and collectors who seem to have fallen deeply in love with the 275GTB-4 and they are not inclined to tolerate any criticism of it. But if a later Ferrari outperforms the 275GTB-4 in almost every way and has a vastly more beautiful body, will the 275 still be high in esteem of postwar classic car collectors? Will it be in a rising price trend? Will it be at the top of Ferrari collector preference?

The postwar classics have yet to be sorted out, and we can only indicate what cars appear to be the most important investor-collector cars.

For an analogy in *prewar* classics we might go back to the immediate prewar years and to the war years. In this period no one seemed to want any big luxury car or performance car—or a car that embodied both luxury and performance. Again and again I have referred to the Bugatti Royale cabriolet by Weinberger. Nobody wanted this car in 1941, at any price.

The Mercedes-Benz S and SS were dirt-cheap; $500 would buy a very good car of this make and model. A car buff who rented space in the warehouse in which I kept my S and SS Mercedes cars owned an early Rolls-Royce Silver Ghost touring car for which he paid $100. I didn't have a great deal of regard for this car buff. I was a level above him with my Mercedes S and SS. I was also in a class above the owner of an Isotta Fraschini huge straight-eight tourer. I didn't even inquire the price of this car. Nor was anyone much interested in a Duesenberg J or SJ, not even a Dietrich dual-cowl phaeton that was demonstrated to me. I felt its price of $600 was a little high.

Finally, the prewar classics got sorted out and relative values are now fairly stable. It is not likely that the Mercedes-Benz S and SS will drop materially in price in the future. Nor is it likely that the Isotta and the Duesenberg cars will lose much of their popularity or much of their present price level.

The more historical perspective we get from our study of the antique and classic car market, the more cautious we get about future values of postwar

classic cars (and, of course, special-interest cars like the Chevrolet Nomad station wagons of the mid-1950s—extremely popular and high-priced special-interest cars).

The Scarcity of Top Postwar Classics

As I have said earlier, it is very much harder to list the postwar classics. True, time must pass in any automobile era for the great collector cars to emerge. Still, the war ended in 1945. In the almost forty years since, what top postwar collector classics do we have? There is essentially nothing to compare with the prewars mentioned above. Though out of date, they are magnificent machines—in mechanics, in size, in body design, in finish, from wood trim to chrome trim.

The postwar classics are, for the most part, smaller cars. In addition to being smaller, they are mostly sports cars like the Ferrari and Mercedes-Benz. There are few cars to compare with the big impressive prewar greats.

Rolls-Royce has put out a few big, important cars in the postwar period, led, probably, by the Phantom V and later Phantom VI. These cars are designed well from a mechanical point of view and their bodies are extremely finely made with top trim of all kinds.

Still, most of these important Phantom V and Phantom VI cars are large limousines and, at best, sedans. They do not have the styling and the verve of the Isotta Fraschini, the early 1930s Chrysler Imperial with dual-cowl phaeton body, or the Duesenberg speedster. They are conservative, formal transportation automboiles that seem excellently suited to carrying the prime minister from 10 Downing Street to Parliament.

Very few Rolls-Royce cars made in the postwar period are cars of style and verve. The Flying Spur sedans approach these qualities, but they are still sedans with a special body—but not a *very* special or rakish body. The same for the long-wheelbase Rolls-Royce and the coupe.

If we try to compare the great tourers of the prewar period to the open cars put out by Rolls-Royce in the postwar period we arrive at one Rolls-Royce even remotely in the class of the great prewar tourers—the Silver Cloud I, II, and III Mulliner cars and the preferred Park Ward cars—both four- or five-passenger convertible sedans of rather austere design. Aesthetically, they don't compare very well with the important prewar classics.

It is no news when a prewar classic car sells for over $200,000. On the other hand a postwar classic that goes over $100,000 is something of an event, and very few do. All in all, the postwar classics are a little more mundane than the great prewar classics as well as less expensive.

The important investment demand is concentrated on the prewar classics.

In addition to being more "investment cars," the prewar classics are far more numerous—in terms of makes and models—than the postwar classics. When we think of the postwar classics we think of the Mercedes-Benz 300SL Gullwing, the 300S cabriolet and roadster, the Ferrari 275GTB-4 and Daytona, some Ferrari convertibles and a few very special cars like the Superfast, the Lamborghini Miura and possibly the Countach, the Cobras, and a few models of Rolls-Royce. Few of these cars are special-bodied machines like the great Duesenbergs and Chrysler Imperials. They are standard cars with standard bodies, many, if not most, of them high-performance sports cars.

So if we are thinking about classic cars as investments we have to think primarily of the prewar classic cars. On the other hand, if we are interested in postwar classics we think of very few real classics of top quality. But if we are persistent in wanting a postwar classic, we have to move on downhill in price to cars such as the Ford Thunderbird of 1955–1957, the early Chevrolet Corvette, the Bentley Continental, the later Lincoln Continentals—as late as the mid-1950s. There are more of these lower-priced postwar classics, many of them, and these are the cars on which demand for postwar classic cars must concentrate—simply because there are few postwar greats to buy. All of which means that the demand for the lesser postwar classics is likely to increase, simply because there is little else to buy in this area of collector cars.

Mercedes-Benz 300 Series Cars

The Mercedes-Benz 300 sedan made its appearance in 1951. It has a six-cylinder in-line engine with a single overhead camshaft. The engine produces about 115 horsepower out of a capacity of 2,996 cubic centimeters (182.2 cubic inches), about the same size as the engine of the Ferrari 250GT. The Mercedes 300 is a luxury car, not a sports car. It accelerates to 60 miles an hour in 16 seconds, and its top speed is very close to 100. In the early 1950s it sold new for $6,980.

The car is a fine luxury car, and its lines, mechanics, and performance have been improved over the car's life—about twelve years—during which time its list price gradually increased to $10,864.

The 300 sedan is not one of the top collector cars of the postwar era, but two other cars based on the 300 are: the 300S and the 300SL.

The Mercedes-Benz 300S (1951–1957) is a super luxury car, the S standing for "super." Its original list price was about $13,250, certainly in the price range of the Rolls-Royce of that era. *Road and Track* of April 1953 describes the 300S in this way:

"And a true thoroughbred it is. A car which is a beautiful combination of the finest German coachwork, the utmost in passenger and driver comfort, and capable of extremely high cruising speeds. Wherever the Mercedes-Benz 300S has been seen, since its first appearance at the Paris Salon in the autumn of 1951, it has caused a quiet riot of enthusiasm, with its low, sleek lines and its attitude of 'going' even when standing still."

The 300S was made in three models—the cabriolet with cabriole bars, the roadster (but with wind-up windows), and the coupe. Everything about the car is luxury, from the quality of chrome to the walnut paneling to the leather pleated seats and door panels.

There are three Solex carburetors on the 1951–1955 models and fuel injection on the 1956–1957 models. The compression ratio was high for the era—7½ to 1. The valve springs were stiffer and there was a more critical camshaft grind to raise the horsepower of the engine to about 150. There was also a faster rear axle to take advantage of the higher horsepower. The car will do about 112 mph, fast enough for a pure luxury car when the car first appeared—or even today.

One great advantage in the car is its absolute reliability. I have owned one or another 300S for the last twenty-eight years, and often the 300S was my only means of transportation. The 300S cars that I owned were rarely in the shop for anything. Recently I got my 300S out of the garage where it had been "resting" for over two years. The temperature was 15 below zero. The car started immediately and kept on running till I had arrived at my destination 300 miles away.

The Mercedes-Benz 300S stands at the pinnacle of important postwar collector classic cars. It is the most prestigious and most publicized car. It is also the most generally high-priced car.

When it first appeared in 1951 it was beyond the financial reach of all but the wealthy—at almost $14,000—and it merited the price. In 1955 I purchased my first 300S, a cabriolet for $4,500. It was still a much-sought-after car, even though it had been on the market for four years.

From this point the 300S declined further in value, in line with almost all used cars—from Ford to Rolls-Royce. Since I vastly preferred the 300S to any car anywhere, new or secondhand, I purchased my second 300S, a roadster, in 1958 from a New York auto showroom for $4,000.

The "position" of the 300S had changed when I purchased my third such car in 1960. This was a cabriolet I purchased privately from a foreign service officer who had bought it when he was stationed in Lebanon and brought it back to Washington with him. It needed a paint job and some refinishing of the wood and cost me $2,800, about market for the car in 1960. It still had some prestige, but it had been out of production since 1957.

My fourth car, a 1955 roadster, was different. It was anything but a prestige car. It was a very much run-down automobile and in need of drastic restoration. I bought it privately in 1966 for $800, maybe a little under market but not by much.

In 1955, when the 300S was still in production and very much of a prestige car, a 1953 coupe was advertised for $7,150. The coupe was never a popular model car but it was in date. By 1960 the coupe had dropped in value to about $4,000. Sometimes the roadster and cabriolet were in the same price range, but in 1960 a 1956 fuel-injected 300S was priced at $12,000 a car with 10,000 miles on the odometer. The carburetor cars could, however, often be bought for less than $5,000.

In many ways, the recession of 1962 was a deep one, but especially deep from the point of view of the stock market, and gloom pervaded Wall Street. In June of that year, a 300S roadster was advertised for sale for $2,500, and it was mentioned in the ad that the car's original cost had been $13,000. Other 300S Mercedes were priced somewhat higher. A fair price for the roadster and cabriolet was about $5,000.

By 1965 the stock market recession was over but the price of the 300S Mercedes was going down. The 1956 and 1957 fuel-injected models have always been the preferred 300S cars. A 1957 "flawless" convertible was on sale for $5,500 and a 1957 300S roadster for $4,750. An earlier cabriolet was priced at $1,995 and a 1953 coupe at $2,500.

The right time to buy a 300S of any body type was 1970, the start of the upward push in classic car prices. An open car in very fine condition could be purchased for under $4,000 and a good unrestored car for about $2,000, although some mint-condition cars were priced up to $5,000 and a few over $5,000.

By 1974, the 300S was on the move in the market. A 1953 with engine and drive train in good condition, but with poor body, was for sale for $4,000. A 1952 coupe with no description of condition was offered for $6,200. A 1955 300S coupe with low mileage was priced at the very high figure of $13,000.

One year later, by 1975, a fine-condition 300S was selling for just under $10,000, but the average car was selling for from $5,000 to $7,000.

The 300S moved up even more rapidly in the second half of the decade of the 1970s. In 1977 I was offered $19,000 for my 1955 roadster, which was completely restored and in fine, but not mint, condition.

By 1980, the good unrestored coupe was selling for about $20,000 and the roadster and cabriolet for $5,000 more. Mint-condition coupes and open cars were from $30,000 to $35,000. In 1979 I had received an offer of $35,000 for my 300S roadster.

By 1981 prices for the 300S were up about $10,000—to $45,000—

and they kept on rising. In January 1982, the Barrett-Jackson auction sold a mint-condition 300S open car for the unprecedented auction price of $100,000.

One year later, in January 1983, collector car auctions were more or less in the doldrums, despite the start of the bull market in stocks. The important car auctions in Arizona were not characterized by many sales, but a mint-condition 300S open car sold for $100,000—the same price the car achieved at the same Barrett-Jackson auction one year earlier. Another 300S, a coupe, also in absolutely mint condition, brought the unprecedented price for a 300S coupe of $76,000.

At this stage of the appreciation cycle of the 300S Mercedes, it should be pointed out that condition means everything in salability and in price. A 300S in good condition can bring as little as $50,000 and in poor condition even less; but an absolutely mint-condition 300S can exceed $100,000. Three mint-condition 300S open cars were on the market in 1983 for prices ranging from $115,000 to $135,000. It now pays to restore a 300S to mint condition no matter what the cost, as the price appreciation will almost certainly cover the cost of bringing the car up to mint. One 300S owner advertised that he had spent $28,000 on the restoration of his car. I can believe it after examining his car thoroughly. Still, the car was not absolutely mint and it would not achieve an "absolutely mint price."

These are some of the pertinent facts about the Mercedes-Benz 300S:

1. The 300S is not a "fad car." It is in no way an "in car." A "fad car" or an "in car" can be popular as an investment at one time and then be unpopular at another time. The 300S is a highly conservative car, and a conservative investment car.

2. The Mercedes 300S has been on a gradually rising price trend since 1970. It dropped precipitately when it became simply a "used car" but then began rising, slowly at first and then more rapidly. It did not take off the way the Lamborghini Miura did in 1980.

3. The 300S has not shown price weakness at any time since it has been on the price upcurve.

4. The 300S is quality all through. It was built to be the best, and if it was not *the* best it was certainly very nearly the best.

5. Relatively few 300S models were ever built and sold, unlike, say, the 1965–1966 Mustang, so there is no market overhang. While high prices certainly bring out the 300S, there are not many 300S models to come onto the market.

6. The car relates to the prewar classics—and the *best* prewar classics. This throwback character of the car may give it some value that it would not have if it were strictly a postwar classic.

7. The maintenance on the car is very low. It is an uncomplicated car—unlike, say, the Lamborghini Miura. It always runs and is very rarely in the garage for repairs. It does not tend to deteriorate over a period of time.

300SL Gullwing

The Mercedes-Benz Gullwing fluctuates in price. Sometimes it is a little lower than the 300S and sometimes a little higher. However, its price has roughly paralleled the price of the 300S since the cars first appeared.

If there is a "gilt-edged" automobile investment it is the 300SL Gullwing. It is a splendid automobile, recognized as such by everyone. It is a car with dash, even against the ultramoderns like the Miura and the Countach. Yet it is conservative.

A fact of great importance about the Gullwing is that it measures the collector car market probably better than any other car—from Mustang to Bugatti Royale.

Roger Bell in his *Great Marques: Mercedes-Benz*, probably the most definitive work on Mercedes, has this to say:

"It was the six cylinder engine of the 300S that provided the basis for Mercedes' long rumoured comeback to European racing in 1952 with the 300SL, or 3-litre Sport Leicht to interpret the nomenclature. And light it was, with a small closed coupe body with gullwing doors clothing a spaceframe chassis of thin steel tubes powered by an inclined (for a low bonnet line) development of the 300S engine with raised compression and three downdraft Solex carburettors, developing a relatively modest 175 bhp at 5200 rpm. The suspension was similar to that of the production cars; even the flexible kingpost mounting, which allowed slight fore and aft cushioning of the front wishbones, was retained, though the car had bigger drum brakes and a close-ratio four-speed gearbox."

Performance was improved over the years, and the 1955 model had fuel injection by Bosch and a horsepower rating of 215, not much by modern standards but enough to drive the car about 150 mph and do zero to 60 in 7.2 seconds. It was once officially reported that the 1955 model would do 165 mph, but I doubt it.

Any way you looked at it, the car was a great bargain, a top-performance, beautiful, well-designed, and well-finished Mercedes for about $6,800. Even as late as 1956, the list price was only $7,300.

In racing in 1952, the 300SL swept everything before it, although I did not see any 300SL for sale until 1954, when it was officially placed on the market. It continued to be made and sold to 1957. In 1957 essentially the same car was produced but this one a beautiful roadster. The last of the roadster series was produced as late as 1963; but the roadster is not, and never was, in the class of the Gullwing. The Gullwing seemed to handle better than the roadster, and its form was unique. Still, the roadster started out in 1957 with a price tag well above that of the Gullwing—almost $11,000. In 1957 the price of the Gullwing was a little under $9,000.

In 1955 the Mercedes-Benz team swept everything before it in racing with its 300SLR track machines. The 300SLR designation sounds as though the cars were souped-up 300SL's, but they were not. The 300SL's, like the 300S's and the 300 sedans, had six-cylinder engines. The 300SLR's had straight eights. They were placed in the chassis lying down, and the drive was taken off between the front block of four cylinders and the rear block of four cylinders. I would expect one of these 300SLR's that won almost every race in 1955 to sell for at least $250,000, should it ever appear for sale—quite a different machine from the stock Mercedes cars of the 300 series.

In 1960 the 300SL Gullwing was simply another secondhand car, although, of course, a good one and an attractive one. Many such cars were offered for sale at an average price of $5,000. The 300SL roadster, vastly less desired on today's market, was selling for at least $1,000 *more* than the Gullwing.

By the bottom of the stock market drop in the summer of 1962, the Gullwing was selling at almost exactly the figure it was selling for in 1960—about $5,000. Slightly more Gullwings were selling at under $5,000 than in 1960, however.

By 1965 a good Gullwing could be bought for under $4,000, although some were priced at a little over $6,000. In that year, I located a reasonably good 300SL convertible that drove well priced at $2,500, and a 300S cabriolet in good condition priced at $1,900. The good-condition roadsters were generally hovering around $5,000. At that time, it might have been better to invest in a 1938 540K roadster for $6,000 or a restored 1937 540K cabriolet for $5,200 or a 1935 500K roadster for $4,800!

In 1970, five years later, a fine-condition Gullwing might cost $6,000 to $6,500, but an average unrestored, but fair, Gullwing might have gone for as little as $3,500. The 300S might have been bought for about the same price.

Four years later, things had taken off in the collector car market and certainly in the 300SL Gullwing market. In 1974 the Gullwing was at the $12,000 level. The 300SL roadster was selling for about $4,000 *less*. The 300S was a little lower than the Gullwing but above the 300SL roadster. Between 1970 and 1974, there was a noticeable rise in the whole market for collector cars.

In 1975 the general price level of a fine-condition Gullwing had risen to about $15,000 and the average car sold for about $10,000. The best 300SL roadster sold for about $10,000, the price of the average Gullwing. The 300S also sold for about $10,000.

By 1980 the boom in collector cars was in full swing. The *fine*-condition Gullwing was selling for the very much elevated price of $55,000 to $65,000, perhaps at an average price of about $60,000. The *average*-condition Gullwing was selling for around $50,000, sometimes a little less. The roadster was selling for from $30,000 to just under $40,000 for a mint car, and the 300S was at the $30,000 level or a little above if in fine condition.

Business began to deteriorate in 1981, and in 1982 the economy was depressed, but the price of the 300SL Gullwing remained relatively firm. By 1981 an auction price of $100,000 might have been achieved, but a price in the neighborhood of $90,000 for a mint-condition Gullwing was probably more normal. At retail, prices above $100,000 were reported.

During the fall and winter of 1982, the collector car business slumped somewhat, and occasionally fine collector cars changed hands at prices that were definitely under the market of 1980 and 1981. The 300SL Gullwing was not in the great demand in 1983 (early) that it had been earlier. In the early spring of 1983, a fine-condition Gullwing was offered for sale privately for $55,000, and few takers. Still, today a price of $75,000 to $85,000 for a fine-condition Gullwing seems about market. A mint-condition 300S roadster or cabriolet can easily bring prices of this level and more. On the other hand, the 300SL roadster sells for considerably less; as of 1983, $45,000 is a fair price for a good-condition 300SL roadster.

These are some of the pluses and minuses on the 300SL Gullwing-as a collector car:

1. If a person had the money to cover the purchase price and wanted to buy just one car as a collector car, the 300SL Gullwing might well fill the bill. That is saying a lot for any collector car, since almost all collector cars have minuses as well as pluses.

2. It is well established as a collector car in almost every circle, from sports car purists to critical competition car drivers to strict investors. One rarely hears an adverse comment about the Gullwing.

3. Mechanically, the car is excellent. It drives beautifully and it gives a minimum amount of trouble for a strict sports car. The maintenance is low, and I would not hesitate to take such a car, provided it was in good condition, on a 500-mile trip over a weekend. I would expect no trouble.

4. The car is vastly simpler than a good many of the multicylinder Italian cars. It has one overhead camshaft, not four like a number of the Italian greats. It has three reliable carburetors or a reliable fuel-injection system, not six carburetors like some of the twelve-cylinder cars, and six cylinders give less trouble than eight or twelve.

5. The suspension of the car is excellent, even by modern standards, and many times I have heard the comment that it handles much better than the

300SL roadster. It is this preference for the Gullwing as against the roadster that seems to have created and maintained the price differential between the Gullwing and the roadster over the years, since the roadster is most certainly a good-looking car and mechanically very similar to the Gullwing.

6. The Gullwing is an easy car to own. It can sit in the garage with a minimum amount of "exercise" and still not deteriorate over a period of time. When it comes time to start it up, it generally starts up and keeps running.

7. There is enough collector interest in the car so that it is not likely to decline in price much in the down business cycle or stock market phases of the future.

8. Anybody can be proud to own a 300SL Gullwing and to drive it, and anybody can drive it. It is not temperamental or in other ways difficult to drive or own.

9. The design of the car is not out of date, and it looks as good today as when it first appeared.

10. Possibly the only real adverse criticism of the car is that it is a little hard to get into and out of, but one soon learns how to sit on the sill of the car and swing his legs in and out. When the gullwing doors are in place, one might have a feeling of claustrophobia, and also there is not the advantage of windup windows, but that is not the most serious drawback, at least for most people.

11. There is a ready market for the car, and it can easily find a buyer at most foreign car dealerships and collector car auctions. It is the type of car dealers are inclined to take on consignment, or buy outright, as well as the kind of car auctions tend to reach for. Thus, the liquidity of the car is good— at least compared with many other collector cars.

300 Four-Door Convertible

Five years ago, I probably would not have considered the Mercedes-Benz 300 four-door convertible as one of the top postwar classics. Ten years ago, I most certainly wouldn't have considered it in the category of the 300S or the 300SL Gullwing. As a car I still don't, but times change and now the four-door convertible is an important and quite high-priced investment automobile, a classic. While the convertible four-door sedan is essentially a 300 and not a super car like the 300S or the Gullwing, it has all the qualities of the excellent 300 sedan plus a four-door convertible body, and in the market of the early 1980s, the four-door convertible sedan and the phaeton were the cars that were priced the highest of any body style. The Duesenberg phaeton, the Chrysler Imperial phaeton, and the Packard phaeton were the highest-priced cars of any body model.

The 300 convertible is not the most beautiful convertible sedan ever built. In fact, fifteen years ago the car was not in the running with the 300S open cars and with the Gullwing or the 300SL roadster. At that time the car seemed somewhat ungainly. We must, however, recognize the judgment of the market in the price paid for a car, and if the market says a car is valuable, it is.

The price of this car is about $40,000, which puts it on the borderline between an important postwar classic and a medium-grade postwar classic. The price has, however, been rising rather steadily and rapidly, especially in the past two years.

In 1960 the price of a four-door 300 convertible was about $2,500, and some were for sale for less. The car was certainly no favorite of the market.

In the stock market recession of 1962 the 300 four-door convertible was at about the same price as in 1960. The preferred later-model car, the 1956 model, was selling for under $3,500.

By 1965 the stock market recession was over, but the price of the 300 four-door convertible had moved little. A 1954 model was for sale for $2,700, although a few were priced higher.

In 1970 a fine 300 four-door convertible could be bought for $3,500 and a good unrestored car for about $1,500. Even at this low price, few wanted this car. One could pay $2,000 to $2,500 for a premium car—the 300S cabriolet or roadster.

Four years later, by 1974, prices of the car had risen materially, and a 1956 (late-model) 300 convertible four-door was advertised at $7,500. Older cars were selling for a little less money.

Prices kept on rising, and by the mid-1970s a fine-condition 300 four-door convertible would bring $8,500 to $9,500 and a good unrestored car $5,000 to $7,000.

In the next five years, the 300 convertible four-door came into its own and the fine-condition car was selling for about $25,000 and the good unrestored car for $20,000.

Although business conditions deteriorated into 1982, the price of this car continued to rise, and in that year a mint-condition car sold for about $40,000, but an average good unrestored car for $20,000—quite a spread between "good" and mint.

The recession took its toll, however, and there was little or no rise to early 1983. When the cars appeared at auction in the early part of 1983, there was little demand for them, but owners refused to sell them at prices under what the market had been.

The cars are good mechanically and reasonably good-looking but not great, and they will probably continue to rise in value as business conditions improve and as sales of classic cars generally increase.

Ferrari

The Ferrari is a "must" for almost any collection that includes postwar classics. The big question is *what* Ferrari or Ferraris to invest in. There are many many highly desirable collector Ferraris, and several of these cars will no doubt emerge as definite investment automobiles. I feel that two such cars are investments right now.

Daytona and Daytona Spyder

The first of the two postwar investment cars is the Ferrari Daytona put out from 1968 to 1973 (when they were "discontinued" in the United States). In 1970 the first Daytonas were sold in the United States with a price of $19,500. In 1973 the price on new Daytonas had risen to $25,000.

The Daytona coupe is a magnificent sports coupe with Pininfarina body. It is a beautiful but conservatively designed car with the V-12 engine in the front and the drive through the rear wheels. Although conservative, it has a somewhat streamlined look about it and is certainly not dated, even in comparison with the very much later Ferrari Berlinetta Boxer 512 with rear engine.

The Daytona Spyder is the open version of the car, a car at least as good-looking as the Daytona coupe but open, and this is very much a preferred car in the collector car market.

The Ferrari Daytona is a top performer even by today's standards. In a fairly recent test against the latest high-performance Ferrari 512 Berlinetta Boxer, the Daytona accelerated faster up to 150 mph. Still, this beautiful Daytona is a docile car and can be driven to and from work.

By 1975 the Daytona coupe was in the $35,000 range. Unlike most "second-hand cars," the Daytona did not decline in price year by year, after its sale in the United States was discontinued in 1973.

From here on, the price of the Daytona rose steadily, but not at a very rapid rate until the 1980s. The Spyder forged ahead, and in 1980 a fine-condition Spyder was bringing about $45,000.

By 1982 the price of the coupe was about $65,000, and for this price a mint-condition car could often be purchased. The Spyder was pushing $100,000.

The rise in price was not over. In late spring 1983, the Daytona coupe tacked on about $10,000 to its 1982 selling price, and $75,000 was more the market for a mint-condition car.

One near-mint-condition Spyder sold for $115,000, and advertisements as high as $175,000 were noted. The Spyders in original form, not conversions from coupes, are probably the best investment—at least for the individual who has $100,000-plus to invest in one car and wants a Ferrari.

275GTB-4

This is the other "bulletproof" car from Ferrari. No one ever seems to criticize this car—and with good reason. It is a fantastic road machine, as I indicated earlier, and a reliable car. It appeared in 1966 as an improvement over the 275GTB, since the GTB-4 had double overhead camshafts on each bank of cylinders. The car was produced until 1968, when it was replaced by the Daytona, a car with a bigger engine and 350 instead of the 300 horsepower of the 275GTB-4. Is the Daytona better than the 275GTB-4? No Ferrari aficionado will say that, although one might say that the GTB-4 with its double overhead camshafts was a definite improvement over the 275GTB with single overhead camshaft on each bank of cylinders. Perhaps the comparison boils down to the fact that the suspension of the Daytona is a little softer and a little less like that of a road-racing car than the 275GTB-4.

The performance of the 275GTB-4 suits me somewhat better than that of the Daytona, but for driving every day I would prefer the Daytona.

As late as 1975, an excellent-condition 275GTB-4 could have been bought for a little over $10,000, certainly not over $12,500, and at $12,500 the price

The Ferrari 275GTB-4, one of the great sports cars of all time, appeared in 1966. The 1967 car pictured here, belonging to Nick Soprano of Motor Classic Corporation, has a market value of about $65,000. In 1970 such a car might have been purchased for about $10,000. (Julia Rush)

was about double that of the 275GTB with single overhead camshaft. In early 1974 a 1968 275GTB-4 was advertised for $11,500.

In 1980 the price of a fine-condition 275GTB-4 was about $25,000, about $5,000 less than a Daytona in the same condition. A good unrestored 275GTB-4 could have been bought for $10,000 less.

In early 1982 the GTB-4 was selling for about $65,000, even a car in mint condition. The finest 275GTB-4 I have ever seen for sale (and I have seen many) could have been bought for $75,000, but the high price reflected the condition and very low mileage of the particular car.

Toward the end of 1982 and in the first months of 1983, the classic car business was in a slump and even a fine-condition 275GTB-4 did not move very rapidly off the showroom floor. The price of the car at that time was certainly not over $65,000. Sales of these cars at auctions were not at all active, and an owner of a 275GTB-4 might well have held on to his car for a while if he wanted to move it at any decent price.

The 500 Superfast and the second-series Super America are still not well established as collector cars of top rank. If I had to make a guess, I would say that time will prove both of these cars as important collector automobiles and a person would not go wrong to buy a Super America for $35,000 and a Superfast for $40,000. Superfasts can bring up to $55,000.

Lamborghini Miura

I would place the Lamborghini Miura right behind the Ferrari as a top-notch collectible postwar classic. Sometimes I think I would place the car ahead of the Ferrari, but the Ferrari has a great name, a long background of engineering, and a proven "track record" on the race course. Lamborghini has never raced, at least to my knowledge.

The Lamborghini Miura was first manufactured in 1967, and my own Miura is Number 11 of all the Miuras manufactured. The car was meant to be produced slowly, with corrections being made as the automobiles were delivered to buyers. Only the car was such an instantaneous success that sales took place too rapidly for improvements to be made, and the problem faced by the factory was filling the orders. It took literally years to make improvements to the Miura. Finally, in 1972, when the last run of the Miura was being made, the kinks seem to have been worked out and the car was relatively trouble-free and engineered close to perfection.

The Miura is a sensational-looking, streamlined car 41 inches high with a V-12 transverse rear engine. With double overhead camshafts and six carburetors the 4-liter engine can turn out up to 400 horsepower with no indication that the engine is being overloaded. The car can accelerate, under the right conditions, to 60 mph in under six seconds and will hit a top speed of perhaps 170. It is low and wide and the springing is excellent, and at 100-plus mph one feels little instability or fear. In traffic it is absolutely docile. The clutch, carburetors, and everything else about the car are suitable to city as well as superhighway driving.

The drawbacks are a slightly harsh suspension and a whine of the gears that can be improved to a degree. Actually, sports car enthusiasts often like the harsh suspension and the whine of the gears.

There is a great difference in value between Miuras by year. Today, a late SV mint car with improvements can go for $100,000, although one may still be lucky enough at times to buy one for $85,000. The earlier cars can be bought for from $35,000 to $50,000.

The Miura started life in 1967, selling for about $20,000, not a low price by any means. In 1970 I saw a good Miura for $24,000, about market at the time. By 1975, $12,000 would have bought a good Miura. In 1981 the last-model SV Miuras were up to $60,000, but the earlier ones were selling for somewhere in the $30,000 range; 1980 saw the big rise in the value of this car.

In 1981 and early 1982, relatively many Miuras appeared for sale in many automobile publications, while in early 1983 almost no Miura appeared for sale. Only 720 Miuras in all were manufactured, not a great number, and people seemed to be holding on to them. My own car was bought in 1980 for $20,000, but before it suited me I had an additional $6,000 invested in it. It is not mint but it is near it. The car on which to concentrate is the last run of the last model—the 1972 SV with separate crankcase and transmission *or* an earlier model that has been completely modernized by Bob Wallace, a Lamborghini engineer and test driver who operates a shop in Phoenix, Arizona. I would just as soon have a Bob Wallace modernized and completely restored 1967 Miura as a mint 1972 last-run SV.

Rolls-Royce

In many ways the Rolls-Royce Silver Cloud series represented the last of the great Rolls-Royces. The first Silver Cloud was put out in 1955, the six-cylinder Silver Cloud I, and it was continued until 1960 when the V-8 Silver Cloud II made its appearance. In 1963 the V-8 Silver Cloud III with its four prestigious headlights appeared and was continued to 1965. In 1966 a completely different automobile appeared, a "more normal-looking" car, smaller, more boxy, and less regal-looking. This smaller car is the one continued up to the Silver Spur of the 1980s. It was called the Silver Shadow and later the Silver Shadow II, and to date this has not developed into a strict collector car. To a certain degree the Silver Cloud series has—but by no means all Silver Clouds. Three Silver Clouds stand out as collector cars. Perhaps they are borderline, but they seem to be moving over into the collector car category.

Silver Cloud Convertibles

These are elegant machines turned out by Mulliner and Park Ward. The Mulliner convertible is essentially a Silver Cloud sedan sawed off and converted to a five-passenger convertible. It is an impressive-looking car but by no means the best car. All the Silver Cloud convertibles—the Silver Cloud I, II, and III—look about the same, although the hood line of the Cloud III is lower than on the earlier cars and the Cloud III has the four headlights.

The Mulliner Park Ward convertible is a car designed to be a convertible, not a sedan cut down to a convertible. It is probably a better-looking convertible than the Mulliner, although even the former is not the ultimate in beauty, by any means. The car is, however, like almost every Rolls ever made, a quality automobile and thoroughly reliable.

Today the Silver Cloud III Mulliner Park Ward car is probably the most wanted of the Silver Cloud convertibles and the highest in price.

In 1955 the Rolls-Royce Silver Cloud I with six-cylinder engine made its appearance and with it the corresponding Bentley, essentially the same car, the six-cylinder SI. The radiators of the Rolls and Bentleys were different; the Rolls-Royce Palladian radiator cost about $250 more to make than the rounded Bentley radiator. Otherwise, except for the nameplates, the cars were about the same, with the Rolls priced about $250 above the Bentley.

At the 1959 Earl's Court Motor Show in London, a Bentley SII eight-cylinder convertible left-hand-drive with a Park Ward body was on display for about $15,000. Landed in New York the price might have been $1,500 more to cover shipping, insurance, and import duty. The corresponding Rolls would have been about $250 more.

In the recession of 1962, I was offered a "current" Rolls-Royce Park Ward convertible. The asking price was $11,500, and this was about the bottom of the market for any Rolls-Royce convertible with Park Ward body. In 1962, with the bottom dropped out of the stock market, there were many Rolls-Royces of all descriptions for sale. I tried out a very nice Silver Cloud II eight-cylinder sedan in New Jersey priced at $9,500, and a corporation in Boston called me repeatedly to see if I would buy its Silver Cloud I for $5,500.

In 1965, after the close of the stock market recession, a 1961 Cloud II Mulliner-bodied convertible was offered for $13,500, a car reportedly in perfect condition. This was about the market on the Cloud convertible at the time.

There was little movement in the price of these Cloud convertibles to 1970, but between 1970 and 1973 prices doubled. I made an intensive survey of

Rolls-Royce Silver Clouds and Bentleys of the corresponding series through the 1970s, both in the United States and in England, and ended up in 1973 buying a special long-wheelbase Silver Cloud I with James Young body, but not a convertible.

In 1975 a fine Silver Cloud II convertible was selling for about $25,000 and an unrestored, but good, convertible of the Cloud II series at about $18,000 to $20,000. A Cloud III convertible was selling for a little more than $25,000. All of these quotations were for left-hand-drive cars, the cars preferred in the market in America.

By 1980 the convertible had skyrocketed to the $60,000 to $70,000 range. The Cloud III tended to be in the $70,000 range if mint, the Cloud II in the $60,000 range, and the Cloud I convertible, the six-cylinder car, between $60,000 and $70,000. The average good unrestored cars were selling for $10,000 to $15,000 less.

By 1982 there was a slide in prices of the Silver Cloud convertibles, and at times a Cloud I, II, or III convertible could be bought for under $50,000, sometimes as low as $40,000 for a fine-condition car. In 1982 I was inclined to buy a Silver Cloud III convertible in very good condition for about $50,000. In England the price of all Rolls-Royce cars had dropped, and $40,000 would buy a mint-condition right-hand-drive Cloud I, II, or III convertible. The pound sterling had gone to pieces and was as low as $1.44, and nobody in England seemed to be in the market for a Rolls-Royce.

Phantom V

The Phantom V was a super car put out between 1959 and 1968 and billed as the largest Rolls-Royce ever built. The bodies were mostly sedan and limousine, and although the new cars sold when first produced at about $25,000, a very high price at the time, they quickly dropped in price as they became simply oversize, conservative, secondhand cars. In 1967 I turned down a fine PV limousine that had had its front and rear left-hand doors dented in badly, for sale for $4,000. The sellers stated that for $7,000 they would deliver the car in perfect condition. My own body shop would have done the repairs for perhaps $1,000. Although many people looked at this car, no one seemed to want to pay $4,000 for it.

At about the same time, the DeKay estate came onto the market in Greenwich, Connecticut, and the DeKay Phantom V, powder blue, and perfect, was offered for sale for $7,000—again with few takers.

By 1975 the Mulliner-bodied Phantom V in fine condition was selling for about $25,000 and demand was active, even though the car was certainly a very conservative sedan or limo.

By 1980 the price was up to $65,000 to $70,000, whether the body was limousine or sedan and whether made by Mulliner, Park Ward, or James Young. It is possible that the James Young bodies were preferred, with prices of these cars closer to $70,000 than $65,000.

By 1982 the Phantom V in fine condition was pushing $90,000, although original and unrestored PV's were selling at auction for half this price. The wanted cars at top prices were the left-hand-drive cars for use in the United States.

In England a right-hand-drive Phantom V could have been bought in mid-1983 for relatively little money. One PV, a 1965 chauffeur-driven car with a new engine, was for sale for $29,500. For $38,000 one could have bought a 1964 limo with a $17,000 overhaul job just completed by Rolls-Royce.

If we move to the ultra-rare ultra-high-priced PV convertible sedans, we are on the very exclusive Rolls-Royce level. I saw one such car, a mint-condition PV four-door convertible in London, priced at $175,000. No such car would sell for under $100,000 on the present market in any condition.

There is one other sedan that I might mention, and this is the James Young long-wheelbase sedan or limousine. The car that is the most wanted of these James Young cars is the Silver Cloud III rather than the earlier Cloud I and II. The Cloud III with left-hand drive has a price pattern and price level something like the Phantom V's and is one of the most-sought-after Rolls-Royces. Ten years ago I was offered a right-hand-drive Cloud III James Young long-wheelbase car in London for $15,000. The car was not mint but it was not in poor condition either. Today this same car might sell for $45,000 to $50,000 in London, probably above the London price of the PV. The left-hand-drive car in America might approach $100,000.

There are many cogent reasons for considering a Rolls-Royce "super car" like the convertibles and the PV's as collectibles, and also a few cautions:

1. The car almost always has a market in America, at dealers' showrooms and auctions. In the recession of 1982, one car that always seemed to sell at auction and to bring a good price was the very ordinary Rolls-Royce Silver Shadow of the late 1960s, a good car but certainly no great or rare Rolls-Royce. The rare and expensive cars held up in price pretty well in the recession when many car auctions went flat.

2. The Rolls-Royce is an excellent car in every way and makes a worthwhile addition to any collection. In fact, a case can be made for including some Rolls-Royce in any collection of any size at all.

3. The Rolls-Royce can be used for transportation, and it can be used regularly. Many of the Silver Cloud series are on the road all the time in the United States and certainly in England.

4. Repairs are easy to make and parts are available. Bob's Auto Parts of

Kingston, New York, will supply any part from a hubcap to an entire engine on short notice and at a reasonable price.

5. The market is good—both the buying market and the selling market—and it is not hard either to buy or to sell a fine Rolls-Royce.

6. The Rolls-Royce for sale must be absolutely mint; condition is more important in a Rolls-Royce than in perhaps any other car. Particularly the wood must be perfect as well as the paint, chrome, and leather. But it does not cost a great deal to put these things in order in a Rolls-Royce. Many shops handle Rolls-Royce restoration and Rolls-Royce parts.

7. The year 1983 offered a big buying opportunity, particularly in England.

8. On the other hand, the "buying opportunity" means that prices were off for Rolls-Royce. Prices did not simply halt or pause in their upward climb in 1982 and 1983. They declined.

9. There are few "sensational" Rolls-Royce cars as collectibles, at least in the postwar era, and there are many cars available, and so the postwar Rolls-Royce price potential probably can never be like that of the Duesenberg or the supercharged Mercedes-Benz or perhaps even the postwar Mercedes-Benz 300S.

Shelby Cobra

Perhaps the Carroll Shelby Cobra is the best sports competition car ever produced in the United States. Whether it deserves this distinction or not, it was a splendid development and a car that was, and is still, praised by everyone. It represents almost the ultimate in simplicity—a small car, essentially the British AC, and a powerful but standard engine, the Ford 289 or the Ford 427. The car weighs little. The engine produces up to 375 horsepower (some later modified engines produce perhaps as much as 600 horsepower), and the mechanical design is up-to-date and straightforward—independent four-wheel suspension and four-wheel disc brakes. About two years ago a German was advised that since he wanted a car that would outperform everything else on the autobahns, he purchase a Shelby Cobra with 600 horsepower. He did.

This is, of course, not the standard Cobra that one can generally buy. The car on the market is the 289-cubic-inch or 427-cubic-inch roadster, the former costing $45,000 to $50,000 and the latter $65,000 to $75,000.

The Cobra appeared publicly in 1962 and was continued to 1965 with the 289 engine. The volume sold was low—100 in all in the year 1962 despite the fact that the price was only $5,995. The larger-engined car, the 427, was continued to 1967, and 356 of this car were produced.

There is much to be said in favor of each of the two engine sizes. It is possible that the smaller-engined car handles a little better than the larger-engined car. The larger-engined car has a shattering performance, however, with a time of 14 seconds from zero to 100 mph and back again to a standstill. In the modern economy cars, a time of zero to 60 in 14 seconds is not bad (with no return to a standstill).

The Cobra is by no means a refined-looking car with luxury features. It has no double overhead cams or six carburetors or walnut trim, etc. It is just a simple car with shattering performance and at the same time a car that is dependable and can be repaired easily and inexpensively.

As recently as seven years ago, a Cobra in mint condition sold for about $17,500. By 1981 the price of the 427 was about $65,000 and the price of the 289 $45,000. Today these prices have been elevated by about $10,000 each—in a period in which classic car sales have not been noted for their strength. The cars will probably not decline, at least in the immediate future.

To a certain extent the "top postwar classics" are an arbitrary category of automobiles. Who says these are the "top classics"? Aren't there any other top classics?

To begin with, we have not included some major makes of cars, such as the BMW and Porsche. Although there are many excellent cars by these two manufacturers, there are very few cars of top quality *plus* high price, and quality and high price are major considerations in the establishment of the category of the top postwar classics.

Certain real standouts could have been included, such as the Maserati Ghibli Spyder, possibly the most beautiful convertible of sports car design ever made. We will include this car with the Ghibli coupe.

Then there are two major sports car makes, Jaguar and MG. The cars are well-established collector cars and investment cars. The reason for their non-inclusion in the category of top postwar classics is their price. Should the XK120 or the MG TC rise tremendously in value, then they might be included. As it is, they are included in the lesser-priced or medium-level postwar classics.

7

The Medium-Level Postwar Classics

THERE IS A tremendous price differential between the important prewar classics and postwar classics. A price of $250,000 for an important prewar classic, such as a Cadillac V-16 convertible of the early 1930s, is not unusual. A price of $100,000 for any postwar classic, no matter how important the car, is unusual. Possibly the most prestigious of all postwar classics is the Mercedes-Benz 300S roadster and cabriolet manufactured from 1951 to 1957. Two of these cars sold at auction in the early 1980s for an even $100,000. This is the price of an absolutely prime-condition open car. The general price level of the car in average condition might be $25,000 lower.

The top postwar classics sell for about $60,000 to $65,000, some a little less. The "medium-level" postwar classics sell for under $50,000, some for under $30,000.

For under $30,000 one can buy almost any classic Jaguar, the XK120, XK140, XK150, and XKE, both the six-cylinder and the twelve-cylinder car. For under $15,000 one can buy a six-cylinder Aston Martin in very fine condition and possibly a Maserati Ghibli, or a very fine Rolls-Royce Silver Cloud I sedan, a right-hand-drive model, particularly in London.

For under $5,000 one can buy a 1971–1974 Cadillac Eldorado convertible in good, but probably not mint, condition.

The big advantage in collecting postwar classics of medium price is that the cash outlay and the cash risk are not great. If one is trying to buy a "good piece of machinery" with a limited cash outlay, the postwar classics of moderate price level offer a number of opportunities. Of course, buying such a car may not be a straight road to a capital gain. A lot depends on the individual make of car chosen for investment.

The less expensive postwar classics are easy cars to own and maintain. Parts do not cost a great deal and are not so hard to get, and knowledgeable mechanics are not scarce.

The less expensive postwar classics can be used, at least occasionally. There is a constant movement in the category from "use," or transportation, cars to classic cars. What is the status of the Lamborghini Countach? It is a sensational automobile, but it is not yet classic. It is still made, but when it stops coming off the assembly line, what then? How long will it take the car to become a postwar classic like its predecessor, the Lamborghini Miura, which is certainly a postwar classic?

Thus it is possible to take a certain gamble on postwar cars—that they will gradually turn into postwar classic cars that will start to move up in price. One can gamble to a degree on the less expensive cars. If they turn into appreciating collectibles, well and good. If they do not, then the cars can still be used and enjoyed and there is no great cash loss.

This chapter must of necessity be a summary and a sample. It cannot include all of the medium-level postwar classics. Still, it does include most of the important ones.

Why did we leave out the Aston Martin? Because the six-cylinder car tends to be low in price and does not seem to rise in price very fast. Within the past twelve months I have found, as indicated earlier, two very good Aston Martins with the very fine Superleggera bodies, one priced at $7,500 and the other for $6,500, prices on the low end of the value scale.

A 1956 Lincoln Continental Mark II that Christie's auctioned in Beaulieu, England, in 1980 for the equivalent of $10,750. In 1970 it might have brought $3,500, and today it would be valued at about $16,000.

On the other hand, is the V-8 a collector car at all or is it still an expensive secondhand car like the Rolls-Royce Corniche?

What about the BMW? The Model 507 is a top car and a collector car, but very few appear on the market. When they do they can reach $18,000 to $20,000.

Then what about the Cadillac convertible of 1947? I owned four 1947 convertibles at various times. The car can sell for as high as $20,000, but is it a postwar classic or is it a special-interest car? This make and model car still has to be sorted out. The same can be said about the Lincoln Continental Mark II of the mid-1950s.

Some very special prewar and postwar cars do not seem to fall into any category, because of their rarity, such as the 1939 Phantom Corsair. Some

This 1949–1950 Italmeccanica custom car, with body by Farina and with a Cadillac engine, an auto-show prizewinner, was purchased by the author in 1951 for $3,750. Today it would be valued at $25,000.

This magnificent 1948 Alfa-Romeo GC-2500 Super Sport two-passenger sport roadster, which sold at Christie's in Los Angeles for $36,000 in 1980, now resides in the National Motor Museum in Beaulieu, England.

of these cars are absolutely unique because of their bodies, mechanics or both. In this category I would place the 1948 Alfa Romeo now in Beaulieu, England. It is one of the most beautiful cars I have ever seen. Essentially a two-passenger roadster, it is superior to the Ferrari in *body* design. It sold at auction at Christie's in Los Angeles in 1980 for $36,000, and today might reach $100,000 or more!

A second "special" is an automobile I owned and developed to a certain extent—a 1950 Italmeccanica, made in Italy. Its chassis was unique but had a five-passenger body by Farina, a souped-up Cadillac engine, and a Mercury drivetrain.

To sum up, there is a certain gamble in buying a medium-grade postwar classic as an investment. There is probably less gamble in buying a top postwar classic like the Mercedes-Benz 300S and 300SL. On the other hand, these top postwar classics cost a great deal while the medium-level postwar classics do not. Although their prices seem high in relation to what they were ten years ago, or even five years ago, prices are not high compared with those for the established collector cars.

Criteria for Selection

1. Somewhat arbitrarily, I have defined "medium-level" as being under $50,000. Of course, values are changing each year. A few years ago an SV Lamborghini Miura of the last model might have been bought for under $50,000. Today a price of $85,000 to $100,000 is about standard for a fine-condition SV. Sometimes values change very fast, perhaps touched off by a price "breakthrough," and these price breakthroughs occur in almost all collectibles.

2. I have tried to select cars that come onto the market in sufficient numbers so that one has a chance to buy them or buy at least one of them without a great deal of trouble. Thus the postwar Italian Isotta Fraschini with rear engine would have to be ruled out, as I have never seen even one of these cars for sale anywhere, at auction or by a dealer.

3. Some cars seem at the present time to be "fully priced"—that is, they are not moving up in price much, or moving at all—while others do not seem very good buys at their present price levels. I have excluded these and chosen cars that seem to offer good values plus a good opportunity for price appreciation. At the present time it seems that the Jaguar XK120, 140, and 150 offer very good values and hold forth the prospect of price appreciation. When one can buy a fine-condition XK140 for about $18,000—and I saw one such car at the 1983 Barrett-Jackson auction—I am inclined to include the XK140 as a medium-priced postwar classic. For $18,000 one gets a fine and beautiful automobile plus a real prospect for price appreciation.

4. I have placed the Chevrolet Corvette high on the list. Down a bit I have placed the Rolls-Royce Silver Cloud series. A little lower down I have placed the Mercedes-Benz group of cars from the 190SL to the 450SL. This placement is somewhat arbitrary.

5. I have tried to be careful about selecting "headaches" and troublemakers. There are some fine cars that require constant repairs and the replacement of very expensive parts—and replacement regularly. These problem cars are not dear to my heart and I have not been inclined to include them.

6. I have to a certain extent concentrated on the cars that the market wants— that the auction houses and dealers like to have for sale. Such cars can be disposed of easily, cars like the Lamborghini Miura and the Jaguar XK120.

Buying Policy

Here are the factors to consider in selecting a collector car:

1. Roadster or convertible. These are generally the premium cars, the most-

wanted body styles, and I have almost always concentrated on these open cars in my price tracing.

2. Two-passenger. These cars are preferred in general to four- or five-passenger cars, certainly including Ferrari.

3. Use for competition, like the Mercedes-Benz Gullwing and the Shelby Cobra.

4. Illustrious ownership of the car or an illustrious driver, such as the Rolls-Royce Silver Ghost owned by Edward VIII.

5. Number of cars turned out. The fewer the cars, theoretically, the higher the price, because of fewer cars to satisfy demand.

6. Number of cars still around to buy. The fewer the better, as long as the buying public *knows* the car and it isn't a very obscure automobile.

7. Low mileage. This is of tremendous importance if the car measures up to the mileage in its appearance and condition mechanically.

8. High original price.

9. Original popularity. The Mustang of 1964–1966 was an immediate success saleswise and every college kid seemed to want to own one. It is just as popular today.

10. Ford or Chevrolet standouts. These are the most popular makes of all the mass-produced cars, and the specials developed from these two makes are popular and high-priced, like the Shelby Cobra and the Pantera.

11. High-performance cars when new.

12. Low serial number of the particular car. My Lamborghini Miura is Number 11 of the 720 Miuras made—maybe a plus for the car. On the other hand, if one has a great make and model like Silver Ghost Rolls-Royce Number 3, he really has a premium car.

13. Technical innovation, or at least high technical development, like the Lamborghini Miura with transverse engine combined with rear drive—everything behind the driver.

14. Italian or British, and possibly German. These are the exotics today.

15. Out of production. The Lamborghini Countach has a good deal of value now. When it goes out of production, then a curve of price increase may develop.

16. Sponsoring club, like the Porsche owners' club, to help owners of the make and model and develop interest in the car.

17. Beauty of styling, like the great Maserati Ghibli, a car that literally takes your breath away.

18. Famous engineer or designer, like Giugiaro and his Maserati Ghibli.

19. Historical importance of the car. The Shelby Daytona Cobra owned by Nick Soprano is one such car, an American Le Mans winner.

20. A trend-setting car like the great Jaguar XK120.

21. Famous body builder like Giugiaro on the BMW M1, one of the greatest postwar competition-sports cars.

22. The reputation when it was new of being a great car, like the Ferrari Daytona.

A particular make and model collector car might well appear in one or more chapters—in one or more lists. The Rolls-Royce Silver Cloud is certainly a top-quality car. At the present time it is also an underpriced car for what it is. In addition the Silver Cloud sedans are medium-priced cars—the standard sedans and even some of the specials.

On the other hand, the Corvette in general is a lower-priced car, but not all Corvettes, and the popular and finer models of Corvette are moving above the $20,000 line, a line that probably puts the car into the medium-priced level rather than the lower-priced level. In addition, as time goes on more and more cars will move up in price. While the Rolls-Royce Corniche convertible is a medium-priced car at about $35,000 in London, how long will the car remain at that level, as long as it is not changed in body style? Perhaps we should not even use the Corniche as an example of a collector car. It is still made, and when it is out of production, then what? Will the price of the present Corniche models that will be out of production drop, stay the same, or rise? Will the car become a collector car? How long will it take to become a collector car?

Chevrolet Corvette

Possibly the "hottest" car in the collector car auctions is the Chevrolet Corvette of 1953–1963, the first ten years of production. The cars were not so remarkable when they first appeared, except perhaps in appearance, but they got better and better mechanically and in performance as they matured over the years. Still, we are talking about values primarily, and the early Corvettes are in great demand and at substantial prices.

Currently a 1953 convertible in class 2 condition can easily bring $25,000 and a class 1 car as much as $35,000. The 1954 and 1955 models run about the same in price, the 1956 a little less. After 1956 all the Corvettes are eight-cylinder cars, and they were improved substantially in both mechanics and apparance. Still, the six-cylinder cars of 1953–1955 are collector cars at relatively high prices. Ford's Thunderbird of 1955 no doubt pushed General Motors into competition with a serious Corvette sports car.

The 1957 cars sell for up to $25,000 for a class 1 car and $18,000 for a class 2 car. Then prices for the Corvette slide off through the model year 1962. The 1963 car, particularly the split-rear-window coupe, was, and is, a classic, and currently could bring well over $20,000. The Grand Sport had an extremely limited production and only estimates are possible on price. One price service estimates that it might bring as much as $125,000.

The Corvettes of the 1950s sold new for about $3,500, not a low price for the era, and the 1960 Corvette was only a little higher at $3,800 for the convertible. From here prices rose somewhat to $4,200 for the 1963 sports coupe and $4,037 for the convertible. This price pattern is, of course, the opposite of the usual price pattern in which the convertible is priced above the coupe.

In 1969 the Corvette was a collectible, but prices were certainly not running away. The earliest convertibles were selling, if prime cars, in the $2,000 range. A 1959 prime convertible was reported sold at $1,275 and a 1961 coupe at $1,350. There was little change in prices to 1970 and there was no 1963 model, the "great Corvette," even reported as sold as of the early 1980s.

By 1975 the Corvette was well up in price. A prime 1953 Corvette was reported sold for $5,750, a 92-point car. A 1954 roadster in comparable condition bought $5,500 and a coupe the same price. The 1955 model was in the same price range. The 1956 and 1957 models were comparable in price. The 1963 cars were selling for a little less, about $4,500.

For the 1972–1973 season Corvettes did not rise at all in value as compared with 1970, although the collector car boom had started by 1972.

By 1975, the middle of the collector car boom decade, the Corvette still had not moved up in price. Five years later, however, the Corvette boom was on. A 1953 unrestored coupe was bringing $11,000 or a bit more, if in sound shape. A good unrestored car was selling for around $15,000 and a 95-point (mint) car $25,000. The same prices were found for the 1954–1955 Corvettes, while the 1956 models were bringing a top of about $17,500. From here on, up through the model years, prices dropped, even to 1963, and a 1963 coupe in the best condition was bringing a little over $10,000. A 1963 fastback, however, was bringing up to $15,000.

By 1982 prices of Corvettes were well up. A 1953 95-point car, a coupe, was reported to have sold for $30,000, and $25,000 was not an unreasonable price for a good-condition 1953. Prices were lower by only a little up through the 1955 model. A 95-point 1956 was reported sold at $17,000. A prime-condition 1963 coupe was selling for about $12,500. Prices were up for 1983.

Rolls-Royce

The Rolls-Royce sedans of the Silver Cloud series are excellent automobiles, majestic-looking and, in my opinion, underpriced, although prices seem to have renewed the upward push that started in the 1970s. On a *price* basis I would look for a Rolls-Royce Silver Cloud sedan in England, and particularly London. True, most of the Rolls-Royce cars sold in England are right-hand drive and these are a little harder to drive in the United States as well as harder to sell, but in England one can still buy an absolutely mint Rolls-Royce for far less money than in the United States.

The car I would very much prefer is the Silver Cloud III sedan of 1963–1965. It is a better car than the Cloud II of 1960–1962 and is more sophisticated and with more power than the six-cylinder Cloud I of 1955–1959, although the mechanics of the Cloud I are excellent.

In 1970, the base year for measuring the rise in prices of collector cars, one could buy a fine-condition Rolls-Royce Silver Cloud I, the six-cylinder car, in America, a left-hand-drive model, for about $6,000. The Silver Cloud II (V-8) could cost perhaps $8,000 and the Silver Cloud III about the same. It would hardly pay to look in England for a right-hand-drive Silver Cloud, to the price of which transportation, insurance, and import duty would have to be added (and damage and pilferage as well).

By 1973 the Silver Cloud III in America was selling for $15,000 to $20,000. In England it was selling for $7,000 to $7,500. The Cloud II in America was bringing $10,000 to $15,000 and in England $6,200 to $6,800. The Cloud I in America was bringing $7,500 to $10,000 and in England about $5,000.

One year later in England prices spurted to $9,500 to $11,500 for the Cloud III, but prices were double this figure in America. In England the Cloud II was $7,500 to $10,500, and in America $12,000 to $15,000. The Cloud I sedan was as high as $9,000 in England and very little more in America. In 1974 I purchased a good Silver Cloud I with the much-wanted James Young body on a long-wheelbase chassis for $9,500. The car came from the Viceroy Carriage Company in London, now Laurence Kayne. In 1977 I sold the car for $14,500. Today it would bring about $30,000.

In the British recession, prices of the Silver Cloud series dropped and demand dropped. In addition the pound sterling dropped in relation to the dollar. In early 1983 a low was reached for Silver Clouds in London, and only in mid-1983 were prices again on the rise with demand burgeoning. Almost every year since 1973 I have been looking at Rolls-Royce cars for sale in England as well as in the United States. While prices are a bit on the rise, the cars are most certainly a buy; it seems prices must rise, and rather rapidly.

In the summer of 1983 a great many cars came onto the market in England and dealers were pushing them hard with many ads in American publications. Demand had increased almost to boom proportions for London dealers, as well as other English dealers, with most demand coming from the United States, and I examined a number of Rolls-Royces for sale in London in July 1983. Laurence Kayne had a very good Cloud III sedan advertised for £12,950—

about $20,000—and for £30,000 ($45,000) he had a Silver Cloud I long-wheelbase James Young sedan with 16,000 miles since new. It was similar to the car I purchased in 1974 for $9,500 but in better condition. In just the two summer months, demand for Silver Clouds in London seemed to increase enormously.

While fakes are hard to discover in paintings, they may be even harder to detect in collector cars. Bentleys are often "converted" to Rolls-Royces through the substitution of the angular Rolls-Royce radiator. The fact that the car is a Bentley can be determined by the serial number, but sometimes these are ground off and the Rolls-Royce serial number is substituted. Usually, these conversions are identified by the dealer selling them and they will bring slightly more than a "normal" Bentley but nowhere near a Rolls-Royce.

Tips on Buying Rolls-Royce Silver Clouds

1. The best time to buy might well seem to be when the rise has started. When one buys at a low point he can never be sure how long that low point will last.

2. The cars to buy are the Silver Cloud III of 1963–1965, then the six-cylinder Silver Cloud I produced from 1955 to 1959, and then the Silver Cloud II produced from 1960 to 1962, with the best Cloud II the 1962.

3. In England right now it is possible to secure an absolutely mint Silver Cloud, either completely restored or with very few miles on the original car and always maintained well. These mint cars, strangely enough, sell for only slightly more than the "good-condition" cars.

4. Ten years ago any kind of restoration in England cost little. Today paint costs about £2,000 ($3,000) and leather interior £3,000 ($4,500)—no small sums.

5. Of all makes and models of collector cars, condition is by far of the greatest importance in a Silver Cloud Rolls-Royce. A Silver Cloud in mediocre condition is difficult to sell, as well as very expensive to restore perfectly. A perfect Rolls-Royce Silver Cloud can usually easily be sold for a good price. Rolls-Royce collectors and other buyers of Silver Clouds (those who buy the cars to use them) will usually not touch anything less than a perfect car—perfect in every way.

6. It is sometimes possible to get a premium Silver Cloud in England for a price not greatly above the standard sedan price, such as the long-wheelbase car, the Chinese Eye Silver Cloud III coupe, the Flying Spur (similar to the Bentley Flying Spur), the James Young long-wheelbase Cloud I (the Cloud III James Young long-wheelbase sedan is almost priceless), or a few Hooper-bodied Rolls-Royces of the Cloud I era (the later Clouds with Hooper bodies are very expensive).

These super cars are not as expensive as the convertibles or the Phantom V and Phantom VI cars. The so-called super cars that we have listed may sell for £10,000 ($15,000) more than the standard sedan and sometimes for as little as £5,000 ($7,500) more. They are worth this premium because they are specials wanted by Rolls-Royce collectors and users.

Mercedes-Benz Cars of the 200 Series and the 190SL

The immediate predecessor of the famous 200 series cars put out by Mercedes-Benz in the postwar period was the 170S. This was a small, well-built car with good suspension and a luxurious ride. The engine was far from a competition engine. It was a four-cylinder with side valves that produced 52 horsepower from a little over 1,700 cubic centimeters. The literature on the car states that it will go 75 mph indefinitely. At turnpike speeds, however, my 170S cabriolet developed serious engine faults and the engine had to be rebuilt completely, not once but twice over a period of six months. The car was beautiful, however, a sporty little car. It first appeared in 1949. My car was a 1950 that I purchased in 1952 for $1,500. In 1983 it would sell for close to $30,000. The 170S cabriolet is a much-wanted collector car and is scarce.

The 220 actually grew out of the 170S, but it was a six-cylinder car. It first appeared in the Frankfurt automobile show in 1951 along with the great 300S luxury sports car and the large 300 sedan. The 170S reestablished Mercedes-Benz in the car business following the devastation of the war, and the 220 and 300 models entrenched the company.

The 220 cabriolet was a 2.2-liter six that developed a modest 80 horsepower, and even when it first appeared it was a great beauty and a quality product with interior comparable in some ways to Rolls-Royce. Today, of course, it is a classic that borders on "the great."

The beautiful and fine 220 was continued to 1954, when a larger and more sophisticated 220S was introduced. (The S in this case stood for "sport.") The 220S does not have the clean, flowing lines of the earlier 220, but it is a good car and also is much sought after by collectors and by car "users," and although it is fairly plentiful, its price compares with that of the earlier 220 cabriolet. Both cars are high in price. In the 1970s the 220S cabriolet was simply a secondhand car but a handsome and very good secondhand car. It sold in the mid-1970s for about $2,500, certainly a secondhand, rather than a collector car, price. In 1984 a fine-condition 220S can easily bring $25,000 and sometimes as much as $30,000.

In 1956 the 190SL (for "Sport Leicht") appeared, a car that turned out to be very popular throughout its history, and even today. It had a 300SL engine (a bit smaller than the 200 series) but with two of the six cylinders cut off and with the overhead camshaft. From this point on, Mercedes-Benz concentrated on overhead-camshaft cars. The 190SL is a sporty little car with rather clean lines, not the greatest performer, but there are those who love the car, and its price and popularity have increased steadily. It has, as suggested by the designation, an engine of about 1,900 cubic centimeters and of then modern design.

At the Geneva Show of 1963 the successor to the 190SL was shown, the 230SL, which, as the designation indicates, had a larger engine (2,300 cubic centimeters) and was a compromise between the old 190SL and the real sports 300SL.

In 1961 the 220S was improved through the addition of fuel injection and designated 220SE (E for *Einspritz*) and was continued to 1966.

In 1967 the 230SL grew into the slightly larger-engined 250SL and in 1969 into the still larger 280SL (2,800 cubic centimeters).

In June 1971, a new V-8 designated the 350SL was introduced. Two years later the 4.5-liter 450SL appeared, and essentially this same car was produced into the 1980s.

The collector cars with a history of definite collector interest and price appreciation are the so-called 200 series cars including at the lower end the 170S and the 190SL and at the upper end the models up through the 350SL. The 230SL looks, to the Mercedes-Benz enthusiast, like a first attempt to produce an effective and reliable sports car with performance, an attempt that culminated in the very-well-received 450SL with a V-8 engine, instead of the 230SL's six-cylinder engine. So the 230SL was a first attempt, but it is now most certainly a collector car, selling for well over $20,000 in fine condition. Even the very late convertibles for five passengers, more or less standard-chassis cars with convertible bodies and hardly sports cars, are in great demand and at prices in excess of $20,000.

In the 1960s the 220 and 220S series Mercedes cars were in no great demand. In the recession of 1962 a 1959 220S, "perfect," was for sale for $1,850. A 1955 model was offered for $2,495.

By 1965 the 220 series had moved up in price. A 1957 convertible was offered for the low price of $1,195, but 1962 and 1963 models were for sale for $2,595, $3,095, and $3,895, the last being about $1,000 under the price of a 300SL roadster. The now very desirable 170S convertible of 1950 was for sale for $1,500, the exact price that I paid for my 170S convertible of 1950 when I bought it in 1952. For comparison purposes a prewar 1938 340 cabriolet was offered for sale for $3,800. Today that car would be selling for $50,000, perhaps more. It should be remembered, however, that as of 1965, the 1962 and 1963 model cars were not collector cars but rather late-model high-quality used cars of an important make and rather "sporty." The cars of the 1950s were, in 1965, the collector cars, or at least were becoming the collector cars.

In 1970 the 190SL in top condition might have sold for $1,800 to $2,000. The 220S of 1957 might have sold for $2,250 if in the same fine shape. There was not much interest in this medium-grade category of Mercedes cars at the start of the investment car boom period.

By the end of the 1972–1973 season the 220S had taken hold in the market, perhaps more than any other of the medium-grade Mercedes cars. A perfect 1954 220S sold for $13,250, while a 1953 in lesser condition (but good) brought $7,500. The 190SL was still less desirable and was selling for as little as $2,500 and sometimes as little as $2,000. By comparison a 300SL Gullwing in fine shape sold for $8,200 and a 1953 300S convertible in fine shape sold for $7,500. The Gullwings and the 300S open cars are now practically in the $100,000 category.

By 1975 the 190SL had moved up to $3,750 to $4,250. The 220S and 220SE convertibles were in the $7,000 to $7,500 range, but the 300SL roadsters were at $10,000 to $15,000 and the Gullwings a little over this price level. Now, of course, the Gullwings are far above the 300SL roadsters.

By 1980 the 170S convertible and the 220 convertibles of the earlier years were close to $30,000 in price. The 190SL could be bought for $10,000, a car in good condition. The later 220S cars could be bought for $15,000, as could the 230SL, the 250SL, and the 280SL. The 300S convertibles were only slightly above the $30,000 top price of the 170S and the 220.

By 1982 the 190SL was about at the $13,500 level. The 170S was a little *down* to under $25,000. The earlier 220's were still pushing $30,000, but the later 220S cars were $10,000 less—under $20,000. The 230SL was nearer to $15,000, but the 280SL cars were selling for about $20,000. Some 230SL's and 250SL's even went $5,000 over this top figure if in the finest condition. There is no price weakening in this group of Mercedes-Benz today.

The 200 series of Mercedes-Benz cars, including the 170S and the 190SL as well as the later and larger-engined 230SL and subsequent cars, are fine-looking, conservative semi-sports cars. They are well made and can be run without a great deal of mechanical difficulties or costly repairs. They will very likely continue to rise in price gradually.

Jaguar XK120, XK140, and XK150

The Jaguar XK series of cars are not the equals of the 300S Mercedes, but they are excellent cars. If for some reason the market valued them at $75,000

This beautifully restored 1953 red Jaguar XK120 is valued at $18,000, but as late as 1970 it might have sold for as little as $2,500. (Julia Rush)

or more in 1970, when collector cars began to rise in price in earnest, they might well be considered *top* postwar classics, but they are far from this price level now. In fact they are still in the "underpriced" category in many ways.

There was a good deal of speculation about the "brand-new sports car" that Jaguar planned to develop right after the close of World War II, and the Jaguar XK120 did appear with considerable glory in 1948. It was far and away the best sports car for the money that probably had ever been produced. It cost $4,800, but soon the price was reduced by about $1,000 because of the devaluation of the pound sterling, and this intrinsic value of the car as a sports car plus the dollar-pound exchange ratio opened up a vast market for the car in the United States. The XK120 was the fastest series production car in the world when it appeared, without any question. It would do an honest 115 mph; my own XK120 that I bought in 1949 easily got a 115 reading on the speedometer, which was probably not far from the actual mph.

If the original engine of the XK120 were developed today and placed in a new sports car that had never before been manufactured, or placed in an existing make of sports car, it would not be considered out of date. It was a straight six with twin overhead camshafts. There were also two S.U. carburetors, and the combustion chambers were hemispherical—the latest chamber design at the time, and still a fine configuration.

The XK120 was far in advance of its day, not only mechanically but in appearance, and it is still a beautiful, streamlined, low car. Moreover, it will run all day long at high speed and give very little trouble—more than can be said of many of the Continental top-performance cars made right now.

The Jaguar progressed in an orderly manner without great innovation from 1948 to 1971, each series being a little more refined, a little more powerful, a little faster than the previous series; but up until 1971 the car was basically the same as it was when the XK120 first appeared in 1948.

JAGUAR POSTWAR SPORTS CARS

Model	Years of Production	No. Cylinders	Horsepower
XK120	1948–1954	6	160
XK140	1954–1957	6	190 (210 optional)
XK150	1957–1962	6	210 (250 optional—disc brakes, BW automatic)
XKE	1961–1971	6	265
XKE V-12	1971–1975	12	272
XJ-S	1975–	12	285

There was little overlap in some models, the old model being phased out while the new model was being introduced. The V-12 engine did not have hemispherical combustion chambers and had only one camshaft per bank of six cylinders, but for a long time neither did the Ferrari V-12 have more than one camshaft for each bank of six cylinders.

The six-cylinder cars were well made and reliable, and quality control was high. The V-12 engine put out in the XKE V-12 had problems (and has problems). Possibly quality control was poor early in the game. At any rate, the engines were not reliable and the cars were too often in the shop for repairs—and they still are. Overheating seems to be a perennial problem of the early V-12 engine.

In 1950 the XK120 was simply a secondhand car, but a good one, and not overabundant, and its value was not sharply under what it cost new. In contrast, in January 1950, a prewar SS100 (Jaguar) in "superb condition" was for sale for $975. The following month another SS100 was for sale for $1,450. In July 1983, Coy's of Kensington, London, had an SS100 for sale for £28,000 ($42,000)—far above any price today on the XK series.

By 1960 the Jaguar was at no great price level. A late-model XK120 (1954) was offered for $995 and another for $1,295. Three XK150's were offered for $2,395, $2,195, and $3,900, the last being a "special XK150S" and described as "impeccable."

Two-cylinder 1894 Peugeot offered at Coys of Kensington, London, for $45,000.

1913 Rolls-Royce Silver Ghost roadster, built for Mr. C. S. Rolls, offered for $125,000 at Coys of Kensington, London.

1928 Packard convertible coupe which brought $40,000 at the Barrett-Jackson auction in 1983.

1931 Chrysler Imperial phaeton reached $125,000 at auction in 1983. In 1970 it might have sold for only $15,000.

1930 Bugatti Royale, Type 41, with Weinberger Cabriolet body, offered to the author in 1942 for $600. Today, one of the world's rarest and most highly valued cars, it would bring in excess of $2.5 million and is now in the Henry Ford Museum. (Edison Institute, Henry Ford Museum & Greenfield Village, Dearborn, Michigan)

1930 Mercedes-Benz SS phaeton similar to one owned by the author for which he paid $550 in 1939. The car was sold for $225,000 in 1983.

This 1933 Auburn boattail speedster, a rare V12 model, sold privately in 1983 for $125,000. Several years earlier it was sold for about half that figure. (Photograph by Koppes, courtesy of Tom Barrett, Scottsdale, Arizona)

1932 Stutz Super Bearcat roadster from the Briggs Cunningham Collection, auctioned by Christie's in Los Angeles in 1981 for $72,000. (Christie's, New York)

1934 Mercedes Benz 540K cabriolet with body by Graber of Switzerland, certainly a candidate for a list of the world's most beautiful cars, was sold in 1983 for $325,000.

1936 Duesenberg convertible sedan, valued at $150,000.

1941 Buick convertible coupe, sold in the 1983 Grand Old Cars Museum auction for $11,100.

1950 Delahaye series 180 custom-bodied car, built for the King of Morocco, valued at $75,000.

1955 Mercedes Benz 300S roadster, purchased for $800 in 1966 by the author. Now fully restored, it is valued at $90,000.

The author purchased this 1960 Rolls-Royce Silver Cloud II sedan in 1977 for $7,000 and restored it. Today it is valued at $32,000.

1966 Ford Mustang convertible which the author purchased fully restored for $1,600 in 1978. It is valued today at $6,000.

A postwar classic, this 1970 Ferrari Daytona coupe was the first one made for export to the United States. It was sold in 1983 by Motor Classic Corporation for $58,500.

In the recession of 1962 an XK140 was for sale for $1,200 and another for $1,150. Several XK150's were for sale for prices ranging from $1,800 to $2,295.

In 1965 an XK120 was for sale for the very low price of $400. The XK150 was selling for prices ranging from $950 to $1,895. A 1962 XKE, "like new," was for sale for $2,850, while a prewar SS100 sold for $4,500—now a collector's car.

Five years later, in 1970, the XK series was still not much in demand. The XK120 was selling in top condition for about $2,000. The XK140 was selling for a little more, and the XK150 for a little less.

After five years of the collector car boom, Jaguar had moved up well in price. The XK120 roadster was selling for about $5,000, the XK140 for about $4,500, and the XK150 for about the same price, perhaps a little less than the XK140.

By 1980, the last year of the fierce rise in collector car prices, the XK120 was up to $15,000. The XK140 and XK150 were a few thousand dollars less and the XKE was selling for around $11,000, sometimes a little less.

Still the climb in XK prices continued, even to 1982, when many other collector car prices had leveled off and even declined. The XK120 was pushing $20,000. This was now the preferred car of the XK series. The XK140 was selling for $11,000 to $12,000. The XK150 was at almost the same price level, and so was the XKE.

In late 1983 an excellent XK120 was offered for sale for $18,500. There had been no rise in the value of the XK models since the onset of the recession. In January 1983, a magnificent-looking and fine-running red XK140 with chrome wire wheels sold for $18,000. In the Christie's summer sale at Beaulieu, England, a very-low-mileage XK150 sold for the equivalent of $24,000, indicating a possible new price rise for the XK series.

The XK120 and all of the subsequent six-cylinder cars are not only good runners and high-performance cars but beautiful cars. They are sports cars that can be used, and without a great many mechanical problems. To a degree they are underpriced, and they will likely rise in price in the future.

The twelve-cylinder cars are performers, and are sophisticated. There is some pride in being able to say, "My car is a V-12." But one pays for this distinction, and a V-12, unless of the late XJ-S series, can be a real problem. Still, the problems of this car do not seem to affect its market value, and it is in demand, the XKE V-12 roadster bringing up to $20,000.

The Medium-Priced Ferraris

The Ferrari 275GTB-4, the Ferrari Daytona, including the Spyder, the late Super America, and the Superfast are top-grade and high-priced postwar

1972 Ferrari 365 GTC-4 coupe (seats four) offered in 1983 by Motor Classic Corporation for $39,500. (Julia Rush)

collector cars. There are other top-grade, top-priced collector Ferraris, most of them limited-production cars. On the other hand, there are medium-grade, medium-priced Ferraris, and there are many of these cars on the market.

One such automobile is the Ferrari 365 GTC-4 coupe, one of the most reliable and maintenance-free of all Ferraris. It is a beautiful car of considerable use and can be purchased for under $40,000.

The most plentiful of the medium-grade Ferraris is the 250GT, and it comes onto the market frequently. The usual model offered is the coupe, but the convertible also appears from time to time.

The 250GT is a good car. It did most of the winning for Ferrari in the period from 1949 to 1955, at least in the Gran Turismo category. In early 1956 it began to be sold to the public, and I had one of the fairly early models, which were sold from 1956 to the 1960s, a long run for a sports car used for competition—but the car was certainly worth the long run. The engine was not big—3 liters—but it turned out a very big 240 horsepower. My Mercedes-Benz 300S had the exact same engine capacity and turned out 150 horsepower.

It is very hard to find a top-performing strict sports car that does not give a good deal of trouble. The Ferrari 250GT is one such car.

The 250GT is a joy to drive. In fact it is one of the two best-driving cars I have ever owned. One has an absolutely safe feeling driving the car; it feels equipped to handle any emergency. At 90 mph one does not tense up and worry that the brakes may not be up to their job in an emergency or that the car is going to turn over on a curve.

The convertible is the preferred model, particularly the car that has both soft and detachable hard top. It sells for up to $30,000 today, while the coupe can sell for as little as $10,000 to $12,000 and a little more. A few super-bodied 250GT open cars were built, the most notable being the California—the 250GTS of 1958. As far as lines went it had everything that a sports car should have, and it is as up-to-date-looking now as it was in 1958—and a whole lot more valuable now than it was in 1958. But this car is not a medium-level, medium-priced collector car. It can well sell at the high end of the collector car price range, sometimes in six figures.

We need go back only to the early 1970s to be able to buy an inexpensive 250GT convertible, and one in this period might have been bought for $2,500 to $3,000. My own 1960 convertible was bought in 1967 for $2,500. These prices were far down from what they had been in 1960, when a coupe ran around $7,500 and a convertible $10,000, although a California roadster was advertised in 1960 for $7,850.

As the collector car boom progressed in the 1970s, Ferrari was at the forefront. By 1975 the coupe was selling for $5,500 to $6,500 and the convertible for about $1,000 more. The high-performing Berlinetta was at about this price, and the still more wanted high-performing and fine-appearing Berlinetta Lusso was selling for about $7,500 to $8,000.

By 1980 the coupe was selling for around $17,000, if prime, and the convertible in the same condition for $22,000 to $23,000. The Berlinetta and Berlinetta Lusso were selling for close to $25,000 if prime.

In 1982 there had been virtually no change in price, perhaps even a weakening. By 1983 the convertible in good condition might have been bought for $25,000 and the coupe for a top of $17,000 to $18,000. The Berlinetta and Berlinetta Lusso were often at the $40,000 level or even $45,000. The year 1983 did not show much of a price increase, if any. Buyers were certainly interested in Ferraris, but the Ferrari had risen too far and too fast and buyers wanted the most exclusive models, not the more common 250GT.

Porsche

It is difficult to visualize this car: flat twelve-cylinder engine with four overhead camshafts, 5,374 cubic centimeters displacement, two turbochargers, 1,100 *brake horsepower* at 7,800 rpm, and a top speed of 230 *mph*. This, of course, is a racing Porsche, the Type 917–30 of 1973.

Over the years Porsche never lagged in competition, but the make never seemed to get much publicity. The street cars are, for the most part, very inconspicuous, and I think I would describe Porsche as the most quietly effective sports car ever produced.

When the first Porsche appeared in 1948 it created a sensation, and car aficionados could hardly wait to buy one. I traded my Mercedes-Benz 170S cabriolet for a 1951 Porsche 356 coupe with a rather small 1,300-cubic-centimeter engine, and I drove this car everywhere and almost every day, including on long business trips. The worst thing that happened to the car was that it once broke a fan belt and, since the car was air-cooled, there was no cooling at all. But I carried a spare belt with me and in thirty minutes I was on my way. The next worst thing was a blowout; even though I was not traveling particularly fast the car almost turned over. The best thing that happened to me in my Porsche was 850 miles in one day, a trip in which I often drove over 90 mph. The repairs? Literally nothing, not even for a valve grind. Maintenance costs were extremely low.

The question is which Porsche is a *medium-level* postwar classic. To some extent almost all Porsches are desirable, and either are or will likely be collector cars. On the other hand, there are many Porsches on the road and many used for everyday transport.

Probably the 356, the model Porsche that I owned, is a major collectible Porsche. The car was developed by the great Ferdinand Porsche in 1948 and was more of a "category" than a single car with relatively fixed specifications.

It was developed further and further until 1965. It started out as a flat four with very limited horsepower. My own 1951 was rated at 46 brake horsepower. Its 1,300 cubic centimeters were up from the 1,100 with which Porsche started, using to a great extent Volkswagen components. Side valves finally gave way to overhead valves, and in the mid-1950s any one of five engines could be ordered for the Porsche 356, the 1,500GS Carrera having four overhead camshafts and producing 100 horsepower. Almost all early Porsches were four-cylinder cars.

In the fall of 1954 Porsche came out with the fantastically popular Speedster, a roadster using the 1,500-cubic-centimeter engine, and by March of the following year this little open car's production had reached 5,000 units. The Speedster had a relatively short life and was soon phased out. Apparently it was priced too low to make money for the firm.

In 1960 the Speedster was simply a secondhand car, although a fine and popular car. It ranged in price on the secondhand market from perhaps $1,500 to $1,650. The Model 356 generally sold for less money, unless it was one of the late and very sophisticated models.

In the recession of 1962 the price may have *risen* by a few hundred dollars, but prices were so low that a few hundred dollars one way or the other was not significant.

In 1965 a 1957 Speedster was advertised for $995, but a Carrera "racing car" was advertised for $3,000. The 356 models were under this latter figure.

In 1959 two average-condition Speedsters sold for $800 and $895 and two prime Speedsters at $1,850 and $1,900. It was hard to find a 356 model selling for a price high enough for any pricing service to record it.

By 1970 the Speedster was selling for around $2,000, some a few hundred dollars more and some a few hundred dollars less. By 1975, five years into the collector car price rise, the Speedster was selling for from $5,000 to $7,000 if in fine condition. The Model 356 was selling for $3,000 to $4,500.

By 1980 the Speedster was selling at prices from $11,000 to $13,000 and the Model 356 from $6,000 to $8,000. By 1982 the early Model 356 coupe was at about the $7,500 level and the roadster at $10,000. The late 356 convertibles were over $10,000 by a little. The Speedster was selling for $14,000 to $16,000. A few Speedsters sold for as little as $11,000 at auction in mid-1982 and as high as $13,500. In July 1983, Christie's at Beaulieu, England, sold a very nice Model 356B cabriolet, 1962, for £7,000—a little over $10,000.

MG TC, TD, and TF

In July 1983, a 1932 MG Magna F2 sports two-seater was offered for sale by Christie's in its Beaulieu, England sale. It was a stark little car with big

This 1953 MG TD roadster, with doors and paint in only fair condition, sold at Christie's in 1981 for $6,000. Today it would bring more than twice that amount. (Christie's, New York)

wire wheels and narrow tires, hardly streamlined. It had a little engine, 1,271 cubic centimeters. It was estimated to bring £6,000 to £9,000 ($9,000 to $12,000). It didn't find a buyer.

The point in all this description is that this *prewar* car is very similar to the 1945 MG TC. This model car first appeared in America—exported from England—in 1947, fifteen years after the production date of the 1932 MG Magna F2. As a matter of fact the Magna F2 was a six-cylinder car, and the much later TC was a four-cylinder car.

The MG is hardly in the class of the Ferrari Daytona or Lamborghini Miura with their twelve cylinders and overhead camshafts. The MG was a simple little "fun" car, most models made to seat two people, and the TC did not have wind-up windows, so that the two passengers were pretty much exposed to the elements. Still, the MG TC gave the owner and his passengers a good deal of satisfaction, and the car would easily go 75 mph.

Appearancewise the postwar MG was out of date when it was first manu-factured. A few years later the Italian Cisitalia appeared, and this super sports car was up-to-date in appearance and certainly in performance. But the MG has remained, and the Cisitalia has not. In fact, the MG is more in demand and at much higher prices today than when it first appeared at a price of about $1,700 in the United States. It was an out-of-date car to begin with and it is an out-of-date car now; but the car has tremendous appeal, possibly because of its simple, basic, fun look.

Actually the TC went into production in England in 1945 in roadster form. In 1947 a coupe and an open four-seater were also made. In 1949 the TD was produced as the successor to the TC, but aside from a very few improve-ments the car was the same. In 1953 another similar car was introduced to replace the TD, and this was known as the TF. This model was continued to 1955, when MG finally caught up with the times to some extent with the MGA, a real postwar automobile.

The collector MG cars are, for the most part, the TC, the TD, and the TF. These are the MG cars in demand at good and rising prices. The later cars are not in such great demand and prices have not risen so much.

In 1950 an MG TD was advertised for a then high price, $1,875, but the car was described as "like new"and it had a supercharger.

In 1955 the TC had dropped in price. Three were for sale for $895, $1,250, and $1,200. The TD's were selling, for the most part, at under $1,000. One "excellent" TD was advertised for $1,085. These are all strictly secondhand car prices.

In 1960 there had been absolutely no change in price level of the MG. Possibly the older TD's sold in the $700 range. Nor was there any change in price by 1965, although many "less than excellent" cars were offered for sale.

One "first-class" TD was advertised for $1,650. By 1970 the TC and TD were selling for $1,500 to $1,900—up somewhat. The TF rarely appeared on the market.

By 1970 the early MG's were to a certain extent collector cars. The TC was the preferred car, followed by the TD and then the TF. A fine-condition TC approached $3,000. The TD in similar condition sold for $1,250 to $1,800, the TF for about $1,250. It might be mentioned that in 1970 the great Mercedes-Benz 300S cabriolet and roadster might have been bought for $2,500 and sometimes less.

By 1975 the TC in fine condition could bring as much as $7,500, although some of this model sold as low as $5,000. The TD was selling for $3,500 to $5,000 and the TF for about $4,500.

By 1980 the MG was selling for "classic car prices." A first-class TC was bringing $13,500 to $14,500. The later TD was bringing less, about $10,000, but the TF was well up—one selling for $17,000 and another for $17,500.

In 1982 a fine-condition TC was bringing about $17,000, the TD's around $14,000, and the later TF's about the same as the TC's—$17,000. There has been little change in price to date.

The MG's of the TC, TD, and TF series are easy cars to own in this era of collector cars. Some collector cars are staggeringly expensive to own and tend to deteriorate, requiring costly restorations. The MG's of the early postwar series are relatively inexpensive to buy and very inexpensive to maintain. The parts are not many and not complicated. Many can be supplied from England at small expense, and there are U.S. sources of parts for little money.

It does not require any great skill to do mechanical work on a small four-cylinder car with simple transmission, brakes, and accessories like carburetor and distributor.

The MG is a two-person, open car. In the 1960s many MG's were used as "station cars." They were run-down and therefore no one would bother to steal them, as they didn't have a great deal of value.

Now values are building up and the car is gaining in appeal, even to a collector of large sophisticated automobiles. In the summer of 1983 I located an average-condition TC in a gas station for sale for $14,000, but the garage owner pointed out that this particular car was "no less than a Model TC," and he was surprised that I did not instantly recognize what a fine car it was and what a favorable price it was.

Medium-Level Fords

The Shelby Cobra is one of the *great* collector cars of the postwar period, and, of course, it is based to a considerable extent on Ford parts. There are

1957 Ford Thunderbird convertible, red with white interior, totally restored, sold at auction in 1983 for $22,000. (Julia Rush)

many other Ford collector cars, not the least important being the Mustang of 1964–1966 and the Boss Mustang, the performance Mustang. The Mustang is, however, not yet a middle-level car but an inexpensive car; how long that will be true we do not know. Here are the middle-level cars put out by Ford.

Thunderbird of 1955 to 1957

While the Thunderbird collectibles are designated as 1955 to 1957, the preference is for the 1955 and the 1957 Thunderbirds, with the 1957 model usually the highest-priced of all three—1955, 1956, and 1957.

The mid-1950s Thunderbird is a very sporty-looking and fine-driving automobile. It is overall a Ford, but good mechanically and well styled. It seats two people in comfort and is certainly not temperamental. It is most certainly not a competition car, nor is it strictly a sports car. For many of us who are used to colossal bills for the maintenance of sports and competition cars, the Thunderbird is a relief. In addition, in the past decade the car has become both a collectible and a legend. It is highly thought of and is now sometimes glamorized by being used in TV shows, particularly those in which the hero drives a red Thunderbird convertible.

The car was made as a hardtop and a convertible, with the hardtop selling today at a slightly higher price than the convertible. I don't know exactly what Ford was trying to do in coming out with the Thunderbird but the company accomplished two definite things. First, it built a good car that, although maybe not a sports car, sold well—52,000 cars in total from 1955 to 1957. Second, it kept General Motors producing Corvettes, epic cars for GM. Beginning in 1957, the Ford Thunderbird tapered off. From 1958 to 1962 the Thunderbird is known as the "Squarebird," and this is not the preferred two-seater. It is a much bigger, square-shaped four-seater. Until recently few people wanted the Squarebird, but now it is in greater demand, although still not in the class of the 1955–1957 Thunderbird in preference or in price.

The Thunderbird was not an expensive car. Its price new was about $3,000. In 1960 it was simply a popular secondhand car and sold for about $2,000.

In 1965 many Thunderbirds were offered for sale, but now they were very much older secondhand cars. The Thunderbird rarely sold for as much as $2,000, and for $1,500 one could easily get one in fine condition.

By 1970 the price of the car had moved up to $2,250 to $2,500, some cars offered for as much as $500 more.

Five years later "giveaway prices" were a thing of the past. The range was $6,000 to $7,500 for a fine-condition car. One "100" supercharged coupe with 12,000 miles on the odometer was advertised for $11,000—very much a special.

By 1979 the 1955 and 1956 cars were selling for $14,000 to $15,000 and the 1957 cars for $15,000 to $17,000. Prices did not move up again until 1981, when the 1955 and 1956 models were selling at above $19,000 and the 1957 cars at about $22,000. By 1983 the 1955 and 1956 cars were at about $20,000 and the 1957 around $22,000. The Thunderbird seems to have a fairly determinable price, even at auction, and the 1983 Barrett-Jackson auction secured $22,000 for a Grade 1 1957 Thunderbird. The 1983 Kruse Scottsdale auction secured $21,000 for a class 1 1957 Thunderbird. In the stronger market of 1984, a superbly-restored 1956 Thunderbird convertible brought $32,500 at the Barrett-Jackson auction, establishing a new auction high for the car.

Mangusta and Pantera

Another classic collector car of medium price level from Ford is the DeTomaso Pantera. This was an "Italianate car" but with basically Ford components. The immediate predecessor of the Pantera was the Mangusta, and this car was also designated the DeTomaso Mangusta after the "inventor" of the car, Alejandro DeTomaso. In 1966 the Mangusta first appeared. It had a Ford V-8 engine and a five-speed transmission, disc brakes on all four wheels, independent suspension, rear engine, and rear drive.

The body on the Mangusta was beautiful, as is to be expected, since it was designed by Giorgetto Giugiaro. The Mangusta was marketed in the United States by Ford dealers and priced at about $10,000.

In 1971, Lincoln and Mercury dealers got the new (or revised) car for sale— the Pantera, a similar-bodied car but a little less sweeping in line and smaller. The Pantera is a performer—145 mph and zero to 60 in 5.5 seconds, the kind of performance one might expect from a small car carrying 310 horse-power. By 1974, 5,269 cars had been built and production ceased.

Since many components are Ford, the car might be considered to combine Italian styling and performance with reliability and low maintenance. Actually the car is not quite the very best in every way. The seating position is cramped. The body tends to rust, and there are several minor faults. Still, the car is a splendid sports car and a collectible.

On the present market the Mangusta is the rarer, and probably the more beautiful, car and it sells for a little over $25,000. One totally rebuilt and power-boosted Mangusta was for sale in 1984 for $30,000. A good-condition Pantera might sell for as much as $23,000 and for as little as $20,000.

In 1978, $10,000 to $12,000 would buy a good-condition Mangusta or Pantera. These cars at the time were not much wanted in Italy, and a fine-condition car could have been bought there for half this price.

One year later, prices of both cars rose to about $13,000 to $15,000. By 1980, $15,000 to $17,000 would buy a good-condition Pantera in America, but the Mangusta was at about the $20,000 level.

So the DeTomaso cars have risen in price fairly steadily but not spectac-ularly. They are beautiful Italian-bodied cars, but they are also Fords with some problems that place them in a quality category very much behind the Shelby Cobra with its Ford components, and there are, of course, far fewer Cobras than Mangustas and Panteras.

Maserati Ghibli

The Maserati Ghibli was Giorgetto Giugiaro's masterpiece. It is a car of such beauty and refinement of line that it is hard to see how the body can be improved in any way. It also seems to be Giugiaro's own opinion that this was his masterpiece, even though he designed such exotics as the BMW M1, the great competition car of the 1980s.

The Ghibli was made during the same period as the Lamborghini Miura (1967–1972). The Miura was innovative in the extreme from a design point of view—body, placement of the engine, frame. The Ghibli was a front-engine, rear-wheel-drive V-8 with double overhead camshafts. The Miura would probably outperform the Ghibli, but not by much. Both engines were of about the same horsepower, but the Ghibli had a refined, luxurious body, and the car could be secured with automatic transmission, power steering and brakes, power windows, and air conditioning. It was perhaps overrefined for a sports car and thus may tend to give more troubles than it should. But the car and its performance and ride are no less than wonderful, and when I drove my first Ghibli prior to buying it I wondered why other sports car manufacturers could not come up with a suspension like the Ghibli's—firm and yet luxurious.

The Ghibli cost new about what the Lamborghini Miura cost—$20,000. In 1973 I paid $6,800 for my car, perhaps under the market by a few thousand dollars. In 1977 I sold it for $9,500, about $1,000 to $1,500 under the market at the time.

In 1980 I bought my second Ghibli for $10,900, about $2,000 under the market, but I had to spend about $3,500 to get it in excellent condition inside and out. Today a car in similar condition can be secured for $16,000 to $18,000. There has been a rise in the value of the car but not nearly so much as in the value of the Lamborghini Miura. In performance the cars are very similar—about 165–170 mph from an engine that can turn out 350-plus horsepower. The acceleration times are not far different.

Still the Miura is vastly preferred to the Ghibli, and whereas there are very few Miuras for sale there are generally many Ghiblis.

While the Ghibli coupe may be the most beautiful sports coupe ever built, the Ghibli Spyder may well be the most beautiful convertible ever built, particularly with the top down. There were far fewer Spyders built than coupes, and they are far more in demand than coupes, with the result that the Spyder has shot ahead of the coupe in value. Today the Spyder can bring from $30,000 to $45,000, still not a tremendous amount as quality postwar classics go and certainly not in comparison with the price of the most-sought-after Ferraris.

8

The Top Prewar Classics

THE TOP PREWAR CLASSICS (automobiles manufactured between approximately 1925 and World War II) are in many ways not only the top classics but the top investment and collector cars. They are not necessarily the best cars or even the best collector cars, but they are the most-sought-after and valuable collector cars. While there are relatively few postwar classics and antiques in the six-figure price range, there are a number of prewar classic cars in that range. To put it in a slightly different way, few postwar classics and antiques sell for as much as $100,000, but a number of prewar classics sell for over $100,000 and even over $200,000, such as the Duesenberg J and SJ, the Cadillac V-16 convertibles, the early 1930s Chrysler Imperial tourers, the Isotta Fraschini large eight tourers, and the Hispano-Suiza V-12 convertible coupes. Surprisingly, for the individual looking to invest a sizable sum in a collector automobile, it would not be difficult to locate a suitable $100,000-plus car today.

Characteristics of the Top Prewar Classic Cars

1. The vast majority of top prewar classic cars of today were luxury cars in their day. The Duesenberg and the Mercedes-Benz S series and 500 series cars were extremely high-priced, as were almost all of the other top prewar classics. The cars were large and impressive, for the most part, far larger than the middle-level cars and particularly the lower-level cars, principally Ford and Chevrolet.

The interiors of these luxury cars were far more luxurious than they are

141

today. I remember examining one car for sale that had upholstery in watersnake skin. Hides of African animals were used for upholstery as well. The finest leather was often used, and on earlier cars pure silk was sometimes installed.

The paint was flawless and the interior was trimmed with fine woods like burl walnut. The interiors were far different from the interiors of the middle-level cars such as Buick.

2. They were innovative in their day, in many cases, and often extremely innovative mechanically. The standard engines were flathead (L-head or side-valve) engines. Overhead valves were not the general rule, although some cars, like Buick, had had overhead-valve engines for many years. Very few cars had overhead camshafts.

One of the greatest and most-sought-after of all prewar classics today is the Duesenberg. This car had a straight-eight engine. It had not just overhead valves but overhead camshafts, and two camshafts at that. There were not simply two valves per cylinder but four valves. The last Duesenbergs, the SJ models, were even supercharged.

The Mercedes-Benz prewar had an overhead camshaft in the larger models of the K, S, and 500 series. The cars were also supercharged in a very effective way.

Multicylinder engines were used, with Cadillac going to twelve cylinders and even sixteen cylinders. Marmon too went to sixteen cylinders in an aluminum engine.

3. The bodies in many cases were fantastically beautiful. The Mercedes-Benz 500K and 540K series, when they appeared in the mid-1930s, were so far ahead of any sports car bodies, and possibly even luxury car bodies, that they tended to take your breath away. The roadster of the 500 series that took my breath away in 1937 was the car that in early 1979 brought $400,000 when Christie's auctioned it in Los Angeles, at that time the highest price achieved at auction for any car.

Perhaps the main feature of the Chrysler Imperial of the early 1930s was the magnificent bodies, particularly on the touring cars with dual cowls. This car seems to me to be the favorite of car price recorder Quentin Craft. On two of his annual price guides a Chrysler Imperial of the early 1930s is pictured, and each of the two cars is more beautiful than the other!

4. Most of the prewar classics were extremely good performers. The Mercedes-Benz S of 1927 had a conservative top speed of 95 mph. The SS of 1928 had a top speed of at least 105 mph. Perhaps the Duesenberg SJ would do 130 mph.

In 1927 the Model T Ford would do about 45 mph with its 22 horsepower. The Mercedes-Benz SS with 160 horsepower without supercharger and 200 horsepower with supercharger engaged was a vastly better performer. The

Duesenberg SJ with supercharger had about 320 horsepower, quite a contrast with the Ford of the era, even the later V-8.

The 2.9 Alfa Romeo had "everything." It was low and long and beautiful. It was an overhead-cam straight eight. It had not one but two superchargers, and its road holding was hard to believe.

5. The preferred prewar classics are often multicylinder cars. A 1931 Cadillac V-8 two-seater, a highly desirable car and a beautiful car, in mint condition may bring $80,000. The V-12 convertible two-seater of the same year, will bring somewhere in the region of $90,000. The V-16 two-seater of the same year will bring about $140,000.

At the Barrett-Jackson auction in January 1983, in Phoenix, a fine Auburn V-8 speedster of 1933 went for $21,200. A V-12 speedster of the same year might bring $125,000.

6. The top prewar classics are generally those cars recognized in their day for their all-around excellence. Rolls-Royce had as its slogan "Best Car in the World." (The new models are still advertised as such.) Maybe it was. There were few rivals for all-around excellence, and only one car seemed to be preferred for its excellence, preferred at least by some foreign car mechanics of the prewar period—the Hispano-Suiza.

Autocar of October 4, 1935, reviews the new Rolls-Royce twelve-cylinder Phantom III in this way:

"Certain cars have acquired a prestige so great that any radical change in their design is a great moment for the industry as a whole. This is why the decision to give the latest model Rolls-Royce Phantom a twelve-cylinder V engine and independent suspension for its front wheels is so very interesting."

When E. L. Cord took control of the Auburn-Cord-Duesenberg Company in 1926 he gave instructions to his staff to "produce a new car which, in terms of style, engineering and sheer panache, should rival the best car the world has to offer." Mr. Cord and his plant succeeded, and the car they produced in the 1920s probably stands at the zenith of all top prewar classic collector cars—the Duesenberg J.

There seems little question that the man who was probably the greatest innovator in sports and racing cars of his era, Ettore Bugatti, designed and built the Type 41 Royale to be the ultimate in luxury cars. The production car had a three-valve-per-cylinder overhead-cam engine with displacement of 12,763 cubic centimeters. The testing program on this car extended over a period of two years before Mr. Bugatti felt the car was ready to offer to the public. The car was enormous. The bodies were in many ways sensational. The 300 horsepower meant that the car, for its size, was a real performer on the highway. Today it is no doubt recognized by more of the cognoscenti as being at the top than any other car, although I am not quite of that opinion.

The Top Collector Cars

Why collect or invest in the top prewar classics? There are several reasons to prefer these cars as investments to other categories of investment cars like special-interest cars and elite-cars, for instance.

1. The prewar classic cars have a history of solid investment. The Duesenberg J and SJ and the Mercedes-Benz 540K roadster are certainly solid investments. Such a car may decline in price a little at times, but, like IBM, the price seems on an up plane. A banker could well invest some trust funds in these cars.

2. The group of prewar classics is characterized by a fairly steady increase in value over the years. Even in 1962 the Duesenberg was selling for sums in the five-figure range. The 500K and the 540K Mercedes have gone up fairly steadily. So have the important Packard convertibles and the early-1930s Cadillacs—all of the convertibles.

3. The buyers of these cars are relatively conservative collectors and almost certainly collectors who have an eye on values. True, the Mercedes-Benz 500K roadster that Christie's in California sold in early 1979 for $400,000, a record price for a car sold at auction, was a magnificent-looking car that the buyer no doubt treasured. Yet the car has been resold to a European buyer for a sum in excess of $600,000. The owner no doubt loved the car but he also had an eye on investment value.

In the 1983 Barrett-Jackson auction, the car I wanted to have, personally, was a Mercedes-Benz 540K with Graber body. I knew the owner, Tom Barrett, would not take less than $300,000 for the car, yet it tempted me. My Mercedes-Benz 300S is also a beautiful car and will perform at least as well as (and more reliably than) the 540K. My 300S in mint condition could possibly hit $100,000 at auction, certainly no more and possibly less. Why then would I consider a car that would cost at least three times the value of my Mercedes? Because of the investment value of the 540K. The car rose in value steadily in the past and it will probably continue to rise in value.

4. There are relatively few of the important prewar classics available for purchase. The 540K's are definitely limited to a small number of cars. We did find out in the case of Duesenberg that there were quite a few of these cars around, because they made their appearance when prices rose. Now probably most of these Duesenbergs are known. In the case of the 1964–1966 Mustang convertible there are literally thousands around and more are being restored all the time. This great number of cars must limit the height to which values can go. Not so in the case of the great classics. If you want a 1930–

1931 Cadillac V-16 roadster there are only a few available—anywhere. This limitation of supply of a much-wanted prewar classic must act as some assurance that the price of the car will rise in the future.

5. The cars are less subject to fad buying than cars in other categories. Currently, the 1955 and 1957 Chevrolet Bel Air convertibles (also the hardtops) are in immense demand and at rising prices. A price of $20,000 for one of these cars is not unusual. Will this preference continue? Maybe, but it is a lot more certain that the preference for a Duesenberg dual-cowl phaeton or speedster will continue.

6. Most of the cars are in fine (many in mint) condition, so there is not the problem of getting repairs performed and locating missing or worn-out parts.

7. Almost down the line the prewar classics are good, conservative investments, from the Darrin Packard to the Duesenberg Model A (not necessarily the J) to the 1931 Auburn 12 speedster.

8. These important investment cars are not very well known to the public. The general public is being educated on them very gradually through sales items in the newspapers, as background for advertisements of various products from expensive perfume to jeans.

The general public is not yet aware of the important classic cars—as investments or as anything else. They do not know much about the 540K Mercedes, the Duesenberg J, the Marmon 16. Right now there is still a good deal of antagonism to these cars and the high prices they bring. How can anyone be so foolish as to pay $300,000 for an automobile?

The answer is that an automobile is worth what someone will pay for it, no matter how much; and this is the same way the value of a Picasso or a Renoir or a Rembrandt is established.

9. It is easier to make a large investment in an important prewar classic car than in a car or cars in other categories. The 1966 Mustang has certainly proved to be a very good investment. Today a fine-condition Mustang convertible can be bought for $6,000 on occasion, possibly even a little less. To invest $60,000 one must buy ten Mustang convertibles. Where will they be stored? Does anyone have a garage for ten additional cars? Public storage, insurance and cosmetic and mechanical upkeep can add up.

For the same $60,000 a collector might purchase one Auburn 851 boattail speedster. He can store this car, insure it, and keep it in repair all for a reasonable total cost.

For the individual with $100,000 or more to invest, few cars are better than many cars—at least as far as trouble of "managing the investment" goes.

Of course, there are reasons for diversifying the investment and diversifying the risk of investing in automobiles by buying several less expensive cars rather

1932 Rolls-Royce Phantom II convertible sedan, Brewster body, made in Springfield, Massachusetts, reached $200,000 at auction in 1983. In 1970 it would have been valued at about $10,000. (photograph by Koppes, courtesy Tom Barrett, Scottsdale, Arizona)

than one expensive one, but there is a definite advantage in not having too many investor-collector cars.

When we talk about the top prewar classics we are talking about the top cars *for investment*, not simply the top cars. Two of the "gilt edged" cars that I described earlier in the book are the Bugatti Royale and the Mercedes-Benz SSK of 1931. There is no point in considering either of these cars in this chapter, because of their extreme rarity.

Choosing "top prewar classics"—the category of investment cars—depends on where the market is. If I had to start at the top and pick the first top prewar classic and I lived in Europe, I might well pick the Mercedes-Benz 540K roadster or convertible. It is possible that if I lived in England instead of on the Continent I might pick the Rolls-Royce Phantom II convertible or touring car, and the four-door convertible in England is a great prewar classic.

On the other hand, in the United States, the top prewar classic is probably the Duesenberg J or SJ, especially the tourers with dual cowl, and that's where we will begin.

Duesenberg

From 1920 to 1926 the Duesenberg Brothers produced an excellent but rather austere car called the Model A, the first straight eight to be produced in this country in any quantity. The car was a performer, and a Duesenberg won the Indianapolis race in 1924, 1925, and 1927. It was, however, not until E. L. Cord got control of the company in 1926 that the "the great Duesenberg" was designed. Both chassis and engine had a racing background, and if the engine were produced today and put into a performance car, the car would not be out of date. In fact, no stock American car having an engine of the advanced design of the Duesenberg is produced today. The same firm, Auburn-Cord-Duesenberg, turned out the high-performance Auburn at the same time it turned out the Duesenberg, and the 1935 and 1936 Auburn boattail speedsters all had a plaque affixed to the dashboard stating that the car had actually been driven over 100 mph. Yet the Auburn with this performance had a straight-eight flathead (L-head) engine of the old type and side valves operated by one camshaft inside the engine, not overhead.

The new and "great" Duesenberg had a straight eight but with overhead camshafts—not one but two, one to operate the intake valves and the other to operate the exhaust valves; and instead of one exhaust valve and one intake valve per cylinder there were two exhaust and two intake valves. The engine (and the rest of the car) was constructed with the greatest precision. On the chassis was placed a custom body by one of the great builders of the United States or Europe, so each car was in effect custom-built. The car was turned

Known as "The Twenty Grand," this 1933 Duesenberg Torpedo sedan was designed by Gordon Buehrig as a show car for the 1933 Chicago World's Fair. The asking price was $20,000 in 1933 (at the time, a Ford V-8 was $560). The value of the award-winning car today would be at least $275,000, and it is the centerpiece of the Merle Norman Classic Beauty Collection.

out from 1928 to 1936, the J model and the SJ model with supercharger that was supposed to secure 320 horsepower from the engine and drive the car 130 mph, quite a speed for the time—when the Model A Ford would do 55. Four hundred and seventy of these great J and SJ cars were built and sold.

In the April 1983 Christie's sale in California, a magnificent Duesenberg tourer sold for $320,000. This Duesenberg was the best that had been on the auction market for a long time, but $320,000 was a premium price even for a fine Duesenberg.

To trace prices for the Model J and SJ Duesenberg we might go back to the immediate prewar years—1939 and 1940. In 1940 two Duesenbergs were offered to me. The first was a magnificent convertible coupe, an SJ, priced at $750, owned by a racing driver. The other was a dual cowl phaeton in average condition, priced at $600. The cars were fine, and in line with the market for Duesenberg J and SJ at the time, but I was more interested in finding a Mercedes-Benz 540K, which I eventually did find, but for this car I had to pay much more—$1,500.

Not all Duesenbergs went at these low prices, however, and in March 1941, a few years later, an SJ torpedo convertible coupe with Walker body and low mileage, and one of only two of these cars in the country, was advertised for $1,850. This may be one of the two torpedoes or boattails known to exist today, cars that might well sell for $500,000 each or even more.

During the war Duesenbergs did nothing pricewise, and they stayed at a low price up to the beginning of the 1950s, no matter how fine the Duesenberg. My first chance to drive one of these cars came in 1946 when a delegation from the Sports Car Club of America, of which I was a member, drove out to the 1946 Indianapolis race.

The leading Duesenberg mechanic lent me his Model J and he drove my Auburn 851 boattail. His car was in top-notch condition, as might have been expected, but I felt it was a heavy car to drive. At about this time I sold my Mercedes-Benz 500K convertible with Corsica body to the Chicago Duesenberg dealer. Even the dealer in Duesenbergs did not seem to be 100% convinced that the car he sold was the best, and he described the car as a "lumber wagon." In any event, in this era people did not swoon when they saw a Duesenberg and the car was hardly a prestige builder for its owner.

In September 1951, a Model J roadster with body by Murphy was offered for sale, a car described by the seller as being in "first-class condition." The price was $2,500. Today the price would probably be $250,000. At about the same time a Murphy-bodied coupe in "excellent" condition was for sale for $1,600.

By the mid-1950s prices had moved up, but not greatly. The very desirable roadster was for sale for $3,200 in 1955. An "excellent" Murphy-bodied town

One of the finest examples to come onto the market, this maroon and cream-colored 1933 Duesenberg SJ La Grande phaeton was auctioned by Christie's in Los Angeles in 1983 for $320,000. In 1970 it might have brought $60,000—a high price for the time.

car was for sale for $2,400. At the time, town cars of any make with the chauffeur sitting out in front in the open were not much wanted by collectors.

In 1951, Quentin Craft, publisher of *Old Car Value Guide*, bought one of the greatest Duesenbergs, the 1937 SJ, the La Grande dual-cowl phaeton. He states that this car was the last Duesenberg assembled in this country before production ceased, and rated this car at 90 points—Show Class. With 36,000 original miles on the car the price of $2,000 he paid seems reasonable enough. In 1981 this same car in the same condition would have sold, by his estimation, for about $260,000.

By the 1960s prices began inching up. Toward the end of 1960 a convertible roadster was advertised for $5,500. A Model J Judkins-bodied coupe was for sale for $7,000. It had a rumble seat, so was somewhat sporty. A 1930 Murphy convertible sedan (four-door), one of the most-wanted body styles today, was for sale for $10,000. The seller was located in Missouri and his advertised price was "firm." This was the shape of things to come. A few Duesenbergs had moved into the five-figure price range, and there they were to stay, ahead of most other prewar classics.

Two years later a 1934 J with Murphy convertible body, restored, was priced at $13,500. A 1932 Dietrich-bodied J convertible was, however, priced at under $10,000—but at "$8,500 firm." Ken Purdy, editor of *True* magazine, began writing about Duesenbergs at about this time; he was so highly respected in sports and collector car circles that his "endorsement" of the Duesenberg must certainly have fueled the market for them. He reported that the cars when new had sold for the then enormous prices of $13,000 to $20,000, a few even as high as $25,000. The cars went down virtually to nothing on the secondhand market prior to the war and during the war; but they were, and are, quality—and beauty—and for that reason they came out on top in the market.

In early 1965, prices had risen a fair amount and were above the prices of almost all other collector cars of any era. A 1929 Holbrook-bodied brougham was priced at $12,500. A 1929 town car was for sale for $12,500, but a four-door convertible Berline, a national show winner, was for sale for $16,500, a car with the much-wanted Murphy body. This was a 1930 Model J.

By 1968 the Duesenberg was on its way in the market. A 1937 Derham SJ phaeton sold for $27,000, a 1936 LeBaron phaeton brought $25,000, and a 1933 Model J roadster brought $22,500.

For most collector cars prices started their big upward climb from the recession bottom year 1970—but not Duesenberg. It was well on its way. A Model J roadster sold for $38,500, and this was about the price level for any open car of the J and SJ series in 1970.

To indicate how high this level was in 1970 for Duesenberg, two of the great Cadillac V-16 open cars of 1931 changed hands at $35,000 and $36,500— and no Cadillac approached $60,000. Two early-1930s Chrysler Imperial open cars sold for $16,500 and $21,500.

By the year 1975, Duesenbergs were at a peak—an enormously high peak. A 1931 Model J phaeton sold for $142,500, a 1931 phaeton for $172,000, a 1931 Model J phaeton for $207,000, and the much-wanted 1936 SJ La Grande phaeton for $210,000.

In 1980, at the turn of the decade, a La Grande SJ phaeton of 1936 brought $285,000, a 1935 La Grande two-passenger roadster brought $265,000, a 1937 La Grande SJ phaeton brought $285,000, and a 1937 SJ Derham tourer brought $270,000. Sedans brought $137,000, $135,000, $145,000, and

1935 Duesenberg Victoria two-door sedan which reached $180,000 at auction in 1983. (Julia Rush)

$220,000—prices not far behind those of the finest-bodied open cars. No fewer than fourteen sales of J and SJ open cars at over $200,000 were recorded.

The following year, 1981, prices rose perhaps a little, but very little—and we were not in any recession for most of 1981, nor had the stock market retreated significantly. Fourteen more sold between $200,000 and $250,000. Trading volume, as they say in the stock market, was immense for Duesenberg with gainers outnumbering losers.

1982 was not a record year in particular for Duesenbergs. One explanation was that everyone who wanted a Duesenberg had managed to buy one by 1982, much of the buying done possibly for nostalgic reasons. Duesenbergs were not noted for their high prices at auction in Arizona in January 1983; but later in the year the important La Grande tourer was sold by Christie's in Los Angeles for the strong price of $320,000—in a generally lackluster collector car sale.

As of 1981–1983 Duesenberg prices were on a plateau, but a plateau with a slight upward tilt. It is my guess that they will not decline in price but—in general—rise, if less rapidly than in the past.

Mercedes-Benz 540K and 500K

It required a good deal of deliberation to determine which top prewar classic car to place at the head of the list of prewar classics for price tracing—the Duesenberg J and SJ or the Mercedes-Benz 540K and 500K. The Duesenberg won by sheer popularity. As far as my personal preference goes, Mercedes would have been considered first. I have owned eleven Mercedes cars in all, including a 540K and a 500K, cars which were my regular transportation at the time I owned them. Aside from personal preferences, however, I think Mercedes cars of these two models have forged ahead of the Duesenberg J and SJ pricewise; and as early as early 1979 there was an indication that the Mercedes car was going to top Duesenberg.

I bought my first 500 series Mercedes in 1942, for $1,500, a five-passenger 540K coupe, not the most desirable body style for a 540K by any means. Still, in 1942 the 540K was not a seasoned classic but rather a recently made top-quality used car. I paid a lot for it; I could have bought a 540K cabriolet that a fellow student at my university offered for sale for $550. Or I could have bought a car that today is much wanted and high-priced, a 770K convertible four-door sedan, for $750.

By 1950, well after the close of the war, a high-priced 500K was offered for sale—a "perfect-condition" car—for $3,500, a high price for the time.

Five years later prices for the 500K and 540K had not moved much, not even for the much-wanted roadsters. In 1955 a 1938 540K "in mint condition" was offered for $3,000. A 1941 540K with removable steel top, overhauled the previous year but in need of paint, was offered for $1,100—not an unusually low price for the 540K at this time.

There was an upward push for this model classic as of 1960, although one car, a four-passenger coupe, was for sale for $2,250 and a two-seater coupe for $3,950. Closed cars were in little demand, but open cars were coming into their own. A four-passenger 540K convertible in "mint" condition was for sale for $9,000. Another such car was for sale for $8,500. A 1940 open tourer with slots for guns was offered for $3,500. This was the very big and impressive 770K. One 500K convertible was, however, offered for $2,000. This seemed to be the period for price breakthroughs.

A few years later—1962—and prices were the same. The Vintage Car Store, a top-quality car dealer, offered a 540K 1937 four-passenger cabriolet, completely restored, for $4,500. A 540K convertible was offered by another seller for $4,950.

The stock market was certainly not booming in 1962 or in 1965 either, but Mercedes prices did not drop off. In 1965 a 540K short-chassis convertible, completely overhauled, was offered by Classic Cars of St. Louis for $6,200. The Vintage Car Store offered a 540K roadster for $8,400.

By 1968 prices were on the upward move. A 1937 540K convertible was reported sold for $15,000. The five-figure barrier had been pierced. The 1935 500K roadster was reported to be selling for $14,500 and the 1935 770K convertible four-door for $14,000. This is the same model car that I could have bought in 1942 in Cambridge, Massachusetts, for $750.

Several 500K and 540K open cars sold in 1970, but the price level was not over 1968, and it was to be expected that the recession year of 1970 would show few strong classic car prices. By 1975 the price rise in collector cars in general that was taking place in America had not passed by the Mercedes. A perfect 500K roadster sold for $72,500—possibly the same roadster that Christie's sold in early 1979 for $400,000. The rather unattractive four-door 540K convertible sold for $23,250 and a four-passenger tourer brought $32,500. The average price was about $37,000 to $42,000. The 770K eight-passenger phaeton (the Hitler-type car, maybe belonging to Hitler himself) brought the tremendous price for the time of $170,000, and the eight-passenger convertible, the 770K, brought $125,000.

Collector cars took off from 1975 to 1980, certainly the Mercedes included. In 1980 many 500K and 540K Mercedes cars were sold and prices were at an all-time high. A 1934 500K two-door phaeton brought $167,000. A 1935 500K cabriolet brought $170,000. In Duesenbergs any body style brings high prices, even limousines and town cars; but not in Mercedes. The closed cars are definitely not wanted in the market.

The following year, 1981, saw prices still high, and prices for the sale of 540K convertibles ranged from $145,000 to $190,000. For the 500K convertibles recorded sales prices are $180,000, $150,000, $140,000. In this year too, closed cars were not much wanted; a sport saloon in top condition was reported to have sold for $35,000.

Prices were weak during the recession of 1982 and even up to January 1983, when the Barrett-Jackson auction offered two superb 540K cabriolets for sale, one with special body that had belonged to Prince Mdvani, the other a Graber-bodied two-passenger cabriolet. Neither of these cars sold at the auction, but a short time later, the Graber 540K sold for $325,000. This was a car far above the average 540K open cars. The Mdvani car should fetch close to $600,000. The Christie's 500K roadster that in 1979 brought $400,000 was reported resold privately to a European buyer for $620,000, and this is about the price level of the very finest and most beautiful 500K and 540K open cars, but not the average-bodied (but mint-condition) car, which might still be bought for $250,000 or even a little less. The superb Mdvani car was sold after the Barrett-Jackson auction, but what it actually brought is difficult to determine, as it was sold with some cars traded in on it.

The Mercedes-Benz 500K and 540K are excellent automobiles from an engineering point of view and excellent performers. They are heavy cars to drive and a bit hard-riding, but they can be used for transportation. They are not trouble-free cars; they require maintenance. Their value depends to a considerable extent on the body, and the more beautiful the body—open body—the more valuable the car, the most valuable cars being the two-passenger roadsters with Sindelfingen body. Body style is far more important in the Mercedes than in the Duesenberg, and, as I indicated, a Duesenberg closed car will bring over $100,000 and perhaps over $150,000 but a 540K closed car hardly tops $50,000 today.

The Mercedes-Benz S and SS

These are stark semi-racing machines put out between 1927 and 1931, supercharged six-cylinder overhead-cam cars. The straight-eight overhead-cam supercharged 500K and 540K were very much more refined sports cars, whereas the S series cars in their heyday dominated European road racing. The open S and SS cars were just that—open with perhaps side curtains but rarely wind-up windows. They were noisy, and the supercharger, when turned on, sounded like a loud siren. The car was difficult to drive. The clutch was hard to depress, the steering was direct and very hard, shifting was a major operation, and springing was hard in the extreme. The cars were, and are, real fire snorters, especially when one opens the cutout. The supreme cars of the S series are the very rare SSK with short chassis and the "light SSK" for racing with high horsepower—the SSKL. The SSKL will probably never appear on the collector car market.

The S is the earliest of these cars, making its appearance about 1927. It was rated at 120 horsepower without the supercharger and 180 with the supercharger turned on. In 1928 the SS appeared, essentially the same car as the S but rated at 160 horsepower without the supercharger and 200 with the supercharger. In 1928 the celebrated SSK came out with about 225 horsepower, and then the super car, the 1931 SSKL with short chassis, lightened and with a larger supercharger that was supposed to boost the horsepower to 300. To all intents and purposes the SSK and SSKL are off the market.

In 1938 and 1939 one could purchase most S and SS cars, some with extremely fine bodies, for about $500, some less and some a bit more. One SS was advertised for as much as $1,000, and I saw at least two dozen good S and SS cars priced at under $1,000 in this period. Duesenberg J and SJ models were selling at about the same price.

These cars were not popular during the war and immediately after the war. In fact, as recently as 1955 they were out of favor and could have been bought for a maximum of $1,500. In 1952 a just-overhauled SSK roadster was offered to me for $3,200, but this was the premium car, not the S or SS.

By 1960 these premium cars occasionally came onto the market, and one was offered in "near-mint" condition, with the much-wanted Saoutchik body with side mounts and disappearing top, for $5,000. At this time the Duesenberg was about twice as high in price as the Mercedes-Benz S and SS.

In 1965 an S convertible was offered for sale for $7,900 and a roadster for the same price. Duesenbergs were far higher in price—from $12,500 to $16,500.

By 1968 a Mercedes sports roadster of 1928 was sold for $12,500 and the J and SJ Duesenbergs were selling for $10,000 more.

In 1970 an S speedster sold for $14,000 and an SS roadster for $19,000. At this time a price of $60,000 for a classic Duesenberg was certainly not unknown.

Ten years later Mercedes-Benz of the S series had come into its own in the market. Model S roadsters sold for about $50,000. Three SS models sold for $50,000, $55,000, and $68,000. An SSK brought $78,000, but one SSK brought the then huge price of $135,000. In this year, however, many J and SJ Duesenbergs sold for over $200,000 and some exceeded $250,000. Duesenberg was clearly ahead of the Mercedes S series, even the SSK, in the market.

In 1981 the S and SS models were selling for about $85,000 to $90,000, well above 1980 prices. Three SSK models were sold in the range of $95,000 to $120,000. These super cars didn't show much appreciation from 1980 to 1981. Duesenbergs, on the other hand, were selling for $200,000 to $250,000.

From 1981 to 1982 there was a down market in both Mercedes S series and Duesenberg. Neither car sold well except the super Duesenberg La Grande tourer that brought $320,000 at Christie's Los Angeles sale in 1983. In the Arizona auctions of January 1983, a fine SS Mercedes-Benz was offered for sale, an attractive tourer in prime condition. The owner told me he would take no less than $300,000 for the car. The bidding came nowhere near $300,000. I would expect the car to sell for a maximum of $225,000, about the price of a fine Duesenberg in the Arizona auctions.

A big price jump took place at the 1984 Barrett-Jackson auction. A Gangloff-bodied 1927 Mercedes S brought $410,000—a great price breakthrough.

I would regard the Mercedes-Benz 500K and 540K roadsters as the highest-priced collector cars, along with a very few prime convertible coupes. Duesenbergs might be a little less, and the S and SS Mercedes-Benz cars in third place. Which is the better series car as a collectible and which has the most positive outlook is anyone's guess. I would think Duesenberg in general, but

1929 Mercedes-Benz Corsica-bodied Model SS touring car, offered by Christie's in Los Angeles in 1983 with an estimate of $225,000–$250,000. A similar car was sold in Arizona in the same year for $225,000. The author purchased an almost identical 1930 SS in 1939 for $550.

exceeded by special-bodied Mercedes 500K and 540K, followed by the more usual 500K and 540K cabriolets, followed by the SS and finally the S—open cars of these last two series, of course.

Cadillac V-16

After the Duesenberg and Mercedes-Benz of the 500 and S series, the selection of the most important, best investment cars is more difficult. I have as my next choice the great Cadillac V-16. In fact, a good case can be made out that the Cadillac V-16 should stand at the head of the list. Pricewise maybe it should. Rarely does any Cadillac V-16 open car of the early 1930s sell for less than a huge price. On the other hand, what is the price outlook for a top-dollar car? And how many V-16's are there for the investor-collector to buy? Certainly not as many as of other of the top prewar classics. Still, there are V-16's to buy, and some sell every year. The car is a real investment possibility.

Just before the war the Cadillac V-16 was not in the greatest demand. On a used-car lot in New York City in 1939 I saw two very fine five-passenger coupes—not roadsters, not the cars of the early 1930s, but fine V-16 closed cars. They were priced at $250 apiece. Maybe the two could have been bought for $400 the pair. The used-car man seemed anxious to sell. They were late-model cars, around 1938, so they were very recent "used cars" in fine condition.

By war's end prices of the Cadillac V-16 had not declined, although the cars were more or less older used cars, not great classics. Government price ceilings were in effect, on the Cadillac V-16 as well as on most used cars of all makes. A 1939 V-16 Fleetwood sedan was for sale for $3,000—"far below ceiling," as the ad stated. A 1940 model "like new" was priced at $3,500— "$2,476.80 below ceiling."

From this point prices dropped to near zero. Ten years later, in 1955, a 1938 V-16, "well-preserved," was for sale for $125, although the early V-16's brought more money. If we now move along to 1960, prices for any Cadillac— open car or V-16—were low. For $2,000 one could buy choice open Cadillacs at giveaway prices—when Duesenbergs were selling in the five-figure range.

In the stock market drop of 1962 one could buy almost any Cadillac open car for about $2,000, and there was not a great deal of distinction between the V-16, V-12, and V-8. In this year at least one Duesenberg was for sale for $13,500, not at all an unusual price for the year 1962 as far as Duesenbergs went.

By 1965 prices were up for Cadillacs, all Cadillac convertibles—V-8, V-12, and V-16. The Cadillac V-16 was scarce on the market, and early 1930s cars were not much quoted in for-sale ads. For $5,000 one could certainly have bought a mint early-1930s open car. A 1931 V-12 convertible coupe was offered for $3,500.

By 1968 prices had moved up, but the V-16 was in no great demand. The highest price noted at which an early V-16 in top condition had changed hands was $18,000. A good but unrestored roadster of 1931, a prime model car today, was sold for $8,500. A mid-grade roadster of the same year sold for $9,500.

The later cars were not much wanted. A 1937 top-grade formal sedan brought $6,500. A 1939 convertible coupe in good, but unrestored, condition, a fine-looking V-16, brought $1,950, the price of a good-looking older convertible of any leading make as of 1968. Duesenbergs at this time were selling for from $21,000 to $27,000.

Collector car prices in general began to rise by 1970, but the prices of the early-1930s Cadillac V-16 were well on their way, not just starting up. A fair price was reported for a 1930 V-16 roadster at $35,000. Another was reported at $22,000 and a 1931 convertible coupe at $24,500. This was an era of "price breakthroughs." A relatively few cars reached very high prices, but many cars sold at lower prices. Apparently their owners did not see what the V-16 open cars were selling for, either at auction or by dealers. The early-1930s sedans were, however, selling for under $10,000.

When we get to the late-model V-16's of 1938–1940, prices were low, even for top-condition convertibles. A 1938 convertible sedan brought $8,500, and prices of the closed V-16's of this period hovered around $6,000. In this year one Duesenberg open car sold for $60,000 and another for $65,000, and many of the Model J and SJ were over $30,000—well above the price level of the Cadillac V-16.

In the next five years prices took off, as they did in almost the entire collector car market, and in 1975 a 1930 V-16 sport roadster sold for $80,000 and a 1931 phaeton for $81,000. The early sedans were selling for about $15,000. There was still no enormous demand at high prices for the V-16 of the late 1930s. A 1937 convertible coupe sold for $22,500 and a 1938 of the same body style for $18,500. At this time several Duesenbergs topped $150,000 at least one was reported sold for $207,000, a 1929 Model J phaeton. Duesenberg was still well above the Cadillac V-16 in the market and in price level.

From 1975 to 1980 prices surged in the collector car market even more than they did in the first half of the decade of the 1970s. By 1980 the Cadillac V-16's of the early series often topped $100,000, some by a good deal. A 1930 sport roadster sold for $130,000. This early roadster was the preferred Cadillac V-16. The late-1930s convertible sedans were selling for about $60,000. The early-1930s closed cars were selling for under $50,000. On the other hand, the Duesenbergs were often selling for over $200,000 and in several cases for over $250,000.

From 1980 to 1981 there was a little upward movement in the prices of the V-16, but not much. Two 1931 phaetons brought $150,000 and $130,000, while a 1931 roadster brought $130,000 and a 1932 roadster $140,000. The late-1930s convertibles did not move up in price. Duesenberg prices seemed to firm up a bit, more cars selling for over $250,000 but many selling for prices from $200,000 to $250,000.

For much of 1981, 1982, and some of 1983, prices of Cadillac V-16's did not go up a great deal, but they did some. The prices of Duesenbergs may have weakened a bit, and the V-16 and the Duesenberg J and SJ were fairly comparable.

Chrysler Imperial of the Early 1930s

Currently the early-1930s Chrysler Imperial rates in the market right behind the Duesenberg J and SJ, the Mercedes-Benz 500 series and S series, and the Cadillac V-16. It is a tremendously preferred car and it is on the market in some volume. The preferred Chrysler Imperials are the eights of the early 1930s, the touring cars, particularly with dual cowls, and the cars with custom-made bodies. There is a vast difference in value between an Imperial with four-door convertible body, a standard car, and a long dual-cowl custom phaeton. This last car is in the highest demand and at high prices.

Chrysler was a pioneering car, appearing on the market in some volume in 1925. It was a car in advance of its time. The engine was high-compression and high-speed, and it had four-wheel hydraulic brakes. Both of these braking features were much criticized when they first appeared. It was thought the application of brakes to all four wheels might cause the car to slew or to turn over. The hydraulic feature was thought to be dangerous, since if a leak developed there would be no brakes. Mechanical brakes did not have this "dangerous" feature; the rods could develop no leaks.

Chrysler was the pacesetter in lower- and medium-priced cars. The top-of-the-line Imperial was not that expensive with its straight-eight flathead engine unless it had a custom-built body, which body cost the same thing whether it was on a Chrysler or a Duesenberg.

The Imperial was, and is, a smooth-looking car as well as a smooth-running and reliable car. It is the height of elegance, and its shape suggests speed. In the 1930s it was my dream to drive up to my high school at the wheel of a Chrysler Imperial. I had to be content with the next best thing—a Chrysler 70 roadster with rumble seat that would outrun any standard American car in its price class.

As late as the 1960s the Chrysler Imperial was in no great collector demand. In 1965 a 1933 Imperial convertible sedan was offered for $1,200, a price far below the price range of the collector cars that we have talked about thus far. In 1970, however, prices started up sharply. LeBaron-bodied Imperials began to go high.

In 1968 a 1932 LeBaron convertible coupe in unrestored, but good, condition sold for $2,000. A 1931 LeBaron convertible sedan brought $2,750, a car in comparable but unrestored condition. Fine phaetons, however, were selling for $12,000, $12,500, and $15,000—near-mint cars.

By 1970 the Chrysler Imperial had gained recognition as a top collectible in the classic car market. A 1931 phaeton sold for $18,500, a 1933 phaeton for $16,000—still half the price of the Cadillac V-16 then. The *Old Car Value Guide*, which first appeared in 1968, was by 1970 a full-fledged store of price information on classic and antique cars. The cover of that first big issue in 1970 had an illustration in color of one car, a "1933 Chrysler Imperial 'LeBaron' Phaeton, Built by Chrysler Corporation, Detroit, Michigan. Straight Eight L-Head engine 135 HP; 385 CID, four forward speed transmission. A limited production model known as the parade car, only 36 were built in 1933. The cover car photo courtesy of The Museum of Automobiles, Petit Jean Mountain, Morrilton, Arkansas, where the car is presently on display."

To say the photo showed a beautiful car is putting it mildly. For beauty the car is at least the equal of the Duesenberg SJ phaeton. Still, in 1970 this great car might not have brought over $35,000—double the price of other more ordinary Imperial phaetons.

Five years later, in 1975, a 1932 Chrysler Imperial phaeton with LeBaron body sold for $61,000—a mint car. The 1970 cover car would no doubt have sold for more than this figure. On the other hand, a "good unrestored" 1932 LeBaron phaeton would have brought possibly $25,000 and an unrestored but good LeBaron Imperial $12,500. There was an enormous price difference between an average LeBaron and a great LeBaron in mint condition. In 1975 a 1932 roadster in top condition brought $51,000, a 1931 phaeton $55,000, and a 1931 convertible Victoria $55,000—top-condition cars.

In the classic car bull market from 1975 to 1980 the Chrysler Imperial did more than well in comparison with other top classics. One of the "great 36" 1933 Imperials illustrated on the cover of the *Old Car Value Guide* for 1975 sold in 1980 for $175,000. In the same year, however, most fine-condition Duesenberg J and SJ open cars sold for over $200,000 and several over $250,000. Still, from 1975 to 1980 the price of the Chrysler Imperial increased by a much greater percentage than that of the Duesenberg.

The next year, 1981, saw one of the great LeBaron Imperials of 1933, of which only thirty-six were built, go for $160,000—a slight drop in price perhaps. Prices were in the range of $120,000 to $150,000, with one car reaching $155,000. The Cadillac V-16 early-1930s open cars were at an almost identical price level, and Duesenberg was at a level of $200,000 to $250,000.

In 1982 business was slack, even as late as January 1983, and, although some good Imperials were offered at auction no truly great Imperial phaeton was offered. Prices showed no increase and maybe a little drop. The lesser-bodied Imperials, the convertible sedans, were in little demand.

Packard

The number of Packard cars sold in America per year was immense compared with sales of all the other top prewar classics. The number of Packard collectors is also very great. Some classic car collectors seem to think the sun rises and sets on Packards. The car is certainly the equal of the Chrysler Imperial mechanically. The Packard is, in general, a majestic-looking car, although few if any are the equal in body style to the Chrysler Imperial LeBaron phaetons. In price the Packard is not so high as the Duesenberg, Cadillac V-16, and Chrysler Imperial—in general. Here we are talking about *average* price, not top price; for an absolutely top Packard with magnificent body the price is as high as for the finest American prewar classics, Duesenberg included, even the La Grande Duesenberg phaeton sold in 1983 for $320,000.

Packard has always been a collector car. Perhaps for sentimental reasons it became an important collector car after the war. A number of us were brought up on the Packard Straight Eight—the ultimate in the 1920s for the average person, who rarely saw a Rolls-Royce or Duesenberg or supercharged Mercedes. It was the dream of many young people to one day own a Packard Straight Eight. No doubt many of those who were young in the 1920s and early 1930s are now buying Packards for nostalgic reasons.

Packard over the years has made all types and grades of cars from top-quality down to cars that to me didn't seem to be the equal of Ford. When we talk about the top prewar classics we are talking about (1) the big Packard Straight Eights, mainly the open cars, and (2) the V-12 open cars of the early 1930s. Sometimes the later cars turn out to be important classics, the special-bodied V-12 tourers and the Packard Darrins—bodies designed by Howard Darrin— and these were produced almost up to the onset of the war.

In 1939 even the big and important Packard eights and V-12's were nothing on the market other than late-model quality used cars. In 1939 a Dietrich-bodied convertible sedan that had cost $4,340 new was for sale for $1,750— a top-quality 1937 used car. One of the cars that on today's market would be very high in price was offered for $1,500 in 1941—a 1939 V-12 Victoria convertible coupe with 13,000 on the odometer, a car that had cost $6,000 new. Still, this car would not bring as much on today's market as a V-12 of the early 1930s. It was in 1939 that I bought a Packard Light Eight convertible coupe with rumble seat for a friend of mine. It was in fine condition and drove beautifully. I paid $125 for the car, a 1932 model of some quality. Today the car should bring an easy $35,000.

By war's end in 1945 many Packard convertibles were offered for sale. Many of these were simply quality transportation cars purchased while people were waiting for the brand-new cars to come off the assembly lines.

In 1945 a 1935 Packard Straight Eight seven-passenger touring car, "motor perfect," was for sale for $1,400. A 1939 Super Eight convertible was offered for $1,257. A 1941 Darrin convertible coupe was offered by a leading New York dealer for $3,800. On the other hand, a used-car lot in an inexpensive section of Washington, D.C., offered a similar car for sale, a car in good condition, for $1,500.

In 1951 the war was long past and so was the big demand for secondhand cars pending the conversion of the auto industry to peacetime production. In September 1951, a great prewar classic Packard was offered for sale—a 1935 V-12 convertible sedan with Rollston body. The car was advertised as "perfect." The price was $700—and this was about market at the time for what are now great Packard collectibles.

By 1955, prices of Packard classics were still at the "nothing" level. A

V-12 convertible with Dietrich body was offered at $1,200 and a 1940 Packard Darrin Model 180 at $795—a big drop from the immediate postwar years. My friend Hemp Oliver, Curator of Land Transportation at the Smithsonian Institution in Washington, sold his very fine, very rare, and today much-wanted Packard 745 tourer for a small sum. He then was offered the car back at this time for $1,100. He put $50 down on the car, then decided he didn't want it back after all—and lost his $50. In 1980 an almost identical 745 touring car was sold for exactly 100 times this figure.

Five years later, by 1960, Packards were still cheap, even the Super Eights and the V-12's—the phaetons and convertible coupes. One of the most desirable of all Packards was offered for sale—a 1932 Model 902 six-wheel phaeton (side-mounted wheels), a dual-cowl car, "excellent, beautiful," for $2,500.

A 1939 Darrin Victoria was offered for $1,245. In this year Duesenbergs were hitting the $10,000 level.

In the recession of 1962, Packards were in the doldrums. A 1929 Packard Straight Eight convertible with engine completely restored was for sale for $1,500. A 1935 convertible coupe with rumble seat was priced at $500, a car in need of restoration.

1934 Packard V-12 Dual Cowl Phaeton brought $125,000 at the Barrett-Jackson auction in 1983. This choice classic could have brought $30,000 in 1970. (Julia Rush)

A 1937 Dietrich convertible sedan was offered at the somewhat elevated price of $3,700 in 1965. The "cheap" Packard convertibles were still selling for essentially nothing in 1965. A 120 convertible of 1941 was for sale, for $950, "mechanically rehabilitated." A 1937 Model 110 convertible, "mostly restored," was for sale for $575.

By 1968, Hemp Oliver's 1930 Packard 745 touring car was selling for $12,500 in fine condition. A 1941 Darrin convertible Victoria in top condition brought $8,500.

The average-condition cars brought far less. A 1934 Dietrich V-12 convertible Victoria in unrestored but acceptable condition brought $1,100. The premium cars were going at premium prices. The rest were still not wanted.

At this time the Cadillac V-16 was in roughly the same price class, but the Duesenberg was selling at about $25,000.

By 1970 Packards had pretty much come into their own as collector cars and at high prices. A 1930 custom eight dual-cowl phaeton brought $19,500. A 1932 V-12 dual-cowl phaeton brought the very high price of $28,500, and a 1933 V-12 convertible Victoria brought $10,000. Late-model V-12 convertibles were at about the $8,000 level. A 1941 Darrin convertible brought $9,500. At this time two Duesenbergs sold at over $60,000 and Cadillac V-16's sold as high as $35,000.

To 1975 Packards rose moderately. A 1930 Model 745 speedster, a most desirable Packard, brought $52,750. A 1937 Darrin convertible brought $21,000, and late-model V-12 convertibles brought prices in this range.

By 1980 prices for classic Packards were very high. A car like Hemp Oliver's Model 745 sport phaeton brought $165,000. A Model 745 speedster brought $135,000. The V-12 "arrived" in 1980. A 1932 Model 905 dual-cowl phaeton brought $185,000. The late-model V-12's were not preferred collector Packards—as usual.

Even the "economy-model" Packard, the 120, brought a fair increase as compared with all earlier prices. A 1936 convertible sedan brought $23,000 and a convertible coupe $19,500. A 1941 six-cylinder convertible coupe, the Model 110, brought the big sum—for the car—of $21,500.

The following year, 1981, saw a little price weakness. The top price seemed to be $145,000 for a 1932 dual-cowl phaeton. A 1931 Model 840 sport phaeton brought $115,000. The number of classic Packards coming onto the market in 1981 was immense. The cheap Model 120 convertible sedan and convertible coupes were selling for $21,000 to $25,000 for cars in top condition. The Model 110 six-cylinder was selling in the same price range.

In 1981 the vast majority of Cadillac V-16's were selling for well over $100,000 and many Duesenbergs were selling for over $200,000 and some over $250,000.

In 1982, Christie's sold out the Florida Wings and Wheels Museum. In this sale was an extraordinary Packard V-12 early Rollston-bodied phaeton. This car brought the unexpected price of $350,000. Some months later a pair of Packard V-12 convertibles (with replaced bodies) brought $450,000 the pair—$225,000 each. These may have been fluke high prices for super cars, but the prices of Packards did not seem to be down in the recession of 1982.

Rolls-Royce

Rolls-Royce has been known as "The Best Car in the World." At least this was—and is—the claim of its manufacturers, and they may well be right. In any event, in the prewar era the claim had a good deal of merit. The Rolls-Royce is essentially a "good car" in that it was, and is, dependable, far more so than many less expensive cars. Still, it had all of the luxury features, including mechanical features, that anyone would want. I have used a Rolls-Royce or its sister car, Bentley, as my only car that I ran every day, and once I ran one for 15,000 miles without servicing it, including trips of 1,000 miles. I expected to get there in luxury and I expected to get back, and I did. I didn't expect that service from a Ferrari, a Lamborghini, or a Maserati and certainly not from such prewar greats as Isotta Fraschini, Hispano-Suiza, Alfa Romeo, Mercedes, and especially Bugatti.

Rolls-Royce has always lagged behind the other main makes of quality prewar cars pricewise, particularly in the American market. There are several reasons. First, the Rolls-Royce did not seem to capture the imagination of most collectors. For the most part the cars were conservative-looking and modest in performance, very different from, say, the Bugatti Royale or the 540K Mercedes-Benz roadster, cars with flair and performance. Second, there were many Rolls-Royce cars on the American market, many used cars, and this big supply of conservative cars meant low prices. The car was never for young people or for those who felt young. It was more suited to the chairman of the board or the rich widow. Rolls-Royce custom bodies are not unknown, and the names Park Ward, Mulliner, and James Young mean quality, but they also mean conservative elegance, not line and flair.

Prior to World War II many used Rolls-Royces sold for a few hundred dollars, even ones only, say, three years old. The old Silver Ghost often sold for $100 or thereabouts; and a Great Gatsby convertible in prime condition, a Phantom I, yellow, was offered to me in 1939 for $550. Instead I bought a Springfield-made Riviera town car with left-hand drive, a Phantom I, for the same price—$550.

From 1906 to 1925, Rolls-Royce specialized in the Silver Ghost, which had a six-cylinder flathead engine of conventional design for the era but a marvelously developed engine, quiet and dependable. This car was used in taxi service when I first arrived in Canterbury, England, in 1959. The engines of these much-used taxis were barely audible, even at relatively high speeds.

Nevertheless the Phantom I of 1925 was a radical innovation for Rolls-Royce. The new engine was an overhead-valve engine, not the more or less outdated flathead engine used for so long.

Here we will consider the Phantom series as prewar top collector cars. The Phantom I was put out until 1929, then was replaced by the Phantom II. The Phantom II had the same size engine as the Phantom I and was very little changed from its predecessor. It had elliptic springs instead of long cantilever springs and there were a few other improvements, but nothing radical or even very innovative.

Between 1936 and 1939 the Phantom III was manufactured, a far different automobile. The engine was an overhead-valve V-12 and very quiet; but the engine was far less reliable than the old six-cylinder engine of the Phantoms I and II—and the Silver Ghost. These are the three investment cars whose prices I trace—the Phantom I, II, and III.

In the immediate prewar years the Phantom series of cars was in no great demand at high prices—to say the least. A 1930 Phantom II was advertised for $150.

By war's end the market became more discriminating and the finer Rolls-Royces brought more money, particularly the fine-looking open cars. In 1945, a Phantom II brougham sedan, English-made, not Springfield-made, was advertised for $3,800, but a Phantom I seven-passenger sedan was still cheap at $850, even though it had an overhauled engine. A late PI with Brewster convertible coupe body that had cost $27,000 new was for sale for $1,750.

In 1951 a PI 1927 cabriolet that had cost $19,500 was for sale for $2,950— "or make offer." At the other end of the price scale a PII was for sale for the low price of $995.

In 1955 the very desirable Phantom III V-12 with canvas top and aluminum custom body was offered by America's leading Rolls-Royce dealer, J. S. Inskip, for $2,750.

Even as late in collector car history as 1960, Rolls-Royce was not of great importance in the market. A PIII limousine, completely overhauled, was offered for $3,200. A "magnificent" convertible body by Gurney Nutting was offered for $4,000.

Five years later, prices hadn't gone up much. A PIII V-12 with Hooper body, a fine body builder with characteristic flair to the body, this car a sedan, was offered at $4,850. A Phantom II Barker-bodied convertible on which some restoration was required was for sale for $4,500. A PI convertible was for sale for $3,900. Two PII convertibles were offered at $4,700 and $4,880. In the recession of 1962 a Phantom I convertible with side-mounted wheels was offered at the very low price of $2,000.

By 1968, top-notch, top-condition cars were selling at much higher prices, and a PIII convertible cabriolet sold for $9,000. A PI cabriolet sold for $7,800 and a PII five-passenger convertible for $7,500. Lesser cars brought lesser prices, however, and an unrestored, but good, PI touring car sold for $2,600.

By 1970, Rolls-Royce had moved into the five-figure price range, at least at times. A PI touring car brought the very high price of $17,500 and a PI roadster $10,000. A PII Brewster-bodied roadster brought $23,500. The PIII V-12 was weak in the market, however, and a price of $10,000 for this car was rarely, if ever, reached. A PIII convertible sedan sold for $7,000 and a convertible coupe for $8,700.

After the first five years of the classic car bull market, Rolls-Royce had graduated to the big league pricewise. A 1926 PI touring car brought $50,000 and a PI roadster $51,000. The great PI Ascot phaeton sold for $41,500. A 1932 PII Henley roadster brought the high price of $71,000. All PIII V-12's held back in price, and none sold for as high as $50,000, at least to the best of my knowledge. One PIII convertible sedan sold for $39,500, about market for the PIII convertible at this time.

In the second half of the bull market of the 1970s the prices of Rolls-Royce cars rose, but not a great deal. In 1980 no Rolls-Royce hit $100,000. At least no six-figure sale seems to have been recorded. A PI Brewster cabriolet reached $72,500. Now the V-12 PIII was catching up in price to the PI and PII. A PIII tourer hit $75,000. A PIII convertible sedan hit $72,000, and a very special PII boattail roadster with Labourdette body, a car that didn't look very much like a Rolls-Royce, brought $95,000. For price comparison, in 1980 many Duesenbergs were selling at prices over $200,000 and some for over $250,000.

Prices were much the same the following year—1981. The same Labourdette boattail seems to have sold again, this time for $100,000, but this is the only recorded sale of a Rolls-Royce for as much as $100,000.

For the next two years there was no great demand for Rolls-Royce prewar classics. Sales at auction weren't doing well and there were many "non-sales" of Rolls-Royce cars.

It may be that low prices reflected the fact that top-quality beautiful Rolls-Royce cars of the Phantom series simply did not come to market. In January 1983, a prime-condition, beautiful Rolls-Royce Phantom II Brewster speedster came up for sale. It sold right after the Barrett-Jackson auction and brought $220,000. The car was one of two such speedsters built.

In the January 1983 Barrett-Jackson auction a Brewster convertible Phantom II brought $68,000, no standout price.

At the same time a private seller in Texas offered a magnificent-looking Phantom III convertible coupe for $75,000. The car had a replacement body and was probably in need of a complete engine overhaul, as it smoked. In mint condition this car too might have gone over $200,000.

Hispano-Suiza and Isotta Fraschini

Without much question the Hispano-Suiza is one of the greatest auto-mobiles ever produced, not because it had verve, not because it outperformed other cars in competition, but because it was a top-quality piece of machinery, possibly *the* top. It had that reputation among foreign-car mechanics when it was new, and it probably has that reputation among those who knew the car when it was current and those who today examine the prewar cars for me-chanical excellence. Until recently the Hispano-Suiza was not in the top price category of the top prewar classics. Now it seems to have moved into that category.

1925 Hispano-Suiza phaeton, sold at Christie's Los Angeles auction in 1979 for $60,000. The value today would be about double that figure. (Christie's, New York)

There is another reason for not placing the Hispano-Suiza higher up in the list of top prewar classic cars, and that is that there are not a lot of them around. And the same can be said about the Isotta Fraschini.

The Hispano-Suiza and the Isotta Fraschini are in the same category from another point of view. They are both big prestigious cars. The Isotta Fraschini is even more impressive-looking than the Hispano. The Isotta has flair and, in general, is a larger car than the Hispano. Very often it carries a magnificent and impressive touring body made by one of the finest body builders in the world.

From 1919 to 1931 the dominant type of Hispano-Suiza engine was an overhead-cam engine, a sophisticated design, particularly for the era. This is almost certainly the design preferred by Hispano-Suiza enthusiasts and collectors—the earlier car with the overhead-camshaft engine. In 1931 the Type 68 came out. This car had a V-12 engine with overhead valves, but the valves were opened with pushrods, not by an overhead camshaft. The engine was less sophisticated than the earlier engines in this respect, but it was quieter. Taken as a whole, the V-12 is probably not so good an automobile as the earlier overhead-cam cars, but multicylinder cars are preferred in the present-day collector market and bring the highest prices.

Mechanically the Isotta is more primitive than the Hispano. The engine is, however, large, and it is a relatively quiet side-valve engine, a straight eight and very much like the straight eights of the American cars of the period, Packard and Auburn included. The Isotta Fraschini is an enormous car, and this size plus top coachbuilt bodies make the car an important collectible.

Just prior to the onset of World War II a huge Isotta Type 8A was for sale in New York City. The price seemed high at the time for this phaeton—$750. At the same time a Hispano-Suiza could be bought for about $500. The important collector Hispano-Suizas are the 32CV, the 64CV, and two models of the great V-12—54/220 and 54/250.

Three of the model Hissos prior to the V-12's were advertised for sale in 1960—a convertible by Henri Chapron for $3,000, and two sedans, both with van Vooren bodies and both 1937 models, one for $3,850 and the other for $2,480. The Isotta did not seem to come onto the market at this time in any great volume.

There was a big spurt in price to 1965. A 1927 Hispano-Suiza with body by Freestone and Webb, a town car, sold for $7,500. A 1926 Isotta Fraschini Model 8A, a phaeton, sold for $9,500, and this was the model that is the main attraction at all classic car auctions today when it is offered for sale.

In 1968 very few Hispano-Suizas and Isotta Fraschinis were recorded as having been sold. Two 1929 V-12's were sold, but these were both sedans and they sold for $7,500 and $9,000. A 1936 K6 roadster, not the V-12, in unrestored condition, sold for $5,000. An Isotta Fraschini Type 8A speedster of 1926 brought $10,000, and a Type 8A convertible brought $12,000.

By 1970, prices of both makes were up. In Hispano a 1925 KB6 phaeton brought $15,000, and a 1926 convertible sedan of the same series brought $12,500. A 1930 H6B convertible sedan brought $16,000, but a 1934 V-12 cabriolet brought $35,000. This car was at least at the price level of the Cadillac V-16 at the time.

In Isotta Fraschini, two 1926 Model 8A cars were sold. A cabriolet brought $18,500 and a roadster $15,000, about the price level of the earlier Hispano classics.

By 1975, Hispano Suiza was pushing the $50,000 mark.

A 1929 Isotta convertible brought $51,000 and a 1931 two-door phaeton brought the substantial price of $75,000.

These prices were about at the level of the Cadillac V-16 at the time, although one Cadillac V-16 sold for $82,500 and another for $85,000—high prices for the V-16 in 1975.

Prices of Hispanos rose somewhat from 1975 to 1980 but not as much as many other cars rose in this boom period. In 1980 no Hispano apparently

1932 Isotta Fraschini Model 8A limousine, offered in 1983 for $120,000 at Coys of Kensington, London. In 1970 it would have been valued at about $20,000. (Coys of Kensington)

sold for as much as $100,000. A 1926 H6B phaeton brought $90,000 and a convertible Victoria $75,000. A 1934 V-12 cabriolet brought $92,500, apparently the high price for a Hispano in 1980.

Isotta Fraschini was, however, into six figures. A 1926 dual-cowl phaeton brought $120,000 and a 1928 eight-cylinder convertible brought $115,000. A 1930 Model 8A convertible brought $120,000 and a 1931 two-door phaeton $135,000. The price level of both Hispano-Suiza and Isotta Fraschini did not change from 1980 to 1981. The Cadillac V-16 open cars were running at prices up to $150,000, above both Hispano and Isotta.

Perhaps in 1982 a new era dawned—as it may have dawned in the stock market with its all-time highs. At any rate, an open four-passenger Hispano-Suiza in good unrestored condition, but with rebuilt engine, sold for $275,000 in Phoenix, Arizona. In 1982 the James Leake auction sold a V-12 convertible for $350,000. These prices may represent the dawn of a new era not only for Hispano-Suiza but for top-quality cars that are rare.

The 1984 Barrett-Jackson auction was a positive follow-up. A 1935 Hispano-Suiza V-12 brought $400,000, and a 1935 Isotta Fraschini two-door cowl phaeton brought $410,000. These were two of the three cars bringing $400,000 or more in the three-day sale. The third was the 1927 Mercedes S, which sold for $410,000. The sale, which totaled $7.4 million, was the greatest in the firm's history, and the great strength of the sale was in the top prewar classics.

9

The Medium-Level Prewar Classics

AFTER CONCLUDING THE last chapter, one might ask why the Bugatti, Bentley, Alfa Romeo, Lincoln, Pierce-Arrow, and Stutz were omitted from the "top prewar" category. The answer is that "top" and "medium-level" are market-oriented terms. To be a top classic the car must (1) be high in price as of today and (2) be sold in the market in some volume. The Bugatti Royale is almost certainly the highest-priced of all prewar classics, but it virtually never comes onto the market. The rest of the Bugattis do make occasional appearances on the market in the United States but not in great volume, and most of the Bugattis are still a long way from being the highest-priced cars.

Until very recently, Bentley has not been one of the highest-priced prewar classics. Only now has the biggest of the great Bentleys, the 8-liter, broken through the six-figure level.

The Alfa Romeo is a superb car, and the 2.9 has always been a dream car as far as I am concerned. Not a great number of Alfas have been sold in the United States, and those that have have not changed hands at the highest prices.

Lincoln might have been included in the top prewar classics except that prices are still not that high and it is not clear just which models of Lincoln are bringing the high prices.

Pierce-Arrow and Stutz are not high-market-volume cars. I might point out here that the Stutz DV32 is probably the engineering equal of any of the top prewar classics. It probably doesn't take second place even to Duesenberg, and the engine is certainly superior to most of the flathead engines of some of the important and high-priced prewar classics.

There are other cars that are top-quality and unique as well as very high in price that have not been included in the great prewar classics, such as the Horch, Maybach, and Ruxton.

A 1938 Horch that sold in March 1974 at Christie's automobile auction in Geneva for the equivalent of $18,500. This is a rare car whose value today would be $125,000. In 1970, this car would probably not have sold for more than $6,000, but by 1980 the value had reached almost $75,000. (photograph by A. C. Cooper, Ltd., courtesy Christie, Manson & Woods International, Inc.)

At the time the Horch and Maybach were built they were almost certainly considered superior to Mercedes-Benz, even in Germany. They were not the performers that Mercedes-Benzes were but they were the ultimate in luxury in German cars, their engineering design was advanced, they were multicylinder, and they had beautiful, big bodies. These cars are both in the six-figure range or close to it.

The Ruxton, a unique front-drive car, was very limited in production and does not often appear on the market. When it does it brings prices at the six-figure level. But why consider the Ruxton when maybe three cars are sold per year?

Medium-Level Prewar Classics Versus Other Collector Cars

The top-level prewar classics at roughly six figures apiece are the *real* investment cars, the ones a banker might approve for a loan. The banker might well approve a loan to a dealer to carry a 1930–1931 Cadillac V-16 convertible, or a Chrysler Imperial phaeton of the early 1930s, or a Duesenberg S or SJ phaeton, or a Mercedes-Benz SSK, or a 500K or a 540K open car, or a Packard 734.

But these cars are very high in price, remembering that they are not bought by investment funds, insurance companies, and banks as stocks and bonds are. They are bought by individuals. Just one individual will have to plunk down $150,000, $200,000, or more for one of these prime cars or have a credit rating good enough so that the bank will lend him money to carry the car—but hardly to keep it indefinitely as an investment.

Then, too, it is a matter of the car investor's conception of what a car is worth or can be worth. It is hard to explain to anyone that a top-condition 540K Mercedes-Benz convertible is worth $300,000. Even the quoting of a price on the car sparks antagonism in people who have high incomes and a relatively high investment portfolio. You can certainly put $300,000 into a "good sound portfolio" of stocks and bonds, but into just one automobile? Hardly!

And how high is up? Will the $175,000 1930 Chrysler Imperial phaeton rise to $350,000 and then on up to $500,000 or more? It never has so risen. Maybe it will and maybe it won't. There is a real doubt in the minds even of the car collectors that prices will move up materially from their present levels.

Thus the stage is set for the so-called medium-level prewar classics. To a degree these lesser-priced cars are like the stocks that people seek out in a bull market after "Big Computer" has hit 150 or "Big Electric" has hit 108. The investor looks around to try to find some company in some industry that hasn't risen as much as Big Computer and Big Electric.

Everybody reacts emotionally to a degree to cars and their prices, and I am no exception, even though I have been looking at collector cars for fifty years and have been buying real classics like the Mercedes-Benz S and SS since 1938. I would hesitate to sell some of my other things to buy a Mercedes-Benz SS for the asking price of $300,000, the exact same model car that I bought in 1939 for $550. Even if I hadn't known the historical price of these cars on the used-car market and later on the collector car market I don't think I could write out a check for $300,000 for any car.

On the other hand, I could certainly gladly write out a check for many of the lesser-priced prewar classics and would be delighted to drive away in any one of them, firm in the knowledge that I had bought a fine collectible for a reasonable sum of money that I could take out of my stock investment portfolio. I would also feel safe in the knowledge that the car would hardly go down in value in the future but would probably go up in value.

These are some of the medium-level prewar classic cars that have recently come on the market:

A 1933 Auburn boattail speedster in excellent, but not mint, condition for $20,200.

A Cord 810 mid-1930s four-passenger convertible in very good condition for $40,000.

A 1937 Packard V-12 convertible coupe for $58,000—a great car in excellent condition.

1931 Model A Ford roadster that sold at Christie's in 1980 for $12,000. In 1970 the value would have been about $4,500, and today it would be valued at $17,500. (Christie's, New York)

A 1931 La Salle Phaeton for $44,500, possibly the star of the Grand Old Cars Museum Collection, a car that appeared to me to be perfect in every detail.

A 1935 La Salle convertible coupe in excellent (not mint) condition for $13,900, a car that any collector might buy and either put in storage and forget about as its value rose or simply drive occasionally, since the investment was about the same as a fancied-up four-cylinder Japanese econocar.

Advantages of Investing in the Medium-Level Prewar Classics

Probably the most important "class" of collector car investments is the major prewar classics, those recognized as the best and, on the present market, the most expensive. There are, however, good reasons for concentrating on the medium-price prewar classics:

1. They are less expensive to buy, and so the downside risk is not so great. A 1933 Grade 2 Auburn boattail speedster at about $20,000 (the price achieved for the car at a recent auction) is a modest investment.

2. One can afford to wait for a market rise with a less expensive car. If one is *investing* he cannot hold on to a car forever before selling—at least most

of us cannot. A $300,000 investment means, in the present money market, a loss of about $27,000 per year in interest not earned in money market funds or in bills and notes. If one invests in a $20,000 car his interest loss is $1,800 a year—vastly less.

3. For the less expensive prewar classics the potential market is much bigger than for the important prewar classics. The less something costs the more people can afford it. In antique furniture the watchword of the dealers is, "Buy the most expensive antique. That is the best investment." Maybe it is for antiques, but on the present market there is something to be said for investing in the less expensive prewar classics.

4. It is possible to make a quick profit on the less expensive cars whereas it is much harder to make a profit on the top-price cars. The $20,000 Auburn speedster could easily have been resold at a profit after the auction sale. So could the Cord convertible that sold for $40,000 at the Grand Old Cars Museum auction in 1983.

5. Sometimes the less expensive, or middle-level, prewar classics can be bought for not much above the cost of restoration. An Auburn boattail speedster of 1933 in poor condition might easily cost $20,000 to restore. An average-condition boattail might cost $10,000 to restore. Thus for the car of the make, model, and condition of the 1933 boattail, $20,000 was, in one sense, a "bargain price."

6. To a degree the top-level prewar classics have already had their price rise. The Duesenberg J has been at high price levels for three years. Many lesser cars have been rising in this same period, "catching up" to the important classics. It is also a matter of getting out of high-priced items and seeking out lower-priced items that may well show a rise in value. It is like the churning that took place in the bull market in securities in late 1982 and early 1983. When the market for consumer products like Brown Group and Sears and May Department Stores had a big runup in price, then money shifted to the high-technology stocks, particularly after the close of 1982 and during the early months of 1983, and this later market saw big rises in IBM and GE, to name just a few stocks. Then the oils came in for selling with the OPEC crisis—and so on.

In 1980 the Model 851 and 852 Auburn boattail speedsters rose to quite high values—about $70,000. The earlier boattails were vastly less expensive, even the Auburn 12 boattails of 1932–1933. Then these twelves started to rise, and before long they passed the eights. In 1980 a 1932–1933 Auburn 12 boattail could be purchased in mint condition for $50,000. Today it is doubtful if one could buy one of these cars for under $100,000.

7. The prewar medium-level classics are well established as investment cars, better established than the postwar classics, both high-priced and medium-

priced postwar classics. All postwar investment cars are still in a state of flux. Some will emerge as true investments, while others may be less recognized as investments as time goes on. The Mercedes-Benz 300S will almost certainly remain a firm investment car in the postwar classic group; but what will happen to the innovative Lamborghini Countach? Will it emerge as an investment car or not? Time will tell.

On the other hand, almost every prewar classic that we have mentioned is an investment car and will remain an investment car. In addition, many prewar cars not recognized as investments will, as time goes on, become investments.

8. In general there are far fewer prewar classics of middle level available for anyone to buy than there are postwar cars—and the fewer the available cars the firmer the prices.

Auburn and Cord

It has been said that the automobiles of the Auburn-Cord-Duesenberg Company of Auburn, Indiana, are the "yardsticks" of the collector car market. In many ways these cars *are* the collector car market, as they are the most desirable collector cars—from the most expensive collector cars to the least expensive collector cars. They were among the most desirable collector cars when they were first made, and they are today. By "most expensive" to "least expensive" I mean just that. The Duesenberg was the most expensive collector car when it was built, and it is the most expensive (or nearly the most expensive) collector car today. When new the Duesenberg cost on the average about $17,000. The superb Auburn speedster cost new $1,150 in 1931. Actually, Auburn-Cord-Duesenberg seemed to have the idea that the Auburn should be a competitor to the Ford!

The Auburn boattail speedster was a stylistic phenomenon. It was the nearest thing to a guided missile (on wheels, of course) that could have been designed over half a century ago—and it first came out well over half a century ago, in 1928. As the years progressed the car design became more fleet-looking. The company didn't put too many baffles in the muffler of the Auburn, and there was a mild roar to the exhaust, a sound which fitted the appearance of the car.

I used to think the Model 851 boattail of 1935 and the 852 of 1936 were the ultimate Auburn speedsters. Now I am not so sure and I would be inclined to buy a boattail of the early 1930s, especially a V-12 boattail of 1932. I would want a car with a paint job like the original—beige with heavy red trim. This was the trademark of the early boattails, a superb combination.

For a price history we can start with 1945, the year I bought my 1935 Auburn 851 Auburn speedster for $800. The car was in excellent condition, and I bought it from another member of the Sports Car Club of America. The paint was the only weak feature; it was not the best repaint job. The V-12 might have cost a little more at the time.

For the next decade nothing much happened to prices, at least as far as upward movement went. In January 1955, a 1934 Auburn V-12 speedster with "motor completely overhauled" was offered for sale for $1,600. The seller pointed out that in 1934 only twenty of these V-12 speedsters were manufactured.

Five years later and still not much upward price movement. In February 1960, a 1936 Model 852 speedster was offered for sale for $1,850. This was the last boattail made and supposed to be the ultimate in the series.

By 1970, prices for the sales of Auburns were well recorded, particularly by Quentin Craft. Here are some of the sale prices for the boattail speedster by year of manufacture:

1928	$12,500
1929	15,000
1930	14,500
1931	12,500
1932	16,000
1932 V-12	20,000
1933 V-12	22,500
1935 (851)	16,000
1936 (852)	12,800

By 1975 the price of the earlier boattails was about $25,000. The 1932 and 1933 V-12 boattails were selling for prices from $35,000 to $40,000. The 1935 and 1936 851 and 852 were in exactly the same price range. These Auburns were a little less expensive than the Chrysler Imperials of the most-wanted years—1931 to 1933.

Prices were up strongly in the second five years of the 1970–1980 bull market in collector cars. The boattail of the early 1930s was selling for about $50,000, the boattails of the late 1920s, slightly less streamlined, for about $40,000, and the early-1930s V-12 boattails for about $65,000. The "preferred eights" of 1935 and 1936 were selling for from $60,000 to $65,000.

From this point the eight-cylinder boattail rose just a little to 1983. In 1981 prices might even have weakened a bit.

In two of the January 1983 Arizona auctions a 1933 boattail was offered, a red car not far from mint. I had thought it might have brought as much as $40,000 but it sold for only a bit above $20,000—not the "shape of things to come," but a real bargain price and well under the market. At the same time a Greenwich, Connecticut, dealer had a mid-1930s boattail for sale for

$70,000—about market at retail. On the other hand, the early-1930s V-12 boattail was priced at about $125,000. This car had developed into a prime collectible.

The Auburn may not be the most sophisticated automobile ever made, and its engineering is out of date with its flathead straight-eight engine. I did, however, drive my 1932 Auburn sports coupe that I had bought in 1936 for $195 with 4,500 miles on the odometer from Washington, D.C., to Mississippi—1,450 miles—and back again without five cents in repairs; and I would not hesitate to try this trip again with the same car, particularly since the dirt roads of Mississippi are now paved. The body of the boattail was, and still is, superb by any standards, and it is the most copied today of any classic car ever made anywhere. It was Gordon Buehrig's masterpiece, and it was he who designed the Duesenberg body and the Cord body.

The Cord L-29 is a real collector's car, one to rival a Duesenberg J or a Cadillac V-16. It is the kind of investment the well-heeled collector could consider if he wanted just one car—until he got the hang of classic car collecting.

The Cord L-29 first appeared in August 1929, and it was continued to 1931. It had a straight-eight flathead Lycoming engine made in Williamsport, Pennsylvania. The car had front-wheel drive, and the transmission was forward of the engine just behind the radiator. Straight eights were the pattern in this era—Buick, Packard, Duesenberg, Auburn. The hoods on these cars had to be long enough to cover the long engine, but the hood of the L-29 had to be even longer to cover both the engine and the forward transmission and shifting mechanism. The grille was a beauty and very much like the grille of the Duesenberg.

Shifting the L-29 was a real problem. The shift rod came out of the dashboard. It twisted right and left and pulled in and out to change gears. The shift rods traveled the entire length of the straight-eight engine and twisted into the transmission forward of the engine. It was almost impossible to shift easily, and there was almost always a grinding of gears with each change. When the car was in gear, however, it really moved. Because there was no driveshaft through the car to a rear drive, the car was very low. I would bet the L-29 I rode in in 1930 hit 90 mph that showed on the speedometer. I would be delighted to own an L-29 Cord today.

As recently as the early 1950s the Cord L-29 was almost at the "throwaway level." In September 1951, a 1930 Cord brougham in "exceptional condition, very fine throughout" was for sale for $350.

By 1955 the car had a good deal more collector interest attached to it. A 1931 L-29 sedan was advertised in "concours condition, new engine, show car. Cars of this condition are selling at $2,000—priced at $1,200 for quick sale."

Five years later, collector interest in the L-29 had developed even more, although the price was still not high. In 1960 a 1930 L-29 cabriolet, "completely restored, 1st place winner," was offered for $2,450. Still, the great Bugatti Type 57 convertible at this time was selling for about the same price and hadn't moved up much.

In 1962 a mechanically good, but unrestored, L-29 phaeton was offered for $1,350, a car that would be in top demand today.

In 1968 two L-29 convertible sedans were sold at $7,500 and $8,500. The L-29 was moving close to the five-figure mark, a fairly high price range at the time.

Two years later, in 1970, Cord had moved into the five-figure range for the desirable body styles. A 1929 cabriolet brought $9,500. A 1930 convertible sedan brought $10,500. A 1931 convertible brought $11,000, and a 1931 cabriolet brought $12,000. This is the body style that is perhaps the best style designed for this car.

The L-29 was a real performer in the first half-decade of the bull market of the 1970s. A 1930 cabriolet brought $55,000 in 1975, and a 1931 cabriolet brought $47,500.

At this time there was a vast difference in price according to condition. A convertible in good *unrestored* condition could sell as low as $7,500 to $9,000.

In the second half of the bull market of the 1970s the Cord L-29 certainly held its own among the risers. In 1980 a 1929 cabriolet sold for $75,000 and a 1930 convertible sedan for the same price. A 1930 cabriolet sold for $87,500. The sedan was selling for about $40,000, and the unrestored, but good, convertibles at about $30,000. Packards of the wanted models, Cadillac V-16's, and Chrysler Imperials of the early 1930s were all well ahead of the Cord L-29 in price level in 1980. There was some rise in the L-29 market in the next few years. In 1982 one L-29 went for $90,000 and one for $95,000, and a mint-condition car went for $115,000, and this was a time of slack demand for collector cars of the mid-1930s.

The Cord 810 and 812 were V-8's with flathead Lycoming engines of very good design and great reliability. I ran one as my only car every day and had no trouble with the engine. The transmission was something else, as was the steering gear box, which broke so regularly that I carried a spare steering gear box with me in the car. The transmission regularly gave trouble, but I got a rebuilt one quickly as an exchange from Auburn-Cord-Duesenberg for $250— in 1950!

The 810 and 812 are not big cars. They are not low, long, streamlined cars. They have a compact appearance, and there is a rounded front of the hood with no grille. The design to me is most pleasing, and I would be delighted to own one of these cars. Today one can easily be bought in good condition, a convertible, for $50,000. The car is far under the L-29 price but will almost certainly rise in the future.

Many Cord 810 and 812 models have been on the market over the years, from the time they became simply secondhand cars to the era of the 1970s when they developed into collector cars.

In 1945, at the end of the war, when cars were still not available for purchase new, a Model 812 supercharged five-passenger convertible was for sale for $1,366, probably the OPA ceiling price at the time.

By 1951, prices were down, however, and a 1936 convertible was offered for sale for $795 with new paint and recently overhauled. This price was well above the level of the L-29; an L-29 brougham was offered at the same time for $350. The year 1951 probably represented the bottom of the market for the 810 and 812 since the outbreak of World War II. Two of this series of the mid-1930s were offered for $525 and $395.

In 1955 a completely restored 810 phaeton was offered for $2,650 and a "very good" 812 phaeton for $1,150. On the other hand, a "fair" 1936 sedan was offered for $200. A 1936 sedan was offered as a trade for a Volkswagen!

By 1960 the 810 and 812 had pushed up in price a bit. A 1937 roadster, "immaculate," was for sale by a dealer for $2,500. A "partly restored" 812 phaeton was for sale for $1,295 and an 812 sedan for $750—no great prices.

By 1968 the Cord 810 and 812 were just about in the collector car price range. They were no longer simply attractive used cars. A 1936 phaeton in fine condition brought $7,500 and a 1937 in good unrestored condition brought $5,000. Sedans in fine condition were in the $3,750-to-$5,000 range.

By 1970 prices had moved up, but not a great deal. A 1936 phaeton sold for $8,500 and a 1937 phaeton for $9,200.

Five years into the boom decade of the 1970s, Cords were well in the five-figure range. In 1975 a 1936 phaeton brought $19,500 and a 1937 phaeton $24,500.

By 1980 Cord was at the $50,000 level. A 1936 phaeton sold for $47,500 and a 1937 for $52,500. Sedans were going for $25,000 to $30,000. In 1980, Chrysler Imperials of the early 1930s were selling for well over $100,000.

In 1981, the Cord 810 and 812 were not up much in price if at all. In 1982 one Cord sold for $60,000 and one for $65,000. At about this time the L-29, as I indicated, did sell, but privately, for a reported $115,000, a convertible coupe in Arizona. In January 1983, the Grand Old Cars Museum sold a Cord for $40,000.

Lincolns

Lincoln has been one of the best cars put out in America from the time the car was manufactured by Leland as well as after it was taken over by Ford.

The car has always been quality at a price, except for two cars—the Lincoln Continental and the Lincoln Zephyr, lower-priced cars but with fine-looking bodies and verve.

One of the two most-sought-after Lincolns was the V-8 of 1929–1932, a big, regal-looking V-8 that was well engineered and well constructed, drove and rode well, and gave a minimum of trouble. I bought a 1930 five-passenger touring car in 1940 for $32, a good-looking car in very good condition but not mint. It never required any repair. The body was aluminum and I sold it for scrap in the government's aluminum drive. It brought $50. The price today of this car in very fine condition would be about $50,000.

The other important Lincoln is the V-12, another fine car, manufactured from 1932 to the war. Like the Packard V-12, the early cars were worth the most—far more than the late V-12's.

At war's end the V-12 was selling for prices above the "giveaway level." In 1945 a 1937 V-12 with convertible sedan body by LeBaron, "excellent," was for sale for $1,500—"below OPA ceiling." A 1938 was for sale for $1,700.

In 1951 the great Model K, a LeBaron convertible roadster—"virtually unused, one of the finest in existence," a 1935 model—was offered for $1,000. A 1937 V-12 roadster, "perfect," was offered by a dealer for $500—"no offers."

In 1950 and thereabouts these big and fine Lincolns were hardly collector cars. They weren't doing much better pricewise in 1955. In that year a convertible phaeton with Derham body was for sale for $800, another car in the $50,000 price class today if in top condition—maybe more.

By 1960, Lincolns were in a much different category. Now they had moved up in price materially. A 1931 dual-cowl phaeton was offered for $4,000 and a 1939 Model K Brunn-bodied Victoria convertible with a recent engine overhaul was for sale for the big sum of $8,500. These prices were close to those of the Duesenberg at the time.

By 1965, prices, if anything, were down, although the 1960 prices may have been extraordinarily high.

There was, in the 1960s, a vast difference in price between a Lincoln in fine condition and a Lincoln in average unrestored condition. In 1968 many Lincolns sold under $1,000. In medium condition they sold for about $2,500. But a top-condition 1930 phaeton brought $7,500. Lincoln convertibles with fine bodies of the *late* 1930s were selling for prices in the range of $5,000.

Two years later, in 1970, prices had punched through the $10,000 mark. A 1931 sport phaeton sold for $18,500 and a 1932 dual-cowl phaeton brought $17,500. Both of these cars were eights.

At this time the V-12 generally sold for less money—well under $10,000, although a 1933 convertible Victoria brought $10,500 and a 1937 phaeton brought $13,500. Now the later-model V-12's did not seem to be so underpriced as they had previously been.

After five years of the bull market of the 1970s Lincoln had arrived on the collector car scene without any doubt. In 1975 a 1928 dual-cowl phaeton sold for $32,500.

Very few V-12's were at this level. A 1933 LeBaron roadster did, however, sell for $39,500, a near perfect car; but a 1935 Dietrich-bodied convertible coupe brought $19,000. A 1937 V-12 phaeton, near perfect, sold for $25,000. At this time the Cadillac V-16's of the early 1930s were 50% higher in price than the Lincolns of the early 1930s, especially the V-8's. The later Cadillac V-16's were selling in roughly the price range of the Lincoln V-12's of the late 1930s.

By 1980 the collector car boom had climaxed, and Lincoln was in the forefront. A 1929 Locke club roadster sold for $70,000. A 1932 V-12 four-passenger sport phaeton brought $95,000; in addition a 1932 V-8 LeBaron roadster brought $86,000. Three V-12 1933 cars sold for $71,000, $75,000, and $80,000—a cabriolet, a four-passenger phaeton, and a LeBaron roadster. A 1937 Brunn convertible Victoria brought $62,500. In this year Chrysler Imperials of the early 1930s were selling above $125,000 and often above $150,000. The Cadillac V-16 of the early 1930s was almost at this level.

From 1980 to 1981, prices of the great Lincolns did not change much, and they certainly did not move upward. Nor did they move upward in 1982 and 1983 in the recession in the collector car industry.

I did not include Lincoln among the "top prewar classics." The cars certainly moved upward in price, and many Lincolns changed hands on the collector car market every year. Still, many Lincolns sold for under $50,000, even at the peak of the market, and a number sold under $25,000. Only the "best of the best" even remotely approached $100,000. The outlook for the price of the great Lincolns would seem to be positive. The cars are quality all through, and most of them are fine-looking vehicles.

Lincoln Continental

The Lincoln Continental came out in 1939 and was continued to the war. Essentially the same car appeared right after the close of the war and was continued to 1948. It was based on the inexpensive Lincoln Zephyr with a very small V-12 flathead engine, not outstanding, but more or less adequate to move the car from place to place. The looks of the Continental were superb, particularly for the prewar era.

In 1950 the 1948 Continentals were simply used cars, and they sold for about $3,000 or a little less, even the convertibles. The 1941 models could be bought for about $1,000—sometimes more and sometimes less.

In 1955 a 1946 Continental convertible "like new" was for sale for $1,495, about market at the time, with very little interest on the part of collectors.

Prices in 1960 were no better. Then prices seemed to firm up, even in the stock market recession of 1962, when a 1948 cabriolet, "a consistent prize-winner," was sold for $2,100 and another 1948 cabriolet for $1,375. At least now the Continental was out to take prizes!

Prices hadn't moved up by 1965, and a 1946 "never run winters, excellent" car was for sale for $1,250.

In 1968 a 1940 Continental convertible coupe in very good condition sold for $3,750 and a 1948 for $2,500.

In 1970 a 1940 Continental convertible coupe brought $4,200 and a 1941 $4,500. A 1942 brought $3,800 and a 1946 only $2,800.

In a ten year period, prices about doubled, but until 1975 the main price recorder of the era, Quentin Craft, paid little attention to the value of the Continental. In 1975 prices were up and pushing $10,000, and he recorded a 1947 convertible sold at $8,500 and a 1948 convertible at $10,750, but he recorded the price of only four Continentals in total. In 1975 the big Lincolns were selling for three times these figures.

By 1980 an average price for a prewar or postwar Continental convertible seemed to be a little over $20,000 if the car was in fine condition. By 1981 prices might have moved up $1,000 but hardly much more. By 1984 prices might have moved up to $25,000 for a fine-condition convertible. At this figure the car seems underpriced.

Cadillac V-8 and V-12

The Cadillac V-16 is a top prewar classic, as high in price as any prewar classic. The Cadillac V-8 and V-12 are medium-grade or medium-priced, prewar classics, far less costly than the V-16. How inferior stylewise and mechanically are the V-8 and V-12 to the V-16? Not very.

In 1945 the Cadillac was an expensive and luxurious used car. A 1939 V-8 convertible sold for $1,848 and a 1940 convertible for $3,750, both convertible sedans. The V-16 was not very much more expensive at the time.

Not many Cadillac open cars were on the market *as collector cars* for the next ten years, and in 1955 a 1928 roadster in need of some restoration was for sale for $325. The car today would sell, in good condition, for about $40,000.

As late as 1960 no one seemed much interested in the prewar classic Cadillac. A 1932 V-12, today a very choice car, was offered for $650.

There is little need to compare these prices with the prices of other collector cars of the prewar era. The prices of these Cadillac cars were at the strictly used-car level.

In the 1962 stock market drop the price of Cadillac V-8's was up a bit, but

1932 Cadillac V-12 roadster, white with red trim, would cost $75,000 today. In 1970 it might have brought $12,000.

still not at the collector car level. A "restored" 1931 V-12 convertible, a most-sought-after car today, was for sale for $2,200. We might add another $10,000 to these prices to get up to the price level of the Duesenberg J and SJ at this time.

By 1965 the 1931 V-12 convertible coupe, which is today very popular, was up to $3,500 but a 1934 convertible sedan was priced at $500.

By 1970 the Cadillac car was "well organized" in the collector car market

1931 Cadillac Fleetwood roadster with rumble seat, sold by Kruse in 1980 for $78,000. In 1970, roadsters like this one rarely brought as much as $10,000. 1984 value: $90,000. (Kruse International)

and now prices were quoted for (1) the V-8, (2) the V-12, and (3) the V-16. The fine V-8's were over $10,000 in 1970. A fine 1929 sport roadster brought $13,500. The late-model V-8's were not in great demand, despite the fact that many of them were very good-looking and good-running cars. A 1938 convertible sedan sold for $5,000 in fine condition and a cabriolet for $5,200. The V-12's were selling in the same price range as the V-8's. A 1931 V-12 roadster sold for $10,500. A 1937 (late) V-12 convertible sedan brought $8,200 and a 1936 $6,500.

Five years into the bull market of the 1970s, Cadillac V-8's and V-12's were far up. Four 1928 cars were sold for high prices, at least high in relation to prices five years earlier. A 1928 cabriolet brought $12,500, a phaeton $29,000, a sports roadster $21,500, and a seven-passenger touring car $16,500.

The 1930 cars sold even higher—a dual-cowl phaeton at $29,000 and a sports roadster at $35,000.

The 1931 cars were, and are, choice. A 1931 roadster sold for $37,500, a phaeton for $35,000, and a dual-cowl phaeton for $44,000.

The 1937 Cadillac was a beautiful car but it was in no great demand in the market. A convertible coupe brought $13,500. The later V-8 open cars brought even less money.

In this same year, 1975, the V-12 was higher in price. A 1931 roadster sold for $47,000 and a phaeton for $47,500.

The later the V-12, the less it was worth. A 1936 convertible sedan, a very good-looking car, sold for $17,000. In contrast the Cadillac V-16's of the early 1930s were in the $80,000 price range.

In the second half of the bull market decade of the 1970s the prices of Cadillac V-8's were up, but the price rise was not so steep as it was in other collector cars. A 1929 phaeton brought $60,000.

The V-12 was very much higher in price. Two 1931 phaetons brought $72,500 and $73,500. A 1932 dual-cowl phaeton brought $96,000. The late-model Cadillacs were far lower in price; a 1937 convertible sedan brought $37,500.

In contrast the Cadillac V-16 was very high in price, at least twelve cars selling during the year at over $100,000, and a 1932 phaeton brought $165,000.

In 1981 an immense number of Cadillacs were sold, but there was no increase in prices.

Both V-8's and V-12's pushed up in 1982 and 1983, countering the down-trend in the collector car market. Now the "floor price" seemed to be $90,000 for the V-12's. Four 1932 cars easily topped $100,000. A V-12 phaeton brought $125,000, a V-12 roadster $115,000, another V-12 phaeton $125,000, and an all-weather V-12 phaeton $120,000. Top prices for the V-8 were far less— about $75,000.

La Salle

The La Salle was Cadillac's "cheap car" but it was not that cheap or that lacking in quality. Packard in its 120, 115, and 110 models put out a really cheap but good-looking car that could be identified with the body style of the great Packards. Cadillac's La Salle looked different from the Cadillac, at least in most model years, and often the mechanical setup was radically different. The La Salle made its first appearance in 1927, and 1940 was the last year of its manufacture. In this period the engineering of the La Salle changed radically, while that of the Cadillac did not. To begin with, in 1927, La Salle had a flathead V-8 engine of 340-cubic-inch displacement. In the depression years a larger engine was installed, 353 cubic inches, but it was the same type flathead V-8.

In 1934 a completely different car was made under the name of La Salle. The new La Salle had a straight-eight flathead engine from Oldsmobile. The price of the V-8 La Salle had been $2,500 to $3,000, not a low Depression price. In 1934 the new car carried a price tag of $1,595 to $1,695. In 1937 the car was extended and a Cadillac V-8 engine installed. Still the car was offered at only $1,155.

Over the years La Salle has never been a popular car with collectors, and when I saw a 1937 convertible coupe in excellent condition sell for $17,000 at auction in 1983, I felt this was one of the best buys offered by the auction house, and a good-looking car.

Even as late as 1955 people didn't seem to collect La Salle and few were offered for sale. I found one offered, a 1939 model, in "excellent condition," with no body description, for $350.

Five years later a 1939 convertible, partly restored, was offered for $300—maybe the same car! In 1962 a 1939 in "excellent condition" was for sale for $275—maybe the same car again! A 1940 sedan was advertised for sale for $150. In 1965 a 1940 sedan was offered for $95. Now a more wanted La Salle appeared on the market—a 1928 V-8 convertible coupe, priced at $2,000.

In 1968, $3,000 would buy a fair convertible of the early series, 1927–1931, and $5,500 a roadster. A fine-condition phaeton of 1930 brought $7,500. The late-model La Salles were not of much account in the marketplace. A fine-condition 1940 convertible sedan sold for $3,500 and a convertible coupe for $2,400. A fine four-door sedan sold for $1,250.

By 1970, La Salle prices were up somewhat, and a 1927 phaeton sold for $10,500 and a 1929 roadster brought $12,500, but most other sales of the 1927–1933 cars were at price levels of $5,500 to $8,500.

By the end of the first part of the rising collector car decade, La Salles of the early years were well up in demand and price. A 1927 phaeton brought

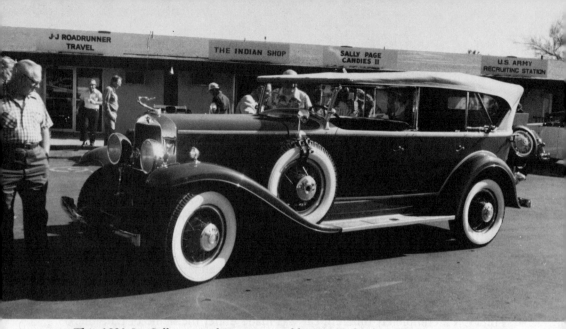

This 1931 La Salle sport phaeton was sold in 1983 for $44,500 in the Grand Old Cars Museum auction. (Julia Rush)

$25,000, a mint car. A 1927 roadster brought $22,500, and a 1928 phaeton brought $26,500. The fine-looking 1931 cabriolet brought $16,500. Most of the late-model La Salle open cars brought much less, however. Sedans, late models, went for under $5,000.

By 1980 the early La Salles were well up. A 1927 dual-cowl phaeton brought $67,000 and a 1928 $65,000. Most of the early-series open cars were at the $50,000 level. The late-model La Salle open cars sold from $23,000 on down to about $16,000 for a fine-condition 1940 convertible coupe.

In the next year prices did not change much for the early and late La Salles. Perhaps they were a little lower. They did not increase to 1983.

To me the star of the Grand Old Cars Museum auction in Arizona in January 1983 was a 1931 La Salle sport phaeton. It appeared to be mint, although the auctioneers rated it class 2 condition. It brought $44,500 and was well worth the money. The car should certainly bring much more if it is ever offered for sale in the future.

Bugatti

Anyone might ask why the Bugatti should be placed in the chapter on prewar classics after the La Salle, particularly the La Salle straight-eight flathead. Bugatti put out overhead-camshaft cars, cars with four valves per cylinder, and supercharged competition cars. Anyone who has driven the Bugatti Type 57 would hardly place it in the class of La Salle.

But my consideration of various prewar classic cars depends on the market.

La Salle has been considered as a division of Cadillac, and there are far more Cadillacs and La Salles sold on the collector car market than Bugattis. Of course, in Europe very few La Salles and Cadillacs are sold but a number of Bugattis.

In regard to prices, La Salle is a low-priced Cadillac, and Cadillac is the top level of the Cadillac–La Salle group pricewise. Unless we are talking about a very few Bugattis, Cadillac is higher in price, and there is no Cadillac *consistently* higher in price than Bugatti than the Cadillac V-16 of the early 1930s.

We can forget about the Bugatti Royale and concede that this is probably the most valuable make and model car in the world, and we can, for all intents and purpose, forget about any appearance of this car on the market for sale.

Which year and model Bugattis are in demand on today's collector car market? All of them! Any Bugatti is a collector's car, even if it has a stubby body or looks like a boat; and no Bugatti goes for nothing.

There is one model of Bugatti, however, that dominates the collector Bugatti market, and this is the Type 57, of the late 1930s. It has an eight-in-line engine with twin overhead camshafts, so its engineering was certainly not behind that of the Duesenberg J and SJ. The engine displaces 3,200 cubic centimeters. There were several variations of the 57—the 57, 57S, 57C, and 57S45. The last three types were supercharged, and the 57S45 had a larger engine, 4,700 cubic centimeters. The top speed of the series was about 125 mph. The body model most wanted is the convertible coupe or cabriolet, and certainly the very special lightweight Atlantic streamlined coupe.

There is another great Bugatti that occasionally appears on the market, a stark powerhouse known as the Type 35, a very compact strictly open speedster.

Few Bugattis were on the market before World War II, and few were seen on the road, even compared with the great supercharged Mercedes cars. In 1945 I noticed one car for sale simply referred to as a "speedster" for $1,750.

Ten years later a Type 57C (supercharged) convertible "restored as new" was offered for sale for $1,800. Other Type 57's were for sale for $750 up by the same firm in Elmira, New York. A 1938 Type 57 coupe was offered for sale by Russ Sceli of Hartford, Connecticut. It was he who in the same year offered me a magnificent 57 convertible in near-mint condition for $1,500. He wanted the same price for the coupe.

By 1960, Bugatti 57's came flooding onto the market. A 57 convertible was offered for $2,000, one for $2,950, a four-place for $4,500, a roadster for $2,950. A 1934 Gangloff-bodied drophead with pigskin upholstery, but in need of work, was for sale for $1,850.

The important Type 35C roadster was for sale for $2,900 and a Type 35C

Grand Prix for $1,500, a supercharged speedster with engine and gearbox overhauled.

This was the price level of Cord at the time.

In 1962 a 57 Atlantic coupe was offered for sale for the very low price of $3,400, but the car required paint, carpets, and a rewiring job. In mint condition today this car would be well into six figures.

A Type 57 Gangloff two-door drophead, "excellent," was offered at $2,750.

The price recorders picked up very few Bugattis that had changed hands in 1968. A Type 35 Grand Prix in fairly good condition sold for $6,200 and a car that was almost certainly a Type 57, a car in near-mint condition, sold for $8,500.

Prices moved up a little by 1970, but few cars were recorded as sold in that year. A Type 57 roadster brought the high price of $12,500, and a Type 57 two-passenger speedster brought $9,500.

In five years of the classic car boom, prices moved up sharply for Bugatti. A Type 57 roadster sold for $46,750, a cabriolet for $31,500, and a drophead for $31,500. It is possible an Electron coupe, an ultramodern coupe, sold for $60,000. Prices were at the level of the Cord L-29 and far above the prices of the Cord 810 and 812.

At the end of the "growth decade" prices had moved up but not a great deal. Bugatti price increases did not seem to keep up with the market. A Type 57 roadster sold for $58,000, a cabriolet for $48,500, and a speedster for

1925 Bugatti, Type 35 Grand Prix, sold for $28,000 at Christie's in 1975 and would bring more than $100,000 in today's market. (Christie's, New York)

$39,500. The important Electron coupe did register a relatively high price—$77,500. The next year, 1981, an Electron coupe was recorded as sold for $71,000. A Type 57 roadster sold for $65,000. In this year the Cadillac V-12 was a little higher in price.

In 1982 a Type 57 coupe sold for $70,000, a 1937 model. A 1939 Type 57 coupe brought $75,000, and a 1939 Type 57C drophead coupe brought $90,000. Bugatti certainly countered any backoff in the collector car market in the recession.

A fine-condition Bugatti with short body was offered for sale by the Barrett-Jackson auction in January 1983, but it did not sell. It is felt that the reserve price was about $85,000.

Alfa Romeo, Types 1500, 1750, 2.3, and 2.9

The Alfa Romeo is a top-level car from an engineering and style point of view. However, its price level is not at the very top, and few Alfas are on the market.

There is one Alfa that is at the top in every way, price included, although few of them come on the market, and this is the 8C2900—the 2.9 Alfa of the late 1930s. The car has an overhead-cam straight eight with two superchargers. It was low and long and, by today's standards, is still. The lines of the car are superb, and it is a performer. Its value is probably far above that of almost every other prewar classic Alfa Romeo.

The first really important sports Alfa Romeo was the 1927 1500 six with one overhead camshaft. Then came an almost identical car but with a 1,750-cubic-centimeter engine. There followed a 1500 and a 1750 with two overhead cams, and some of these cars were supercharged. In 1938 came the great 2.9 with two superchargers. There was also a 2300-cubic-centimeter straight eight. The six-cylinder 6C2300 was the main road car that was continued to the war. The firm also made a few competition V-12's, and these have occasionally appeared on the market. I watched the time trials and the race at Indianapolis in 1946 in which three Alfas were entered, the team led by Luigi Villoresi. The cars, called Alfettas, had tiny 1500-cubic-centimeter engines and would not stand up against the big-engined cars entered in the race. For a long time the supercharged Alfettas competed against the 4500-cubic-centimeter Ferraris in Europe, and beat them. Ferrari finally won, hardly ever to be beaten again until decades later. The Frank Griswold 2.9, a blue coupe, won the first Watkins Glen race and won it easily.

In the late 1930s, the Alfa Romeo was a most desirable car, particularly among young collectors. Actually, at that time buyers were simply purchasing secondhand quality automobiles, used sports cars, for the most part, and trying to get a real bargain in a luxury car that had once cost, say, $10,000 and that could now be picked up for considerably less.

Alfa Romeo, small, high-powered, well sprung, was also a glamour car. It had been winning in European racing as well as in the United States, and it was making the news fairly regularly. People wanted it and would pay more for it than they would for a big Mercedes-Benz S or SS or a Rolls-Royce Silver Ghost or Phantom I or II.

Ray Gilhooly, the former Indianapolis driver, who sold me my Mercedes-Benz SS, had a beautiful small Alfa for sale, a 1750, for $3,000. All I could do was look, at least in 1938 when this car was offered for sale.

In March 1939, he advertised an Alfa for sale, a twin-cam supercharged Alfa, "like new," for $1,650, about the market at the time.

A decade and a half later the price of Alfas hadn't moved up. A 1936 1750 with body by Touring, "completely refurbished" and "mint," was for sale in the early part of 1955 for $1,900.

Five years later Alfa Romeo was still not much in demand, and in November 1960, a 1934 model 1750 Gran Sport was offered for $2,595.

By 1965, prices had moved up. A sprint Zagato racing car was offered for $3,000, but an 8C2300 in "fine condition" was priced at $6,900. Quite a choice car was offered in the same era—a 1937 grand prix aerodynamic rear-engined experimental car for the very low price of $2,100. In the 1950s and 1960s, specialized racing and other competition cars and experimental cars were often for sale very reasonably, cars that today are in demand at high prices.

In 1968 one of the great 8C2900 roadsters was sold for $10,500. An unrestored 1930 sport roadster was sold for $2,000 and a 1925 for the same price. Most Alfa Romeos were not in demand. Only the top Alfas commanded a high price. The price of $10,500 was about the same as the price of the Auburn boattail speedster of the mid-1930s.

The next year a 1933 Model 8C2300 tourer in top condition sold for $18,500 and a 1938 8C2900 for $11,000.

By 1975, a boom year for cars, prices were well up. Two of the great 8C2900 roadsters brought $19,000 and $19,750. Of ten sales recorded by Quentin Craft, the price of the cheapest car was $17,500 and the most expensive $24,500 for a 1933 8C2300 roadster in fine condition.

In the next five-year period prices very nearly doubled. A 1930 Gran Sport brought $47,000. A 1938 Model 8C2900 brought $37,500. For comparison purposes the Auburn boattail speedster of the mid-1930s was bringing $60,000 at the time and more.

During the next two years, to 1982, in which the country went into a recession, the price of Alfa Romeo cars declined a bit, possibly as much as 10%, and nothing seemed to bring as much as $40,000. On the other hand, no great car seemed to change hands in this period. An advertisement did appear of a very famous competition 8C2900 coupe, and the price was an astronomical $220,000. What the car sold for, if it sold, is not known.

The Alfa Romeo seems to be an undervalued car, particularly in the United States, and as the country moves to prosperity, the price of these cars should rise materially.

Chrysler 70–80

The Chrysler 70–80 series were epoch-making cars. They had the Chrysler innovations of the high-compression, high-speed engine and four-wheel hydraulic brakes, and in addition, were very fast, highly styled cars compared with the competition. The 1925 Ford Model T, Chevrolet, Buick, Oldsmobile, and Pontiac hardly compared with the Chrysler 70. Nor did the Ford Model A roadster with rumble seat compare with the Chrysler 70 of 1925 for performance or looks.

The first important car of the new six-cylinder Chrysler series (the first Chrysler was simply a dressed-up old Maxwell four with a new name) was the Chrysler 70—with 70 horsepower and able to achieve 70 mph.

By 1928 the Chrysler 70 was in need of a facelift, and it got it in the Chrysler 72, a bigger, more impressive-looking car, particularly the sports roadster.

In 1929 the essentially same car became the Chrysler 75, and in many ways this was the ultimate in the "medium-priced" sports car ($1,555 for the Blue Boy roadster).

In 1930 the sales of these sports models had proved so successful that three sportier cars were produced—the Chrysler 66, 70, and 77, the larger numbers indicating a bigger and more impressive-looking sporty car. The cars were well styled, with narrow bands for the trim over the radiators, and louvers in the form of wings, plus bright colors and some fancy two-toning. My 1930 Model 70 coupe with rumble seat was a great satisfaction to me and gave me a good deal of prestige with my college friends, even though I had bought it secondhand in 1935 for under $100.

The Imperial 80 (1926–1930) was a kind of super Chrysler that may have been designed to compete with the Packard. All of these Chryslers had six-cylinder flathead engines, but they were excellent.

Chryslers were late in arriving at the stage of collector cars, and only very recently has the Imperial become a collector car. Here the Imperial eight of the early 1930s separated itself from the Chrysler Imperial 80, the six-cylinder car that ended in production in 1930. Even as late as 1965, however, an Imperial eight of 1933, a convertible sedan, was offered for sale for $1,200. In 1960 a 1927 Chrysler 70 roadster was for sale for $600, and this was the approximate price level of the 66, 70, 72, 75, and 77 until well into the boom market of the 1970s.

In 1968 a Locke-bodied Chrysler Imperial 80 roadster of 1928 was recorded as being sold for $8,500, but the price of a good unrestored car was about $2,000.

By 1970 the Imperial 80 of 1926–1930 was selling for about $7,500 on the average, and the eights of 1931–1933 at over double this figure. A Chrysler 75 roadster sold for $4,500 and a Chrysler 72 roadster for $3,800.

By 1975, five years into the boom period, a 1928 Imperial 80 roadster brought $18,500 and a 1929 $18,750. The later eight-cylinder cars were selling for $40,000 to $55,000, and a mint-condition 1932 LeBaron phaeton went for $61,000. Now a 1929 Model 75 roadster sold for $14,500 and a 1928 Model 72 for $11,500.

By 1980 the Imperial 80 had arrived at a clear collector status. A 1926 Locke roadster sold for $42,500, and a 1928 LeBaron convertible sedan brought $57,500. Something over $50,000 seemed an average price for the six-cylinder Imperial. The eight-cylinder cars of the early 1930s were all over $100,000, and some were over $150,000. These latter are all, of course, top-level prewar classics.

Two years later the Imperial bucked the downtrend in business. A 1929 sport roadster brought $62,500, and four 1930 open cars brought $65,000, $62,000, $57,000, and $62,500. The great classic eight-cylinder Imperials of the early 1930s had not risen in price.

In 1982 the Chrysler 70 roadster of 1925–1926 was selling for $12,500 to $15,000. The Chrysler 72 of 1928 was at the $15,000 to $16,000 level and a 1929 Model 75 sport phaeton sold for $26,000. Two Model 77 open cars brought $32,500 and $36,000. Some of the less distinguished four-cylinder cars of 1924–1926 were bringing over $10,000. All Chryslers had become popular in the market.

From 1930 to 1933 the great Imperial eight was produced, and we consider this car a top prewar classic. It is top in body design and certainly in price. In this same period, however, and through 1933, a welter of finely styled Chryslers were built. The open cars are now in great demand, including a "secondary" Imperial, the CQ model. The great models are the LeBaron-bodied custom cars and the CL series. Sixes and eights were excellent cars in every way; I spent many happy hours riding in a 1931 CD series eight-cylinder sports coupe. All of these cars seem to hover around $25,000 today, and also seem to be pushing upward in demand and in price.

Pierce-Arrow

If one were asked in the 1920s what cars were the finest made at the time, particularly in the late 1920s, he might answer "Packard, Pierce-Arrow, and Cadillac," in that order. Rolls-Royce and Duesenberg were super cars that the ordinary person hardly ever saw. Nor did the ordinary person see the great

Continental cars. In the United States, Packard was the prestige car, probably followed by Pierce-Arrow and then Cadillac. Lincoln might have been included but it did not have a great deal of public exposure at the time.

The "trademark" of Pierce-Arrow was the set of headlights which protruded through the front fenders, patented in 1912, and the 1913 model carried these "fender headlights." If the buyer of a Pierce-Arrow didn't want these characteristic lights (and there were few that didn't) then he could order the car with conventional headlights, and the company permitted this option up until 1932.

The Pierce-Arrow was a big, impressive, top-quality, but conservative car. Some of the cars of the teens were absolute behemoths. I recall pushing the starter on a great 13,500-cubic-centimeter Model 66 that sounded as though I were starting the engine of a diesel-powered ocean liner. The sound was far more impressive than pushing the starter on the largest diesel truck made today.

Up until about 1960 very few Pierce-Arrows were offered for sale. The car was considered "dated" and secondhand, unless it was a true antique, and true antiques were rare. In 1960 a 1936 convertible was offered for sale, "overhauled, body mint," for $2,650. A V-12 sports sedan was offered for $1,200, a car with a LeBaron body. For comparison, at this time Duesenberg was selling for over $10,000.

By 1965, prices of Pierce-Arrows were up. The Vintage Car Store offered a V-12 1933 convertible for $5,800, not a low price for a classic car at the time. It also offered a 1928 convertible coupe for $3,700. A great car was offered for sale at this time, the Silver Arrow, "a national overall winner, very rare," for $6,500. This was a very streamlined car put out in 1933, a V-12 closed car, developing 235 horsepower. On the market in 1983 it would be an easy six-figure car.

In 1968 a Silver Arrow sold for $7,500, a 1935 V-12 convertible sedan for $5,500, and a 1930 LeBaron phaeton for $8,500. Lesser-condition cars did not sell well. Two 1930 phaetons, unrestored but good, sold for $1,800 and $2,000.

By 1970 prices had risen. A 1930 dual-cowl phaeton brought the high price of $18,500 and a 1931 roadster the same price. The V-12 car did not seem popular at this time. A 1932 V-12 convertible sedan went for $8,500 and a 1933 V-12 cabriolet for $6,500. In 1938 the Pierce-Arrow firm went bankrupt and its assets were sold for $40,000. As I recall it, the brother of the dean of my university was president of Pierce-Arrow when I started in college, and this relationship gave the dean a good deal of prestige with us students, prestige which, I guess, disappeared upon liquidation of the company. In any event the nearer we get to the date of liquidation—1938—the lower the price of the collector cars in 1970. In 1970 the price of Pierce-Arrow was in the same range as the price of the great Chrysler Imperials of the early 1930s, some of the highest-priced prewar classic cars today.

In 1974 an "excellent" 1928 Pierce-Arrow roadster was offered for sale for $14,500, a price in keeping with 1970 prices.

By 1975, Pierce-Arrows were high in price. The great Silver Arrow of 1933 was now up to $45,000. A 1933 V-12 cabriolet sold for $24,500 and a 1935 V-12 for the same price. A 1932 V-12 phaeton brought $42,500, a dual-cowl car. The earlier open cars ran around $20,000 or less. Now it was the V-12 that was in favor in the market.

At this time the Chrysler Imperial of the early 1930s was selling for perhaps 50% more than the Pierce-Arrow.

By 1980 there was something of a reversal in preference. Now the earlier eight-cylinder cars were in favor. A 1929 phaeton eight in top condition brought $82,500 and another in top condition brought $70,000. A 1936 V-12 roadster brought $52,500, a high price for any V-12. A 1935 V-12 cabriolet brought $55,000.

By 1982, prices for Pierce-Arrows were definitely down, not just maybe down a bit. A 1929 dual-cowl phaeton brought the high price at the time of $70,000. A 1930 car of the same body style brought $72,000. A 1938 V-12 convertible coupe brought the same price. The V-12's seemed to be out of favor. Christie's auction in California offered a superb 1929 phaeton for sale in April 1983, a car that had received first place in the national competition of the Classic Car Club of America. The car had been completely restored. It was estimated to bring $65,000 to $75,000 but it did not sell. This seemed to be a down period for Pierce-Arrow.

In the April 1983 Christie's sale in which the Pierce-Arrow did not sell, a 1929 Stutz Model M speedster with LeBaron body, a car reportedly in excellent condition and with side-mounted wheels, and estimated to bring $68,000 to $70,000, also did not sell. Two years previously one of the greatest of all Stutz cars was sold for a little over $70,000, this one a 1932 Super Bearcat, a car of some renown from the Briggs Cunningham Museum.

Stutz has always been a glamour car and performance car. In 1929 I looked at a boattail speedster in the East Hartford automobile section. I didn't even inquire the price but was told the car would do 105 mph. On occasion I saw a Black Hawk open car on one of Hartford's fashionable streets, where it seemed to belong naturally, no doubt owned by one of the high flyers in the boom stock market of 1929—before the crash.

In 1928 a new stock car record was set when a Stutz Black Hawk speedster was driven at Daytona at 106.52 mph. A special-built Stutz with a special Miller sixteen-cylinder engine of very limited size, 3.2 liters, it clocked 225 mph in a record attempt.

In 1931 Stutz introduced a great car, the DV32—four valves per cylinder—

for better aspiration, a straight eight with dual overhead camshafts, essentially the same type engine as the Duesenberg's. Its nine-bearing-crankshaft engine turned out 155 horsepower, and the car was guaranteed to do 100 mph. In 1946 I bought a 1932 Stutz DV32 sedan for $175. In 1948 I had the pleasure of working with Frederic Moskovics, who had been made president of Stutz in 1925. It was he who developed the straight eight with single overhead camshaft shortly after his ascent to the top position in Stutz. Moskovics had been a racing driver and was interested in top-performance engines. His cars certainly had them.

Very few Stutz cars were offered for sale prior to the 1960s and even to the 1970s. In 1965 a DV32 two-seater convertible with rumble seat and side-mounted wheels was for sale for $3,750. In 1968 a 1925 Weymann-bodied roadster was sold for $7,500. The Weymann body was unique in that it was fabric stretched over a frame. It was thus very light. A 1926 speedster was sold for $5,500 and a 1932 DV32 cabriolet for $2,600, not a top-condition car, but in good condition.

By 1970 Stutz was well up in price. A 1928 phaeton brought $12,000, a 1930 boattail $17,500, and a 1932 DV32 convertible Victoria $18,500. This was about the price level of the Chrysler Imperial of the early 1930s, a top-value car in the 1980s.

Five years into the boom of the 1970s, Stutz was higher up in value. A 1928 dual-cowl phaeton sold for $42,500. Two 1925 open cars sold for $21,500 and $22,500. This was about the level of the early-1930s Chrysler Imperial open cars.

By 1980 the Stutz was up in price, but other prewar classics were up more. The great 1932 Stutz Super Bearcat roadster sold for $95,000, the most desirable Stutz and one in top condition. No car seemed to hit $100,000, at least in a recorded sale. A 1928 boattail speedster sold for $78,000 and a 1928 phaeton for $85,000. Now, however, the Chrysler Imperial of the early 1930s was selling for over $100,000 and some for over $150,000. They seemed to have left Stutz behind, at least in the marketplace.

In 1982 a few Stutz cars punched through the six-figure level. A Super Bearcat roadster was reported to have sold for $120,000, a car in top shape. A 1933 four-passenger LeBaron roadster was reported sold for $130,000. A 1932 DV32 speedster was sold for $110,000. The open cars up through 1928 were selling for well under $100,000. The Chrysler Imperial of the early 1930s had backed off a bit in price but was still well over $100,000, and a few sold for over $150,000.

Marmon V-16

The Marmon V-16 was a unique car with twin banks of eight cylinders and an aluminum engine of relatively light weight. Maybe the Cadillac

V-16 was a better engine, but I am not so sure. I am only sorry that I did not keep my Marmon V-16. It was, however, a sedan, and at the time I took it in part payment for my Offenhauser-engined Cisitalia I wasn't interested in anything but sports and competition cars.

The Marmon V-16 first came out in 1933, in more or less the bottom of the Depression, and three years after the Cadillac V-16 appeared. The enormous engine of 9.1 liters, compared with 8.2 liters of the last big Cadillac Eldorados, was supposed to turn out 200 horsepower, quite a rating for a car designed in 1933. The cost of the entire car was under $6,000, a low price for the car but too high a price for the Depression bottom.

As late as the 1960s, Marmons were not in great demand, not even the V-16. In 1968 a 1931 V-16 cabriolet in unrestored, but good, condition sold for $2,500, but a 1930 sedan in top condition brought $7,000. The following year a fine-condition 1931 V-16 sedan sold for $10,500 and a 1931 LeBaron town sedan for $12,000.

Prices were about the same in 1970, with relatively few Marmon V-16's being sold. In 1975, however, prices were well up. A 1931 sedan brought $18,750, and a 1931 convertible sedan brought $25,000. This was about the price level of the Cord 810 and 812 of the mid-1930s, no huge price for an important prewar collector car.

By 1980 the Marmon V-16 had forged ahead in price, and many came onto the market. A 1931 convertible sedan sold for $70,000. A 1932 convertible sedan sold for $75,000 and a 1933 for $72,000. This was the general price range of the Pierce-Arrow at the time, and the Cord 810 and 812 had been left behind. The Auburn boattail speedster was certainly not more expensive than the Marmon V-16.

There was no change in price to 1983—up or down.

Bentley

Here we will concentrate on two great Bentleys, the Speed Six and the Eight Liter, two of the finest of all classic cars. Many Bentleys come onto the market, and many are very different, from the cars made by W. O. Bentley to Rolls-Royces simply sold under the "Bentley name." Both "Bentley Bentleys" and Rolls-Royce Bentleys were and are excellent cars, and I have driven and ridden many miles in both.

In 1925, W. O. Bentley put out a big-engined 6.5-liter overhead-cam car. In 1929 it was made more sporty-looking and had fewer luxury features and was known as the Speed Six. This car was a monster and sounded and drove like the Mercedes-Benz S and SS of the late 1920s.

In 1930 a really big-engined car was put out by W. O. Bentley to replace the 6.5-liter car (the Speed Six). This was the Eight Liter Bentley, its engine about the size of the big Eldorado engine. The hood was massive and gave the car a very important appearance, at least as important as the S and SS models of Mercedes. In 1931, Rolls-Royce took over Bentley and began soon thereafter to turn out Rolls-Royces but with the name Bentley.

Very few Speed Six and Eight Liter Bentleys are offered for sale in this country. In 1965 a 1929 Speed Six, "magnificent, restored," was for sale for $5,850. In 1968 a Speed Six four-passenger tourer was sold for $7,500. In the following year a Speed Six sold for $9,000, a touring car. In 1970 a four-passenger Speed Six tourer changed hands at $14,500. An 8-liter cabriolet brought $10,500.

Five years later a Speed Six tourer sold for $27,000 and an Eight Liter cabriolet for $35,000.

In 1980 a Speed Six tourer sold for $41,000 and a roadster for $45,000. An Eight Liter cabriolet brought $85,000 and a sedan $72,000.

The following year prices were about the same. In February 1981, Christie's in California sold an Eight Liter four-door sport sedan with replaced body by Mulliner, a car sold by the local Rolls-Royce and Bentley dealer, who had restored it well. It brought $90,000—under expectations.

In 1982 a Speed Six roadster brought $50,000 and a Speed Six tourer brought $55,000. An Eight Liter cabriolet brought $90,000.

All Bentleys brought prices in this general range, at least the Bentleys made before the Rolls-Royce takeovers, but the Speed Six and the Eight Liter are the most popular cars. Recently, in Greenwich, Connecticut, a dealer in foreign classics offered a beautiful Eight Liter Bentley roadster for $175,000. High-priced, perhaps, but the car was a standout, and this price may well be the shape of things to come for the great Bentleys. The cars may well move into the category of top prewar classics—if they are not there already.

10

Antique Cars

WHAT EXACTLY IS an antique car? One commonly used definition is all cars made before 1925. Those made from 1925 on to World War II or through the war are defined as classic cars. Sometimes antique cars are considered those made up to 1942—with the exception of those automobiles considered classic. Then there are subdivisions of old cars according to era of manufacture—from the very early one- and two-cylinder cars of the late nineteenth century to the multicylinder super luxury cars made into the first half of the 1920s. Certainly these two kinds of car are radically different.

It might be easiest to use the 1925 cutoff year as a general part of the definition, and then make certain exceptions. Within the category of cars made before 1925 we might divide the cars into (1) general categories of cars and (2) market preferences for these early cars. For instance, in the early sports cars, the antiques, two make and model cars stand out—the Mercer Raceabout and the Stutz Bearcat of the early teens. These are in a category by themselves. They are very similar as far as construction and performance go, and they were turned out in the same era. They form a category of antique cars of their own. There are other very similar cars, like the Simplex in the Smithsonian Institution and the early Packard Speedster, but these two cars are in a different category from the point of view of the market. The market *vastly prefers* the Mercer and the Stutz Bearcat, and the price of these cars has reflected this preference through the years. They are higher in price by far than almost all similar cars of the period, and they do not often come onto the market.

These are the categories of antique cars that I will use:

1. The early sports cars—Mercer Raceabout and Stutz Bearcat
2. The somewhat similar early sports cars

3. The *pioneering* one- and two-cylinder cars (and a few fours) of the late nineteenth century and early twentieth century
4. The simple cars of the first two decades and a few to 1925
5. The big multicylinder cars of the first two decades and to 1925
6. The "transportation cars" of the 1920s like the Flint and the Jewett
7. Rolls-Royces of the Silver Ghost model
8. The Model T Ford

The Pluses and Minuses of Collecting Antique Cars

1. Antique cars are, in general, low in price, and later I will discuss exactly why they are low and which cars are particularly low. In the January 1983 Barrett-Jackson auction there was a 1912 Ford Model T roadster in very good condition that went for $14,500. In the Grand Old Cars Museum auction of the same month and year a 1912 Ford Model T Speedster in splendid condition and with a fine red paint job brought $18,500. A 1908 Hupmobile roadster in class 2 condition brought $12,000. The car was driven onto the auction platform on its own power and sounded fine. In general, classic cars cost far more.

2. Most of these cars need restoration, which can cost a great deal. During the war a junker Mercer Raceabout was bought for $25. It was totally restored to mint condition. What would the restoration job cost today? Its present value is $150,000. At any rate, a restored antique usually does not cost as much as one would have to spend to put an antique in poor or average condition into good condition.

3. The supply of these cars is small. There will certainly be bargains. Still, the downside risk is minimal in antique cars because many are relatively low in price.

4. Preferences for antique cars may remain constant over the years; not so for other categories of collector automobiles, such as classic or special-interest cars.

5. The price trend of antiques is up, but not very sharply. This is the general rule—the classics outperform the antiques in steepness of price rise.

6. Parts are extremely hard to find in antiques. Sometimes unique firms like Hoffman and Mountfort of England produce a batch of scarce parts like Bentley pinion gears (and I have seen the excellent products they make), but parts are, and always will be, a headache.

7. Most antiques cannot be used for transportation, probably not even for a short Sunday drive. They are fragile and cannot keep up with the traffic on any road today. They are thus hazardous to drive.

8. Suitable storage space must be found for these cars, and this may not be an easy job. Wherever the car is parked, people are apt to open its doors, open the hood, crank it, etc., and even a door opened too often may give problems. So the cars must be well protected.

9. There is not a very large collector market or investment market for these cars.

10. It is hard to build prestige with these cars. The Clenet, the elite convertible, will probably do a much better job along this line!

11. Antiques, the ones with few cylinders, are unique, and the automobile authority in England, Michael Sedgewick, sums them up in this way: "To a great many people, car enthusiasts and collectors included, the primitive cars are not automobiles at all, and for that reason demand for them is limited."

When one looks at an early Rolls-Royce Silver Ghost he often wonders how it rides and drives. When he looks at a Peugeot of the late nineteenth century he tends to think of it as a museum object and not so much as something to ride in or drive. It is something that sits rather than goes!

The Early Sports Cars: Mercer Raceabout and Stutz Bearcat

The Mercer Raceabout and the Stutz Bearcat are very similar cars—big four-cylinder cars, fast for the time, with a minimum of bodywork and no top. A circular glass "monocle" was used for a windshield. Both cars were glamour machines when they first appeared and they have remained such ever since. The Raceabout was first produced in 1911, but by 1920 a completely new car was produced. The early cars seldom appear on the market but the later models often do. There is a world of difference in the price of the two models; the early model is preferred.

The Stutz Bearcat appeared in 1914, and by 1923 this early-model car had ceased to be manufactured. I remember a neighbor of ours who owned this car when I was in school in 1928. It was almost fifteen years old at the time but it created a sensation when it roared along the highway, as did a Mercer Raceabout that was parked outside my school.

One can pore over the early issues of the *Antique Automobile* of the Antique Automobile Club of America or the *Bulb Horn* and the *Horseless Carriage* of the 1950s and find few or none of these great cars offered for sale. In 1932 I found a magnificent yellow Stutz Bearcat for sale for the then huge price of $200, and during the war one of the early members of the Sports Car Club of America restored a wreck that he bought in a junkyard—a Raceabout—and then offered it for sale in about 1945 for the enormous sum of $7,500.

In 1969 a Mercer Raceabout was recorded to have been sold for $20,000, a prime-condition car. By 1970 the Mercer had risen only slightly in price, and only one was recorded by Quentin Craft as having been sold. A 1914

Stutz Bearcat was recorded as sold for the same price, $21,000, a car in comparable condition.

In the following year a Mercer Raceabout apparently sold for the very much elevated price of $40,000. A Stutz Bearcat in comparable fine condition sold for $22,500, very much under the Mercer.

The next year the Stutz Bearcat may have risen to $25,000, but the Raceabout probably didn't rise from its then lofty level.

By 1974 the Raceabout was up to about $45,000, but a fine-condition Bearcat sold for $51,000—above the usually preferred Mercer Raceabout.

By the middle of the car boom of the 1970s the Mercer Raceabout in top condition was up to $75,000 and the Stutz in comparable top condition was up to $50,000.

By 1976 one top Raceabout apparently sold for $125,000, but a prime-condition Bearcat sold for half that price—$60,000. For the next year the Raceabout held at about the same level, but two very good (but not mint) Bearcats were recorded to have been sold for $45,000 and $37,500.

In 1979 a Raceabout was reported sold for $160,000, a nearly top car. A perfect Stutz Bearcat apparently went for $65,000. In 1980 the Raceabout stayed about at its very high level but the Bearcat had risen to $85,000.

In 1981 there was perhaps a slight drop in the very high price of the Raceabout, to $140,000, and the Bearcat was at $72,500.

In 1982 the Raceabout was at about $150,000 and the Bearcat was at about $75,000. It is expected that as of the latest year the Raceabout is up to about $150,000 and the Bearcat is not far under this figure. The market is somewhat up as of 1984.

Other Early Sports Cars

To the Mercer Raceabout and Stutz Bearcat aficionados there are probably no "other early sports cars." Still there were, and are, cars with comparable looks that do appear on the market from time to time, and they probably merit consideration because of their antiquity, their similar rakish lines, and their price in comparison with the very high present market price of the preeminent Raceabout and Bearcat. It is also possible that these automobiles will rise in value simply because they relate to the Mercer and Stutz. I, certainly, would look at them.

One such comparable early sports car is the 1913 Simplex 75-horsepower chain-drive roadster with an enormous 10-liter four-cylinder engine. (One such car is in the Briggs Cunningham Automotive Museum in California and another in the Smithsonian Institution in Washington, D.C.)

Another car is the 1914 Apperson Jackrabbit. Another is the 1907 Buick Model S roadster. The 1913 Cadillac roadster is in something of the same class. The 1914 Overland Speedster is more certainly in the class of the Mercer and Stutz, as is the beautiful 1911 Stoddard-Dayton Racer.

I cannot trace prices of any one make and model through the years, because too few of any one make and model were sold in the period I reviewed, but we can get a very good idea of trends of these antique sports cars by noting various ones that sold each year together with their prices.

We might start with 1955, a year before antique cars became in demand. A 1916 Crane Simplex six-cylinder seven-passenger touring car (Berline) with Derham body was for sale for $1,050. To be sure, the car was not the famous speedster model, but it was a Crane Simplex and a desirable car.

In the same year a Pierce-Arrow Model 38 C-4 runabout, "beautifully restored," was for sale for a bid over $2,500, and this was a car that was in many ways comparable to the Bearcat and Raceabout. We can get an idea of values of collector cars at the time by noting that in 1955 an L-29 Cord phaeton was for sale for $1,850. The car might sell for $75,000 today. Of course, Duesenberg at the time was "way up" to over $3,000.

Two years later a Cadillac roadster of 1912, fully restored, was offered for $2,750. A 1912 Simplex Model 38 sport touring car, driven only 5,000 miles, was for sale for $4,500. Of course in the same year a 1929 Mercedes-Benz SS roadster with Corsica body was for sale for $2,000, a car that today would sell for possibly over $200,000. So antique sports cars were not all that low by comparison.

In 1960 a Buick 1908 runabout, unrestored but in very good condition, was offered for $2,000. A Buick 1915 torpedo roadster, restored, was offered for $1,500. A 1905 Pope Toledo race car was also offered for $2,500—a car in "running shape."

In 1965, five years later, prices were up. A 1909 Stevens Duryea runabout, restored fifteen years earlier, was for sale for $7,000. A 1912 Speedwell, "restored and complete," was for sale for $6,500. A Hupmobile Model 32 roadster, a 1913 car, was for sale for $4,000. A 1912 SGV sport roadster, completely rebuilt, very much like the great Mercer Raceabout, was for sale for $5,500.

In 1970 an American La France 1924 Speedster, "excellent," was for sale for $3,250. This was in many ways a car comparable, at least in appearance, to the Bearcat and Raceabout. A 1910 Locomobile Model 30L was for sale for $25,000, and this car was a comparable car. In fact in the same year a Mercer Raceabout was offered for sale for $22,000.

By 1975, five years into the car boom decade, prices were up, as was to be expected. A 1914 Buick Runabout roadster, restored six years earlier, was for sale for $12,500, and this was not the greatest or most-wanted car.

In the Leake sale held in Dallas on June 1, 1975, a 1919 Pierce-Arrow Dual Valve Roadster brought the substantial price of $17,500. This was a more sophisticated car than the Raceabout and Bearcat but not a great deal more. It was certainly a car of quality equal to the Bearcat and Raceabout.

A car made earlier than the Raceabout and Bearcat came up at auction at Geneva, March 20, 1975, a 1905 Mercedes 40/45CV two-place roadster, four-cylinder and 6,800 cubic centimeters. It had no top or windshield, and this was the way the car was made. It was in apparently fine condition, fully restored, and it brought the then high price of $22,000.

In the same sale a car comparable to the Stutz and Mercer did appear—a D.F.P. E4 Series E roadster sport two-place 1-liter 600 of 1910, a four-cylinder car. It was in excellent condition and brought $7,900.

At about the same time a 1910 Overland roadster 90% restored was for sale for $7,500.

In February 1979, Christie's in California sold the Bud Cohn Collection. Lot 49 was a National 1913 Model 40 two-passenger sport roadster, four-cylinder and 7.3-liter—a big-engined car, excellent in appearance and condition. It brought the high price of $40,000.

In 1980 one of the great speedsters was offered for sale, a 1911 Simplex Speedster, for $40,000, about the price to be expected at the end of the decade of the big price rise.

In 1980 a splendid very early sports car was offered for sale, a 1906 Packard Model S Runabout, for the not small sum of $60,000, but well under the Mercer Raceabout.

In the same year a 1914 Apperson Jackrabbit in fine condition brought $28,000, and a 1907 Buick Model F Touring Runabout brought $18,500.

Two years later, in the recession, prices were not down but up. A 1910 Reo Model R of 30 horsepower was offered for $30,000. A 1916 Scripps-Booth Model C3 Cloverleaf roadster was offered for $20,000, and a 1919 Cole Arrow Eight Speedster was for sale for $28,000—not quite comparable to the Mercer or Stutz.

In 1983 a "Mercer-type" car was for sale, this one a 1909 Buick big 50-horsepower T-head Model 6 or 7 with an old restoration. The price was $17,500. A 1910 Hupmobile runabout in "excellent" condition was for sale for $14,000 and a 1913 Metz roadster, "completely restored," for $16,000.

Two 1914 speedsters were for sale, an Abbott Detroit Model G roadster, six-cylinder, for $27,500 and a Grant Model M roadster for $16,000, the Grant being fairly rare but not the best car ever, at least in my experience. A 1917 Reo four-cylinder roadster was offered for only $5,995.

Collecting the Early Sports Cars

1. By almost any standards the early sports cars are good-looking, which can hardly be said about the primitive one- and two-cylinder cars.

2. The cars are good mechanically and rugged. They thus require a min-

imum of maintenance and relatively few replacement parts—unlike the present-day competition cars with four overhead cams and six carburetors.

3. The cars can be run, at least on occasion. Most of them can keep up with turnpike traffic and not beat themselves to pieces.

4. They seem "underpriced," starting with the Mercer Raceabout at $150,000 and the Stutz Bearcat at a little less. This is about the price of a new Rolls-Royce Corniche and less money than an early Rolls-Royce Silver Ghost. The early sports cars other than the Raceabout and Bearcat seem very much underpriced, and even today they do not seem to be priced in accordance with the other collector cars.

5. The Mercer and Bearcat are very salable, and dealers and auctions will take the cars and generally advertise them, so they are relatively liquid.

6. It is entirely unlikely that they will decline in value. There is no element of fad in these cars.

7. The investment is not the greatest, so many can afford to buy such cars, particularly the less-known early sports cars.

One- and Two-Cylinder Cars of the Late Nineteenth Century

These are the very primitive first attempts to produce an automobile in the last century and in the beginning of the present century. They are a breed all their own, and they are, in general, hardly usable for any purpose except specialist rallies and displays. In some ways they seem to be bargains. They are rare, but they do not seem to bring the huge sums of money that many other rare and good collectibles bring.

We might in the case of these primitive cars move from the present back, as far as values go. One standout pioneering car I saw in mid-1983 was a Peugeot two-cylinder of 1894. One wondered, when he looked at the car, whether it could ever be used to transport anybody anywhere—it was that primitive. It did not use spark plugs but rather a gas burner that was always on. This was called a hot-plug car; the flame was "pushed" into the combustion chamber when it was necessary to ignite the gas at the top of the compression stroke. The car needed complete restoration, which its owners, Coys of Kensington, could no doubt arrange. The price was £30,000 (about $45,000). For this type of car the price was not low, but the car was very early and unusual.

A little earlier a less illustrious early car was sold by Christie's in its England sale, an 1896 Whitney 4/5-horsepower two-seater Stanhope, for £11,000 ($25,000). Steam cars, even early ones, do not seem to command the high prices that the gasoline cars do; a Stanley Steamer of 1899 was reported to have brought $16,000, a car in fine condition.

In the summer of 1982 an early car was advertised for sale for the high price of $58,500—an 1896 Lutzman Model Arrow One, four-horsepower, one-cylinder.

If we go back a few years to the February 25, 1979, sale of the Cohn Collection in Los Angeles by Christie's, an epic car sold—an 1893 Benz 1½-horsepower Velo two-passenger Sociable. This was a trophy-winning car in the great London-Brighton Commemoration Run in 1975. It was used in the Daimler-Benz seventy-fifth anniversary celebrations in 1961. In the 1979 sale it brought $65,000—a price that seemed low for the historic importance of this car. It was one of the earliest of all automobiles still in operable condition.

In 1979 an 1899 De Dion–Bouton 3½-horsepower Type D four-passenger Vis-à-Vis was offered for sale by Christie's in Madison Square Garden in October 1979. It was estimated to bring $30,000 to $40,000 but was withdrawn prior to the sale.

If we move forward just a few years and down a few notches in quality, a 1903 Humberette one-cylinder two-seater was sold by Christie's in Beaulieu, England, for £7,000 (about $14,000). The car had not been run for nineteen years, while the De Dion–Bouton had successfully competed in the 1967 and 1970 London-Brighton Run.

When one combs over past sales of the real antiques, the cars seem very scarce. If we go back to 1975, halfway into the boom decade of the 1970s, we find a restored 1899 Decauville 5 CV Vis-à-Vis four-place selling in Geneva by Christie's for $6,000. In the same year the same auction house conducted the Beaulieu sale. A 1900 M.M.C. Princess four-seater Victoria, two-cylinder, with overhauled engine, sold for the equivalent of $10,350—4,500 guineas.

We hardly need to move back in years prior to 1974 to arrive at the period in which the true antiques were selling at low prices compared with almost any group of collector cars. In Christie's Beaulieu sale of 1972 one car in particular was featured in a full-color photo—a 1903 Panhard et Levassor 10-horsepower rear-entrance tonneau with four-cylinder engine. It competed several times in the London-Brighton Run with no trouble and was a fairly good-looking five-seater. It brought the equivalent of $16,800, and the make was very important.

In 1974 also an 1896 Leon Bollée 3-horsepower tandem tricar sold for the equivalent of $7,680, a famous make and a very early car, a one-cylinder machine. The car was described as "excellent."

In the same 1974 Beaulieu sale another preeminent car sold for the equivalent of $8,400—a 1901 Clement-Panhard 4½-horsepower Stirling "Dog Cart." It was a one-cylinder car with rear-mounted engine. The car had not run in fifteen years and the condition was described as "fair."

In the same sale a unique vehicle sold for the low price of $2,880—a

1903 Humber 2 3/4-horsepower Olympia tandem tricar, a single-cylinder with a motorcycle frame but with two wheels in front of the handlebar in front of which was a big wicker seat for two people. The "car" was in the 1967 London-Brighton Run.

In Christie's March 1974 Geneva sale, several pioneering old cars were auctioned, and this sale represented something of a low point for this type of collector car. An 1897 De Dion–engined 1 3/4-horsepower light two-seater car in relatively good condition, although not run for some time, brought £3,380 pounds—$8,100.

Another De Dion–engined car, this one an 1899 (circa) with front and rear seats, single-cylinder, but not in running order, brought only £2,535. A 1901 Dumont single-cylinder rear-entrance tonneau, in generally good condition although not run in a long time, brought another low price— £2,394, or $5,700.

In the United States in 1970 the oldies brought little or nothing, unless extremely eminent or great cars or both. A Schacht of 1898–1902, a runabout, was offered for $2,500. In 1970 a 1903 single-cylinder Cadillac was advertised for $6,500.

If we go back to 1960, a fine-condition, restored De Dion–Bouton of 1898 was for sale for $3,000. A 1901 two-cylinder 12-horsepower Panhard-Levassor was offered for $3,000 and a 1901 De Dion–Bouton single-cylinder 8-horsepower in "excellent condition" for $3,500.

In 1957 a great, rare, and "almost new" car, a Larraine-Dietrich limousine, was for sale for the then big sum of $8,500. But a 1900 Loco-mobile steamer, fully restored, was offered for $2,500. A 1903 one-cylinder Cadillac was offered for $5,000. In 1955 an unrestored 1903 Cadillac was offered for "best offer over $3,500." A 1903 Humberette was for sale for the low price of $1,200.

Buying a Pioneering Car

1. The pioneering cars do not have the same strong uptrend in prices that most of the other types of collectible cars had in the decade of the 1970s. As late as 1975, prices of these early one- and two-cylinder cars were not high. From 1977 on, prices were certainly not strongly up, and from 1977 to the past two or three years the prices of the pioneers more or less stabilized.

2. In the last two years, prices have resumed their upward direction, but not strongly.

3. The "new" buyers in the market do not seem to be interested in the earliest cars, probably because there is no element of nostalgia in these cars for them.

4. Very few of these cars come onto the market, and when they do, demand is not great. Should demand increase just a little bit, prices would have to rise, because of the limited supply of these cars.

5. The cars cannot be run very much at all. They are far too slow to keep up with any traffic, and they are very hard to keep running. Repairs are hard to secure, and so are parts.

6. The cars are more or less museum pieces to be kept in a display area of one's garage, or even in one's house, or possibly lent to a car museum.

7. It is just possible that demand for these small old cars will never approach the demand for the big, impressive multicylinder cars of the immediately following era.

The Simple Cars of the First Two Decades

A large number of collectors concentrate on the simple (or simpler) cars produced in the early part of the century and up as far as the cutoff year of 1925, when another category of automobile—the "transportation car"—came into existence.

In this section we are considering cars that were, and still are, somewhat unique, not necessarily the important pioneering cars of the late nineteenth century and early twentieth century, but interesting cars of the early part of the century through the decade of the teens and a little later.

Four examples of the "simple cars" are the curved-dash Olds of about 1903, the Maxwell two-cylinder of about 1909, the Sears high-wheeler of about 1907, and the Schacht high-wheeler of the early years of this century.

Everything about these four automobiles is similar—from price pattern to the appearance to mechanics. The so-called curved-dash Olds was put out from 1901 to 1906. It was a one-cylinder car that looked like a carriage without a horse in front, and its price new was the same all through its history—$650. The car was made in some volume and appears on the market fairly frequently. This is the price pattern of the car:

Curved-Dash Olds Prices

1957	$2,250
1960	2,900 (completely restored)
1970	4,000
1975	6,500
1980	10,500
1982	15,000

The Sears high-wheeler was a very similar high-wheel buggy type of car put out in generally the same era as the curved-dash Olds, just a few years later. It is not as popular in the market as the Olds and generally sells for less than the Olds.

Sears High-Wheeler Prices

1955	$1,000
1957	2,600
1970	2,500
1975	7,500
1980	9,000
1983	12,500 (restored)

Between 1957 and 1970 the price of the Sears certainly did not decline. The car was simply not in the greatest demand, and a market price was not as determinable as it was in other makes of collector cars.

The Schacht was put out in the same era as the Sears, but it was a more sophisticated "primitive." It was also a high-wheeler. It had a two-cylinder engine. Since there are quite a few of these Schachts, they come onto the market from time to time, very often in fine condition.

1905 Schacht runabout, which brought $8,500 at a Christie's sale in 1979. The value of the car today is probably $15,000. Some of the early cars are among the most reasonably priced automobiles available. (Christie's, New York)

In Christie's Bud Cohn sale of February 1979, a fine-condition 1905 Schacht sold for $8,500, and this was about market price at the time.

The early Maxwell is on the market in some volume and has come onto the market fairly regularly in the past. The Maxwell of the last part of the first decade of the present century was a more sophisticated car than any of these cars already described. It was not a "buggy without the horse in front." The hood was in the front, and many of the models had a windshield and top. It looked like an early ancestor of the cars of the 1920s. It had a two-cylinder engine and could do 30 mph on the highway.

Schacht High-Wheeler Prices

1957	$ 775
1970	2,500
1975	3,700
1980	9,200
1982	9,000

Early Maxwell Prices

1955	$1,650 (perfect)
1960	1,750
1965	3,750 (restored and excellent)
1970	2,000
1975	9,000
1980	10,750
1983	16,500

I know this car pretty well as a "fish that got away." It was put up for sale in 1965 for $1,200, a car in restored condition and priced under the market.

These four makes of car are on a rung below the epoch-making, pioneering cars of the latter years of the last century. At the same time they are not the more sophisticated cars of the first two decades of the present century. Still, we are talking about a very diverse group of antique cars in this general group, and generalization is very hard. For instance, there are plenty of early Cadillacs for sale, but there are also plenty of buyers. A 1903 roadster will sell for over $16,000. A 1905 four-cylinder touring car will sell for over $20,000. The 1910 and 1911 tourers will sell for $25,000. Many Cadillacs up to and through 1920 will sell for $20,000, and prices seem to cluster around this $20,000 figure.

On the other hand, the 1909 De Tamble, a car that often appears on the market, sells for half this figure. The Italian Fiats from 1909 to 1915 are much wanted and sell for $30,000 to $35,000. At the 1982 antique fair at Casale di Scodosia in Italy, not far from Padova, I saw a very early Fiat closed car offered for about $40,000. The early Franklins from 1905 to 1911 sell for $20,000 to $25,000.

When we get into the big names the early cars can bring more money. A 1910 Hispano-Suiza tourer can sell for $50,000 and more if in fine condition. An Isotta Fraschini of 1910–1915 can bring $40,000 to $45,000. A 1906 Mercedes double-chain-drive seven-passenger touring car in fine condition brought $85,000 as reported by Quentin Craft.

But to get back to the simpler early cars, an Orient Buckboard of 1903 can bring $9,000 to $9,500. The above price curves pretty well represent the earlier simpler cars, the cars without the biggest names.

The Big Multicylinder Cars of the First Two Decades

There is a vast difference between the simpler cars of the early twentieth century and the multicylinder cars. These latter are the big, important luxury cars of the era, and they are the cars of the well-to-do collector today. In general these big, sophisticated machines do not go cheap. We are not talking about the great cars of the first two decades—the Rolls-Royces, the Hispano-Suizas, the Isotta Fraschinis, the Mercedeses—but there are plenty of other makes that are important collector cars and are becoming more important each year.

If we go back to 1957 we find some of these more important, bigger early cars selling for substantial sums, not the lower prices realized by the simpler cars of the same era. A 1909 White steamer Model 0 in "number one running condition" was advertised for the big sum of $16,000.

A 1900 Larraine-Dietrich limousine was offered for $6,500. This same car may have been advertised earlier for $8,500.

At the other end of the price scale for big important early cars was a Packard Twin Six of the first year of manufacture of this model—1915—"asking $4,000." A 1914 Renault Big Six convertible sedan was offered for $1,750. Both cars are much sought after today.

For comparison purposes a Mercedes-Benz SS with Corsica roadster body was offered for $2,000 (we have cited this car before) and a 1931 Bentley Eight Liter Gurney-Nutting coupe for $980, a car that today might bring $98,000 or more—a hundred times as much.

In 1960 a 1913 Renault five-passenger tourer, "restored," was offered for $4,950. A 1917 Crane Simplex five-passenger tourer, "excellent," was for sale for $4,500. At about the same time a 1919 Cadillac Type 57 phaeton in "show condition" was offered for just $1,000. A 1916 Crane Simplex six-cylinder seven-passenger soft-top Berline with body by Derham was for sale for $1,050, a car from a famous collection in Chicago. A 1911 Delauney-Belleville six-cylinder, "like new," from the same collection, was for sale for $3,200.

A great car was offered for sale in 1960—a 1917 Pierce-Arrow Model 48 six-cylinder tourer, for $4,800, not much by today's standards but not cheap as of 1960. For the same price a 1914 Renault tourer, "restored," was for sale. Still, for about the same price an open 1910 Cadillac could have been bought, "engine rebuilt and restoration nearly complete." The body could be converted from a touring car to a roadster by removing the back seat. A 1915 Cadillac Model 51 seven-passenger tourer was for sale for $2,800.

By 1965 a really important car was offered for sale, a 1909 Napier seven-passenger six-cylinder car, unrestored, for $10,000. A 1907 White steam roadster was for sale for $9,000, a Model H.

In the same year a 1917 Packard Twin Six seven-passenger touring car, "fair original condition," was for sale for $5,500. A 1915 Crane Simplex, "restored like new," was for sale for $6,500.

The Model 48 Pierce-Arrow had caught on in the market by 1965, and a first-place winner, a tourer, was for sale for $12,000.

A 1910 Thomas Flyer, a great car on today's market, a 6–90 roadster, was for sale for $6,500; but an important-looking 1914 Renault town car was offered for $3,500, a car that looked very good in the illustration in the ad.

By 1970 the really important collector cars had caught on, and prices were very high for the time, and for today's market too. A 1919 Locomobile dual-cowl phaeton with a Farnham and Nelson body, "fully restored," was priced at $55,000. A 1913 American Underslung touring car, Type 56, in show condition apparently, was for sale for $40,000.

Still, in 1970 not all prices were high for the big important cars of the early part of this century. A 1918 Cadillac, an eight-cylinder seven-passenger tourer, was for sale for $6,500. Of course, this was the exact model I had bought in 1929 for $25. By 1970 the Crane Simplex was up to $10,500 and the Pierce-Arrow Model 48 to $14,000.

Five years into the classic and antique car boom and the Crane Simplex was up to about $25,000, the Pierce-Arrow Model 48 to $18,000, the Packard Twin Six to $20,000, and the early Cadillac V-8 of 1915 to just under $20,000.

The real standouts were going up in price very rapidly. A 1917 Winton Big M five-passenger four-cylinder, "mint," was for sale for $45,000.

By 1980, the end of the decade of big boom, the Crane-Simplex was in the $40,000 to $45,000 range. The Pierce-Arrow Model 48 was selling for around $40,000, the Packard Twin Six at the same level, and the early Cadillac V-8 at $21,000 to $23,000. A 1917 Locomobile six-cylinder seven-passenger touring car, "rebuilt completely," was for sale for $34,500. On the low end of the price scale was a 1908 Delauney-Belleville, "restored," for $12,000.

As of now the Crane-Simplex is about at its 1980 price. The Model 48 Pierce-Arrow may have gone up $1,000 or $2,000. The Packard Twin Six may have backed off by about $5,000, to $35,000, and the early Cadillac V-8 is about at the same level as a few years earlier.

In early 1983 the antique car market was not strong in America. In the January 1983 Barrett-Jackson sale a 1919 Hispano Suiza in reasonably good condition reached a high bid of $40,000 and no more, and the car looked very good. A 1915 Simplex tourer reached $42,500 and also did not sell.

The "Transportation Cars" of the 1920s

At the Beaulieu, England, collector car "complex" there is a car that visitors can drive around a course for a small fee. This is a 1927 Jowett two-cylinder touring car. Its value is about £3,200 to £4,000 ($4,800 to $6,000). It is a plain little car, not luxurious, not very fast, hard-riding and a bit hard-driving. Its main quality is that it is "old," or at least somewhat old.

In the 1981 Christie's Los Angeles sale was a 1923 Nash Model 691 five-passenger six-cylinder touring car. It was in good running order, and the paint and interior were fair. It had big disc wheels. The car was neither good-looking nor bad-looking. It was essentially a piece of transportation for the middle-income car buyer of 1923. It was estimated to bring a price of $12,000 to $14,000. It brought $7,500.

These two cars are typical of the great group of "transportation cars" that are always on the market.

1923 Nash Six Model 691 Five Passenger Touring Car, in good running order, but with paint and tires in only fair condition, was bid to $7,500 at auction in 1981. The estimate was $12,000–$14,000, but the market was softening. Cars of this kind and model are not in great demand. (Christie, Manson and Woods International, Inc.)

These are the cars that went at giveaway prices relatively few years ago. We might start by tracing the prices of one such car, the 1921–1923 four-cylinder Essex. I bought one of these cars in very good condition in Deep River, Connecticut, from a garage owner in 1931 for $35. I immediately drove it to Washington, and although I had tire troubles, I had no mechanical troubles. I drove back and forth several times to Washington and drove to school and about town every day. I kept the car for two years.

In 1968 it was a quoted collector car and it sold for about $1,000 if in reasonably good condition. In 1969 the car might have brought $1,500, but the open car sold for about $2,500, double its value of a year earlier.

In 1970 the two-door coach like my car was selling for about $3,500 and the tourer for a few hundred dollars more, a very high price at the time, a price a Mercedes-Benz 300S cabriolet or roadster in very fine condition would bring then.

By 1975 there was absolutely no upward movement in the price of this car despite the fact that most collector cars were in a boom. In fact, the Essex four may have declined in price.

By 1980 the coach was up to $5,000 but the touring car of 1921–1923 was up to about $10,000. From 1980 to 1983 the price of this car didn't seem to move up at all. It may have been a situation in which the price of the car rose too far too fast and the quality was not there to back up the market price.

I have selected three cars that I classify as "transportation cars" for price trend and to verify the slide in price (or price plateau) of the early 1980s.

The first car is the Buick 1923 six-cylinder touring car, one of which I purchased in 1930 for $35. I liked this excellent car (I was "brought up" in a relative's 1919 Buick six touring), and although it was not in the fine condition of the 1919 car, it ran and gave very little trouble.

Now by 1969 this model car was up to a high $3,000, more than it would have taken to buy a 1951–1955 Mercedes-Benz 300S cabriolet or convertible. Here is the price trend:

1923 Buick Six Touring Prices

1969	$3,000
1970	4,000
1975	9,250
1980	19,000
1983	16,500

My next selection is a less renowned automobile, but comparable to the 1923 Buick, a 1921 Studebaker Special Six touring car. This car was the same in each of the years 1921, 1922, and 1923. My car was a 1921 model, in fair condition, and it was purchased in 1928 for $15, a fair price at the time.

1921 Studebaker Special Six Touring Prices

1969	$2,500
1970	2,500
1975	5,100
1980	15,000
1983	13,500

Prices of this car proceeded much as the Buick's did from 1969 to the present. It is also interesting to note that in the early 1980s the price was off as it was in the Buick.

The third car is a 1928 Chevrolet coach, the two-door model. This was no luxury car. It was a workhorse and not highly styled. It was the last of the Chevrolet fours and was succeeded by the very much more advanced six-cylinder car of 1929, which my family owned. I could compare the 1928 and the 1929, since I spent many hours riding in the 1928 four. This is the price trend of the 1928 coach:

1928 Chevrolet Two-Door Coach Prices

1969	$1,150
1970	2,100
1975	4,000
1980	7,000
1983	6,200

The four-cylinder two-door Chevy coach is obviously a less desirable collector car than either the 1923 Buick or the 1921–1923 Studebaker. The chassis and engine were more rudimentary and the Chevy was a closed two-door car, not the generally more valuable touring car. I have deliberately chosen this prosaic car to see what the price trend is for an ordinary "transportation car" of the 1920s. The price did rise to $7,000, a collector car price. It also dropped back in the 1980s as the other two cars did. I did not choose these cars to show the drop in the early 1980s. This is simply the way the figures developed.

When I say "transportation cars" I am talking about the average-to-good automobiles of the 1920s used for transportation by people with low and medium incomes. These cars too have risen in price along with the important collector cars. On the other hand, they may in some ways resemble the "go-go" stocks of a stock market boom, those stocks that are carried upward with the important stocks in the high-tech field or the advanced retailing field or whatever field or fields seem to be booming in recovery periods and in prosperity periods. Then when a reaction sets in it is often the go-go stocks, selling at 50 to 100 times annual earnings, that plummet. These transportation cars did not plummet by any means, but they did slacken off, and they did not keep up with the leaders in collector cars—the Rolls-Royces, the Mercers, the Mercedes-Benzes, the Packards. As collectors became more discriminating they tended to buy the important collector cars and to shy away from the simply "older cars."

No doubt in our big amorphous group of transportation cars some will emerge as real collector cars and their prices will rise. Right now it is hard to tell which such transportation cars may move into new and significant collector car groups and rise in price. One should, however, look for quality of the car, beauty, rarity, high price, and luxury status when the car was new, and increasing interest in the marketplace as evidenced by a price trend that is picking up.

The Rolls-Royce Silver Ghost

The Rolls-Royce is possibly the biggest seller in the entire field of collector cars. More Silver Ghosts by far are offered for sale than Model T Fords. In fact, in the really important collector auctions there are probably more Rolls-Royce cars offered for sale than all models of Ford—Model T, Model A, and Ford V8. In England and on the Continent, Rolls-Royces predominate at the auctions.

The Silver Ghost spans the years in which the automobile was developed—almost from the start up through the years in which it developed into both a useful and dependable vehicle and at the same time an ultimate luxury. Rolls-Royce stood, and still stands, at the top of the quality and luxury pyramid.

The Silver Ghost represents the "one-model" policy of Rolls-Royce, and for many years the Silver Ghost was the "one model." The Silver Ghost is a flathead (side-valve) six-cylinder car. The car first appeared in 1906 with a big 7,036-cubic-centimeter engine and weighed a fairly light 2,464 pounds for the chassis. In 1909 the size of the engine was increased to 7,428 cubic centimeters and the chassis weight to 3,800 pounds. In all, 6,173 Silver Ghosts were made from 1906 to 1925, an incredibly long life span at a time when automobile technology was developing rapidly. Electric starting was introduced in 1918, fairly late, and four-wheel brakes were installed early, in 1924. Otherwise the car remained very much the same throughout its life. I will say, however, that as time went on the car became more sophisticated and modern-looking, and it also drove in a more refined manner. In the 1930s I

1921 Rolls-Royce Silver Ghost, with Labourdette body, that brought $60,000 at Christie's Leake sale in Arlington, Texas, in 1974. The car might bring $175,000 today.

remember driving a Silver Ghost tourer of the late teens. It was noisy and fairly hard-riding, and it was a job to change the gears without a clash. In 1959 I rode in a Silver Ghost taxi of the 1920s, a cab that was constantly in use. The ride was soft and the engine was smooth and quiet. The same car could be used today for a taxi. It was that refined an automobile. In 1959 the taxi company used only Silver Ghosts in its fleet of cabs.

No matter what year the Silver Ghost was, at the outbreak of World War II it had little value unless, perhaps, it was an exemplary model or a historic car. For $100 one could have bought a very good Silver Ghost of the teens.

In 1983, Coys of Kensington, London, offered a Silver Ghost touring car that had been owned by an Indian maharajah. The price for this 1913 car was £100,000—over $150,000—even though it was not exactly one of the earliest Silver Ghosts. The same firm had another 1913 Ghost for sale, this one having belonged to C. S. Rolls himself, a roadster with a platform behind the one seat for carrying a hot-air balloon. (Mr. Rolls was a balloon enthusiast.) Three of this model car had been made, and the price in 1983 was £85,000 ($130,000), which seemed low for the appearance and near-perfect condition of the car plus its historic association.

One can make an inverse correlation between year of manufacture of the Rolls-Royce Silver Ghost and the price. The earlier the year the higher the price, and as we approach the earliest year of manufacture, 1906, the price skyrockets. The Silver Ghost tourer painted silver, the very early car that is frequently used in films and in illustrations, would probably be worth at least

$500,000 on the market. All Silver Ghosts of the first decade of the century are in more or less the priceless category today.

On the other hand, very fine classic Silver Ghosts in good condition, cars of the 1920s, often seem to go surprisingly low. At the Barrett-Jackson sale of January 1983, a 1923 sedan in class 1 condition achieved a high bid of only $31,000. I examined the car and it was as classified. On the way to the auction platform, however, the plug in the bottom of the carburetor bowl fell out and was lost, so the car had to be held up a long time before it could move to the auctioneer under its own power. Had the car been an open car instead of a four-door conservative sedan, the high bid would no doubt have been higher. In the Leake auction of 1982 a class 2 1924 touring car sold for $51,000.

In the July 1982 Christie's sale at Beaulieu, England, a 1922 four-seater Silver Ghost tourer with body by Haywood of Wolverhampton was sold for £16,000—about $25,000, not a big sum for this car. The car was in good condition, but the body, although certainly not new, was not original, although it was an attractive design.

In the sale of the collection of Rolls-Royce cars owned by Mr. Tony Frey by Christie's in 1980 a superb early Rolls-Royce Silver Ghost brought the equivalent of $150,000. It was a 1910 seven-passenger limousine with body by Fuller of Bath. It was a car used in rallies, a car in excellent condition, and an original car, not an altered car.

In the same sale for $40,000 one could have bought a 1920 sedan de ville with body by Hibbard and Darrin of Paris. It had been altered over the years and was not in prime condition, but it was a very good-looking car.

The unique car of the sale was not a Silver Ghost but an earlier Rolls-Royce, a 1905 30-horsepower six-cylinder roadster with body by Jarvis of London, a very attractive and very early Rolls. The car brought only about $116,000 because when it was found in Australia in 1957 it was very nearly a wreck and required extensive rehabilitation, including the manufacture of many parts. The restoration job was superb, but the car is to a degree non-original. Had it been original and in top condition it should have brought $250,000.

In London in December 1979, Christie's auctioned a 1921 torpedo tourer for £30,000—about $66,000 for a fairly good-looking low-mileage open Silver Ghost.

If we move back five years we find much lower prices. In Christie's March 1974 Geneva sale a 1922 sedanca cabriolet for six by Hooper brought £9,859—about $23,000.

In the 1974 Leake sale in the United States a reasonably good-looking 1921 seven-passenger double cabriolet brought $38,000. The car was almost entirely original and completely restored.

In the 1974 Beaulieu sale three superb Silver Ghosts were sold. The first was a 1912 seven-passenger enclosed-driver limousine with Mulliner body "in outstanding condition." The interior and coachwork were restored. The car brought $45,600.

A very good-looking 1920 five-passenger torpedo tourer with Barker body brought $33,600. The car was apparently in excellent condition.

The best Silver Ghost, however, was a 1915 London-Edinburgh four-seater sporting torpedo with Wilkinson body. Although the car, including body, was excellent, the body was a reconstructed one. The price was $62,400.

If we move back to 1970, the year the car boom started, the Silver Ghosts of the teens were selling for about $30,000, cars with open bodies and fine appearance. The cars of the early 1920s were at about the $20,000 level, and the latest-model Silver Ghosts were at about the $10,000 level. An immaculately restored 1914 town car was for sale for $14,500.

If we go back five years to 1965, prices were very much lower than they were in 1970. A 1913 semi-boattail roadster was for sale for $8,750. In 1960 a comparable car, a 1913 Mulliner town carriage in concours condition, was offered for $6,750. A 1922 tourer with Grosvenor body was for sale for $6,000. A 1923 Brewster-bodied cabriolet was offered for $3,750.

In 1955 the Silver Ghost had hardly started up in value and a 1924 car, a Locke four-passenger tourer, "generally restored," was for sale for $2,350.

In 1950 many Silver Ghosts were at the "nothing level." A 1922 Silver Ghost coupe was offered for sale in a publication of one of the car collector clubs for $385. It was about at this time that the Edward VIII special-bodied Silver Ghost was offered to me for $1,200, a streamlined car built for the king, a car with oval doors. It was bought by the collector Max Obie, who displayed it in a special booth at various exhibitions for many years. He restored this unique car completely.

So we have a very gradual uptrend in the prices of Silver Ghosts. We find almost no pre-1910 car for sale, but the later cars rose from a few thousand dollars to perhaps a peak in 1977 or thereabouts. Then interest in the Silver Ghost seemed to flag and the prices of this model Rolls-Royce seemed to slip, and they have not recovered.

Investing in a Rolls-Royce Silver Ghost

1. In many ways the Rolls-Royce Silver Ghost exemplifies collector cars, particularly the antiques. If one knows little about antique and classic cars or their prices and price trends he might well concentrate on buying a very original, good-looking Rolls-Royce Silver Ghost in very fine condition. It is a conservative investment that is moving up fairly steadily in price.

2. The Rolls-Royce Silver Ghost had a setback in price in the late 1970s, but not a serious setback.

3. Prices are firm and are likely to move up in the future.

4. The Silver Ghost can fairly easily be maintained, and parts are available, although sometimes they are expensive.

5. A poor-condition Silver Ghost should be avoided, as elaborate restoration can be extremely costly.

6. There is a fairly readily determinable market price for the Silver Ghost, and auctions and dealers want the Silver Ghost to sell, particularly the cars with attractive bodies and in good condition.

7. The cars can be driven. They are rugged and reliable and not temperamental.

8. The Silver Ghost is a Rolls-Royce and an impressive prestige collectible car.

The Model T Ford

At one end of the collector car scale is the Rolls-Royce and at the other end the Model T Ford. The Rolls-Royce was the ultimate in quality and prestige. The Model T was the cheapest possible piece of transportation, designed and built to make Americans "wheelborne." The quality that sold

1916 Ford Model T touring car which would value today at about $15,000. (Christie's, New York)

the car was simply transportation at a price many people could afford. The price was achieved through mass production and assembly-line operation. Henry Ford was a bug on economy and volume.

The car was simple in almost every way. The windows were opened and shut by means of a belt attached to each window, not a windup handle. There were certainly no four-wheel brakes—only one brake on the driveshaft plus an emergency brake that operated on the two rear wheels. There were only two forward speeds and no clutch, only friction bands that moved the car when the driver pressed down his foot and tightened them up. The reverse was by another pedal. There was no accelerator on the floor, only on the steering column, so that the driver always had one hand, or at least some fingers, on the lever to the right of the steering column. On the left side of the steering column was another lever, this one for the "spark." It was an advance and retard lever. There was no automatic advance and retard. The later cars had starters, but they were not very powerful, and so a crank was fitted in front of the engine as well as a choke, in addition to the choke on the dash.

The car usually started in the morning, except in cold weather when the oil was thick. Then sometimes one had to build a bonfire under the crankcase and also pour boiling water over the intake manifold so the gasoline would vaporize.

The bands in the transmission frequently wore out, resulting in no brakes, no reverse, and no low gear—or at least not all of these necessary elements. But new bands, a set of all three, often could be bought for $1.75, and sometimes this $1.75 included installation by the garage. Repairs were very little and parts almost at a giveaway level.

While Rolls-Royces possessed beautiful bodies or quality coachwork, the Model T Fords were standard, and all black. The roadsters were all alike. So were the touring cars, the standard model car. A few speedsters were available, but these were specials and, as far as I know, never manufactured by Henry Ford. So we do not have the job of trying to compare a Barker-bodied landaulet with a Hooper-bodied tourer in Rolls-Royce.

In 1930–1932 a good Ford open car could be bought for $5, and at that price one had some choice. Of course the car might have cost $250 new or even more—up to $460. The last Model T that I owned was a 1925 touring car, and this car listed new for $290. I bought the car in 1929, in fine condition, for $35. I didn't have to spend a nickel on restoration.

All Ford Model T cars are more or less alike. They all had four-cylinder engines that produced about 22 horsepower. The engine had approximately the displacement of the engine in the Ferrari 250GT, only the Ferrari engine produced 240 horsepower. Between October 1908 and May 1927, just over

1912 Ford Roadster Model T which sold for $14,500 at the Barrett-Jackson auction in 1983. (Julia Rush)

15,000,000 Model T Fords were produced. Then the company turned to the Model A. The time span of the Model T Ford is not so different from that of the Rolls-Royce Silver Ghost—1906 to 1925 (and a few made in 1926).

The price trend of the Model T Ford is not very important, because even today we are not talking about any sizable investment. Only the very earliest Model T's are at any significant price level. In the Grand Old Cars Museum auction in Arizona in 1983 a fine-condition speedster painted red, a 1912 model, sold for $18,500, and this was a "special," not a production car. At about the same time the Barrett-Jackson auction sold a 1912 roadster in class 2 condition for $14,500. The Kruse Arizona auction at about the same time sold a fine 1911 roadster for $11,500 and a fine 1914 roadster for $9,900.

The same auction sold an average-condition 1927 roadster, the last year of the Model T, for $4,700, and this was certainly about market price for a late and average Model T.

The year before, many Model T Fords were sold, and this was about the price range depending on year of the car:

1909 touring	$17,000
1912 roadster	11,750
1923 roadster	8,500
1926 touring	6,500
1927 touring	5,500

These are actual selling prices for particular Model T's at auction, cars in good condition but not necessarily Grade 1 cars.

If we move back to 1975, prices of Model T's were lower but were by no means at the giveaway level. A 1920 custom-bodied speedster, professionally restored, was for sale for "offers over $3,200." A 1923 speedster, "professionally restored," was for sale for $2,600. Two early touring cars were for sale—a 1911 touring car for $5,000 and a 1914 tourer for $4,500. Still, even in 1975 there was not an enormous price distinction between the early and the very late Model T's, and the 1927 tourers in top condition were bringing, at times, just under $5,000.

In 1970 a 1914 tourer, restored, was for sale for $3,000 and a 1921 for $2,500. The 1926–1927 open cars were at the $2,000 to $2,500 level. In 1970, however, these prices might have secured a good Mercedes-Benz 300S cabriolet or convertible.

Even in 1965, five years earlier, Model T's cost at least something. A 1915 touring car, "excellent," was offered for $2,200. A 1922 tourer, "excellent," was for sale for $1,500 and a 1923 tourer for $1,150. My Mercedes-Benz 300S roadster cost at this time $800. Of course, it was in need of restoration.

In 1960 a prizewinning, completely overhauled 1918 tourer was for sale for $1,850. A 1915 roadster was priced at $1,750 and another 1915 roadster, "restored," at $850.

In 1957 a 1915 "restored" Ford was offered for sale for $800. A 1923 tourer in "A-1 condition" was offered for $400 and a 1922 roadster, "completely restored," for $400. At this time a Mercedes-Benz SS roadster with Corsica body was for sale for $2,000.

Investing in a Model T Ford

1. There are many Ford Model T's on the market, or potentially on the market.

2. Still, the price of the Model T is rising—not as fast as some other collectible cars but rising nevertheless.

3. The Model T can still be bought for a reasonable sum—under $5,000 for a late one and something over $10,000 for an early one.

4. If at all possible, Model T Fords made prior to 1910 should be located.

5. Condition of the car is important, but not all-important. All parts can be secured easily, and the cars are not hard to work on.

6. The cars do not have to be babied or stored as carefully as, say, a Duesenberg Model J or a Ferrari.

7. The cars can be driven fairly regularly. They are not inclined to break down or deteriorate rapidly.

8. The only trouble with regular driving is that they will do only about 45 mph flat out. They go up steep hills rather slowly, and one must sometimes change into the only other forward gear.

9. The steering is direct, and there are transverse springs, so if one whips around the wheel too sharply he might turn over. I have.

10. The investment is small and it is conservative, and more Model T collectors are coming into the market every year. The car has great nostalgia value.

11

Special-Interest Cars, Prewar and Postwar

A FERRARI 1960 250GT coupe in excellent condition is priced today at $18,000. The car is, in many ways, perfection. It looks good, drives extremely well, and is excellent mechanically.

A 1934 Ford roadster in exactly the same condition may very well sell for the same amount—$18,000. It too is a good car, is well made, has power, looks good, and is desirable.

While I have owned both of these cars and have had many years of enjoyment driving both, one can hardly compare a 1934 Ford that sold for $525 new with a 1960 Ferrari that sold at about $10,500 new. One was a well-made utility car with some sportiness about it. The other was a strict sports car of very advanced mechanical design.

Yet today the cars sell for about the same price. There is certainly no shortage of either car on the market. In fact, there are far fewer Ferrari 250GT convertibles on the market than 1934 Ford roadsters. The explanation of the relatively high price of the 1934 Ford is that a lot of people want the 1934 Ford roadster and, at least at the present time, are willing to pay somewhere around $18,000 for it. At the Grand Old Cars auction in January 1983, held at Apache Junction, Arizona, a 1934 Ford roadster sold for $30,000, not $18,000. To be sure, it was in mint condition, but $30,000 is a lot of money for a 1930s Ford of any description and very much above the market price of a Ferrari 250GT coupe of the late 1950s and early 1960s. In fact, for $30,000 one could easily have bought a Ferrari 250GT convertible, not just a coupe.

Now to turn to the special-interest cars. A 1933 Chevrolet sport coupe in excellent condition, can be bought for $10,000, a car that cost $535 new, while a new Aston Martin may have cost new twenty times this figure. James

Bond (007) cut a fine figure in his Aston Martin that would sell today for $10,000.

In analyzing automobiles as collectibles and as investments one must recognize *what is*, not what might be or what should be. Maybe a Ferrari is a vastly better car all around than a 1934 Ford, and maybe an Aston Martin is better than a 1933 Chevy coupe, but market price is what we are interested in, not abstract judgments.

In very early 1983 many of the segments of the collector car market were dead, or very nearly dead, and a sale in which only 40% of the cars auctioned actually found buyers was very acceptable from the point of view of the collector car auctions. When, however, a good special-interest car of the prewar period, or of the immediate postwar period, came up a lot of buyer interest appeared, and we have the situation in the Grand Old Cars auction in Arizona in January 1983 in which the 1934 Ford Roadster brought $30,000. When the 1934 Ford roadster sold for $30,000, far above any reasonable estimate of what it would bring, the audience, mainly dealers from all over, clapped. They didn't comment that the car wasn't worth that much.

"Special-interest cars" is a very satisfactory designation of this category of collector-investor car. The cars have attracted some special interest. The Duesenberg and the Packard V-12, two examples of great collector cars, *are* great cars. They are classics, and they stand out in almost any collector's eyes as prime cars, fine pieces of machinery with beautifully designed bodies. Special-interest cars, at least as we have used the term, are not necessarily great collector cars. They may not be particular standouts as automotive design goes. They are simply automobiles that have attracted buyer interest.

Perhaps time will prove them to be great cars, but for now it is sufficient that the market recognizes them—by high prices.

Top Prewar Special-Interest Cars

Ford Open cars, 1931–1940

Ford convertibles, roadsters, and touring cars of this period are extremely popular and, if in good condition, almost always bring high prices—from the low five figures to about $30,000. If I had to pick the *most* popular Ford of this period and the highest-priced car I would select, at least tentatively, the 1934 Ford roadster. We are of course talking about a car in excellent to mint condition. In fact, one has only to see a fine-condition 1934 Ford roadster in an auction to be fairly certain that it will achieve a high bid or an actual high sales price. In 1982, Ford roadsters of 1934 sold for $18,500, $20,000, $24,500, and $30,000—all at the major car auctions. A convertible brought $18,000.

The 1935 model was also popular in the marketplace, and a roadster of this model year sold for $18,750.

The convertibles of 1936 were more popular with the buying public than the 1936 roadsters, and two convertible sedans brought $19,750 and $25,500. Convertible coupes with rumble seats brought $15,000, $15,500, and $24,000. Two phaetons brought $14,600 and $20,750. The rest of the years of the 1930s up through 1939 were less popular, and prices did not run in general in the five-figure range.

If we go back from the "banner Ford classic year" of 1934 we find 1933 roadsters sometimes selling in the low five figures. In 1932 both a four- and an eight-cylinder car were turned out by Ford. The four-cylinder car of this year was essentially the same as the famous Model A, only it was called the Model B. Two Model B four-cylinder roadsters sold for $18,000 and $22,000 at the major auctions. A V-8 roadster sold for $27,500, and one sold for $19,000. Phaetons sold for $10,000 to about $27,000.

The last of the Model A's were turned out in 1930 and 1931. These were reliable, simple automobiles, and I went to high school every day in a 1930 model. In college I bought a fine 1931 deluxe Ford convertible with rumble seat for $35. In 1982 a 1930 convertible brought $14,500 and roadsters brought $8,000 to $13,000. These were, of course, all Model A four-cylinder cars. The 1931s ran higher and were a more elegant car with a more artistic radiator. Two rumble-seat convertibles brought $12,500 and $13,000. A standard phaeton brought $14,000, but a two-door phaeton brought the large sum of $28,250. Many roadsters of the year 1931 were sold, at least twelve, and these ranged in price from $7,600 to $17,500. In all, twenty-three roadsters were offered for sale by the major auctions and about half of them actually found buyers.

The number of Ford cars of the 1930s up until the war cut off car production was enormous, and the number coming up today in classic car auctions is still enormous, even though the cars are about half a century old. They are popular and they almost always seem to bring high prices. In the Ford cars of the 1930s up until the war, buying interest always seems to be present, at all major auctions.

Chevrolet, 1931–1932

The Chevrolets of 1931 and 1932 were very smooth-running and smooth-looking cars for the period and for inexpensive cars. Chevrolet came out with its six in 1929. I owned one of these early sixes and it was a most satisfactory car. Ford was still putting out its Model A four-cylinder car and even continued this more or less out-of-date car into 1932, when the Ford V-8 was introduced.

The 1931 Chevrolet open cars were pretty cars, and they ran well. In 1982 one of these cars, a rumble-seat convertible, brought the big sum of $24,500, and a deluxe phaeton brought $21,000, also a big sum. The 1932s were even more stylish with their hood panels instead of the customary hood louvers and resembled the Cadillac V-8 of 1932. When these panels were plated the car had a very fine appearance. Several of these 1932 open cars were offered for sale but the owners wanted close to $20,000 for them, or above $20,000 in general. One phaeton did sell for $15,000. From 1933 up until the war the Chevies were not nearly so popular as the Ford V-8's, and far fewer Chevies came onto the market.

Buick, 1940–1941 and the 1930s

One of the most desirable of the prewar special-interest cars, and at a favorable price, is the 1940 and 1941 Buick convertible. Mechanically this car is excellent. I ran a 1940 sedan for many miles during World War II. It is also a fairly good-looking car, and finally, for what it is, it can be bought with limited cash outlay. I prefer the appearance of the 1940 car, particularly the convertible, and for a short time I owned and ran a 1940 Buick Special convertible, not as good as the Super, but good nevertheless. In the Grand Old Cars Museum sale of 1983 a 1941 Buick Special convertible sold for $11,100. A small collector of cars in Connecticut bought such a car in 1981 for $3,500—a steal! During 1982 another 1941 Special convertible sold for $9,100. Two Roadmasters were offered for sale, big convertible sedans, and they had reserve prices on them of $45,000 and $39,500, probably well above market, although both cars could have sold for well into five figures. Possibly they reached high bids of $42,000 and $28,000. The 1940 model may have been of smoother design, particularly the radiator, and it should sell for about the same price as the 1941 model. A Super convertible coupe of 1940 or 1941 should sell for about $15,000. A car in very fine condition might sell for as high as $25,000.

When we look at the Buicks of the 1930s the price of convertibles is mostly the same year by year. The top-grade convertible sedans and convertible coupes are generally at the $25,000 level. The lesser cars are at the $15,000 level. The 1933–1936 models are a little less popular. Then when we get back as far as 1932 we get to a fine-looking automobile, not far behind the much-wanted 1932 Cadillac. The 1931 Buick convertible is at about the same price, a wanted car like the Cadillac of the same year but at a vastly lower price level than the Cadillac. The Cadillacs of the years 1930–1932 are classics, and the V-16, a great classic, in the $200,000 range. In fact, almost all Cadillacs are now true classics rather than special-interest cars, and so are La Salles.

Top Postwar Special-Interest Cars

Special-interest cars of the postwar period are really where the action is in today's collector car market. These are the cars of the 1950s and 1960s, not the great and recognized collector cars like the Mercedes-Benz Gullwing and 300S cabriolet and roadster, not the Ferrari 275GTB-4 coupe, but the Fords and Chevies that collectors have decided in earnest to collect. *Motor Trend* magazine for February 1983 contains an article entitled "American Cars" and includes a 1955 Chevrolet Bel Air sport coupe and a 1955 Ford Crown Victoria, a two-door closed car, among those illustrated. The Bel Air coupe sold for $2,166 new and the convertible for $2,302. Neither car was a real pioneer like the early Fords nor a true sports car.

If it were not for these so-called special-interest cars of the postwar period the auction business for automobiles would be far smaller than it is today and there would be far fewer car collectors.

In the postwar period the cars that seem to me to be of the greatest collector (or buyer) interest are probably Chevrolets, *followed* by Fords—just the opposite of the situation with prewar special-interest cars. (Among "special-interest" cars I have not included such Chevrolets as Corvettes and Sting Rays. These are postwar classics and they are becoming more classic all the time and will undoubtedly continue to attract major collector interest.) What will happen to the special-interest Chevrolets we do not know, but right now these cars are extremely hot in the market and they account for a good many collector cars sold and a good many dollars of sales.

Chevrolets, 1955 to 1957

In Middleburg, Maryland, not far from Baltimore, there is a car shop that specializes in the repair and restoration of Chevrolets. The owner and operator of the shop, Mr. J. P. Bostian, was a Chevrolet owner. He seemed to prefer Chevrolets as his own transportation. And they were well suited for that. I drove them long distances when they were new—from New York to this restoration shop in Maryland—not as my own collectible car but rather as transportation to get down to the shop to see how work on my own collector cars was progressing.

Mr. Bostian's son, Rodney, still does my work as he has been doing it for the past thirty years. I asked him recently what he thought of the collectible 1955 and 1957 Chevies. He replied, "They are certainly good cars, but I don't quite see their tremendous popularity."

The fact of the matter is that these cars are extremely popular with collectors, and their price is anything but low in relation to their cost new and certainly anything but low on an absolute basis. The Chevrolet Corvair, the pioneering rear-engine car, can be bought for well under $5,000, for a fine-condition convertible. A Bel Air of 1955 certainly cannot be bought at any such low price if in good condition.

As in the case of so many other cars, the preferred collector car model is

The Chevrolet Bel Air hardtop of the mid-1950s is valued today at $15,000 in top restored condition. In 1970 it would have been valued at $1,000 or less. (Julia Rush)

the convertible. In 1981 and 1982 a great number of these cars were sold. The summary of sales for 1981 indicates that one Bel Air convertible of 1955 brought $15,900 and one brought $13,800. These were both prime cars. Lesser cars, cars in class 2 and 3 condition, brought sums below $7,000, and two sold for under $5,000. In all, twenty-three of these two model cars were offered by the major auction houses in 1981.

The much-illustrated 1955 Chevrolet Bel Air hardtop was in demand, but at prices lower than the convertible. In all in 1981 twenty-five hardtops were offered for sale, in all degrees of condition from mint to poor. The high-priced hardtop brought the big sum of $13,000, and from here prices ranged on down to $1,200 for a class 4 car—"Could be used as transportation. Needing paint or major mechanical repair." Such a job could cost up to $10,000 or more.

There is some reason for the immense demand for Chevrolet Bel Airs of 1955 and 1957. *The Great American Convertible* by Robert Wieder and George Hall has this to say about the Chevrolets of this period:

"In 1955, Chevy merged its early '50s rounded lines with the Ford strongbox look and came up with this. One of the most immensely popular American cars ever, the Bel Air was the mobile icon of youth for ten years. When new, it was an affluence car, but it was as a *used* car that it endured for a decade in persistently large numbers on the highways. With Chevy's first V-8 power unit, it was GM's definitive attempt to create a factory-built, all-purpose hotrod. It was considered perfection in design, and adolescents saved money for years for one. Bel Airs lent themselves marvelously to alteration and power-beefing, and with them customizing and street-racing came of age. It also became the first *cruising* car. Like the Mustang and VW, it defied obsolescence long after production ceased. The classic youthmobile, it went like a thief in the night and was *the* car to own among the *Happy Days* generation. Although all were hot, the 1955–1957 years were the apex, and now unique, since Chevy totally abandoned the design in 1958."

In all, thirty-one Chevrolet convertibles of the year 1957 were offered at auction in 1981 by the major auctions. Seven of these cars sold for $14,000 on down to $10,000, and not one of these cars was in mint (class 1) condition. No fewer than seventy-seven Bel Air hardtops were offered by major auctions, and those that found buyers realized from $11,000 for a class 2 car down to $1,600 for a car in need of restoration—class 4. Two-door sedans also brought good prices. In 1984 some Bel Airs topped $20,000.

While I have selected the two most popular postwar special-interest Chevies for price studies, there are still other Chevies that are in demand, too, although to a lesser extent (with the exception of the Corvette, Sting Ray, and a few other sports cars put out by Chevrolet). One such automobile is a 1948 Chevrolet convertible coupe in fine condition that was bought by a collector in 1983 for the "high price" of $7,500.

Ford Convertibles and Woody Wagons, 1946–1948

The postwar Fords in the greatest demand at the present time are the station wagons with wood and the convertibles (1946–1948). These cars are sold at tremendous premiums over other body models of the same years as well as Fords with similar bodies but of other years that are in demand.

The 1946 Ford super deluxe convertibles and Sportsman convertibles in grade 1 condition can easily bring $25,000 and possibly as much as $35,000. The woody wagons can bring $8,000 to $10,000.

In the next year, 1947, the deluxe convertibles in good to excellent condition bring $8,000 to $10,000. The woody wagons bring $10,000 to $12,000.

For the model year 1948 the price level of the convertible and woody wagon is about the same as for the 1947 model. The later postwar Fords and the earlier postwar Fords do not in general bring these high prices (with the exception, of course, of the Thunderbird).

Other Special-Interest cars to Watch

Chrysler, Prewar and Postwar

A great deal of interest has developed in Chrysler products, both prewar and postwar. Chryslers of the early 1930s are particularly sought after and high in price—not just the Imperials (great classic cars), which are often in six figures, but the lesser cars turned out in these years.

Recently a 1931 roadster, the eight-cylinder model, sold for $33,000. A 1933 coupe brought $12,900. Six- or eight-cylinder open cars of 1931–1933 can easily bring $25,000 to $30,000 if in prime condition.

A great deal of interest has developed in the later Imperial series and the 300 series of Chryslers of the 1960s, although prices are not at tremendous levels. Many classic car auctions offer such cars, some in fine original condition or restored. In the Grand Old Cars Museum auction in Arizona in January 1983, a Chrysler Crown Imperial convertible of 1961 brought $6,600, perhaps a bit above market. A 1965 300L convertible brought $4,700, again on the high side.

Another Chrysler product, the Plymouth, has also developed into a special-interest car, not a luxury car, but a well-designed economy car. The wanted prewar Plymouths are the 1931 and 1932 cars, particularly the roadsters. I didn't think the 1932 Plymouth roadster that the Connecticut policeman was driving was as fast as it was; otherwise he wouldn't have caught me!

The 1932 Plymouth open car in class 1 condition can easily sell for $20,000. The 1933 model sells for about the same figure, the 1931 convertible for a little less. Convertibles up to the war sell for up to $15,000 and sometimes a little more. In the postwar era the 1946, 1947, and 1948 convertibles are selling for over $10,000. From the year 1948 on, Plymouths are not in great demand at high prices.

Dodge 1930–1933 open cars sell in the neighborhood of $20,000 and a little more. The later open cars to the war period sell for around $15,000. The 1946–1948 open cars are around $10,000 if in prime condition, and from the year 1948 value falls off sharply and the cars are not in such great demand.

The 1930–1933 DeSoto open cars hover around $25,000. The later models up to the war are around the $15,000 mark, and no postwar DeSoto open cars seem in great demand or sell at prices in the five-figure range.

Ford's Other Special-Interest Cars, Prewar and Postwar

From the point of view of volume of sales, Ford's "other car" is Mercury, which first appeared in November 1938. It was essentially a Ford but with a different body. In price it stood between the Ford and the Lincoln, so that when the Mercury appeared the Ford Motor Company could cover the price ranges of most American buyers.

Over the years Mercury developed into a powerhouse, the horsepower rating going up as high as 375 for an ordinary production model, not a special. The mid-1963 Mercury Marauder had optional engines which produced up to 415 or 425 horsepower, so it was not quite an econobox.

As far as collecting goes, the Mercury bears the same relationship to the Ford as the Cadillac does to the La Salle. The Mercury tends to bring higher prices than the Ford of the same year and model. A prime 1939 Mercury convertible, the first series produced, can bring $30,000 and even more. The 1940 can bring about the same price and the 1941 only slightly less. The 1942 model brings at least $10,000 less.

In 1946 and 1947, Mercury produced the Sportsman convertible, which has turned out to be a collector's item and in prime condition can be sold for $30,000. Convertibles of these years are $10,000 cheaper. The convertible of 1948 is about at the $20,000 level.

In the January 1983 Barrett-Jackson sale in Phoenix, Arizona, a late-model Mercury, a 1952 Monterey convertible, sold for $14,500, a rather high price, especially when very few cars were being sold at all. In the postwar period interest dwindles off until the model year 1956, for which a Mercury convertible could top $10,000 if in fine condition, but after this few Mercury cars ever hit $10,000 at auction. The majority of these later cars sell for under $5,000 and many sell for under $3,000, particularly the closed cars.

In general, the Mercury has been a serviceable automobile and rather reliable—in that respect something like a Ford. On the other hand, one of

1952 Mercury Monterey, sold at the Barrett-Jackson auction in 1983 for $14,500. (Julia Rush)

three worst troublemakers I have ever owned (and I have owned in all eighty-eight cars) was a 1958 Mercury V-8 station wagon. One garage in Washington, D.C., saw me coming in for repairs with my Mercury and stated that it had a policy to do no work on the 1958 Mercury as it was too much of a troublemaker. Finally, however, I got the valves working on one of the two banks of four cylinders so that the car once again functioned on eight cylinders instead of four. At that juncture I sold the station wagon and was glad to get $200 for it, a seven-year-old car.

The Lincoln V-8's and V-12's are quality automobiles, almost all of them from the time they were built by Leland instead of Ford up through the model year 1960—at least. The Lincoln Continental, 1954–1957, was probably the last great collector car put out by Lincoln, and it remains a collector car. As time went by it did not sink into oblivion.

We are not talking about the great Lincolns here, however, but rather about the Lincoln Zephyrs. These were inexpensive cars ($1,275 when first introduced in 1936) put out from the mid-1930s to 1942. The engine, a very small V-12, was never particularly good, and some of them have been replaced with other sturdier engines in the Zephyrs of 1936–1942.

Whatever the shortcomings of the engine, the Zephyr is in demand in collector circles. The early cars all were apparently closed cars, the 1936 model, and these cars are not in great collector demand at the present, although mint cars can easily reach $10,000 and once in a while possibly a little more.

In 1937 a Zephyr convertible sedan was manufactured, and this car is in collector demand. In very good condition it can bring $15,000 and in mint condition $30,000.

In 1938 both a convertible coupe and a convertible sedan were turned out, and today the convertible coupe, mint, can bring $25,000 and the convertible sedan even more. In fact, all body models except the six-passenger sedan can bring $15,000 and up. Such is the demand for the Zephyr.

The convertible coupe and convertible sedan of 1939 in mint condition can both bring over $25,000, possibly as much as $30,000. One can pay $10,000 less for a convertible of this model year in "very good" condition. Mint condition brings a great premium. If we get down to class 5 cars, the bottom level, even convertibles can sell for under $2,000.

The 1940, 1941, and 1942 convertibles in mint condition all bring somewhere around $25,000. The Zephyr then disappeared from the new-car scene and did not emerge after the war.

The Lincoln Continental was put out from 1940 to 1942 and again from 1946 to 1948. This is not, in my opinion, a special-interest car, but an important classic collector car that is becoming more important and more in demand all the time.

GM's Other Special-Interest Cars, Prewar and Postwar

In a 1983 auction a 1954 Olds reached a high bid of $10,500 and did not sell, as $10,500 was not enough for the seller of the Olds. This was about market price on the 1954 Olds 98 convertible in mint condition, and this car was probably mint, although I did not see it.

In the postwar period almost all mint-condition Olds convertibles turned out from 1946 to 1950 bring roughly the same price—$12,000 to $15,000. The cars in poorest condition are in the $2,000 range.

From 1950 up to the end of convertible production in the mid-1970s, few Olds convertibles, even in mint condition, seem to have reached $10,000 at auction. After the 1955 model, prices of convertibles tend downward. The 1961 cars were at the $5,000 level, even mint cars, and by the 1975 convertible cutoff date they were selling for $4,000 or even less.

When we go back to the early 1930s we get pretty much the same picture that we do in the case of many, if not most, special-interest cars. There was special interest, and enough special interest to result in some substantial prices. The mint 1930–1932 convertibles are in the $25,000 price range, while the coupes are selling for around $10,000 or a little more. For 1933–1939 models the prices of fine convertibles are running around $20,000 or a little less. The 1938 L-38 eight-cylinder convertible is an exception and can bring, mint, $25,000. The 1940 Series 90 eight-cylinder phaeton and convertible in top condition can bring close to $30,000. So can the 1941 Series 98 convertible and phaeton.

In the postwar period the 1946–1950 convertibles in the best condition all seem to bring around $15,000. From 1951 on, prices rarely run as high as $10,000, and they decline slowly year by year, as I have indicated. So there is a sharp contrast between prewar and postwar Oldsmobiles.

Until the appearance of the high-powered models of the 1960s, Pontiacs in the postwar period were not, and are not, very popular special-interest cars. The 1946–1948 series convertibles in mint condition can bring close to $15,000, and the 1949–1950 convertibles close to $10,000. Nothing after 1950 is in great demand as a collector car except a very few of the late-model performance cars, and even these are not generally in the high-four-figure range. The 1947 Torpedo convertible and deluxe convertible can bring around $12,500—at any rate well over $10,000—and no other postwar Pontiac seems to reach this price level.

The Pontiac has been a utility car throughout its history, a good, reliable utility car, but, until the 1960s' big-engine cars, no great performers and with no important innovations in either mechanical design or bodies.

On the other hand, there are some prewar special-interest Pontiacs and some quite good-looking convertibles. The 1930 model can bring $15,000 to $20,000, but only the roadster and phaeton. A fine 1932 convertible can bring up to $25,000 and the coupe up to $15,000 if in mint condition. This same price level holds for the convertibles up through 1942, except that the later in the prewar period we go the lower goes the price—but only a little lower, the 1942 convertible selling, mint, for about $15,000.

The sport cabriolets of the early 1930s were, and are, very good-looking cars, and the V-8 engine was, and is, a good and reliable power plant. Pontiac simply designed a great many cars that turned out to be sought after by collectors.

Postwar Buicks

The postwar Buicks are not among the most-sought-after collector cars by any means, and most of them have not achieved the limited distinction of being special-interest cars. I have owned three postwar Buick convertibles, a 1947, a 1952, and a 1955. The 1955 was a very good car, and the transmission was far better than on the earlier cars. The 1952 and 1955 cars were our only cars for a while and drove beautifully.

The postwar cars rarely hit $10,000, even the mint convertibles. A few of the early postwar convertibles, through 1952, do run at times over $10,000, but not the later ones.

The big exception to this generalization is the Buick Skylark of 1953 and 1954. This was a very well-designed, rather sporty car, often painted bright red, that is getting to be very much of a collector's automobile. A mint-condition one sold in 1983 for $8,000. It is entirely possible that this car was sold under the market. A mint-condition 1954 Buick Skylark convertible can bring up to $15,000. A 1953 model might even bring a few thousand dollars more.

Some other Buicks recently sold include a 1975 Buick Free Spirit for $3,900, no great collector price, but about market for the car; and a 1969 Buick 225 Electra convertible in excellent condition appearancewise for $1,900, well under the $6,000 that a mint-condition car of this make, year, and model was bringing generally.

On the other hand, the prewar special-interest Buicks were going for much more money, a 1941 Buick Special convertible, selling for $11,100 and a 1937 Buick convertible sedan for $14,000.

Special-Interest Cars of Today and Tomorrow

In a sense a special-interest car is one that has not quite "made it" as a classic collector car but will sell at a premium over secondhand, maybe not as much as a true classic collector car, but a premium nevertheless.

The 1955 and 1957 Chevrolet Bel Air hardtop and convertible are most certainly special-interest cars. As time goes on probably these cars will be in the class of the Ford Thunderbird of 1955–1957, and these Thunderbirds are definitely collector cars.

But what about the six-cylinder Bel Airs of 1953–1954? The 1955 and 1957 V-8 Bel Airs were to a certain extent "bombs" and would perform well, even against the Ford Thunderbirds of the same era. The earlier six-cylinder cars weren't exactly bombs that would stimulate the imaginations of the youth, but they were fairly good-looking and extremely reliable automobiles. Maybe they will be among the special-interest automobiles of the future.

The 1955–1957 Thunderbird is a classic, not simply a special-interest car but a classic with value, and value that has persevered for several years.

But what about the Thunderbirds of 1958–1960? These are often called Squarebirds, as they seat four rather than the two that the 1955–1957 Thunderbirds seat. The 1955–1957 cars are neat, simple "packages" with a lot of get-up and go. The Squarebirds are bigger, bulkier, and heavier. They are far less like sports cars. Still, at an auction today when one of these later Squarebirds comes up for sale we look at it and begin to think, "Gee, that's a rather sharp car." Mint-condition 1960 Squarebirds *can* bring in five figures but rarely do. The later in year we go the less these later T-Birds seem to bring— in 1983 a 1964 T-Bird coupe brought just $2,400.

Collectible cars are products of the times. They are not absolutes and they by no means represent absolute and eternal values.

Advantages of Investing in Special-Interest Cars

1. The entire area of special-interest cars is a low-priced area, and almost anyone with expendable money can find some special-interest car within his means. For less than $5,000 one can easily find a good car.

The Grand Old Cars Museum sale in Arizona in January 1983 was a sale of cars from the museum, not a consignor sale. The first car to go was a 1968 Plymouth Fury III convertible in fine condition. It brought $2,200. The next lot was a 1968 Olds Cutlass convertible that brought the same price. Lot three was a 1968 Ford Mustang fastback that brought $2,650. The next lot was a Buick Electra 225 convertible that brought $1,800, and a 1970 Olds 442 convertible brought $2500.

Maybe these are cars of very limited special interest, but they were from the museum collection and in excellent condition. A few lots later a 1965 Cadillac convertible in fine shape (a special-interest car definitely) brought $2,900.

Still later the Chevy Bel Air convertible of 1957 brought a First-class special-interest-car price—$9,750. This was a prime special-interest car and it brought less than a number of Japanese econoboxes cost new—and could be used for transportation every day if need be.

2. There are probably hundreds of thousands of strict special-interest cars on the market or potentially on the market, and one should have little trouble finding a car that suits him. When I bought a car within the past few years I chose a special-interest car—a 1966 Mustang convertible completely overhauled. I paid $1,600 for it. Today it is a "classic," and at the January 1983 Barrett-Jackson auction the owner of one of these much-sought-after cars turned down $10,500!

3. If a special-interest car is bought with any degree of investment intelligence the car almost certainly will rise in value. A 1965 Chrysler 300 series convertible was sold at the Barrett-Jackson auction for $4,700. This is a fine-performing car and much in demand and it should go up in price as time goes on. The particular car sold here was in excellent condition.

4. Cars in excellent condition, even mint, can be purchased. Putting an average-condition car, almost any car, into mint condition can hardly be accomplished at under $5,000. Some of the special-interest cars that sell for a few thousand dollars have paint jobs on them that possibly cost $5,000. Perhaps the paint jobs were put on in low-cost areas or the owners knew how to paint expertly. If to the paint job one adds upholstery, carpets, chrome, top, and engine overhaul, $10,000 is not an unreasonable amount to pay for restoration of a special-interest car. In strict classic cars, top-notch restoration means top-notch prices, and a mint-condition classic usually goes at a disproportionately high price.

5. Because of the price range of these special-interest cars the market for them is very broad. It is sometimes possible to put the cars in a sale with no reserve. If they go lower than the owner expected that is no tragedy. It is a tragedy if the owner expected $250,000 minimum for his car and all it received as a top bid at the auction was $160,000.

6. There is a big risk that expensive cars will go down in value, at least temporarily. In 1980, Duesenberg J and SJ seemed to be the name of the game. Everybody wanted one of these greats. Next year everybody who wanted a J or SJ seemed to have one and the bidding dropped off—and so did the price. Likewise, 1981 seemed to be the year of the Ferrari, particularly the Daytona and the 275GTB-4. In 1982, Ferrari demand slackened off and prices flattened out.

The higher the price the greater the downside risk—in houses, in stocks, and in automobiles, among many other types of investments. There is little risk with low-priced special-interest cars. A $2,000 car doesn't offer much downside risk.

7. As a car develops into a collectible, price tends to rise. Gradually the car becomes more and more of a mature collectible, and as it does its price

curve flattens out. In 1970 the Mercedes-Benz 300S roadster (and cabriolet) wasn't much of a collectible. A good example could be bought for $2,000. My own 300S roadster was bought in this era for much less than $2,000. From that date, about 1970, interest gradually developed in the 300S until in 1981 a mint-condition car was in the $100,000 class. How much more will the car rise and how fast? A 1957 Bel Air convertible may well rise by a greater percentage!

8. Parts for many special-interest cars are available in many places and are relatively inexpensive. Try to buy a radiator star ornament for a Mercedes-Benz 300S convertible or cabriolet of the mid-1950s—at any price! Then try to buy the entire drive train for a 1955 Chevy Bel Air. One should be located in a day and at a reasonable price.

9. Many mechanics and body shops can work successfully on many special-interest cars. Many of these cars are essentially the same cars that mechanics have been working on right along. The Bel Air is a Chevy V-8. The Buick Skylark is simply another Buick with a fancy body. The mechanic and body shop should not charge premium prices for work on such cars.

On the other hand, how many good mechanics are there to work on a Lamborghini Miura? If I had to have my Lamborghini Miura engine overhauled I would have the engine removed and shipped to the shop of Bob Wallace in Phoenix. I would expect to pay a higher-than-average hourly charge for expert work. I would expect to pay far less per hour—and in total—for work on a Chevy Bel Air, and I know where I can get this work done well at $15 an hour.

10. A special-interest car can be run. The most expensive mint-condition cars can hardly be run at all. The superb Jackson Delahaye 1939 convertible with van den Plas Belgian body that sold in 1983 can hardly be run at any time anywhere. It was displayed on a turntable that operated electrically. It should remain on a turntable! It was perfection, and it can hardly be run at all if that degree of perfection is to be maintained.

On the other hand, a Bel Air convertible can be used, at least part-time. From time to time the paint can be touched up and the interior renewed. If the value of the car keeps rising, at some point a fine lacquer paint job can be put on the car and top-grain leather installed. The drive train can be completely overhauled. Then the car can be carefully stored and used only for very special occasions.

Disadvantages of Investing in Special Interest Cars

1. The *real* investment automobiles are classic and antique cars. At best, as far as investment is concerned, special-interest cars are "maybe" investments. *Maybe* a 1953–1954 Chevrolet Bel Air six will turn into an investment car.

A 1955 and 1957 V-8 Bel Air certainly is a special-interest car, but what will it be in the future? A true investment car like a 1955 or 1957 Mercedes-Benz 300S convertible or cabriolet? The Chevy of this era has a long way to go in order to achieve that status.

2. Prestige also exists only in the true classic or antique. A Bel Air hardtop is a fine automobile but hardly a prestige car for the more well-to-do collector. The 1938 Packard 12 convertible coupe is a prestige car.

3. The important classics and antiques are recognized as investments almost everywhere, both in the United States and abroad; not necessarily so with the special-interest cars.

4. The supply of classics and antiques is definitely limited, and hence price can hardly ever be low. Demand for limited-supply cars is usually very great. There were very few Mercedes-Benz 300S cars produced ever, yet many people are constantly interested in this car. Were it not for the fact that price is now about at the six-figure level there would be quite a scramble to buy up these cars in limited supply. While demand for special-interest cars may be great, it is usually not great in relation to supply, which is also great.

5. Restoration on special-interest cars is usually not hard to accomplish. Parts are often readily available, as is repair and restoration labor. In important classics and antiques, parts are often hard to come by and labor is hard to come by. A recent Lamborghini Miura overhaul cost $38,000, twice what the car cost new in 1967.

The real classic or antique is worth the price, because of the restoration cost that went into the finely restored car. The value is there because the funds went into the car. Not so with the special-interest car, which can usually be restored for much less money. In addition, the special-interest car is usually much newer than the true classic or antique and thus requires less restoration, and often less ground-up restoration. In fact, there are many special-interest cars available in original and fine condition.

6. The marketing of a true classic or antique is usually far easier than the marketing of a special-interest car. Try to get a dealer to buy, or an auction to sell, a 1965 Ford Thunderbird. There is usually little interest. But offer the dealer or auction a fine-condition Ferrari Daytona, particularly a convertible, and note the reaction. Dealers and auctions will reach for true classics and antiques, but not for special-interest cars.

7. The marketing costs of special-interest cars are often very high in relation to the cost or selling price of the car. One can afford to truck a Rolls-Royce 1920 Silver Ghost tourer from New York to Phoenix to auction. Trucking and insurance are not great as a percentage of the price the car will probably bring. Such costs are great for a car that may bring $4,000—a special-interest Squarebird, let us say. One trip to the auction and back and enough trucking and insurance will have to be added to the price of the car when next it is

offered for sale to make the necessary price of the car above the market. One might have to wait for years to make up the cost of such a shipment that did not result in a sale. It should be pointed out that *the rule* at classic car auctions is that the majority of the cars offered for sale do not find buyers. A sales percentage of 40% (with 60% of the cars unsold) is quite common.

8. If a person has a sum of, say, $100,000 to invest in a car or cars, it is almost certainly better to invest in one or a few more expensive "investment cars" than, say, fifty cars costing $2,000 apiece. One or two cars are more workable as collectibles than a lot of less expensive cars. The more cars, the higher the annual maintenance—for repairs, garage, insurance, etc.

9. If one can spot future classic cars in the special-interest category, cars that are destined to rise in collector interest and in price, well and good. But this process is like buying Xerox when nobody heard of the company; it is just as hard to pick a special-interest winner as it is a winner on the stock exchange. It is far safer, as well as more conservative, to pick an established classic or antique car.

Price Trends of Special-Interest Cars

Price trends over the years for special-interest cars, prewar and postwar, are difficult to determine. Some special-interest cars that are very popular and high-priced on today's market were not popular a relatively few years ago. In fact, as recently as 1970 prices of many special-interest cars were not recorded. The cars were considered too unimportant as far as the market was concerned, regardless of what intrinsic merit the cars may have had.

In special-interest cars the high risers pricewise are the prewar cars. There are, of course, many of these prewar special-interest cars.

I have selected sixteen cars for price tracing, but in 1968 there were recorded prices for only six of these. As recently as 1970, six of the make and model cars we were tracing had no price recordings or very doubtful prices recorded. It is only in the last few years that we can get a fair sample of cars sold and their prices. Most of the cars that we have traced were sold by private individuals or by used-car dealers, and the prices are recorded nowhere. We note, for instance, in 1981 a 1940 Buick convertible that sold for $15,000. The price of the 1940 model is not far different from the price of the 1941 convertible. In the same year, an excellent 1941 convertible was purchased for $3,500, and for another $1,000 the car would have been near mint; this is quite a distance from $15,000.

Fifteen years ago almost all of these cars sold for "what they would bring," and a 1934 Ford roadster might have sold in one place for $2,500 but in another place for $1,000. Recorded and publicized prices, for special-interest cars anyway, were not very well developed, so a seller was not aware of what his make and model had just sold for somewhere else, or even in his own city or town, for that matter.

With these limitations we might now proceed to present some tentative price trends.

One of the principal special-interest cars of the prewar era is the *1934 Ford roadster*, and this is the car that in January 1983 sold for a little over $30,000 at the Grand Old Cars Museum sale in Arizona, a mint car.

The earliest "collector car price" we have on this car is $2,500 in 1968. The next year a price of $3,500 was obtained, then $3,250, a slight drop into the recession of 1970. Five years later a price of $7,500 was recorded—five years into the collector car boom.

The second half of the collector car boom decade of the 1970s saw an even sharper rise in the price of the 1934 Ford roadster—to $25,000 in 1980, better than tripling in five years. In 1981 the price was still rising, to $27,500 in 1981; and from here the price rose to the $30,000 reached at the Grand Old Cars Museum sale. These are the percentages that subsequent years bear to the first year recorded of $2,500, and this $2,500 is made equal to 100%:

1968	100%
1969	140
1970	130
1975	300
1980	1,000
1981	1,100
1983	1,200

The *1936 Ford convertible sedan* has a very similar price pattern, in a sense proving out the price pattern and percentage of price increase of the 1934 Ford roadster. The 1936 rose from approximately $3,500 in 1968 to $4,000 in 1969 and then dropped a bit (as the 1934 Ford roadster did) to about $3,900 in the recession of 1970, then rose to $10,500 in 1975, to $19,000 in 1980, to $21,500 in 1981, and to $25,000 in 1983.

The *Ford Model B roadster of 1932* was the last of the old Model A Fords, and it was a "dressed-up" Model A. The first price we note is $2,500 in 1970, then $7,250 in 1975, and about $12,000 in 1980. From there the price rose to $25,000 in 1981, where it has remained more or less to the present. The Model B was a latecomer to the collector Ford price rise but it caught up in the 1970s.

The *Ford Model A convertible coupe of 1930* comes next in our price recordings. My "first recording" of this car was in 1932, when my next-door neighbor bought a mint-condition one for $385—hardly a collector car at that time, but a car in which I rode to high school every day.

To move up from ancient history, in 1968 this car brought about $3,000. By 1970 the price was somewhere around $4,400, but in 1970, in the recession, one sold for $2,650. By 1975 the price was way up to $6,250 and by 1980 way up again to $13,500. The next year the price rose about $2,000 to $15,500 and by 1982–1983 to $19,500.

The postwar Fords also had a sharp rise in price, at least the collector Fords did. One of the most popular postwar Fords is the *1946 Ford woody wagon.* The car was not especially popular before 1970, but a price of about $2,500 was recorded for 1969, and the price was the same in 1970. By 1975 the price rose a fair amount to $5,500, but five years later, by 1980, the price had exploded to $21,000. It rose to $22,500 in 1981 and to $25,000 by 1982–1983. It wasn't very much behind the 1934 Ford roadster.

The *Ford 1946 deluxe convertible* started out in 1969 at about the same figure, $2,500, but dropped to about $1,200 in the recession of 1970. By 1975 it was merely back up to $2,500, the price level of 1969. By 1980, however, there was an enormous rise to $12,500. There was a backoff to $11,000 in 1981 and then a rise to $14,000 by 1982–1983. It is possible that the price in the summer of 1983 was up another $3,000.

From the Fords we move on to the very important 1955 and 1957 Bel Air convertibles and hardtops. These cars were really nothing as collector cars even as late as 1970. In 1970 a *1955 Bel Air convertible* was reported sold for $700. Five years later the price was up to $3,250 and by 1980 to $8,250. By 1981 the price was $10,500 and by 1982–1983 to $13,000. It is possible as of summer 1984 for a mint-condition 1955 convertible to bring as much as $20,000.

Not many other of the collector Chevrolets were recorded pricewise before 1970 or even before 1975. In 1975 the *Bel Air coupe* sold for $2,250, compared with $3,250 for the same year (1955) convertible Bel Air. By 1980 the price of the coupe was up to a very high $6,100. The following year a price of $9,100 was recorded and in 1982 $10,000.

The *1957 Bel Air convertible* stood at about $3,750 in 1975 and by 1980 was up to $12,500. It rose just a bit to 1981 but by 1982–1983 was up to $16,000. A price of $19,000 may be the level of 1984.

The *1957 Bel Air coupe* is a little cheaper. In 1975 its price was about $2,600, and five years later the price had risen to $7,250. It was $9,250 in 1981 and $9,500 in 1982–1983. In 1984 it may even have reached $14,500.

We might finish up the postwar special-interest cars with the Buick Skylark and the Olds convertible of the same year, 1954. In 1969 the *1954 Buick Skylark convertible* might have brought $1,550 and in 1970 about the same price, say $1,500. Five years later prices rose to $3,600, but by 1980 the Skylark was a real collector's car at $12,000. A year later the price was $12,750 and by 1982–1983 $15,000. We always price top-grade cars. In the Grand Old Cars Museum sale of January 1983, a Grade 3 Skylark sold for $8,000. I couldn't quite agree that the car was a Grade 3; I thought it might be a bit higher.

We get few prices on the *1954 Olds convertible* until 1975, when a price of $2,800 is recorded. Five years later a price of $6,500 is recorded, then $7,100 in 1981 and $10,000 in 1982–1983.

From here we move on back to the *Buick convertible of 1940*, a splendid-looking car and a splendid-running car, another car I have ridden in and driven for thousands of miles. The question is, which 1940 Buick convertible? The answer is, not the Limited, which is very high in price, but rather the Super, or the Century. The Century is, however, very much higher in price than the Super.

In 1969 a price of $2,400 was recorded and $1,500 in the recession of 1970. The price tripled to $4,500 by 1975 and by 1980 the Super convertible was up to $9,500 but the Century was up by another $5,000. By 1981 the price was up a very big $5,500 to $15,000 and by 1982–1983 to $22,000. I saw a fine 1940 Century convertible coupe at the Barrett-Jackson auction that achieved a high bid of $20,000 for a car in class 2 condition, but the owner wanted more, and probably rightly so.

1933 Chrysler Standard Imperial convertible sedan, sold for $40,000 at auction in 1983. Value in 1970: $7,500. (Julia Rush)

We now move to the more popular Chrysler special-interest cars—not the great prewar classics but the special-interest prewar Chryslers.

The *Chrysler eight convertible of 1933* is the car I have chosen for price recording. It is a little more expensive than the six-cylinder convertible. In 1968 its price was about $1,000, possibly a bit more for the mint-condition cars. By 1969 the price was up to $3,450, although I am not sure this much rise took place. I prefer to think the $1,000 price for 1968 was unrealistically low. The 1970 price was the same as the 1969 price, but by 1975 the price had risen to $9,500. The car became a real collectible and by 1980 it was at $23,500. By 1981 it was at $24,500 and stayed at about this price for the 1982–1983 season. In the summer of 1983 the price might have been $2,000 more.

DeSoto was not the most popular car ever, but our early one, a 1929, was a reasonably good-running and good-riding car and fairly trouble-free. We have traced the *1930–1933 DeSoto roadsters* pricewise. In 1968 an average price was $1,600. In 1969 the price was $2,250 and in 1970 $3,250. By 1975 prices were well up to the $10,500 level. By 1980 this price had doubled to $21,500, where it remained for the next year, but by the 1982 year it seemed to decline to $17,500, an unusual drop for any special-interest car. By 1983 prices of $25,000 were recorded.

We have traced prices for still another car, this one the *Lincoln Zephyr convertible of 1937*. In some cases the year 1938 was used where 1937 prices were not available.

In 1968 this car could probably have been bought for $1,000. In 1969 the price may have been $1,500 and in 1970 $2,600. By 1975 the price had risen, but less than those of many other special-interest cars in this five-year boom period, to $5,500. But by 1980 it was catching up and stood at $17,000. By 1981 a price of $18,500 may have been the norm for a fine Zephyr and by 1982–1983 $21,500.

Price Summary, 1970–Present

Prices prior to 1970 for many special-interest cars, both prewar and postwar, were scarce. Twelve cars have fairly good and reliable price recordings from 1970 to the present. These cars are: Ford Roadster, 1934; Ford convertible sedan, 1936; Ford Model B roadster, 1932; Ford Model A convertible, 1930; Ford deluxe convertible, 1946; Ford woody wagon, 1946; Chevrolet Bel Air convertible, 1955; Buick convertible, 1940; Zephyr convertible, 1937; Buick Skylark convertible, 1954; Chrysler eight convertible, 1933; and DeSoto convertible, early 1930s.

These cars have these combined (added together) values year by year:

1970	$28,995
1975	76,350
1980	194,750
1981	225,750
1982–1983	259,500

With the 1970 combined price of $28,995 made equal to 100% these are the comparative percentages showing the level to which prices of the group of twelve cars rose since 1970:

1970	100%
1975	263
1980	672
1981	778
1982–1983	890

Prices as of 1982–1983 season were 890% of their level in 1970, almost nine times as high as they were at the beginning of the collector car boom of the 1970s. The error in this percentage is probably small, since twelve cars and their prices are combined in each of the years in which prices were recorded. The bigger the sample, the less the chance that it will be distorted by any one price that is not entirely representative of the particular make and model car in one year.

12

The Replicas and Throwbacks

AT THE JANUARY 1983 Kruse auction in Sun City, Arizona, a 1980 Tiger roadster and a 1980 Puma roadster were offered for sale. A 1979 Panther didn't find a buyer. A 1980 Doval speedster brought $29,500. A Mercedes SSK replica didn't sell, nor did a 1981 MG TD replica or an SS Jaguar replica. A 1980 Shay brought $10,250. A 1980 Gazelle sold for $7,000. A 1977 Auburn speedster replica brought $14,000 and a 1982 brought $19,000. Two other Auburn replicas failed to find buyers. A 1982 Mercedes-Benz SSK replica reached the high price of $45,000, but this sum was insufficient to induce the owner to sell. A 1982 AC Cobra replica did sell for $27,000. A 1976 Stutz sedan reached a high bid of $31,000. A Mercedes-Benz 540K replica reached $36,000. A 1980 Kelmark roadster and a '79 Blakeley Bearcat didn't find buyers.

Many of this special type of car, sometimes called the elite car, are emerging into the category of investment automobiles. The specials and the replicas are maturing rapidly, and in another five years maybe even the purists will be interested in "taking a flyer" on one of these cars.

The big trouble with these specials is that they are still imitations of the real thing—and at very high prices at that! They are modern cars, even though they are intended as copies of the greats of the prewar era.

The original Mercedes-Benz S and SS of the late 1920s were temperamental and hard to drive. One had to hold on to the steering wheel with some determination. They rode hard, and they required a good deal of attention. In a way the 500K and 540K of the mid-1930s were no easy cars to maintain. They were frequently in the shop for repairs. Today those repairs would cost a big sum if the cars were used for transportation, and there are relatively few mechanics expert on the prewar Mercedes—even if all the parts were available, which they certainly are not.

Now, if I could drive a genuine original Mercedes-Benz S, SS, 500K, or 540K with ease and with the knowledge that I would be able to get to my destination without a breakdown, I would be happy to own and drive one. The elite cars, the copies of the great prewar cars, overcome the difficulties of owning and maintaining the original cars.

The elite cars are not yet sure investments. The sports cars and luxury cars of today, the postwar classics, and the prewar classics are all advertised in the automotive and sometimes in the public press, particularly Rolls-Royce and Ferrari. *Hemmings Motor News* has thousands of advertisements, some with pictures, of classics and special-interest cars—but very few elites. The elites are put out by very small companies, many of which are in shaky financial condition. One has almost to check monthly to see which of the makers of the important elites are still in business. Small companies are obviously not in any position to advertise, and so the public has not yet become aware of the cars, not even the important cars like the Clenet and the Excalibur.

Vague Replicas

There are a number of elite or special cars that have a vague resemblance to classic cars, usually those of the 1930s. They are very often called by the name of the car they are supposed to copy, but they are different, not only mechanically but in appearance as well.

The leading car in this category is the Excalibur. The car goes back to the automobile designer Brooks Stevens, whose name is known to almost every postwar automobile fan and collector. In 1962, Stevens designed what he called the Excalibur SS, a car with a body resembling that of the Mercedes-Benz SS and SSK of the late 1920s and early 1930s. The chassis was Studebaker. The car went into production in 1964, and Mr. Stevens secured several

One of the replicas offered at the 1983 Barrett-Jackson auction was this Excalibur. Top bid on any Excalibur was $23,500. (Julia Rush)

dozen orders when the car was exhibited at its first motor show. These shows of specials and new cars were prevalent in the 1950s and 1960s.

With the demise of Studebaker in 1966, Stevens switched from Studebaker mechanical components to Chevrolet Corvette components. After the initial design and initial production he took over the firm of SS Automobiles, Inc., to make the new car. The price of the first cars was $7,500, and two models were made, an "SSK-type" two-seater roadster and a four-seater tourer. While the roadster resembled an SSK, the tourer didn't do any more than recall the Mercedes-Benz cars of the late 1920s to the viewer, if he was familiar with these original cars.

By 1970 the price of the Excalibur new had risen to between $12,000 and $15,000, by no means a low price for any new car in 1970. By 1979 the price had risen to $27,500 for a new car and by 1980 to $38,000.

Over the years the car has become more refined in its appearance as well as more expensive. The so-called Series 4 was put out in 1980 and continues to be manufactured today. The touring car, or phaeton, now sells for $55,000 and the roadster for $59,000. The name of the company manufacturing the cars is now Excalibur Automotive Corporation (1735 South 106 Street, Milwaukee, WI 53214). The company's production in 1983 was 200 new cars.

As for almost every car produced today, depreciation sets in the moment the car is sold and the purchaser drives away. Still, the Excalibur Automotive Corporation can point to its minimal depreciation in comparison with other new cars. The roadster is the scarce Excalibur and tends to bring the highest price on the secondhand Excalibur market. In January 1983, *Hemmings Motor News* advertised a 1983 Excalibur roadster for $54,500 as against about $59,000, the advertised price new for the 1983 model.

As I have indicated above, the Excalibur new in 1980 cost about $38,000. In the car auction year that started in the fall of 1981 and ended in the spring of 1982, two 1980 models were auctioned for $41,000 and $46,000. A 1980 was advertised in *Hemmings* for $42,500 in December 1982, and two 1981s were advertised for $43,500 and $39,500.

The 1977 and 1978 tourers were auctioning for about $30,000 and were advertised for $25,000 to $32,000, still healthy prices for late 1982 and early 1983.

In the 1982 season a 1976 model was auctioned for $20,500. The 1974 model was auctioning for $16,500 and $17,000. One was advertised for sale for $21,000.

The 1972 and 1973 models were not bringing so much—$10,000 to $11,000. The earlier models didn't seem to be appearing much at auction.

If we go back to 1980, of course, there are no auction prices or advertised prices for 1981 and 1982 Excaliburs, since they hadn't been made and their prices hadn't been advertised either—the new-car sticker price.

The late-model Excaliburs were, however, selling in 1980 for high prices relative to prices of the Excalibur cars sold at auction and advertised in late 1982 and early 1983. Prices of the 1977 and 1978 cars were around $30,000— $29,500, $30,000, $32,500, some a little less expensive. The 1974–1976 model cars were selling in the range of $21,000 to $23,000. The 1973s were selling in the range of $20,000. The 1970 cars were in the $15,000 range, at least the price that the car sold for new in 1970.

In 1980 quite a few 1968 models were advertised for sale—including one for $16,000 and two others for $16,500 each.

Earlier cars were scarce. One 1967 roadster was advertised for $12,995, but a First Series 1966 roadster was advertised for $24,500. The 1970 price level of the brand-new cars was $12,000 to $15,000, so the Excalibur had graduated from a secondhand car with yearly depreciation to a collector car with appreciation, and these prices were as of 1980, not 1982 or 1983.

These are some of the value characteristics of the Excalibur:

1. The new car declines in value, but not a great deal—unlike other new cars, the standard transportation automobiles.

2. Value keeps going down as the car gets older, as it does for transportation automobiles, but not so precipitately.

3. A point is reached from which there is no further depreciation—at least this is the value curve today for the older Excaliburs.

4. Then value goes up for the older models, finally exceeding their price when new. A 1968 roadster was priced at $16,500 in 1980 and a 1969 tourer at $16,900. The 1970 new price was $12,000 to $15,000. A 1966 roadster, a First Series Excalibur, was priced at $24,500. The price of this particular car new was very likely $7,500 or close to this figure.

5. The price pattern is much the same as for Ferrari. The newer the Model 308 the higher the price, but as the very old Model 308's come onto the market the price tends to exceed the new price. While the Daytona was in production the price pattern was similar to the price pattern of the 308 (and the Excalibur). The original 1969 model Daytona sold in America for $19,000 but as low as $13,500 in Italy (I could have bought one in 1969 for $13,500 at the factory). While the Daytona was being produced the last models secondhand sold at a discount from the new price, but the earliest models did not sell for as low as their price when new. As time passes there will be less and less difference in price between the earliest Daytonas and the last Daytonas produced. The Excalibur price pattern may be the same.

Exact Replicas

Some of the new elite cars are *exact* replicas, or at least very close replicas. Few people look at an Excalibur SS and mistake it for a prewar Mercedes-Benz, although the car is certainly based on the S series of the late 1920s.

On the other hand, even the connoisseurs sometimes have to look very closely at one of the more exact replicas to be sure it is not an original. One such car is the replica Auburn 851 and 852 speedsters of 1935 and 1936. This prewar car is the most copied of any prewar car by far. There are at least a dozen makers of Auburn boattail replicas.

One such Auburn speedster replica was made by California Custom Coach of Pasadena. The body is fiberglass, whereas the original Auburn speedster was a metal car, but the molds for the replica's fiberglass body were made from an actual Auburn 851 speedster of 1935, so the lines are authentic. The chassis and engine are Ford, and the engine is a large 400-cubic-inch model.

The finish of the car is excellent and better than the original boattail had— at least the 1935 boattail that I owned. The trim is chrome-plated brass and stainless steel, and Connolly English leather is used for the upholstery, considerably better than the original upholstery.

Obviously some of the Auburn 851 and 852 replica cars are better than others. Different factories (or shops) that make these cars turn out very different products, even though they may look more or less alike.

One of the preferred Auburn boattail speedsters is the Glen Pray boattail, and perhaps this car is the closest thing to the original boattail of 1935–1936. This replica Auburn speedster generally secures very good prices at auction and when sold by dealers. The auctions will often announce, when the speedster comes up for sale, "This is a Glen Pray boattail," meaning, "This is a good one and you will get a good car if you are the high bidder on this one."

Unfortunately when auction prices are recorded for Auburn boattail replicas there is often no description of what kind of Auburn replica the car sold was, so that prices are not strictly comparable.

In 1982 the Auburn replica boattails sold within a fairly narrow price range at auction, regardless of their year of manufacture—1976 or 1982. For a class 2 car the top auction price was about $25,000 and the low price was $20,000. Two late-model class 1 cars brought $20,000 and $22,000.

In the January 1983 Barrett-Jackson auction a class 2 boattail of 1979 sold for the low price of $14,800. Five other Auburn boattail replicas were bid up as high as $19,000, but none of the five apparently found a buyer.

In the 1977–1978 season at least twenty-one boattails were offered at auction. A really old one, made in 1967, sold for $15,250, a car in class 3 condition, which was a high price for the year sold and for the condition of the car. Others of the twenty-one offered for sale brought $16,100, $23,000, $17,500, and $22,000.

Prices didn't seem to move up from 1977 to 1983, although in 1983 more very late models were sold (1980–1982 cars) and the later the car the higher the new price. New prices of the replicas certainly moved up, and rather rapidly.

Besides the Auburn boattail there are two other close replicas of the cars put out by the old Auburn-Cord-Duesenberg Company—the Duesenberg Model J and SJ speedster and the Cord, principally the convertible 810 and 812 sedan of the mid-1930s. Some of the Cord replicas are so close to the originals that from a distance even a Cord owner, like me, could be fooled, at least at first glance.

(Above) Philip Blake standing beside his Bentley Speed Six coupe before restoration, and the refurbished automobile (below) as a four passenger open car. It's hard to believe this is the same automobile. (Philip H. Blake)

There are two kinds of "new Duesenbergs" on the secondhand car market. The first is a fairly accurate replica of the J and SJ of the late 1920s to the late 1930s. The second, although connected with the Duesenberg family, is nothing like the original Duesenbergs but is a super-luxury modern automobile.

In the January 1983 Grand Old Cars Museum auction a 1981 Duesenberg speedster in mint condition, with Lincoln drive train, brought $56,000. The auctioneer stated at the time this car came to the auction block that a similar Duesenberg replica had sold for $87,500.

In 1981 several of these speedsters were offered for sale at auction. A 1973 car brought the low price of $41,000. Eleven other speedsters were offered, but none found a buyer, although the high bid on one of the cars may have been $100,000 and on the other $101,000. A fair price for 1982–1983 might be $75,000.

Five years earlier only three of the speedsters were offered for sale by major auctions. A 1972 model brought $35,500 and the other two did not sell. One had a reserve price of $55,000 and the other $65,000. Prices in five years ending in 1982 had risen very little, remembering that the price of these replicas new was rising rather rapidly.

The final car in this group of fairly faithful replicas is the Cord 810 and 812 of the mid-1930s, the so-called "coffin-nosed" car. Seven of these replica convertibles were offered in the 1977–1978 season. They had been made from 1966 to 1971. All but one of them sold. The top prices were $10,000 and $10,250. The lowest-priced car brought $6,800.

By 1981 these cars were bringing about $10,000 to $12,000, up a bit from five years earlier. In 1982 they were selling at about the same price level. Two 1970 models brought $9,500 and $12,500.

The early 1983 sales in Arizona saw some higher prices for this car. In the Barrett-Jackson auction a rather good-looking Cord replica made in 1970 brought $11,600, a car in class 2 condition.

These true replicars have not declined in price in the recession, but they are not characterized by any great increase in price or in popularity either, although some of them are almost dead ringers for the originals.

General Throwbacks

Quite a number of the replicars look similar to the automobiles of the late 1920s and the 1930s with their lack of an "envelope look" and their fenders that seem to be added on and not an integral part of the body. Many of them are very large and are characterized by horizontal lines and an absence of streamlining.

The Clenet is one and is probably the car of the greatest prestige of all of the "general throwbacks," if not all of the replicars. The Clenet is an impressive-looking car, large, long, somewhat high, with a very long hood and side exhaust pipes in the tradition of the old S series of Mercedes-Benz of the late 1920s and early 1930s. Perhaps a better generic term for this car is "neoclassic."

The Clenet that was made in California by Alain Clenet, a Frenchman who once worked for American Motors, is essentially a Lincoln—in chassis and drive train, including the 351-cubic-inch small-block V-8 engine and three-speed automatic transmission. Mr. Clenet kept everything stock so that there would be a minimum amount of trouble in servicing and repairing the car. The Clenet's cockpit and trunk are MG and thus somewhat limited in space for a big man.

The interior of this two-seater is luxurious—Connolly English leather for seats and side panels, and Wilton carpets. The dashboard is black walnut. In front are a real radiator, two large detached headlights, two driving lights, and two horns. The outside exhausts are imitation and do not carry off the exhaust gases as the exhausts on the S series Mercedes-Benz cars did.

The Clenet is a prestige car, probably the Rolls-Royce of the replicars. People are willing to part with a substantial sum of money to own one. The media have helped the car enormously, as they have helped the Excalibur. Publicity has had its effect on the market, at least to some degree.

In the January 1983 Barrett-Jackson auction a 1978 Clenet roadster in top condition sold for $35,000—not a huge price but a very substantial one for a replica car. Still, at this well-attended auction the car should have brought more, and it probably would have brought more had it been sold in 1982 instead of 1983, when the country saw few signs of coming out of the recession.

Clenet roadster, 1978, which sold for $35,000 at auction in 1983. (Julia Rush)

In the 1982 season at least four Clenets were sold at major auctions. A 1980 model in class 1 condition brought $65,000, and this is about the price a dealer would have secured for such a car. It was about market for a late-model mint Clenet. The Kruse auction secured this price. A 1979 model was also sold at one of the Kruse auctions in the same season, for $47,000. Two class 2 Clenets also sold for $42,000 and $45,000. The market in 1982 was about as high for Clenet as for any replicar made by any company anywhere.

In the 1981 season no fewer than fifteen Clenets were offered for sale by the major car auctions. Five of these cars found buyers. The others did not. Two class 1 Clenets brought $62,500 and $65,000. Both of these cars were roadsters. Two coupes sold for $38,500 each, class 2 cars. There was actually little price movement from 1981 to 1983, although economic conditions in the country were far worse in 1982 and early 1983 before the upturn got underway.

Five years earlier, in 1977, three Clenets were offered for sale by major car auctions, but none found a buyer. The prestige of the Clenet was still building and the Clenet was far less known in 1977 than in 1982. A mint roadster was apparently bid to $55,000 but the owner wanted $65,000.

There is little evidence that prices rose from 1977 to 1981, 1982, or 1983.

There is another unusual "general throwback," the Sceptre, a car much less widely known than the Clenet. While the Clenet is an impressive-looking car, it does have a "put-together" look, with such things added on as fenders, exhaust pipes that are simulated, large separate headlights, separate driving lights, separate horns, added-on spare tire. The Sceptre, on the other hand, is an "integrated" car that looks as if it was actually made in the late 1930s. It vaguely resembles the great Alfa Romeo 2.9 with double supercharger.

The construction of the Sceptre is extremely rugged but based on Mercury Cougar in frame and drive train. The engine is Mercury Cougar stock placed in a Cougar chassis that is modified and strengthened. The engine is a big 351-cubic-inch V-8. The car weighs only 3,100 pounds, so performance is good.

The Sceptre is not a big car, but because of the disproportionate length of the hood it gives an impression of size. The cockpit is small but luxurious. Connolly English leather is used. The dash is well instrumented. The trim is Brazilian walnut veneer. The steering wheel is leather-covered.

The car is maneuverable, will do perhaps 120 mph, and accelerates well. It was made by the Sceptre Motor Car Company of Goleta, California, and many of the cars on the market sold new for the fairly substantial price of about $50,000 or more.

There have been few recent sales of Sceptres. In the 1981 season four Sceptres were offered at auction but none sold. Two class 1 roadsters were bid up to $25,000 and $27,500, but the owners wanted $35,000 for each car. Two class 2 cars were bid to $30,000 and $38,000, but the owners wanted $45,000 for each car—so no sale.

If we go back to 1978 we find only one Sceptre offered for sale by a major auction, this a class 1 1978 roadster, probably as new. It was bid to $46,000 in a Kruse auction, but the owner wanted $55,000, probably the price he paid for it new.

So we don't know how the Sceptre will make out as an investment car. I do know that although I am a purist who drove a Mercedes-Benz S and SS as the only transportation cars I owned—before the war—I most certainly would not mind owning a Sceptre, or a Clenet either!

Super-Luxury Elite Cars

The super-luxury elite cars are not exactly throwbacks to the prewar era or to any other era. They are automobiles that are made to appeal to the "carriage trade." For the person who has the money and can afford the very best, these cars are made to be the answer.

At the head of the list of these plush automobiles probably stands the Stutz, not a throwback car to the 1930s, not a present-day adaptation of the features of the old and great Stutz, but a completely different car from the original, not particularly a high-performing car like the prewar Stutz but rather a "millionaire's wagon."

The new Stutz was originally designed by the eminent car designer Virgil Exner, and bodies were built by the Italian body firm of Ghia, known for its quality work. The car looks something like a very plush Cadillac but has traces of Chrysler that Virgil Exner no doubt brought with him from his design work for that company.

The car is very long in body and in wheelbase. Two-toning is used in painting as well as plenty of chrome. There is one nonfunctional external exhaust pipe to add to the glamour of the car, and imitation running boards that open with the doors are attached to the doors.

The interior is sumptuous. The seats are a soft Italian leather. The carpets are fur, and interior metal is plated with gold. English walnut veneer is used for the wood trim. The assembly of the car, paint, and chrome are all of top quality and workmanship.

The chassis and power train are stock Pontiac Bonneville—403-cubic-inch V-8 engine and GM Hydramatic transmission. The chassis is completely stock Pontiac, so repairs should be no problem at all.

There are three body models extant: a four-door sedan, the fixed-head coupe, and a coupe with detachable hard top. The sedan was priced at

$70,000 and the convertible at $107,000. A special-order limousine was priced at about $200,000. The car did have appeal for Hollywood celebrities, some of whom paid these prices for the car.

These cars come onto the market from time to time, usually at the car auctions or advertised privately. One 1975 model Stutz Black Hawk coupe, supposedly in immaculate condition, was advertised for sale recently for about $25,000. It was pointed out by the owner that the current price of the Stutz new was over $90,000.

In the January 1983 Barrett-Jackson sale two of these modern-day Stutzes were offered for sale. One was a 1979 four-door sedan in prime condition. It did not sell but reached a high bid of $57,500. The other car was a 1971 model which was brought in at $23,000. It was in class 2 condition and did not find a buyer. In the Kruse Scottsdale, Arizona, auction of January 1983, a 1976 Stutz sedan was offered for sale, but it too failed to find a buyer. It was in top condition and reached a high bid of $31,000.

In the 1981 season a 1975 Stutz coupe did sell at auction, for $32,000, a car in class 2 condition. Three other Stutz two-door hardtops were offered for sale but did not find buyers. Their reserve prices were $27,000, $35,000, and $50,000, quite a distance from their prices new.

In the 1977–1978 auction season, several Stutzes were offered for sale. A 1972 two-door hardtop in class 2 condition brought $24,800, and a 1974 two-door hardtop brought $26,750. There was not much price movement from 1977 to 1983, and the car is not in the greatest demand.

Foreign Elites

I suppose any foreign car has a kind of exotic appeal for American buyers that American cars do not have. The manufacturer of elite cars abroad can use his domestic components, and it is natural that he should, but to American buyers the "foreign domestic components" are exotic—Jaguar, Bentley, and other makes which to Americans have a good deal of exotic appeal.

One highly interesting foreign elite is the Panther made by Panther Westwinds of Byfleet, Surrey, England. The firm has turned out two very different cars, one a large throwback sedan that in a general way resembles the Bugatti Royale and the other a throwback roadster that fairly closely resembles the SS100 of the 1930s, the old Jaguar. This roadster is a very good copy of the old SS100 and might fool a number of people, at least from a distance.

One highly important fact about this car is that it is based on an old Jaguar, although not the original SS100 Jaguar. The engine used in this car is the 1948 Jaguar in-line six with double overhead camshafts, an engine that currently is not out of date; I have driven many miles in the old 1948 Jaguar. It was, and is, a quality car of definite sports car rank.

Many, if not most, of the American elites have fiberglass bodies. The

Panther has a handcrafted aluminum body set off with Lucas P100 headlamps and a "tacked-on" spare wheel and tire at the back. The interior is leather and the instrumentation is excellent. The paint job is top-quality. Many of these so-called J-72 Jaguars sold new in the neighborhood of $35,000, not a high price for a quality car all the way through.

In the 1982 season a Panther roadster in top condition, a 1974 model, sold at auction for $25,500, not a low price in relation to the price of the car new. In 1981 a 1974 roadster in class 2 condition sold for $20,000. Another 1974 roadster in similar condition reached $25,500 but did not sell, as the owner wanted $27,500 for the car. In 1977 a mint-condition 1977 Panther roadster was bid up to $18,000 in a Kruse auction, but the owner placed a reserve price of $30,000 on the car.

The collector car market is not well aware of the Panther and there is no great enthusiasm for it. It does not have much of a price history. On the other hand, the Panther should never sell at a giveaway price. It is a quality car that is low enough in price always to assure some market.

Other Elites

How many car companies there are turning out the new elite cars is uncertain, but there are at least a hundred—from Herman Quint of Waterbury, Connecticut, manufacturing a 300SL Gullwing that is a dead ringer for the original but uses Chevrolet mechanicals, to the Cumberford, originally made in Stamford, Connecticut, using polished wood on the exterior and selling in the $150,000 range. One reason for the cloudiness of this area of car manufacture is that these companies seem to go out of business about as fast as they enter it. Some of the new products I am absolutely certain will never succeed. Others I think may have a good chance to succeed, but with undercapitalization it is possible that even good elites can fall by the wayside as their factories fold.

Most companies turning out the new elites fall into one of two categories. One is the company turning out super cars, like Knudsen Automotive, Inc., of Omaha, Nebraska. Knudsen's automobile looks like a billionaire's sporty Cadillac, but with separate bumpers, a rear tire bulge, individual headlamps, and three chrome-plated pipes out the side. Knudsen makes a coupe, a cabriolet, and a so-called Royale sedan and Royale limousine. The limousine is extremely long and can be purchased with various features, including armor plating. Prices can run into six figures. Knudsen also makes the Baroque, a sporty car, but the company's emphasis is on super luxury, not sports cars.

The other type of company is the one turning out so-called sports car throwbacks. Doval Coach Limited of New Haven, Connecticut, turns out a very sleek roadster called the Shadow based on the Ford V-8 drive train. The body is aluminum and expensive as well as hard to construct. The gauge of the aluminum is heavy. The paint job consists of thirty-four coats of hand-rubbed lacquer. Burled English walnut, Connolly English leather, and wool carpets are used in the interior. The top is hand-sewn mohair. The body is a subdued boattail design with four exterior exhausts. It has a long hood, and the whole car is well proportioned.

Neither the Doval nor the Clenet is important in the car market—at least yet. On the other hand, two cars that are factors in the market right now are the Berlina and the Zimmer. The Berlina, a car turned out by Phillips Motor Car, is a big, impressive-looking convertible obviously based on the 540K Mercedes cabriolet and roadster. It has large separate headlights, driving lights, two side-mounted spare wheels, and a radiator fairly closely modeled after Mercedes. The engine is a GM 350-cubic-inch. In 1982, five of these Berlinas were sold at major auctions. The 1981 model brought $54,500, a more or less princely sum for any elite, even a Berlina. The car was in class 1 condition. A 1980 car of class 1 condition brought $42,100. The other three cars were 1981s and they brought $41,000, $38,750 (both class 2), and $36,500 (class 3). All of these prices were substantial for any elite, but all were very late models (almost new), as the car does not have a long history of manufacture. What they will bring as they age in the market one does not know. Right now they are quality novelties.

In 1981 a Berlina 1981 brought the high price of $54,500, but this was not strictly a "540K Mercedes." Four other Berlinas were offered for sale but did not find buyers. Most owners wanted over $40,000 for their cars. Of course as time went on the new price of all elites rose with rising costs of production.

The Zimmer is a car put out by Zimmer Motor Cars Corporation, Pompano Beach, Florida. It is in the class of the Berlina and about as important in the market (and in the same price range). The car uses a Ford drive train, at least in some of its cars. It sells for somewhere around $30,000 and has been in this price range for the past two years.

Not all of the elites are luxury cars, however. The Gazelle has been put out at least since 1978 and it is an inexpensive but somewhat attractive elite. It is based on several smaller car chassis and power trains, including VW, Ford Pinto, and Chevette. In the 1981 season a class 1 1978 Gazelle brought $7,000 at the Kruse auction. Two 1980 class 1 Gazelles brought $5,700 and $5,200. A class 2 1980 model brought $4,500. Two 1981 cars using Pinto mechanicals sold for $9,000 and $7,000, both class 1 cars.

Elite Cars as Investments

Very few cars are sold new at the retail price and then proceed to rise in price, thus proving themselves to be good investments. Usually the car declines in value, no matter how unique or how fine. After a time it seems to hit bottom, where it stays for a time. Then it starts to rise. At bottom it is simply an old car that looks interesting but essentially no one wants it enough to pay much for it. I remember that in the late 1950s I put my Mercedes-Benz 300S cabriolet, a car in excellent condition, in a concours d'elégance in a town in Virginia close to Washington. When the judging committee got to the car they questioned why anyone would put such a car in a concours d'elégance! The car was worth about $2,500 at the time. The same car in the same condition with the same number of miles on it would now sell for a quick $60,000, and it is one of the greatest, as well as one of the most expensive, of all postwar classics.

These are the factors to consider when judging a replica or throwback car as an investment:

1. There is no clear-cut evidence of a rise in value of such cars, at least no substantial rise. The Excalibur is a well-seasoned car, manufactured since 1964. We do know that the earliest models have shown a definite increase in price, certainly as against their modest price new in 1964. The later the model Excalibur, the less definite the rise in value.

2. The new price of every elite car goes up. If the car started out in 1965, say, to sell for $10,000 and the current new price for essentially the same car is $50,000, then it stands to reason that a good 1965 car will sell for more than its price new of $10,000. The rising *new* price tends to pull up the "secondhand price."

3. The elite cars have not yet found their niche in the collector car market and as investment cars.

4. To a considerable extent the elites are not originals. They are, many of them, throwbacks and imitations of the real thing. The purists still do not like them much if they like them at all.

5. The cars are not engineered, integrated cars. They generally use a standard American power train, almost always Chevrolet or Ford. One then has the idea that he is really driving a Chevy or a Ford dressed up to look like something far grander than it is.

6. No car using American mechanical components has seemed to sell well or has seemed to move up in price much as it aged. The Iso Grifo is a beautiful little Italian car using a Chevrolet power train. The car looks about as good as a Ferrari. It is not, however, popular in the market, and it can be bought currently for $10,000 to $12,000.

Perhaps the Bizzarini is an exception to this general principle that nobody wants a car with American components, at least a collector-investor. The Bizzarini, designed by the great designer Giotto Bizzarini, is beautiful and handles well. Fifteen years ago one could be bought for $6,000. I examined a beautiful Bizzarini for just this price. Today it may sell for $25,000. This is an Italian car, however, not the product of an American shop, and because of its country of origin and its designer it is a collector car.

7. Few of the elites secure much approval from the test drivers who report on them in the automotive press. Typically they say that the driver's seat is too cramped, or the suspension is not right, or the car is underpowered, or too many things are stuck on the car—horns, rear tire, etc. Whether the reviewers for the magazines and newspapers are prejudiced or not is uncertain. In any event these reviews do not enhance the value of these automobiles.

8. On the positive side, the elites do not have the troubles and the temperament of the originals they copy or imitate—the cars of the late 1920s and the 1930s. Many, if not most, of the elites use American mechanicals and are thus fairly reliable—maybe not so reliable as a Ford or a Chevrolet all the way through, but far more reliable than the prewar classics. The elites can be used for transportation.

9. Right now the elites are in an uncertain state, perhaps a state of flux. The public is just getting used to them. It may be that as the cars become better known they will be better accepted by the general buying public so that a value base can be established.

10. As one gets used to seeing these cars more it is possible that he will see their more positive side. He may get used to their lines. He will also learn to recognize a Sceptre or a Quint or a Clenet, and as he does he may develop more positive feelings toward the elite cars.

11. The elites do not decline in value so far and so much as standard American cars.

12. The cars can be disposed of very much more easily than a production American car. The major auctions like to offer the cars for sale, whereas they are not inclined to take a five-year-old Buick or Chevy for sale. There is a certain prestige that attaches to the cars. For that reason dealers should be more inclined to buy them and take them on consignment than ordinary Cadillacs and Lincolns.

13. One of the greatest qualities of the elites is their prestige. They are often used as backdrops for advertisements of all kinds, including backdrops in TV ads. The elites are not unobtrusive cars by any means, and they do create something of an aura for the driver. Passersby see the cars and at least recognize that they are something out of the ordinary and something probably quite expensive.

13

Low-Priced Investment Cars

IT IS SOMETIMES objected that investment automobiles are only for the wealthy few, and that the man in the street can't possibly afford any investment car at all.

In early 1970 the investor with an average income could afford an investment automobile, and a very good one—good as a pure investment and good in terms of design and engineering. The November 1982 issue of the *Robb Report* contains an article on a mid-1950s Mercedes Benz 300S roadster. The color reproductions, if accurate, give me the impression that this particular car would sell for $100,000 at least. The car was one of the finest turned out in the postwar period.

In 1970, a similar car in average condition (but not superb condition like the car illustrated in the *Robb Report*) was offered for sale in Washington, D.C., for $1,900. At that time, to get the car into superb condition might possibly have cost as little as $3,000 to $4,000. My own 300S roadster was bought in 1966 for $800 and completely restored for $4,000.

In 1978 I purchased a finely restored 1966 Mustang convertible for $1,600. In 1983, the car would have brought at least $6,000 in good condition.

Are these good old times over now? Are all the low-priced investment cars gone? Are investment cars only for the rich investor now?

The answer is no. Current times always seem too late for buying investment cars, investment paintings, antiques, and real estate. It also *always* seems too late to "catch the rise in the stock market."

In mid-1982, I went on a specific hunt for low-priced investment automobiles, just to see what I could find—not for myself necessarily, but just to see what the hypothetical investor with limited capital might be able to find in an investment automobile.

The trouble with buying "now" is that one cannot predict what is going to happen to the market and to price. One can only use his best judgment and arrive at the conclusion that this car or that car will probably rise in price over the next several years.

Finding a Low-Priced Investment Car

One might start by reviewing the price reports in the field of collector cars. A number of guides are listed in the Bibliography of this book. Particularly useful ones are *Old Car Value Guide, The Gold Book*, Official Price Guide to Collector Cars, and *Collector's Guide to Car Values.*

You must go through the guides to see the low-priced cars. Avoid the Duesenberg J and Mercer Raceabout! You can then narrow down your field of interest to certain makes and models. Right now there are a limited number of low-priced investment cars on the market—truly investment cars, not simply secondhand cars.

After the preliminary price review has been done, the next step might be to visit some dealers to see what they are offering in the way of low-priced investment cars. Of course, you cannot hold all makes and models of low-priced investment cars in your head. You must concentrate on relatively few makes and models, those available and those you are particularly interested in. This is exactly what I did.

First we must define low-priced cars. Today a low-priced car is one selling for $10,000 or less. A recent survey indicates that the average price of a new car today is a little over $10,000. Even the inexpensive U.S. and Japanese subcompacts, fully equipped, come to well over $7,000.

This 1980 Duesenberg II was bid to $67,000, but failed to sell at the 1983 Barrett-Jackson auction. A similar car sold for $56,000 a few days later. (Julia Rush)

More popular in England than in America, 1961 Aston Martin coupe, sold by Christie's in London in 1979 for $27,000. Cars like this one sometimes appear in the United States in very good condition for about half that amount. (Christie, Manson & Woods International, Inc.)

On today's market, $5,000, and sometimes even less, should purchase an investment car. However, the lower we go in price, the greater the gamble, and the more we get into old secondhand cars that *may possibly* go up in value at some time in the future and become investment automobiles.

The first likely investment car I located in this general range under $10,000 was an Aston Martin DB4 coupe of 1961 with Superleggera body, a beautiful classic car, the finest sports car made in England. The leather was good, the paint, gold, was almost good, but certainly above poor. The car had good chromed-wire wheels and good tires. The chrome on the car was generally good.

The condition overall was no better than good and perhaps a shade under good. The car needed a new clutch, but the engine, transmission, and differential seemed to be in good condition. The price of the car was $7,500, about an auction price but below usual dealer price. The dealer, Motor Classic Corporation, of North White Plains, New York, specializes in Italian sports cars, mainly Ferraris, and handles some German cars as well as outstanding Shelby Cobras and doesn't seem to want to deal in English cars, Aston Martins included.

Estimating the cost of getting the car in fine condition is the next step in determining whether this car is a good investment or not. It is possible that

$4,500 would do the job, including clutch, engine work if necessary, and new paint.

Car number two was snapped up very quickly, and for good reason. It was a bargain, and it was purchased privately. The car was a 1941 Buick Special convertible, in excellent condition all around—with one exception. Had I not looked under the hood, I would have graded the car very good with a real possibility of making it into excellent with an expense of about $2,000 to $2,500. Paint was excellent. Chrome was excellent. The same for the upholstery, top, and carpets. The body was all-around perfect.

An automobile buff purchased the car in Connecticut for $3,500. The reason for the low price, besides the fact that it was sold privately? The engine was not original. It was a Buick V-6, a modern engine installed to make the car usable today.

The buyer had the engine tuned so that it ran well. At this point he was offered $6,000 for the car, including the recent V-6 engine. He estimated that to buy an original 1941 engine in good condition and install it would cost about $800, and there was about another $1,000 needed for other refurbishing—$5,300 in all. At that point, the car would have been near mint, but not quite. It should have been worth about $7,500 and, if mint, about $10,000.

Car number three was offered for sale by Post Radiator Company of Darien, Connecticut. It was a 1928 Ford Model A convertible in original condition and with very few original miles. It was far from being in mint condition, but there were few signs of major deterioration. A paint job and new upholstery and top were required, but the price of $7,000 was not great for the condition. The car sold for $5,000. In all, perhaps $3,000 would have been required to put the car in very good, but not mint, condition. If mint, this particular model car might sell for $14,000 to $15,000.

This is simply a sample of good buys that might be made in investment cars. Had I spent more time seeking out such inexpensive investment cars, no doubt I could have found many more.

Inexpensive Investment Cars by Make and Model Car

Here I'll discuss some cars that the investor with no more then $5,000 to spend should consider—the Ford Mustang convertible, 1964–1966; Cadillac Eldorado convertible, 1971–1974; Chevrolet Corvair (preferably convertibles and later models); Austin-Healey 3000; Datsun 240Z.

Ford Mustang Convertible, 1964½–1966

I have mentioned this car many times in this book because in many ways it has been the biggest bargain in recent years of all collector cars, and certainly of the lower-priced collector cars. I need not dwell on the merits of the car at any length. In the first place, regardless of what the car is intrinsically, the fact of the matter is that it has been rising in value in recent years.

You should choose a Mustang of 1964, 1965, or 1966 vintage, not later, and the car should be a convertible, not a coupe. The car came in three engine sizes: 170-cubic-inch six, 200-cubic-inch six, and 289-cubic-inch V-8. The last car has the power of a junior Ferrari. The six is reliable, quiet, and easy to repair, on those rare occasions when repairs are required. Parts are available virtually everywhere and for very little money. Metal underpans, for example, rust out, but can be replaced at minimum cost. An entire engine can be purchased inexpensively. My own six gets about 24 miles to the gallon, with regular gasoline, and I use it whenever I wish, either around town or on trips.

The first Mustang is known as the 1964½, since it appeared at midyear. The last desirable Mustang convertible is the 1966. From then on the cars became heavier-looking and, with some exceptions, have been less desirable to collect.

The May 7, 1981, *Old Cars Weekly* carried a front-page headline that read: "Mustang Sets Record at $13,000." The Mustang was not, however, one of the convertibles of the mid-1960s, but "a plain fastback." This is not one of the collectible examples we have been talking about, but it does indicate the rapid upward price movement of Mustangs. In June 1981 at the Leake car auction in Tulsa, a 1965 Mustang convertible with 21,130 miles on the odometer and completely original and unrestored brought $21,500, a record price for a Mustang convertible.

You still can find a good mid-1960s Mustang convertible for $5,000 or less, and for $6,000 or a little more you should be able to buy one of these cars in near-mint condition—a car that is rapidly rising in price.

Cadillac Eldorado Convertible

Possibly the most beautiful of the big postwar luxury convertibles is the Eldorado Cadillac convertible put out from 1971 to 1976.

In 1977 there was a run on Eldorado convertibles, and they rose in price well above the new price, particularly the 1976 model, the last manufactured. Many people, particularly car dealers, bought these last Eldorado convertibles and put them away to look at and to watch them appreciate in value. In 1977, a fair market price for one of these 1976 "new Eldorados" was $20,000 + . I looked at a fine Eldorado at that time, one with 3,500 miles on the odometer, for $13,500. The 1975 model, with few miles, would have brought about $10,000. The older the model, the less it would bring, and a 1974 car, the last car using regular leaded gas, sold for $5,000 to $6,000. The older cars, back to 1971, in fine condition, sold at that time for as low as $4,500.

By the end of 1979, the mad rush for Eldorados had worn off to a degree and prices had settled back. The brand-new 1976 Eldorados were selling at the same price as they did in 1977, perhaps a bit more. The simply "used" 1976 cars were selling for about $8,000, with, say, 20,000 miles on them—plain used cars but with very desirable bodies. The older cars were down to $5,000 and below, off a bit.

In early 1983, $4,000 would buy a very good Eldorado convertible, not the 1975 or 1976 model, but an older car. Now, however, condition became more important, as the cars had been around longer, and they began to be separated into two groups: the ordinary used cars and the collector cars in fine condition.

By the onset of the spring buying season in 1983, the Eldorados began to rise. The "new" 1976 cars sold for at least $20,000 and more like $25,000. The used 1976 cars sold for around $10,000, some more, some a little less—not as low as $8,000 (provided they were in good condition).

The 1975 cars were selling for just under this figure. The earlier cars, starting with the 1974, rose to a $6,000-to-$8,000 range. A fine 1974 would bring the $8,000 figure or more. The earlier cars in good condition might bring only $5,000.

The Eldorado is certainly a luxurious car, but it is not a great car from a mechanical point of view. However, it is good, and with proper lubrication the front-wheel drive will not give a great deal of trouble.

All Cadillac convertibles, of any year, are in demand. The cars of the mid-1960s and late 1960s are in the $5,000-to-$6,000 range. Many of them are in good condition, many of them restored. I have owned the 1967, 1968, 1969, and 1970 models, all of which I bought new. They are good-looking, good-running cars, and are rising a little in price and rising in demand.

Chevrolet Corvair—Especially the Convertible

The rear-engine Chevrolet Corvairs, put out between 1959 and 1969, are not moving a great deal in the market, but they are moving. They are collector cars and are likely to move upward in demand and price. They are also, for the most part, inexpensive cars.

The early Mercer Raceabouts are the expensive ones, not the later Mercer Raceabouts. The early Corvairs, on the other hand, are not the expensive Corvairs. The later the Corvair the more expensive it is and the better the car—as a general rule.

The basic Corvair was produced from 1959 to 1964, and this is probably the least desirable of the Corvairs. For $3,000 one should be able to buy a fine-condition Corvair convertible of this era.

The sporty Monza Corvair, a coupe, was put out in 1960. The Spyder (convertible) was put out in 1962 and continued to 1964. This car should be bought for $4,000 or thereabouts.

From 1965 to 1967, the Corvair Corsa was put out, a car somewhat hard to find today. Still, $4,000 might purchase one.

From 1965 to 1967, the Turbo Spyder was manufactured, and for the same price one of this model Corvair might be purchased, a car in good condition.

Between 1962 and 1964, John Fitch turned out a modified Corvair called the Sprint. In 1965 he made a still better car, the "Second Generation Sprint." For $5,000 one of these cars might possibly be located. From 1966 on he made a "super" car, the Fitch Phoenix. From 1966 to 1969, Don Yenko made a "racing" Corvair called the Stinger. Once in a while one of these Phoenixes or Yenkos can be bought, and if one should ever go for $5,000 or less it most certainly should be bought.

Austin-Healey 3000

The Austin-Healey 3000 of the first half of the 1960s is a first-class, good-looking six-cylinder classic. It has been rising in price steadily over the past half decade and it is now pushing over $5,000, although $5,000 might at times still purchase a good 3000. While the car is not a great classic or a top-prestige make, it is a very good and very reliable car that can be used for everyday transportation if necessary. Recently a few of these cars have been advertised at over $10,000.

Datsun 240Z

The Datsun 240Z was an attempt by the fourth-largest car manufacturer in the world to make and sell a sports car. The 240Z was unveiled at the 1969 Tokyo Motor Show, a very good-looking sports coupe with a straight-six 2.4-liter engine. The car was docile but had a good deal of acceleration from its relatively powerful engine—which produced 151 horsepower, the same as my Mercedes-Benz 300S roadster with its 3-liter engine. The car was a performer but highly reliable. It was aimed at the sports car market, mainly at the American market, and the company's aim was good. In three and a half years, 153,000 240Z cars were manufactured. Of this number, 130,000 were sold in the United States, many to the young college student market.

There are many 240Z cars still on the road, and for that reason prices in the market are not high, but there is a definite interest in this car on the part of young collectors, more interest than the later 260Z and 280Z cars attracted, cars with perhaps more refinements but at the same time less performance.

On the present market a 240Z can be bought for $2,500 to $4,000. One of the best 240Z's I saw was restored completely by Rodney Bostian's garage in Middleburg, Maryland. Everything was done to the car, and it was priced at $3,500 a few months ago. The car should not go down in value, at least the restored car. It is probably underpriced and should rise.

Slightly More Expensive Investment Cars by Make and Model

Here I'll discuss some cars that might be bought for $10,000 or perhaps a little more—the Chevrolet Corvette and Sting Ray, the Mercedes-Benz 190SL, the Jaguar XKE6 convertible, and the Porsche (early models). Such cars are apt to be in good condition but not necessarily in mint condition.

Other cars might be bought. Once in a while the Maserati comes up in this price range, a Ghibli or an Indy (the four-seater equivalent of the Ghibli) or a good-model earlier car, but it is becoming very hard to locate any of the very desirable Ghiblis for a price near $10,000. The Indy is rising in price too, but occasionally one can be bought in the $10,000 area. The earlier Maserati Mexico can be purchased for $10,000.

In Lamborghinis the earlier cars are excellent-running and reasonably good-looking cars, but the Miura can rarely be bought at under $30,000. The earlier cars are not preferred in the market and they are not standouts in appearance like the Miura and the later Countach. The 350GTV and the 400GT can at times sell in the $10,000 range. The convertibles are very much in demand and almost never appear in this price range.

The cars I discuss below, however, are on the market in some volume, and their market price is relatively determinable.

1978 Chevrolet Corvette with 15,000 original miles, Indianapolis Pace Car, sold for $12,750 at the Barrett-Jackson auction in 1983. (Julia Rush)

1963 Chevrolet Sting Ray. Four of this model were offered at the Barrett-Jackson auction in 1983, and one sold for $15,000.

Chevrolet Corvette and Sting Ray

The cars of the early 1960s, very desirable collector cars of classic design, can at times be bought for about $10,000. Cars as late as 1962 in good condition, but not necessarily mint, can be purchased for about $10,000. A mint 1962 with a ground-up restoration was offered by a dealer for $15,500 fairly recently.

Cars from 1963 through 1967, the so-called "new series," can sometimes be bought in good condition for about $10,000, but rarely the 1963 split-window coupe.

The latest series, from 1967 on, can be purchased in good condition for about $7,500. As the latest model year is approached the price rises.

These cars are excellent in performance and in design.

Mercedes-Benz 190SL

The Mercedes-Benz 190SL is, of course, a Mercedes, and because it is, its value is fairly high and rising. The 190SL is not a great performer. It has a small four-cylinder engine. The body is of fairly pleasing design. The convertible is in big demand as of 1983. The 190SL was put out from 1956 to the early 1960s. The cars are good, reliable, and fairly easy to maintain. A 190SL in good condition can be purchased for a little over $10,000, but a standout can cost $12,500 or more.

1965 Jaguar XKE six-cylinder 4.2-liter sport coupe, valued today at $12,500, was bid to only $3,800 in 1981 at auction. (Christie, Manson and Woods International, Inc.)

Jaguar XKE Convertible

The six-cylinder XKE was put out from 1962 to 1970. It is an up-to-date-looking sports car, a car of high performance, and a car that can be driven regularly. It is a true sports car but gives far less trouble than the twelve-cylinder XKE.

The car is on a rising price curve but at times can still be purchased, in good condition, for around $10,000. A mint-condition car can easily sell for over $20,000.

Porsche, Early Models

The Porsche cars of the late 1940s were pioneering cars, and none brings as little as $10,000, if the car is in any kind of condition. But the Porsche cars of the early 1950s can be purchased, in good condition, for a little under $10,000. The cars are a pleasure to drive, are performers to a degree, and are reliable. I operated one of these 1950s cars as our only car and one day we drove it 850 miles without a great deal of fatigue.

The popular 356 model appeared in 1952 and was continued to 1964 with upgrading in horsepower and performance. These cars can be purchased for $8,000 to $10,000, although some go higher. The cars are stylized but very popular, and they are fine performers and reliable. Both convertibles and coupes are in demand.

One and Two-Cylinder Antique Cars

In Christie's Los Angeles auction of March 29, 1980, a one-cylinder 1911 Brush runabout in good condition brought $8,000. It might bring more today but not much more. This was about a standard price for one-and two-cylinder antiques.

In the February 1981 sale held by the same auction firm, another 1911 single-cylinder Brush was bid up to $7,500 but did not find a buyer. The estimated price by the gallery was $8,000 to $10,000. Obviously some bid between $8,000 and $10,000 would have been acceptable to the seller.

In the same sale a 1903 curved-dash Olds might have brought a little more, but $10,000 would have been a reasonable price for one of these oldies.

In the 1983 Kruse Scottsdale auction, a 1911 Brush roadster in good condition reached $11,100 but did not sell.

When we go to the four-cylinder antiques, prices are higher, but in the March 29, 1980, sale a good-looking 1910 four-cylinder Hupmobile in apparently good condition, a runabout, sold for $11,000—not far above the $10,000 target price.

This one cylinder Brush of 1911 brought $8,000 at Christie's 1980 Los Angeles auction. Ten years earlier, the car would have sold for about $3,000; today it would be valued at about $15,000. (Christie's, New York)

In the same sale a 1911 Ford Model T four-cylinder runabout in excellent condition, a good-looking car, sold for $9,000. As we move forward in years in the Model T (and the Model T Fords were all pretty much alike regardless of year of manufacture), prices are lower. Those cars might be added to the $5,000-and-under list. In the same sale a 1923 Ford Model T runabout in reasonably good condition brought $4,800. The Ford Model T is a popular car and is rising in price.

In the 1981 Kruse Scottsdale sale a 1908 Buick roadster brought $14,500. A 1912 Ford pie wagon brought $10,600, and a 1912 roadster brought $11,500. A 1914 roadster in top condition brought $9,900.

In the recession a few cars actually rose substantially in price, cars in the less expensive category, but for the most part they have stayed on a plateau. The great and rare cars have been in greater demand by far than the less expensive cars, those at the bottom of the investor car price scale. Investor cars are something like paintings. In the recession of 1981–1982 great paintings sold about as well as they ever did, and at strong prices, even rising prices. Great cars like the Packard convertible sold by Christie's did not show much weakness. In fact, this car went for the extraordinary and unexpected sum of $350,000. In recessions the low-priced buyer often drops out of the market— the buyer of low-priced antiques, the buyer of low-priced collector paintings, and the buyer of low-priced collector cars. This lower-to-medium-income buyer comes back into the market with the return of prosperity.

The Yet-to-Emerge Automobile Investments

The security business is always intrigued by the idea of finding a new Xerox or a new IBM early in the game before the company has proved itself—and then riding the stock up from $1 to $145. It happens once in a while, and sometimes in the automobile industry.

With all of the hoopla about the De Lorean, followed by the big financial bust, one wonders whether the big market overhang of De Loreans might offer an opportunity to make a good investment. These cars were list-priced at $25,000. When the first cars arrived in the United States in April 1981, they were selling to customers at well over $25,000.

By the fall of 1983, brand-new De Loreans were advertised for $21,000. In the 1982 auto auctions, De Loreans were selling at about $20,000. By the fall of 1983, used De Loreans were selling in the $15,000 range and some as low as $13,000. The trend was down—and it was a trend, not a few fluke prices. The question is when the bottom will be hit. And then what? A small rise? A gradual but continuing rise? A price boom for De Loreans?

The De Lorean was, and is, quality. The quality planned for did not quite come through. The massive chassis was treated with fusion-bonded epoxy to prevent corrosion, and the exterior is an enormously expensive stainless steel.

There is certainly nothing the matter with the engine and drive train. The placement of the engine behind the rear axle is in line with the latest sports-car design. The V-6 is an overhead-cam powerplant, essentially Renault. The top end is Volvo and the bottom end Renault; the fuel system is Bosch K-Jetronic fuel injection.

The body was designed by the great Giorgetto Giugiaro of Ital Design and is certainly not bad-looking, although not in a class with his Maserati Ghibli.

The horsepower was a modest 130 and it would drive the car at 130 mph. The zero-to-60 time was 8.5 seconds—no Grand Prix or hot-rod time certainly.

To some car aficionados the body looked like a "corporate design," not the kind of body that Giugiaro, left to his own devices, would have produced. Giugiaro may have designed the body, but was his original idea modified? The position of the driver and occupants of the car is certainly not all that could be wished for. The seating is too low, and thus visibility is far from what it should be.

Car and Driver magazine for July 1982 says in its headline: "Who Says Stainless Steel Won't Tarnish?" This is certainly a major fault with the car. The stainless steel quickly turns a kind of dirty brown. Then when an accident occurs and there is any break or bad dent in the car, the entire panel must be unbolted and a new panel fitted, quite a costly operation.

I think the essence of the failure was the price. It was supposed to be priced at $15,000 in 1978, not $25,000. Sales were targeted at 20,000 per year and possibly as high as 30,000—for a strict medium-performance sports car never before on the market and with a sticker price of $25,000.

At $12,000 or even $15,000, maybe! But at $25,000, no way. The car was no Ferrari. It didn't have the name Ferrari. It didn't have the looks. It didn't have the performance. It didn't have the racing history—or any history, for that matter.

In performance and looks it was certainly no 1983 Corvette. For $25,000 *in 1983* the Corvette gives you a V-8 with 205 horsepower, zero to 60 mph in 7.1 seconds, and a top speed about 10 mph over the De Lorean. No tester rated the road-holding and cornering ability of the De Lorean as even in the same class as the Corvette.

The De Lorean has had its day, and its price has been falling. Yet, on the positive side, it will almost certainly become a collector car and probably an investment car as well, and after the price stops falling it will start to rise and will almost certainly keep on rising.

We can take a look at a far less sophisticated sports car than the De Lorean, the Bricklin of 1974 and 1975. This car too is a gullwing like the De Lorean, but the body is plastic and far cheaper in construction than the stainless-steel De Lorean body. The price on the first-year car was about $7,500 and on the last-year car $9,800. The dealer's cost, $5,400, was very low even at the time compared with the De Lorean's price. Horsepower was 175 for the 1974 model and 162 for the 1975 model. Today the Bricklin is selling for around $10,000. A mint car can bring $13,000 to $15,000.

What does the experience of the Bricklin indicate to us about future values of the De Lorean? The Bricklin is certainly not the equal in quality of the De Lorean, and the Bricklin has been rising in value—not a tremendous amount but rising nevertheless. And so, is the De Lorean likely to rise after it has stemmed the downward price movement? If a mint-condition De Lorean can be bought today for $15,000 it is hard to see how the value of the car will not rise in the future, probably not greatly, but it should rise enough so that the car turns into something of an investment. Had the car sold new for $12,000 to $15,000 then it would be hard to see anything but a good price appreciation for the future.

The October 1983 issue of *Special Interest Autos* has as its cover picture a very fine photograph of a 1935 Nash Lafayette sedan, a rather nice-looking car when it was put out and selling for a medium price. The magazine headlines the article on this car as "Nash's Low-Priced Challenger." The two-passenger coupe sold new at $580 and the finest model, the four-door brougham with integral trunk, for $710. In 1935 the cheapest Chevrolet sold for $550 and the cheapest Plymouth for $570.

Ten years ago I might have paid $1,000 for this car, simply as an old car in fine condition. Five years ago I might have gone to $1,200, but no more. For this sum five years ago I could have bought a good Mustang V-8 289 convertible—a 1965 or 1966. In fact, one was offered to me in 1980 for $700.

Now the question is: What is this Nash worth on today's market, and, if one is considering investment value, what will the value be, say, five years from now?

Will this car be an "emerging investment" or will it simply remain an old car in fine condition? My guess is that it will become an investment, not the greatest investment, but an appreciating investment nevertheless. Today it will bring over $6,000. If one is interested in strict emerging investments that have as yet not emerged or emerged only a bit, then he joins the ranks of those investors, brokers, and mutual fund managers trying to discover a new Xerox or IBM. It can be done in collector cars, and the trick is to find the cars that have not risen greatly but that are quality and in short supply, and were once popular in the market (better still, popular to a degree right now), and try to ride the market up with a piece of machinery that will provide some satisfaction of ownership.

14

Underpriced Investment Cars

"BUY UNDERPRICED STOCKS!" This is the "name of the game" the professional security analysts play—and the portfolio managers and the mutual fund managers. If they can find a stock selling for, say, two and a half times earnings, that is an indication that it is underpriced. If they can find a stock selling for one-third of the underlying assets or net worth of the company per share, then that's another indication that the stock is underpriced. What the professionals are doing is trying to find bargains, stocks that are worth more than they sell for on the present market and stocks that are likely to rise in the future. Sometimes the underpriced stocks are in companies whose sales are likely to boom in the future.

In automobiles, "underpriced classics" is the name of the game. Many dealers will advise a potential purchaser, "Buy right," which means, "Buy a car under the market and you will likely make a profit when you sell it."

The thinking is the same in stocks and in collector cars. Only it is far harder to determine what is an underpriced car. There are few financial measures to use. There is no measure of "times earnings" or "below book value."

To a considerable extent an underpriced car is either a car that is selling under the dealer or auction market by a fairly substantial amount or a collector car that seems subjectively to be low in price for what you get in the car.

On the present market there are certain cars that appear underpriced—in relation to what one gets in the car, to other cars in the general category of the car, and to what the price may well rise to in the future. It may also be underpriced in that restoration and maintenance are unusually low for the make and model car, particularly if one has any intention of driving the car for use.

On these bases there are a number of cars that fall into this category on the present market, and in the rest of the chapter I will try to point out what I feel are the greatest bargains on down to the lesser bargains.

Rolls-Royce Silver Cloud Sedans

The Rolls-Royce Silver Cloud I, II, and III sedans are beautiful automobiles. When they first appeared in 1955, collector car purists commented, "They are too big and two feet too high." As time went on, collectors and other connoisseurs took another look. Today these cars are used as symbols of wealth and taste on TV and in movies.

The Silver Cloud III of 1963–1965, the last of the series manufactured, is probably the preferred car. It is an eight-cylinder automobile and more refined mechanically than its predecessor, the Silver Cloud II and the six-cylinder Silver Cloud I.

The standard sedan with left-hand drive can be bought for about $30,000–$35,000. Sometimes it costs a little more and once in a great while a little less. It starts easy and drives and rides well, and repairs are not extraordinarily great for a car of this complication. It tends to keep going and isn't always in the repair shop. For $35,000 one can get at least a near-mint Silver Cloud III.

The Silver Cloud I is a six-cylinder car put out from 1955 to 1959. It has a rugged engine like a truck and it tends to keep going with a minimum of repair. The car is even more reliable than the eight-cylinder cars of the Silver Cloud II and III series. This car can sometimes be purchased for a little over $20,000, in excellent condition.

The Silver Cloud II is the first eight-cylinder car of the Cloud series. It was made from 1960 to 1962, and the later cars are better than the earlier cars (1960), since there were some bugs that had to be worked out in the 1960 series. These cars can be bought for $20,000 to $25,000.

The long-wheelbase sedan (or limo) will cost about $10,000 more than these quotes—and is worth the extra money. The cars with James Young bodies can cost at least $20,000 more than the standard sedans. They are rare and worth very much more. The Flying Spur is a magnificent sedan which may sell for $65,000 to $75,000 and possibly even more, but there are few of these cars available.

A right-hand-drive car is definitely not preferred in the United States, and therefore a left-hand drive might be the focus of attention. Right now, however, right-hand-drive cars are bargains in the United States and even bigger bargains in England. A right-hand-drive 1963 Cloud III was recently advertised by a major dealer for $24,500. A Cloud II might be purchased for $20,000 to $23,000 and a Cloud I for a little less, although not much less. A long-wheelbase Cloud II with the much-wanted James Young body was advertised for $29,500. The Earl's Court Show Car, a 1956 six-cylinder car with special Freestone and Webb body, was advertised for $15,000 by a dealer in California.

In London a Cloud II was advertised for sale for $14,500 by the firm that sold me my long-wheelbase Silver Cloud I with James Young body. A Lancashire, England, firm advertised a Cloud III for $16,000. The same firm advertised a Cloud I formerly owned by Lady Grosvenor, presumably a mint-condition car, for $10,000. In the same magazine a Cloud III that had been purchased three years earlier for $25,000 was for sale by a British dealer for $18,000. For the same price one could buy another Cloud III, this one with a recent $9,500 overhaul. The Cloud II would fall somewhere between the price of a Cloud I and a Cloud III. It should be pointed out that the price of the Silver Clouds in England is at a low point, partly because of the drastic decline of the pound sterling in relation to the dollar and to almost every European currency.

In Rolls-Royce, only mint and near-mint cars should be bought. Rolls-Royce collectors demand mint and near-mint and will pay for such cars. Lesser cars are not desirable in the market, even at a price.

Ford Mustang Convertibles, 1964 to 1966

Unlike the Rolls-Royce Silver Clouds, which have been declining in price in the present recession both in the United States and in England, the Mustang convertibles of the series 1964½, 1965, and 1966 have been rising in value. From Rolls-Royce, at one extreme, we move to the Mustang, perhaps at the other. We move from a car in a price trough to a car in a price upswing, and a price upswing in a recession.

In the Kruse sale in Arizona in January 1983, one 1966 Mustang convertible in class 1 condition brought $9,750. A 1965 in class 1 condition brought $8,400. A 1964½ convertible in class 2 condition reached $10,250, not enough to induce the owner to sell.

The Mustang convertibles at auction are like Renoir paintings at auction. The auctions do at least as well as dealers do as far as price goes. All of which means that one should try to buy privately or from a dealer a 1964½, 1965, or 1966 class 2 Mustang convertible for a maximum of $6,000 and preferably for a maximum of $5,000.

Rolls-Royce Silver Cloud Convertibles

From the inexpensive (but climbing) Ford Mustang convertible we return to the Rolls-Royce Silver Cloud series, only this time to the convertibles, which are vastly higher in price than the sedans and rather scarce. The kind of car on which to concentrate is the left-hand-drive Silver Cloud III, followed by the Silver Cloud I and finally the Silver Cloud II.

These cars are not inexpensive but they are excellent automobiles and have a classic beauty and elegance to them. Probably no Silver Cloud convertible of the I, II, or III series can be bought for under $60,000. While in the case of the sedans there is considerable difference in price among the Cloud I, II, and III series, there is not so great a difference in the convertible series. The important fact is that the car is a convertible, a scarce item on the market, not that it is an early Cloud I six or a late Cloud III eight.

Curiously, the Rolls-Royce automobiles do not do nearly as well as the Mustang convertibles in auctions. The Rolls-Royce buyers do not seem to frequent the auctions as much as the Mustang buyers do. Therefore once in a while a Cloud I convertible will sell for as low as $40,000.

The car on which to concentrate is probably the Park Ward convertible rather than the Mulliner convertible. The Park Ward may be a little better-looking; it is not made from a sedan whose metal top has been cut off and replaced with a convertible fabric top. Maybe we are being unfair to the Mulliner convertible, but this is what the car appears to me to be. I would prefer buying a left-hand-drive convertible in the United States, not a right-hand-drive.

Jaguar XK120, XK140, and XK150 Roadsters and Convertibles

The Jaguar XK is a beautiful series of cars. The bodies of these cars compare favorably in beauty with the bodies of almost any classic car. The Jaguar, while not big and bulky, is still an impressive-looking car. It drives well and handles well, and the six-cylinder engines certainly don't cause as much trouble as the V-12 engines.

The roadsters and the convertibles are the cars on which to concentrate, and they are worth over double what the coupes are.

I would have as a first choice an XK140 roadster. Next I would select the XK120 roadster, one of which I drove for many miles. Finally, I would select the XK150, a more refined and more "standard-looking" car. I would attempt to buy a car in mint condition all through and with chrome wire wheels. In the January 1983 Barrett-Jackson auction a magnificent 1955 XK140 in class 1 condition with red paint and wire wheels reached $17,250, not enough to induce the owner to part with it.

The XK140 and 120 should be bought for under $20,000, possibly for $17,500—in class 1 condition. The XK150 in the same condition should be bought for around $15,000.

Lamborghini Miura

The 1967 Lamborghini Miura set a new standard for the construction of sports cars, with its transverse engine behind the driver coupled to a rear drive. The car has a fantastic, "out of this world" body. As late as 1980 it sold for about the same price that it sold for new—$20,000 in 1967. Then it began to rise in price, but by the recession of 1981–1982 it was on something of a price plateau at $25,000 for the earlier car, the P-400, but $65,000 for the last model of 1972, the SV with several advanced mechanical features but essentially the same body and trim.

Toward the end of 1982 the Miura became scarce and its price rose again, and by 1983 the early Miura was selling at about $30,000 and up to $35,000 in dealers' showrooms. One firm out West was offering a 1967 model for $50,000 in early 1983. In the East two of the last models were offered for $85,000 and $100,000—not that these were market prices, but they were breakthroughs in a few prices that indicated a probable rise in price in the future, at a time when classic car prices and sales were weak.

The car is not low in price, but it is rare and a great automobile that will stand for a great step forward in sports car design. No Miuras have been made since 1972 or 1973, and only 720 were made in all. The car is a collector's item and a "statement." It is also an automobile for the man or woman who loves sports cars and the ultramodern.

Bentley SIII, SI, and SII Sedans

The Bentley sedans of the S series (equivalent to the Rolls-Royces of the Silver Cloud series) are top-quality luxury sedans but not as attention-getting as the sister car of the Bentley—the Rolls-Royce. The car is beautiful, dependable, conservative, easy to repair, and useful for transportation, should one want to use it for business or shopping on occasion.

Today the Bentley S series is at an unusual low point in demand and price. Over the years it rose tremendously, but in 1982 the price and demand weakened.

The best Bentley of the S series to buy is probably the SIII, the 1963–1965 eight-cylinder car that corresponds to the Rolls-Royce Silver Cloud III, the last of the series that started in 1955 and ended in 1965. The car should have left-hand drive. Today an SIII might be purchased for $18,000, an SII for $16,000, and an SI (the six-cylinder car) for $13,000.

The auctions seem to sell Bentley S series sedans very well and at prices above those of dealers, the SIII sometimes approaching $30,000 and the SI and SII $20,000.

In England the S series Bentley sells at extraordinarily low prices. The SIII with right-hand drive can sell for as low as $15,000 for a car in excellent condition. Recently, Laurence Kayne, an English Rolls-Royce and Bentley dealer, advertised what appeared to be an excellent SII sedan for $14,500. One SII was advertised for $11,000, and he had an SI for sale for $6,750, a car with what was purported to have a first-class new paint job.

1965 Bentley SIII sedan, offered in 1983 by Laurence Kayne in London for $15,000—about half the price of a comparable Rolls-Royce. (Julia Rush)

It would be my objective to buy an excellent-condition left-hand-drive Bentley SIII for a maximum of $20,000. Motor Classic Corporation recently had a mint Bentley SIII sedan with left-hand drive for $20,000. Possibly the car could have been bought for a little less. The SI is an excellent and even more trouble-free car that should be bought for less than my $20,000 maximum for the SIII.

Aston Martin Six-Cylinder Coupes

The Aston Martin Model DB six-cylinder coupe didn't need James Bond (007) to publicize it to be a fine and accepted sports car. It was and is an excellent, reliable, and rugged automobile. It is also a good-looking car. During the 1970s the car was not much in demand, and prices—particularly in England, the native country of the Aston Martin—were very low in relation to almost all other collector cars. At the end of the 1970s, demand began to increase, and so did prices. In the United States, however, where the car is not very well known, prices did not rise much and are not at all high now. Within the last twelve months I found two 1963 Aston Martin coupes with left-hand drive and with the beautiful Superleggera bodies in reasonably good condition. One was priced at $7,500 and the other at $6,500. It would appear that $4,000 might be required to put these cars in class 2 condition—not mint, but very good and very attractive. These prices may have been low for the car, and some Aston Martins of the same era in very good condition are offered for sale at about $12,000 and rarely under $10,000. The V-8 is quite different, and one of these popular cars can hardly be bought for less than $20,000 to $25,000.

The way I feel about the six-cylinder DB coupes is that if I could afford no more than an investment of, say, $7,500 for a sports car I would have an excellent automobile in one of the six-cylinder DB coupes, and a car in which I would be proud to be seen. I would also expect a definite rise in value over the next two or three years.

Cord 810 and 812 Convertibles

The Cord convertibles of the mid-1930s seem definitely underpriced today—by anyone's standards. The car is a unique-looking machine, perhaps not the most beautiful, but it is something of a "statement" and was in the first Museum of Modern Art exhibition that I visited. The car is not bulky and the mechanics are good. The V-8 engine is reliable, and the car can be driven. At one time a Cord 810 was my only means of transportation and I drove it almost every day with very few repairs.

Currently, the auction price is about $40,000 to $50,000 for the very desirable convertible in good or even mint condition. The excellent 1937 four-passenger convertible that was auctioned at the Grand Old Cars Museum sale in Arizona was in almost mint condition except that it had replacement fiberglass fenders. It sold for $40,000.

In the slightly later Kruse Scottsdale auction a similar car brought $36,000 and another similar 1937 car was bid up to $40,000 but not sold. A mint 1937 Cord sold in the Barrett-Jackson auction for $40,000.

This price level is far under the level of a year earlier. Considering what the car is, the price is very low and is not likely to stay at this level.

Maserati Ghibli Coupe and Spyder

Between 1980 and 1982 the Maserati Ghibli was very low in price. It is possibly the most beautiful sports coupe ever built, and the designer, Giorgetto

1967 Maserati Ghibli purchased by the author in 1980 for $10,900 and valued today at $16,000. (Julia Rush)

Giugiaro, seemed to feel that it was his masterpiece. The car is luxurious inside and out and even comes with automatic transmission, power steering, power brakes, power windows, and air conditioning. The interior finish and dash can hardly be improved upon.

Currently, it is possible to get a Ghibli of the early 1967 series for $15,000 or even a little less. For a maximum of $22,000 one can get a 1972 model, the last put out and with a slightly larger engine than the earlier Ghibli. Many of the bugs in the original car were worked out in the later models.

The Spyder with the top down is certainly a candidate for the most beautiful open classic ever made, at least postwar classic. Few of these open cars were made. Demand is high and supplies low. Such a car can cost anywhere from $28,000 to $42,000.

In the January 1983 Barrett-Jackson auction an early Ghibli in fine condition brought $17,500, a rather high price for an auction, and particularly for an auction in which sales were hard to make. The price trend will, no doubt, be up.

Chevrolet Corvair Convertibles

The Chevrolet Corvair is an automobile within the means of anyone who has just enough money to buy an inexpensive car. The one collector car that anyone seems to be able to afford is the Chevrolet Corvair of the 1960s, the somewhat innovative rear-engine car.

At the Grand Old Cars Museum sale a 1963 Corvair convertible in class 3 condition, no sensation of a car, brought $5,800. After having inspected this particular car and noting the knockdown auction price, I think that not only was this car high in price but possibly Corvairs were taking off in the market. To be sure, a mint-condition Corvair convertible can bring up to $7,500, and easily $5,000, but this car was far from mint and was rather uninteresting-looking.

For a maximum of $2,500 one can get a class 3 closed Corvair, possibly for as little as $1,500. This is not, however, the car that is in the greatest demand.

While the car-buying public seems to be becoming well aware of the Corvair, prices have had difficulty rising. The Corvair may be in the price and preference class in which the Mustang convertible of 1964–1966 found itself, say, at the beginning of the decade. It is entirely possible that the Corvair will "take off" as the Mustang convertible did. Right now, however, one might try to get a very good Corvair convertible for a maximum of $5,000.

Cadillac Eldorado Convertibles, 1971–1976

The Cadillac Eldorado convertible manufactured between 1971 and 1976 is one of the most beautiful and impressive-looking luxury convertibles ever manufactured. It is a big and extremely stylishly designed automobile that is reasonably good mechanically, except for the springing and the wheel universals. Otherwise the car is well made and fairly rugged.

There are two facts to keep in mind in regard to the Eldorado convertible. The first is that there is a vast difference in value between the average Eldorado convertible on the road and a fine-condition Eldorado convertible—at least $5,000 difference in value, since that is the least one can spend to put an average Eldorado into fine condition. To achieve mint would cost very much more than $5,000. Today one should buy only Eldorados in very fine condition.

The other fact to remember is that there is a great difference in values between the last model of the Eldorado convertible made—the 1976—and the earlier models. The 1976 model with reasonably few miles can bring $12,000 up. With very few miles it can bring $20,000.

In 1982 a good-condition 1974 model sold for $3,500, and this is the target price of any good-condition (not mint) car from 1971 to 1974. The 1975 model might bring $6,000 to $7,000.

1974 Cadillac Eldorado convertible purchased by the author for $5,200 in 1977 is worth $12,000 today. Some cars of these last convertible models have been seen at prices higher than this, while specimens in poor condition sell for much less. (Julia Rush)

On the other hand, any mint-condition 1971–1974 can bring $7,000 as a minimum, and possibly as much as $9,000, the figure that was offered to me for my 1974 model.

The Cadillac convertible of 1947 is a good car, and I owned four of them at various times—as my only car. These cars, in top condition, sell for over $15,000, as do the 1946 cars, which like the 1947 model are not particularly distinguished. It is possible that the 1971–1974 Eldorado convertibles will head toward this higher figure over the years.

Late-Model Packard V-12 Convertible Coupes

In the Grand Old Cars Museum auction in January 1983, the car I felt was the standout of the entire sale was a 1937 Packard V-12 convertible coupe. It was listed in class 2 condition, but it was certainly close to class 1. The grille was chrome-plated, almost certainly not an original feature, but the chrome enhanced the appearance of the car without damaging its originality very much. This car sold for $58,000, and when one considers how few fine cars might have been bought for this figure in any of the four January 1983 Phoenix auctions, this car looked very good as a buy. There were better cars in these auctions but at vastly higher prices, and this 1937 car was a prime car to add to anyone's collection.

The price of this car is about standard for a late-1930s Packard V-12 con-

1937 Packard Twelve convertible coupe that brought $58,000 in 1983 at the Grand Old Cars Museum sale. Value in 1970: $8,000. (Julia Rush)

vertible in fine condition. The V-12 convertibles of the early 1930s can sell for twice this figure, or at least nearly twice the $58,000 that this car cost, and for $58,000 one could have bought a car that was magnificent and in almost perfect condition—by anyone's standards.

Delage and Delahaye Roadsters and Convertibles of the Early Postwar Period

One of the most exotic cars ever produced is the Delahaye, particularly the convertible. The Delage is on the same order, perhaps not as exotic-looking. In later years in the history of the two cars they were combined in one company under one management.

There are not enough Delahayes and Delages around for the car to be well known in collecting circles. For that reason at auction these cars sometimes can be picked up at what appear to be bargain prices.

A standard retail price for the postwar car, the Model 135M cabriolet, may be the $60,000 asked for a 1948 cabriolet. The particular car was the winner of the 1948 Paris concours d'elégance and had a body by Guillore. The car was one of two of this model and had only 26,000 miles on the odometer. It had been stored for twenty-eight years.

At auction these cars in near-mint condition might be bought for about $30,000.

The postwar cars are not a great deal different from the prewar cars, the latter being perhaps a little more dashing, but the prices of the prewar cars are about twice those of the postwar cars. In the January 1983 Barrett-Jackson auction a 1939 Delahaye convertible was one of the real standouts with superb restoration. It sold for $110,000. In the same month a 1938 Delage D8/120 was offered for sale for $90,000, with Chapron body, a car that had belonged to Barbara Hutton. It too was a convertible but a little less beautiful than the Delahaye and probably not in the superb condition of the Delahaye.

Ferrari Super America and Superfast

In all probability the Ferraris that are popular today will continue to be popular for some time—and will rise in price. These popular Ferraris are the 275GTB-4 and the Daytona as well as almost all Ferrari convertibles. Maybe they are underpriced on the present market, but in 1980 and 1981 they had a big runup in price and did not decline much in the recession of 1981–1982. They are still in demand and perhaps particularly among buyers who want dashing performance and prestige cars, not simply classic cars.

There are few Ferraris that are true classic cars as contrasted to performance and prestige cars. The Ferrari Super America is one such car, as is the Superfast. These cars are not bought primarily for prestige reasons or by drivers who want to have the best performance on the road. They are being bought by collectors who consider they are buying postwar classics. In Italy this is most certainly the primary motivation of buyers of Ferrari Super Americas. Of all Ferraris sold in Italy this car is in the greatest demand and at the highest prices.

The Super America and the Superfast are both big-engined, high-horse-power cars. The Super America was put out from about 1961 to 1964, a coupe with a 4.9-liter engine, one of the biggest engines ever used by Ferrari. When the car appeared it was definitely a prestige car. Currently, it sells for about $35,000.

The successor car to the Super America was the Superfast, another big-engined car of about 5 liters manufactured from 1964 to 1966. Only about thirty-six of these "500 Superfasts" were built. The car sells today for about $50,000.

When any Ferrari of any model or year sells under market, that is an event. Almost every Ferrari is in demand and at rising prices. These two big, high-performance prestige cars are the exceptions.

Model T Ford

The Model T Ford in the present market seems underpriced, but rising in price and in buyer esteem. The best Ford Model T I have seen for sale was auctioned in the January 1983 Grand Old Cars Museum sale in Arizona. It was a magnificent (if this term can be applied to a simple little four-cylinder car with two forward speeds and the brake on the driveshaft) "sports car." The earlier the Ford Model T, the better and the more valuable. This speedster was a 1912. It was painted red and was an attention-getter. It was in at least class 2 condition. The red paint job was very good, and the car had a most sporty appearance. I would not be surprised if this particular car would do 60 or even 70 mph.

The 1908–1909 cars can bring up to $20,000 if in prime condition, and from 1909 to the last year of the Model T (1927), prices decline. The 1927 roadster and touring car in *mint* condition bring about $10,000 to $12,000. It would be my objective to get a Model T of the 1920s in very *good* condition for a maximum of $5,000. At this price the Model T seems underpriced. I would concentrate on the tourers and roadsters.

Rolls-Royce Phantom III, Especially the Convertibles

The Rolls-Royce V-12 Phantom III of the immediate prewar years is one of the most elaborate and carefully made cars ever produced. In many ways

1970 Rolls-Royce Drophead, priced in London at $30,000. (Laurence Kayne)

it is the masterpiece of the Rolls-Royce company. To produce the exact same car today would cost at least $250,000 per car, according to the best guesses. The car has the magnificence of the big Isotta Fraschinis, the Hispano-Suizas (including the V-12's), and the Duesenberg J's and SJ's. Yet for what the Rolls-Royce Phantom III is it seems underpriced on today's market.

The most beautiful car of the PIII series is the convertible sedan, followed by the convertible coupe. The cars were put out from 1935 to 1941, and the cars on which to concentrate are the latest cars, not that they are the best but they are the underpriced ones. The earliest convertibles and open cars easily sell at $100,000 to $120,000. The later models can often be purchased for $50,000 to $60,000, even the open cars.

A 1937 PIII convertible with a magnificent two-passenger body was offered in 1983 (not mint) for $75,000. It might have been bought for around $60,000, and at this price it was underpriced. The PIII is rare but occasionally offered for sale. The closed cars, the late models, can sometimes be bought for $25,000 to $30,000.

Lincoln Continental Convertible, First Series

This first series was put out just prior to World War II (1940–1942) and the same car was put out right after the war (1946–1948). In these two periods 2,227 convertibles were made. They are all "Mark I" cars.

The Continental was based on the Lincoln Zephyr, a forward-looking body style, but the Continental was far more elegant and is an elegant car today with its low, long, horizontal look. The mechanics of the car are not the finest, and the Zephyr was not priced high enough for the company to be able to turn out top quality. The Zephyr and the Continental have flathead twelve-cylinder engines. In the late 1940s no one would pay very much for a used Continental, prewar or postwar, and $1,500 was about standard. Since that time, prices have been rising. A Continental convertible of the 1940–1948 era in very fine condition would sell today for $15,000 and a mint-condition convertible for $20,000.

Ferrari 330GTC Coupe and 330GTS Convertible

Ferraris (as well as other high-performance Italian cars) are not easy or inexpensive to maintain. Some are better and some are worse when it comes to reliability and repairs.

Bob Wallace, a Ferrari expert of Phoenix, Arizona, said this about the

This Ferrari 330GTS Spyder sold new for approximately $16,000 in 1967, but by 1972 the value was half that figure. In 1983 it sold for $49,500 at Motor Classic Corporation. (Julia Rush)

Ferrari 330GTC of 1967–1968: "This Ferrari is the best road car and the most practical." He felt the car should run 100,000 miles without the necessity for doing any major overhaul work. When you get into the car, he states, you are very likely to get where you are going.

Today a mint-condition 330GTC closed car should be purchased for $25,000 or possibly a little more, far less than the $65,000 that a 275GTB-4 or a Daytona coupe would sell for.

The 330GTS is an open car and for that reason very desirable. Still, this car costs far less than the 275GTB-4 and the Daytona; a mint-condition 330GTS might be purchased for $40,000 to $45,000. It too is highly reliable and a low-maintenance car.

La Salle Convertible Coupe, 1935–1940

One of the best buys in the entire Barrett-Jackson car auction in Phoenix in January 1983 was a 1938 La Salle convertible coupe in class 2 condition. It brought $16,000, the price of a good Japanese four-cylinder coupe new.

This was about market price for this car. A 1937 model, also a magnificent car, sold in the same auction for $18,500. In the Grand Old Cars Museum sale a few days later a 1939 La Salle convertible coupe brought $16,000. This car was in less good condition but still was a fine-looking car.

The 1937 La Salles used the flathead Cadillac engines. These engines were quality and reliable and were made for use in the top car line of the company. Prior to 1937 the La Salles used not a V-8 but an Oldsmobile straight eight. This engine was used from 1934 to 1937.

The La Salle of this era has a classic look about it. It is rather large and impressive-looking and is a luxury car, at least in its appearance. Mint-con-

1937 La Salle convertible, red with white top, was sold at the Barrett-Jackson auction in 1983 for $18,500. In 1970 it might have auctioned for $5,000 or a little less. (Julia Rush)

dition cars might cost $20,000 or even a little more, still something of a bargain price for this quality collector car.

Lamborghini 350 and 400

These are coupes of tremendous horsepower and performance, but rather conservative-looking cars that preceded the ultramodern Miura and the later Countach.

The 350GTV came onto the market in 1964 with a horsepower rating of about 360 and a top speed of 160 mph, not far behind the later Miura. Only 250 of these cars were made.

In 1966 the slightly larger-engined 400GT came out. It would seat four people and the car would do about 167 mph. The same number of this model Lamborghini were produced—about 250. Currently, a fine-condition 350 or 400 should easily be purchased for $15,000, and some can no doubt be purchased for $12,000 and even less.

These cars are quality, although very conservative in appearance. They are far more reliable than the later Lamborghinis and cost less to maintain.

Auburn Boattail Speedsters of the Early 1930s

The Auburn V-12 boattail speedster of the early 1930s is generally much wanted and very expensive, and can sell for as much as $125,000. The ultimate design of the speedster was the 1935 and 1936 851 and 852 models, and these cars sell for about $70,000 if in prime condition.

The in-between speedsters are those made in the early 1930s and up to the introduction of the 851 in 1935. These can sometimes be purchased at bargain prices (for what they are) but probably not for long.

In the January 1983 Barrett-Jackson auction a 1933 model Auburn speedster painted red got a good deal of exposure. The car was very fine-looking and in very fine, but not mint, condition. It sold for $21,200, a bargain price. Although the car was around a long time for prospective buyers to examine and was not suddenly sprung on the public at the auction rostrum, it secured little buyer interest although there were at least 1,000 registered buyers, mainly dealers, at the auction.

Two speedsters of the same vintage were offered by the later Arizona Kruse auction, but these failed to find buyers at $21,500 and $31,000. At even $35,000 an early 1930s speedster in mint condition is an excellent buy.

Lagonda V-12 Rapide Convertible of About 1939

The Lagonda Rapide was a beautiful and modern-looking car when it was produced in the immediate prewar years. It is a beautiful-looking car now, a fine classic, as fine in appearance as some of the very high-priced V-12 convertibles like the Hispano-Suiza V-12 and the Horch V-12.

The Columbia House World of Automobiles, An Illustrated Encyclopedia of the Motor Car, a set of twenty-two comprehensive volumes, says this about the Lagonda Rapide V12:

"Into this chassis was also fitted W. O. Bentley's remarkable 75 × 84 mm 4½-litre V12 cylinder Lagonda engine with a single chain-driven overhead camshaft to each bank of six cylinders. This produced 225 bhp on an 8.8 to 1 compression ratio. World War II stopped production and further development of this great car, but not before two Rapide V12s had come third and fourth in the 1939 Le Mans race in a tryout for a bid for outright victory in the 1940 race."

Such a Lagonda Rapide V-12 raced in an early Watkins Glen race, and although it did not win it acquitted itself very well, at the same time appearing to be a beautiful and docile sports car.

Such a car in fine condition should be purchased for under $40,000. For half this price, or at most $25,000, the six-cylinder car might be purchased, a car with the same appearance but a less sophisticated engine, another underpriced car.

Iso Grifo

In the February 1981 auction held by Christie's, an Iso Grifo 5.7-liter sport coupe with Chevrolet Corvette engine was on the block. The car was manufactured in 1969 to use this engine. This model car was first introduced to the public in 1965 and was continued through until about 1974. The top speed of the car with its 295-horsepower Corvette engine was about 165 mph.

This particular car, which we examined in some detail, was quality and was in excellent condition. It reached a high bid of $9,500. This was about market price for this car as late as 1982 and possibly 1984.

The car is a performer. It is extremely fast. It is reliable, with a Chevrolet engine and transmission (and sometimes Ford), and it is inexpensive. It is the kind of car that one can admire in his garage, but at the same time one can get in, turn the key, and roar off down the road without fear that something expensive is going to happen to the car. The car is pure Italian in design and of top quality.

15

The Buyers In The Market:
Important Collectors and Collections

To assess the market and the future potential for collector cars one has to try to determine who is buying. To a considerable extent, the essence of the market for collector cars is the collector car auction—not that all collector cars are bought or sold at collector car auctions by any means, but who buys and who sells are explained by the car auctions.

Old Cars Weekly for February 3, 1983, carried the main headline: "550 Cars Cross the Block at Kruse-Waller Sale. Selling Percentage is 42%."

The article says, "This percent average is better than some past outings with some really good buys available to the serious bidders. . . . The long and short of it is simply that the Kruse-Waller sale reconfirmed itself as a major force in the Arizona new year auctions." This means that the 42% sale was a success.

In the Rick Cole Arizona sale of the previous January, the sales percentage was 36½%. Thirty-three cars out of ninety offered found buyers. This was not a devastating percent as auction sales in this industry go, but the sale was not a great standout.

It costs a great deal to truck a collector car to the auction—and then back again if the car does not sell. The cost is at least $2,000 from the East Coast to Arizona and back again. It can cost as much as $2,000 one-way in a closed car van. Why then do the sellers go into a collector car auction knowing in advance that only 50% of the cars offered will sell and possibly only 42% or 36½%? Or 32%, the percentage reported for the leading 1983 Arizona auction?

At the Barrett-Jackson auction in Arizona in 1983, I talked to a number of the sellers whose cars did not sell, and to a number of the sellers before the sale took place. The fact of the matter is that many, if not most, of the disappointed sellers were not really that disappointed. Certainly their cars did not sell, but the sellers felt that that was no calamity. There did not seem very much pressure to sell or even a tremendous amount of interest in selling. There was at least as much disappointment on the part of would-be buyers who came away empty-handed—and there were plenty of those disappointed buyers.

This is not at all the way it is at the art and antique furniture auctions—or the silver, glassware, ceramics, etc. auctions. Such low percentages of sales in those auctions spell failure. If I offered some of my paintings for sale at Christie's or Sotheby's and I sold only 42% of what I offered I would be in something like disgrace. There would be many collectors, dealers, and auction officials who would think that my paintings weren't very much or else that I had such a wild idea about their value that my reserves (the minimum prices I would accept) were set far too high.

As far as buyers go, they do not generally expect to get the cars they like. At least they do not expect to get them all. They are there at the auctions in case they can buy what they want to buy, but they often come away with a feeling of regret that their bids simply did not come near the reserve prices set on the cars they wanted.

Car purchasers are a unique breed. Russ Jackson owns the Classic Carriage House in Phoenix, the oldest antique car showroom in Arizona. Each January, Russ Jackson and Tom Barrett stage what is probably the biggest and most important collector car auction in the United States—the Barrett-Jackson auction. Mr. Jackson explains the auction business this way:

"Everybody is a collector and at the same time everybody is in the business of buying and selling collector cars, at least everybody who is active in the collector car auctions like ours in Arizona.

"At our auctions there are about 1,000 registered buyers, and probably 50% of these are bona fide buyers. The registered buyers register with us prior to the auction and secure an auction number which they use so that we can determine who made the winning bid on each car sold.

"All of these are collectors, or at least consider themselves to be collectors. They may have three cars or ten cars or a hundred.

"Ninety percent of the people selling are also buying at the same auction. They sell one car and buy one or sell five cars and buy ten. Sell Saturday, buy Sunday. There are hardly any collectors of just one car. They have from one to ten cars, and there are literally thousands of these collectors.

"Everyone buys and sells—refines his collection. That is why I say everybody is in the business and everybody is a collector. They all collect, invest, buy, sell. It is more than rare to find any owner of a collector car who has just one car. I know from my dealership and from the contacts I make in our auction.

"As far as important and larger collections go there are probably fifty important collections in this country—collections with at least a hundred cars. There are probably more big collections in this country than in Europe. In Europe only the very rich collect cars. As for smaller collections, there are thousands of these in this country.

"Why do they buy? Investment is a very important motive. They don't buy because they think it is a pretty car. Nearly everybody buys as an investment—also because they like the cars, but at least 60% of the motive is investment. Long-term investment in collector cars has been great.

"Now people are buying the later cars, the cars of the 1950s and 1960s, but these are the smaller collectors. These people may have from one to ten cars."

Howard Snyder, former president of the Maryland chapter of the Model T Ford Club International, is, to a degree at least, typical of the very large group of car collectors of today. In the August 4, 1983, issue of *Old Cars Weekly*, one of his cars, a 1909 Buick Model 10, Toy Tonneau body, a prizewinner, was offered for the reasonable price of $20,000. He stated:

"I have been in the garage business, and I guess that cars and gasoline are in my blood. I am selling my Buick because I want to buy another car. Three weeks ago I injured my wrist cranking my Buick. I don't think I can crank these cars anymore. People think I am crazy to sell my Buick, and it is an excellent car, but I do need the money."

Mr. Snyder has another car, a 1916 Model T Ford. Over the years he has restored three or four Model T Fords. Mr. Snyder said he always has more than one car and he added that many collectors have more than one car. About three-quarters of the members of his chapter of the Model T Ford Club International have more than one car; about half the members have more than two cars. He felt this proportion of collector car ownership held true of the chapters of the club all over. One member of his chapter has twelve cars and is busy adding to his collection.

"A lot of collectors buy for investment," he said. "If you are interested in automobile investment, you have to be sharp or else loaded with money. Basically, unless you are a sharp buyer or loaded with money and can get a bargain, your main return on the car will have to be the joy of ownership. I get more on my money market certificates than on the sale of my cars.

"Four cars at the same time are the most I have ever had. Some people have ancient vehicles which they store, let sit and deteriorate, and this is very sad."

Possibly to avoid having one such car deteriorate spurred Mr. Snyder to offer his 1909 Buick for sale. He wants to buy a neglected 1924 Willys Knight touring car—a car that "needs tender loving care."

I asked him whether he did his own work on his cars, to which he replied, "Oh, yes. I've fixed up cars for years. I think that most collectors, at least in my club, do a great deal of their own work. I also do some work on other people's cars."

Let's move from antiques to postwar classics. In some ways, Stan Zagorski, the magazine illustrator, typifies a large group of collectors of such cars.

Stan sells and he buys—generally in that order. He sells in order to secure the funds to buy something else. In one year he purchased six collector cars. In other years he purchased no cars, but simply held on to what he had. In all he has owned about twenty-five collector cars, mostly postwar Italian exotics, although he once bought a Porsche Turbo. Sometimes he offers a car he has as a trade with a dealer in collector cars or else sells a car to a dealer, frequently for a good price, above what I think he might have sold the car for to a collector via newspaper advertising.

"I very often buy in Europe, particularly in England," he told me. "Very often I can get a very good buy there, or in the Middle East or in Central America, including Guatemala. For me as a buyer the market is often more favorable there. Of course, my phone bills are enormous. I call all over to locate cars."

When I asked him how many cars he had owned at any one time, he replied, "Once I owned five collector cars at the same time. What a headache! Two is the perfect number. Even three are too many."

Right now he owns three cars:

Lamborghini Miura SV, the last model, put out in 1972, with separate crankcase and transmission. This is the most desirable of all Miuras and the most sought-after. In all, Stan has owned six Miuras, including the one he sold me. It seems difficult to "separate" anyone from his Miura. It is something of an epoch-making automobile.

Ferrari Daytona, one of the smoothest-looking, -driving, and -riding Ferrari powerhouses ever built—from 1968 to 1973—and a great favorite of Ferrari collectors.

Countach 5-liter, the last model made, and still being made, the "earthbound guided missile." He bought the car new in Europe for an amazingly low price, and in so doing followed the principle of collector car buyers to "buy right."

Through his Lamborghini ownership Stan has made himself one of the greatest authorities on the Lamborghini car in the world.

In an interview with Nick Soprano, owner of Motor Classic Corporation, I asked him to outline who was buying and whether or not the buyers owned more than one car. Within the year, one client bought nine postwar classics from him. Among the purchases were a 289 Cobra, a Mangusta, a 280SL Mercedes-Benz, a Jaguar sedan, a Ferrari Boxer, a Ferrari 275GTB-4, and a Ferrari 275GTS. The buyer had a few other cars at the time, so this brought his collection to a total of eleven. At one point, four cars were sitting in the showroom which hadn't been delivered to this buyer.

A new-car distributor who has approximately fifty cars in his collection had also purchased a number of cars from Nick, who sold him a very fine 275GTB-4 Ferrari, a Ferrari Boxer, and a Ferrari Lusso. Nick had been asked to let the buyer know when a 275GTB-4 would be available, and the truck hadn't even unloaded the car when it was sold. Nick said that he had wanted at least the pleasure of getting to know this great car, but that didn't happen. And the collector bought another 275GTB-4 from Nick shortly thereafter. This collector, with about fifty cars, mainly Italian sports cars, has put together an impressive collection.

Nick sold three Ferraris to a first-time Ferrari buyer. "He bought one and then he bought two others: first a 365GTC, then a Lusso, followed by a 308GT-4. He had these and an additional road car for daily use—and that was his collection."

One of his collector clients, a real estate developer, has an impressive thirty-five-car collection that runs from Duesenbergs to road Ferraris. He bought four cars from Nick within two years for his collection: a Ferrari Daytona coupe, a 365GTC Ferrari, a 275GTS Ferrari, and a Grand Prix Bugatti Type 37A.

Some people buy cars that you might not expect them to buy. We were on hand when a rather diminutive woman in about her mid-fifties came by to pick up her Ferrari. She had purchased two Ferraris: a 308GTB and a 365 two-plus-two—for her own use. She had always had sports cars, we were told, but with her first Ferrari, she became quite enthusiastic and bought a second one.

Nick analyzed his market in this way: "In general, the investor-collector-enthusiast is the type who buys these postwar classic sports cars. He is usually a professional, such as a doctor, or lawyer or the head of his own business. A year or two back, buyers seemed to be mainly coming in to buy an "investment car," but with the economic fall-off, this pattern changed and we were back to collectors and enthusiasts. Before the recession, people came in with $20,000 to invest in a car. Now one has to hold the car longer than two years to make a good return on the investment, as the market hasn't risen much. It hasn't dropped, but it hasn't risen either as much as it did a few years back."

He also added the point that the strength of the currency affects the market: "We were selling to Italy for a while, and we were selling to Germany when the German mark was stronger."

In America it is a bit difficult to tell just who is a dealer and who is a collector of automobiles. As indicated, it is often a matter of sell Saturday, buy Sunday. This is different from the art and antiques scene, in which dealers are very separate from collectors or from buyers who want to decorate their homes or simply have some beautiful possessions.

The European market for collector cars is more like the art and antique market. Up to a few years ago, investment was the main motive, as it certainly is in the United States. Collector car sales boomed under the impact of investment buying. Then things cooled off.

The same for cars, but more recently. Jeffrey Pattinson, owner of Coys of Kensington and automobile tycoon in new cars, told us in London, "Cars as investments are finished. They were too publicized as investments. Investment value as a motive pushed prices way up for a time. Now prices are off, and we emphasize love for the car, pride of ownership."

In England and on the Continent there are perhaps two main categories of buyers—the important and very wealthy buyers who want the big, expensive cars, and the small buyers who scrape together enough money to buy just one or a few cars and restore them as they can, often working on the cars themselves. In the Christie's annual Beaulieu, England, sale the sellers are generally not collectors but simply people who want to get rid of a particular car. This summer auction, of course, emphasizes the less expensive cars, and the buyers are car enthusiasts rather than investors. Dealers, for the most part, are not interested in these less expensive cars. They concentrate on buying the expensive cars sold elsewhere at other times in the year.

The English auctions are certainly what they purport to be, but Michael Sedgewick, technical adviser to Christie's car auctions, says this:

"The 'presale' is everything. The bidders know what they want in advance of the sale, especially the bidders on the big important cars. Fifty percent of the cars in our auctions are actually sold in advance of the auction. At the auction we know who will bid about what and we have an idea who will come out of the auction owning which car. We have a reserve on almost every car we are selling. This reserve is generally below our low printed estimate. We will not take cars for auction with too high reserves. We know the biggest buyers, the buyers of the most expensive cars."

Perhaps we can divide the buyers in the European auctions into three groups: (1) the big dealers who sell to the important buyers, collectors, but collectors of a relatively few cars, like 10 cars at most; (2) the new buyers coming into the market, the 'thirty-five-year-olds' who want one or a few fairly important and fairly expensive cars, but not necessarily the most expensive cars: (3) the "poor" buyers after one car that they will do a good deal of the work on themselves and then move on to car number two.

The Auto Museum Phenomenon

The past decade has seen the greatest growth of collector car museums in history. Museums have sprung up almost like mushrooms, and they are somewhat unique, as museums go.

On December 1, 1981, the Imperial Palace Automobile Collection of Las Vegas, Nevada, opened to the public. In 1971 construction was started on the Imperial Palace Hotel and Casino. About ten years later the top floor of the garage was converted into an automobile museum, a large space of 51,000 square feet. Casino, hotel, and car collection were developed by Ralph Englestad, an old-car enthusiast.

When Mr. Englestad decided to start a museum, he put a crew out on the road to buy up cars, cars suitable to a museum of collector automobiles. By the time the museum opened, on December 1, 1981, about $10,000,000 had been spent buying the cars. They were bought restored, since a long wait and a number of headaches were not wanted when the museum opening was contemplated. Mr. Englestad decided on an optimum number of cars at 300 of which 200 would be on display, and from time to time other of the cars would be placed on display and some of those on display removed for a time. It was also his intention to sell off some cars and to replace them with other cars from time to time. He wanted to collect certain celebrity cars, and he got cars that had belonged to Cecil B. De Mille, Al Capone, Douglas MacArthur, and Adolf Hitler. He bought such makes as Duesenberg, Packard, Metz, Rolls-Royce, Ford, Chevrolet, Hudson, and Chrysler. He also bought a few fire engines and motorcycles.

From time to time I have noticed that the Imperial Palace was bidding for collector cars at various auctions. In Tommy Reed's Hot Springs, Arkansas, sale in early 1982, for instance, the Imperial Palace bought the Gloria Swanson 1918 Cadillac phaeton for $30,000. In July 1981, Ralph Englestad bought a 1923 Renault touring car that had belonged to F. Scott Fitzgerald. One can comb through collector car auction news items and see the activities of Mr. Englestad and his museum.

The museum which came on with a big bang very recently is the Blackhawk Collection. In a year, Don Williams, director of the collection, accumulated a major portion of the hundred-car collection. The cars have been exhibited in a warehouse on San Ramon Valley Boulevard in San Ramon, California, the warehouse being fixed up somewhat like a museum. On September 18,

1983, plans were announced to open the Transportation and Automotive Museum of the University of California, which includes the Behring Educational Institute. To date apparently about $15,000,000 has been spent on the collection, and the museum-warehouse was opened in July 1982. Much of the money for the museum and its collection was apparently supplied by Mr. Ken Behring—hence the Behring Educational Institute.

About half of the collection of the Blackhawk Museum was at one time or another owned by Tom Barrett of Scottsdale; Tom has sold many cars to the collection.

The Blackhawk Collection has in it some stars. One such car is the Hispano-Suiza Boulogne model with tulipwood body, a celebrated and much-illustrated automobile. The Blackhawk Collection paid $400,000 for this car. The collection also bought a Hispano-Suiza H6B with coupe body by Kellner, for $50,000. The great Clark Gable Duesenberg Speedster was also bought by the collection for $350,000.

One can scan the automotive press to see the activities of this collection. Very recently a group of five cars were purchased. In August 1982, Blackhawk purchased the 1941 Indianapolis pace car, a Chrysler Newport dual-cowl phaeton, a special made just to pace the Indianapolis race.

The collection also purchased Barbara Hutton's Mercedes-Benz 540K and a magnificent Rolls-Royce Phantom III. Clark Gable's boattail SSJ Duesenberg speedster was also a recent purchase, as was the Kellner-bodied Hispano-Suiza that we earlier cited. The cost of these five cars came to about $1,000,000.

Messrs. Behring and Williams acquire with verve and with a sense of public relations. On April 16, 1983, a reception was given for some of the leading worldwide collectors to celebrate the arrival of no fewer than twenty one-of-a-kind top collector cars, a group of cars valued at $10,000,000. Among the group was an extremely rare car, an Italian Bucciali, worth perhaps as much as $1,000,000. There was also a 1936 Mercedes-Benz special roadster that had been advertised by the factory as the "most expensive Mercedes-Benz in the world."

Heading the list of the great collectors of automobiles in the United States are Dorothy and Jack Nethercutt of Sylmar, thirty miles north of Los Angeles, California. This highly important collection of the finest classic and antique cars is housed in a $25,000,000 museum in the town of Sylmar, California. The display floor resembles a car showroom of the 1920s with marble floors, marble columns, and gold inlay work on the ceilings.

The J. B. Nethercutts privately own their collection of cars, and the collection is shown as the Merle Norman Classic Beauty Collection in Sylmar. The Merle Norman Cosmetic Company is also owned by Mr. Nethercutt.

There are 119 cars in the collection, and several cars were purchased for it in 1983, including two Austro Daimlers of 1932, a limousine and an Alpine sedan, as well as an open Packard of 1904. The collection rarely sells any cars. It buys whatever would add to the collection or is particularly beautiful. There is no set purchasing plan.

The cars in the collection run from a 1904 Packard to a 1972 Rolls-Royce, with everything between, including a 1967 Ferrari and a Mercedes-Benz Gullwing. The collection is heaviest in the luxury prewar classics of the 1920s and 1930s.

The star of the collection is a 1933 Duesenberg that has always been referred to as, and is known as, the Twenty Grand Duesenberg. The collection has owned this great for many years. It is a Duesenberg Arlington Torpedo sedan, a one-of-a-kind car designed by the leading Duesenberg body designer, Gordon Buehrig, for the 1933 World's Fair. The car has a Rollston body and is a closed-model SJ.

The collection also owns Rudolph Valentino's 1923 Avion Voisin. It is a sporting open car.

The collection is rotated in the 1920s showrooms. About forty cars are on display at any one time in this handsome setting.

One of the "older" car museums is the James C. Leake and Antiques, Inc., Car Museum in Muskogee, Oklahoma. It has been in existence for about twelve years. The "nucleus" of the museum is a collection of about sixty cars. These cars have remained in the collection since they first became a part of the museum collection.

Each year Antiques, Inc., and James C. Leake hold an auction. About seventy cars placed in the auction are from the museum collection, so the museum is purchasing cars in the market from time to time during each year, since its "nucleus" of cars amounts to only about sixty.

To these seventy cars offered from the museum collection are added 500 consigned cars.

For thirty years James C. Leake has been a collector of cars, but only in the past twelve years has there been a formal car museum. The name Antiques Inc. indicates something of the scope of the interests of Mr. Leake and his museum. In 1979 his auction included antique furniture as well as automobiles. The annual auctions are offerings of the finest cars available in the country. In the 1983 auction year the Barrett-Jackson auction had a superior group of cars for sale, but in certain years Leake's cars can hardly be beaten for quality, cars like the 1936 Hispano-Suiza V-12 with Saoutchik convertible body that auctioned for about $350,000 in 1982.

The museum collection includes such stars as the Rolls-Royce 1911 Silver Ghost belonging to the Maharajah of Mysore, a 1934 Packard dual-cowl phaeton, a Marmon V-16 touring car, a 1925 Locomobile, a 1903 Ford (chassis number 68—68th off the assembly line), a 1904 Northern, a 1904 Reo, and a 1901 Olds.

There are also Ferraris, including a Berlinetta Boxer 512 and a Ferrari Daytona Spyder, and Lamborghinis and Maseratis.

Harrah's Automobile Collection is the largest such collection in the country. It is located in Reno, Nevada, and until recently was owned by Bill Harrah, automobile collector for many years. The Harrah enterprises were sold to Holiday Inn, including the automobile collection, and that collection is now known as the Harrah Automobile Foundation. The cars were given to the foundation by Harrah's, the gaming arm of Holiday Inn. So far about a hundred cars have been transferred to Harrah's Automobile Foundation. Over a five-year period the rest will be donated. There are on display about 1,000 cars, and in all there may be as many as 1,200. The cars range in year of manufacture from the 1890s through the 1960s.

Harrah's has conducted auction sales for the purpose of getting rid of excess cars and duplicate cars, boats, and airplanes. On September 12, 1981, for instance, Harrah's sold 142 vehicles, by no means all junk and lesser duplicates. One of the cars sold was an excellent Bugatti Type 57C convertible coupe. Another was a 1936 Hispano-Suiza. The former car brought $90,000, the latter $55,000. This was Harrah's Seventh Vehicle Auction, and the 142 cars brought in a total of $1,911,220.

Probably the most notable of Harrah's cars is a Bugatti Royale town car, but this is not all. Harrah's has still another of these top classics—out of a total of only six or seven ever made. Another "great" in the collection is a 1908 Thomas Flyer that took part in the famous New York–to–Paris Race. Still another great car is the Phantom Corsair, the Rust Heinz super streamliner of 1939 built on a Cord 810 chassis and displayed in the 1939 World's Fair and also billed as the Flying Wombat in the moving picture *Young at Heart*. When I owned this great car, I drove it to work almost every day and used it regularly to go out in the evening.

A number of today's great collectors started to collect in a modest way right after the close of World War II. In 1948, Bill Harrah bought his first cars, a 1911 Maxwell, a 1911 Model T Ford, a 1906 Model F Ford, and a 1902 curved-dash Olds—not the most distinguished cars ever, but a start. It was not until 1961 that his collection was big enough or fine enough in his opinion to be placed on public display. The main make of car displayed is the Model T Ford, and Fords make up about 10% of his entire collection, with Packards next. The emphasis is on American cars.

Art Grandlich started collecting automobiles thirty-five years ago, when he was nineteen years old. He and wife, Betsy, in January 1983 put on one of the most successful auction sales of all time—the Grand Old Cars Museum sale in Apache Junction, Arizona, a sale that I have mentioned often in this book.

This sale was the opposite of the usual activity of a car museum—the buying activity. This was a selling activity. On the other hand, maybe it was the logical sequence to building up a museum collection—disposing of it in the end and at a handsome profit. The sale was a "no reserve" sale. The cars sold for what the buyers at the auction would pay for them, and if no one wanted to pay over $1,000 for a near-mint Packard V-12 convertible presumably the car would have sold for $1,000. Only the car did not sell for $1,000. It brought well over $50,000.

So now the Grandlichs and their Grand Old Cars Muesum are finished in the collector car business with a handsome capital gain. They sold all of the 175 cars they offered for sale. In all they sold 3,000 items, including automobile signs, automobile pictures, stationary engines, etc. All these things came from the Grand Old Cars Museum, which had been organized in 1977. The museum opened with thirty cars that the Grandlichs shipped in from Wisconsin.

Betsy Grandlich stated her philosophy:

"It is clear that the key to our sale was that the cars were all American cars, cars that people could identify with, not cars that were made for a few years and then went down the drain—or very old cars, cars that can't be driven and that few people know about.

"An investment, whether diamonds, clocks, or whatever, is a gamble. In fact, a synonym for investment is gamble. If, however, you buy the best product, which the open car was, the most expensive cars and produced in limited numbers, then people thirty or forty or fifty years old identify with these. They are getting cars which they and their parents identify with, perhaps a car on which they learned to drive.

"That's why our sale was so successful. There was something for everybody, and we had 1,066 registered bidders, probably more than any auction anywhere has had. Some cars sold for $1,000 and some for $50,000. The average price ran from $5,000 to $15,000—a good, affordable price range."

Over the years the Grandlichs conducted car auctions and in the meantime were buying for their own collection in the museum. The museum was a kind of attraction carrying an admission charge located in their shopping center. They loved Packard convertibles, and they had many.

The New Museums—What They Mean to the Collector Car Market

1. The new car museums are just that—new. For the most part they are only a few years old and certainly the vast majority of them have been organized well after the close of World War II.

2. These museums have been buying choice cars that are carefully selected.

3. The cars bought are, for the most part, the very expensive, very fine cars.

4. The museums often are the end result of buying by one man, perhaps one man with a financial backer.

5. When the collection gets big, then it is moved to a new structure generally and converted to a museum.

6. A museum is a natural development of the efforts of collectors. Cars take up a great deal of room. A collection of a hundred cars requires a very large storage space, and a museum may be the answer. A collection of a hundred equally valuable paintings can be hung in many homes, and if of sufficient importance, then lent to an art museum, where it can easily be accommodated.

7. A car museum is a convenient way to handle expenses taxwise, especially if admission is charged so that the museum is a business proposition.

8. The collection can be converted to a foundation, and each time the collector gives a car to the museum foundation, this is a contribution against adjusted gross income.

9. Sometimes when museums develop up to a point in the accumulation of cars at appreciating values, a natural development is to liquidate all or at least some cars at a capital gain at preferred capital gains tax rates.

Major Museum Collections

We have described a number of the collector car museums in some detail rather than simply listing them because they are major factors in the market. They have been buying at a great clip and are likely to continue. They have been, and are, an important buyer element. Then, of course, there are the well-established and older museums, the museums that have been in existence for a time, whose collections have long since been accumulated, at least for the most part. They are not at present important elements in the collector car market. They are not out there buying. Still, they are some of the absolutely top collector car museums of the country.

The Henry Ford Museum (the Dearborn Museum), Dearborn, Michigan, is a top collection including the highly important Bugatti Royale with Weinberger cabriolet body.

The Frederick C. Crawford Auto-Aviation Museum and Western Reserve Historical Society, Cleveland, Ohio, has a very large collection of immaculately restored antique and classic cars, with particular emphasis on antiques.

The Smithsonian Institution, Washington, D.C., has a fairly large collection of cars, trucks, and motorcycles that has been completely catalogued and described in a government booklet by former Curator of Land Transportation Smith Hempstone Oliver.

The Auburn-Cord-Duesenberg Museum, Auburn, Indiana, has a large collection of cars, not strictly the products of the Auburn-Cord-Duesenberg Company.

The Long Island Automotive Museum, Henry Austin Clark, Glen Cove, New York, was a museum built up to a size of about 220 antique and major classic cars. In 1979 Austin Clark held a well-publicized auction, and in September 1980, the museum formally closed. Mr. Clark now has thirty-five cars, mainly antiques, in the collection. The museum was in existence for thirty-three years.

The Briggs Cunningham Automotive Museum, Costa Mesa, California, is a fairly large collection of antique and classic cars built up by Briggs Cunningham over a period of many years. Sometimes a few cars are sold in a process of refining the collection, like the 1932 Stutz Super Bearcat that was sold in 1981 by Christie's in Los Angeles to Tom Barrett. There is a Bugatti Royale in the collection.

The Indianapolis Motor Speedway Hall of Fame, Indianapolis, Indiana, has some fabulous racing cars.

The Candy Store Museum, Burlingame, California, has a collection of about a hundred milestone cars, dating as recently as the 1950s and 1960s, going back to the great prewar classics and to some antiques of the 1920s and earlier.

Important Collectors

In the September 12, 1981, Harrah auction in Reno, Arturo Keller of Mexico City bought the top-priced car in the sale—the Bugatti 57C, referred to earlier, for $90,000. He also bought the second-highest-priced car of the sale, the 1936 Hispano-Suiza, for $55,000. He also bought a 1930 Auburn cabriolet, a 1909 Ford Model T touring car, a 1930 Avon-Standard sports two seater, a 1927 Ford pickup truck, a 1911 Maxwell runabout, and a 1936 Singer two-seater roadster.

After the auction Mr. Keller stated, "I already own eighty cars." Mr. Keller is a manufacturer of auto interiors for American cars. He is a big buyer and a big collector.

In 1947, Cameron Peck of Chicago, a very early member of the Sports Car Club of America, took me on a guided tour of his collection of cars. As I recall it, he had about 120 cars, and to keep them in order I believe he had four mechanics. The garage in which he kept the cars was something of a combination of the latest parking garage and an enormous automobile showroom. It contained everything from an Alpine Rolls-Royce to an SS Mercedes-Benz touring car, later owned by a seller in the 1983 Barrett-Jackson auction and valued by this seller at the auction at $300,000.

The collection was dispersed for business reasons. It was certainly one of the finest car collections in the world at the time.

Dr. Samuel Scher, a plastic surgeon, was also an early member of the Sports Car Club of America, and in those early days of the 1940s and 1950s, we all knew one another. I visited Sam's collection in New Rochelle, where it occupied an entire large floor of a garage, and the floor was fixed up and lighted like a museum. The collection was large but probably well under a hundred cars, with some great standouts like a near-new Mercedes-Benz 540K convertible and Charles de Gaulle's staff car. Dr. Scher went to enormous trouble to restore his cars to original condition, just as Cameron Peck and Bill Harrah did.

About twenty years ago, Dr. Scher disposed of his collection. His group of Rolls-Royces he sold to Harry Resnick, but the bulk of his collection was sold to Richard C. Paine, Jr., of the Paine Webber brokerage firm. Mr. Paine's collection of about 300 cars is located in Owls Head, Maine. The collection boasts some superb cars, including, of course, the Scher cars. The collection used to form a museum, but the museum now seems to be closed, so I would have to classify the cars as a private collection.

A short while ago I would have had to classify Dorothy and Jack Nethercutt as possibly the king and queen of American car collectors. Now they have a museum and I must classify their collection as a museum collection; but whatever it is it is the product of painstaking collecting backed up by considerable collector car investment funds.

These are some other major collectors: Robert Bahre, Oxford, Maine; Wally Rank, Milwaukee, Wisconsin; Clifford Oborne, Warren, New Jersey; Brooks Stevens, Mequon, Wisconsin; Philip Wichard, Halesite, Long Island, New York.

There are many big collectors, but many of this group do not care about publicizing the fact that they are either big collectors or wealthy. At the Reggie Jackson Fall Classic at Oakland, California, several big collectors were spotted when this auction took place in December 1982, collectors in addition to baseball player Reggie Jackson himself. These were Art Wahlers, Phoenix, Arizona; Dave Smith, Las Vegas, Nevada; and Frank Negri, Fountain Valley, California. These three are regular auction goers—and auction buyers.

At the Kruse auction in Phoenix of January 1982, Reggie Jackson demonstrated that he was a big buyer. He bid $525,000 on the Granatelli-built turbine Corvette, but he was topped by the $550,000 bid of Milton Verret of Beaumont, Texas. Reggie has a huge collection of performance cars of the 1960s.

In the Annual Greater Dallas–Ft. Worth Collector Car Auction at the end of 1982, a pair of 1934 Packards made headlines when they went for the unprecedented sum of $450,000—$225,000 each for the 1934 V-12s, one a dual-cowl phaeton, the other a boattail. A highly important fact as far as big collectors go is that both of these cars were bought by one man—the reputed Houston billionaire Jerry J. Moore, who had some grand plans to build a $20,000,000 old-car museum in Houston.

When we come to Tom Barrett of Scottsdale, Arizona, I don't know exactly what he is, dealer or collector or both. Tom Barrett and Russ Jackson put on the most important collector car auction in the country each January, and only the Leake auction rivals it. At the same time that Tom is an auctioneer he is a dealer who sells somewhere in the region of $8,000,000 worth of cars in the year. His inventory (or maybe it's his collection) is worth about $3,000,000, the inventory he has on hand at all times. I am inclined to classify Tom Barrett the way Lord Duveen was classified in the field of paintings, mainly Old Master paintings. Lord Duveen was the supreme painting dealer, and I suppose Tom Barrett is the supreme collector car dealer. In any event, he has the reputation among many people—certainly the car authority Henry Austin Clark, for years the owner of one of the finest car museums in the country—of being absolutely honest (which is saying a lot for the car business and car auction business, which has been rocked with scandal). Lord Duveen paid over the market to get the finest and to attach a kind of aura to the paintings he handled. The high price made the paintings of high quality! Maybe Tom Barrett follows this same philosophy. Like great collectors, Tom keeps the cars in near-mint condition and drivable. He told me a short while ago that had I arrived in Scottsdale a little earlier he would have taken me for a ride in the Mdvani Mercedes-Benz cabriolet, an absolute super car; but it was nothing to him to get in and drive it wherever he wanted to go at the time. Tom's sales as a dealer seem to prove his ability. His 1983 sales (not his auction sales) were at an all-time record level—$11,800,000.

16

Where to Buy and Sell: The Structure of the Collector Car Market

HAROLD ELLIS, A Las Vegas dealer in classic cars, recently gave this piece of advice on buying an investment car: "You have got to buy right." By this he meant, "Pay the right price. Don't pay over the market; and if you can buy under the market then you have bought well."

Five years ago I bought a car which I restored. Somewhere along the line I went wrong. I had paid too much, considering the restoration required. The market still hasn't caught up to my total investment.

Mr. Tom Barrett of the Barrett-Jackson auction in Phoenix, Arizona, puts it in a slightly different way. He says, "You can't pay too much but you can buy too soon." This means if you buy above the market value you won't be in too bad a position over the long run. The rising market will eventually catch up to what you paid for the car. Fine advice, as long as the market keeps rising and at a fairly good pace!

Perhaps even more important for the nonprofessional automobile investor is to buy a "wanted" car in excellent condition, possibly even mint condition. If you buy a 1958 Mercury station wagon, you have not made a wise investment. If, however, you buy a 1957 Mercury Turnpike Cruiser convertible, you have something the market definitely wants.

If you buy a 1958 Eldorado convertible in fair condition, you don't have much. If you buy a 1958 Eldorado in mint condition, you have a car worth about four times as much as the car in fair condition. A 1958 Biarritz convertible in mint condition may be worth close to $30,000.

Of course, if someone buys not for investment but just what he wants, and if he is not concerned with selling, then what he buys, where he buys, and how much he pays isn't so important. Still, it is disheartening to most people to pay $10,000 for a car that is worth on the present market no more than $5,000. Why throw your money down the drain?

Buying Through Advertisements

The traditional way to buy a collector car has been to follow the "for sale" ads in newspapers. For example, I have been following ads in the *New York Times* since the 1920s. In the past ten years the antique and classic car sections of metropolitan newpapers have grown enormously.

There is a certain advantage to buying through the newspaper ads. Most of the cars advertised in big-city newspapers are offered by private individuals. When negotiating with a dealer one cannot avoid the feeling that he may be charging the last dollar for the car he has for sale or that he is selling a lemon that he is passing off as mint. This is not quite accurate, and some dealers sell truly mint-condition cars at fair prices. If, however, the seller who advertises in the newspaper states that the automobile is being sold because he is moving to another state, then that seems like a good background for the purchase of a good car at a reasonable figure.

A great advantage to buying from individuals who advertise is that there is no dealer markup involved and no dealer overhead to cover. There is also the vague possibility that the seller is not as aware of the market as the dealer and thus will not ask a "market price."

The individual seller is often willing to cut price. The dealer can cut price only up to a point. He does not often sell below his cost on the car, his restoration, a portion of his overhead, and at least some markup.

For example, I found out in 1977 that the market on my 1960 Ferrari 250GT convertible was about $12,000. I ended up selling it to Nick Soprano, who had answered my ad—for $7,700. He immediately resold it. The new owner found out who I was and called me about the car. I asked him whether he had had to pay over my $12,000 advertised price, to which he replied, "Yes, I did have to pay over that figure." In this case Nick made a *smart* deal and got a good buy, but it might have been a collector who would have bought the car at way under market!

In all fairness to the dealer, years later he advertised a Maserati Ghibli coupe for sale in the *New York Times*. As soon as he saw me walk into his salesroom he lowered his advertised price by $2,000, and he ended up by doing all the work I required on the car at his out-of-pocket cost, not at $35 an hour, his usual rate.

The private seller in many cases is willing to state what the condition of the car is and state it accurately and honestly. He may even tell what he paid for the car and when he bought it as well as what restoration he did and how much it cost. Many car sellers are not out to make a killing but just to realize their investment and move on to something else.

Unless a collector or car investor is a car expert, however, he can make a serious mistake buying from an individual seller just as he can make a serious mistake buying from an unscrupulous dealer.

The *New York Times* is sold all over the country, including the classified sections. Each metropolitan paper has similar car advertisements that should be read very carefully.

There are some tricks that lawbreakers pull in order to make a fast buck. A crook will locate an inexpensive collector car that is regularly parked in the street, probably near the owner's home. The crook will advertise this car for sale in the local newspaper and list a pay phone near the location of the car. The crook then stands by the pay phone on a Saturday or Sunday and waits for calls from prospective buyers. When he gets a call he makes an appointment to show the car.

As the meeting time approaches, the crook starts to wipe off the car with a cleaning rag—looking like an owner getting his car cleaned up to show. The crook may even short the ignition so the car can be started—always hoping the car's owner will be far enough away not to see what is going on.

Strange as it may seem, a deal is often consummated between the crook and the prospective buyer. A deposit on the car may be taken—and that is the end of the crook and the deposit. Sometimes the prospective buyer pays in full and drives away with the car!

The *New York Times* and other metropolitan newspapers are good starting places in the hunt for collector cars, but there are other very important sources of advertising. *Road and Track*, a popular car magazine, has an excellent "Market Place" section on classic cars for sale, many of them illustrated.

An absolutely invaluable source of classic cars is *Hemmings Motor News* (Box 196, Bennington, VT 05201). This monthly, with a subscription of over 210,000, contains some 500 pages of classified advertising of cars, parts, and services. There are cars listed for under $1,000 and on up to $750,000. The cars range from mediocre Chevies to Mercedes-Benz 770K parade tourers. There are many illustrations of the cars offered for sale, and there may be in all as many as 10,000 individual advertisements. In *Hemmings* I once saw a 1965 Silver Cloud III long-wheelbase sedan for sale completely restored professionally, even to every piece of chrome, and the price was $19,000. The owner, located in a little town in Michigan, didn't even know what a "long-wheelbase" model was. He didn't know that it commanded a great premium over the ordinary Silver Cloud III sedan. So sometimes answering private ads can prove interesting.

Buying from Dealers

Over the years, used-car dealers have had less than stellar reputations. There have probably been plenty of cases of misrepresentation. But I have bought about half of the classics I have owned from dealers. Do I feel that I have been cheated by the dealers who sold me the cars? No. Only once was I really angry, at a dealer who represented the Porsche I was buying as a 1952 model when, in effect, it was a 1951 model.

Do I feel that I got better buys privately than I got from dealers? No, I don't. I got just as good buys from the dealers from whom I purchased—from the point of view of both quality and price.

How can one do as well buying from a dealer as buying from a private individual? The dealer is out to make money, and he must add his overhead plus a profit for his markup to what he pays for the car. The answer is that he has "bought right." He has bought low enough to be within the market on his sales. It is just possible that he got a number of low-priced cars—in some cases "real steals" such as the dealer who bought my Ferrari 250GT convertible for $7,700 that I was asking $12,000 for.

However it works out, the dealer is in a very good position to buy right. He is in a good position to trade the seller down, and if he buys my Ferrari for $7,700 he can turn around immediately and make money by selling it for $10,000—still $2,000 under my asking price and about $2,000 under market at the time.

So the dealer can be competitive in price.

There is another way that the dealer can be competitive in price with the individual seller of a car. The dealer can take a car in in trade. Let us say he offers the Ferrari he bought from me for $12,000. Someone wants to buy the car but he has a trade-in—say, a 1963 Aston Martin coupe with Superleggera body. The owner of the Aston Martin wants an allowance of $6,500 on his car. The dealer allows him $5,000, and the buyer with the Aston Martin trade-in gives the dealer his Aston Martin plus $7,000, to equal the selling price of the Ferrari of $12,000.

The dealer now offers the Aston Martin for sale. He is not particularly interested in Aston Martin, or any English car, for that matter, because he deals mainly in Italian sports cars. He offers the car to a buyer at his trade-in allowance—$5,000. The potential buyer offers him $4,000 for the Aston Martin and the deal is done.

The dealer now comes out of the whole deal on Ferrari plus Aston Martin with $7,000 cash from the buyer of the Ferrari plus $4,000 from the buyer of the Aston Martin—$11,000 in all for a car for which he paid $7,700. Had I come away with the Aston Martin for $4,000 I would have been delighted and I would have had a car at under market. This is a very realistic figure, as five years later this particular dealer offered me two such Aston Martins with Superleggera bodies—one for $7,500 and one for $6,500.

Can the car buyer get stuck buying from a dealer? Of course he can, and

I go back to the Maserati Ghibli that I bought from the dealer, a car that cost me $3,500 for repairs even before I took delivery on it. I, however, know at least a little about the condition of a classic car and the cost of restoration, and I estimated what it would cost to get this car in condition. I did this estimating before I ever made an offer on the car, and I offered a price low enough to allow me to have the restoration performed and still have a total investment in line with the market at the time.

It is often far better to buy a car from a reputable dealer than from a private individual. The chances of getting a trouble-free fine-condition car from a dealer may be far better. The dealer has the facilities to find things wrong and to put the car in condition after he buys it. His costs are out-of-pocket costs—his wholesale cost of parts required in restoration and his out-of-pocket labor rate to the mechanics he employs. In addition, he is, no doubt, a regular customer of glass companies, carpet companies, chrome-plating shops, paint shops, and specialized body shops. These shops know, too, that he is in the business of making money, and if he can make money on the work they do and the things they supply, they will get more business from him. In fact, unless they give the dealer a good price he may not long remain in business. In any event, the dealer is one of the "used-car repair and parts fraternity." They all live in the same world and speak the same language. They also all know which one is honest as well as which one overcharges.

Some dealers in classic and antique cars deal only in the best, and some in the very best. One dealer in the Northeast seems obsessed with the idea of buying only the finest classics obtainable. For perfect or near-perfect cars he will pay a premium and he will often outbid every other potential buyer of the car. He is, of course, an expert buyer and knows the condition of cars inside and out. He specializes in postwar Italian sports cars.

When he gets such a car in his dealership he may still go over it in detail, replacing carpets and chrome plating under the hood so that the engine compartment looks like a silver teaset in a museum. He may even replace the tires with Pirellis at up to about $250 apiece. When he gets through the car is often mint, and he has bought the car at a dealer's price, perhaps somewhat above, and restored it to mint condition at *his* cost.

When he sells the car an "implied guarantee" goes with it: If anything happens in the way of mechanical failure he will make some kind of adjustment.

One of the greatest buys that I have ever seen offered by anyone—dealer or private owner—was a long-wheelbase left-hand-drive Rolls-Royce Silver Cloud III that looked brand-new, although it was made in 1965. It was traded in on a Lamborghini Miura that a customer fell in love with.

The dealer was not a Rolls-Royce man, and all he was interested in doing was getting rid of the Rolls-Royce as best he could. He priced it at $35,000, far under the market for an absolutely mint-condition car of this make, year, and model.

When you buy a car from a private seller, that is it! If anything goes wrong, even while driving the car home, you, the buyer, cannot go after the seller for anything; and no one expects the seller to make anything good—in any way.

On the other hand, if you buy a car from a dealer there is an implied warranty. Whenever I had fault to find with a dealer who sold me a car the dealer did something about it. In 1977 I bought a Cadillac 1974 Eldorado from Bay Lincoln Mercury in Brooklyn. It was the dealer's own personal convertible, a specially painted beautiful car. As I drove the car, however, I found things that were wrong. I brought the car back about six months later and complained about some of the shortcomings. The dealer took the car in and repaired it, replacing parts wherever they were needed. He charged me out-of-pocket on labor, which amounted to about $8 an hour, not the usual $25 an hour. When he totaled up the bill he deducted 20%, which he called a discount. Instead of paying about $1,000 for the repairs and replacements, about the retail figure that any repair shop would have charged me, I was charged about $350.

To go back to the dealer who sold me my Maserati, he spent about six months doing various things to the car that I had bought from him but on which I had not taken delivery, and he charged me somewhere between his cost and the retail price of repairs and replacement, but nearer his cost. Some things he did at his own expense entirely.

Another advantage to this relationship is that dealers often have the cars you are interested in, and private individuals may not be selling the cars you want. The individual who owned the Rolls-Royce would never have parted with it unless he had seen the Lamborghini Miura. Apparently, he didn't have the $60,000 purchase price of the Miura or else didn't want to deplete his funds in order to buy it. In any event, I passed up the Rolls, and it is one of my mistakes I will probably not get over.

The dealer's buying policies can help the investor. The dealer buys what will sell, not what won't sell, and he follows the market, buying those things for his inventory that are on the way up. One dealer I know is currently concentrating on Ferrari Daytona, Ferrari 275GTB-4, Lamborghini Miura and Countach, and the later Mercedes-Benz convertibles. He also buys early Corvettes and the most popular Porsches.

Finally, it is somewhat easier to get rid of a car bought from a dealer that the buyer no longer wants. He approaches the dealer he bought the car from originally and says he does not want it. The dealer would, of course, like to have him trade in the car on something more expensive, and the dealer cannot very well say, "I don't want the car. I don't like that make and model!"

The owner of the car may say to this dealer, "I just want to get rid of the car and I don't want to trade it in on any other car." The dealer will almost certainly feel an obligation to accommodate him.

I bought a Maserati Ghibli from a dealer several years ago. I decided after a time that I didn't want the car, and I so informed the dealer from whom I had bought it. The dealer asked me what I wanted for the car. I named a figure in advance of what I had paid for the car when I bought it from him originally. He reached for the phone to call someone who had seen my car in the shop and wanted to know whether I, the owner, was interested in selling it. I did not sell the car, but at that juncture I would probably have sold it with at least some profit.

The dealer could have said to me, "I will sell the car for you on consignment. Bring it in next Monday. If this procedure does not suit you then I will buy it outright from you, but if I buy it outright I can't pay you as much as you will get if I take it on consignment. I will have to tie up my cash for a time, and I need my cash. Besides, my cash costs me interest at the bank, and the interest rate right now is high."

An owner of a Ferrari convertible faced just this choice with the dealer. He chose not to sell the car to the dealer but to consign it for sale. The car went on the showroom floor. It is stored on the floor free of charge. It is cleaned and polished regularly, and it is there for potential customers to see when they walk into the showroom.

All through this chapter I have assumed the potential buyer has cash—all cash. He then picks where he thinks he can best buy a car for all cash— private seller, dealer, or car auction. If the potential buyer does not have cash on the barrelhead he will almost certainly have to buy from a dealer, because the dealer has bank and finance company connections. Of course, the buyer too may have access to bank credit. The dealer does, however, in virtually all cases, have a finance connection that can be activated immediately.

If the potential classic or antique car buyer needs to buy a car on the time payment plan and has a trade-in, the dealer is probably his only source for a collector car. The auctions almost always want *all cash*, and almost all sellers want all cash and will rarely take a trade-in. Besides offering credit purchasing on the time payment plan, some dealers offer leasing for classic cars, even Rolls-Royces. Auctions and private buyers certainly do not as a rule offer leasing of any kind. I once sold a Cadillac convertible on the time payment plan, and I wish I had never thought about this kind of "creative financing." I couldn't even collect the first payment. Then I tried the time sales finance plan on a 1955 Buick convertible with one-third down. I had to repossess the car—in terrible condition. I had to spend a great deal of money getting it back in shape. Then I sold it for cash for not quite enough to arrive at my original sales price.

It seems likely to me that classic and antique car dealers are above the level of the operators on the corner used-car lot. I have found that dealers in classic cars have been honest in describing the condition of the car in detail and stating what they have done to the car as well as what they have not done to the car to improve it. So you may want to hold on to your wallet when you walk into the showroom of a classic car dealer, but not always. If you walk into the showroom of Jack Barclay Rolls-Royce on Berkeley Square, London, you will probably be unable to tell a used Rolls-Royce from a brand-new Rolls-Royce. In fact, when Jack Barclay refinishes one of his used Rolls-Royces, the finish is probably superior to what it was when it came from the Rolls-Royce factory.

Buying at Auctions

The classic car auctions are not as well known to the general public or to the collector-car-buying public as they might be. For some reason the press does not seem to be impressed enough with these auctions to give them much publicity, not even the press in major collector car auction cities like Scottsdale and Phoenix, Arizona. Only when a collector car goes for a really great sum, like the $400,000 that Christie's auction in California got in early 1979 for a 1935 Mercedes-Benz 500K roadster, does the press seem to take any notice.

In the United States in 1981 probably over 10,000 collector cars were offered at auction. Of this total, 5,317 cars actually sold—a little over 50%. This is the estimate of the Collector-Car Auction Reporter, Inc., of Bloomington, Indiana. Brian Jones, president of this organization, estimates that total bids on the collector cars offered for sale amounted to $72,226,700.

The biggest collector car auction firm in the country is the Kruse Company of Auburn, Indiana. Dean Kruse is national sales director for Kruse International, the auction division of Thorp Sales Corporation, a subsidiary of International Telephone and Telegraph. Kruse reports sales of his auction firm at over $60,000,000 for 1982.

Thus the collector car auction business is either already big business or it is on the verge of becoming big business.

One big reason for buying at the collector car auctions is that a great buy may be made, and if not a great buy then at least a "right buy," a buy somewhat under the market. Buying a car at an auction is like buying anything at an auction, art and antique auctions included. The major buyers are dealers, and they must buy at figures which will allow them a markup.

The automobile auctions are much the same. The prices are, in general, wholesale prices. The buyers are mainly dealers who buy to resell at a higher figure. At the Barrett-Jackson auctions in Phoenix, dealers dominate the buying, not private buyers. True, car museums buy, but by far the largest number of buyers are dealers from all over the country as well as from Europe.

At one auction held in Arizona, the Grand Old Cars Museum liquidation auction, dealers predominated. It was a unique auction in which every car was sold without any reserve (minimum price). There were in 1983 very likely over 1,000 registered bidders at this auction of 150 cars held in one day, and the dealers purchased nearly every car offered for sale.

One of the "steals" was a magnificent Duesenberg II speedster, 1981, that sold for $56,000. The *auction* market on this car was almost $100,000.

At the same auction an almost-mint 1966 Mustang convertible brought $6,750. At the previous auction, the Barrett-Jackson auction, a mint Mustang convertible reached $10,500, but the owner wouldn't sell; he wanted more. A 1933 Chrysler Imperial eight-cylinder convertible sedan in excellent condition went for $40,000, well under even auction market price. A fine 1937 Cord 812 phaeton went for $40,000, very much under market.

In the 1981 Christie's sale in Los Angeles, a 1932 Stutz Super Bearcat from the Briggs Cunningham Museum was sold to dealer Tom Barrett for $72,000. He immediately resold this car, without putting in restoration, to a private buyer in Florida for $100,000. Mr. Barrett told me that he did particularly well in his buying at Christie's auctions and he was able to resell to good advantage.

One can often buy at wholesale or even below wholesale at the collector car auctions. There is, however, another reason for buying at these auctions, and that is that what one would like to buy may be available only at one of these specialty car auctions. A Mercedes-Benz 540K of the mid-1930s may be the ultimate collector car at the present time, a car preferred even to the Duesenberg. The January 1983 Barrett-Jackson auction offered not one 540K but two, and both in superb condition. In addition, both cars were of superb design, one being a special made for Prince Mdvani and the other a very special-bodied Graber car. Both were big and stunning. They were not ordinary cabriolets by any means, and cabriolets are rare enough. These two cars were among the rarest of the rare and they were a major reason for the trip that my wife and I made to the Arizona auction.

If one wanted the very finest Delahaye, the Barrett-Jackson auction had a 1939 cabriolet with van den Plas Belgian body, a superb-looking car in better condition than when it came off the showroom floor originally.

At least two absolutely mint Mercedes-Benz 300S cars were offered, better than new. One, a roadster, brought $100,000. The coupe brought the unprecedented price of $76,000—very high for a 1953 300S coupe; but if one wanted the best it could have been here at this auction.

If one wanted a fine 1934 Ford roadster, the best, it was at the Grand Old Cars Museum auction, where it brought $30,000.

I myself look vaguely for a Mercedes-Benz SSK. I passed up one years ago at a very favorable price, and I guess I am just trying to bring back that past opportunity when I look for such a car now. The auctions will one day offer an SSK and they may well be the sole source of this highly rare, much-wanted, extremely valuable car.

Kruse offers more cars for sale at auction than any other auction house— by far. The firm holds twenty-five auctions throughout the year and adds other auctions to the group it manages. For the most part these auctions are held in the Southwest and the central West. Relatively few auctions are held in the East. One gets the idea that auctions should be located in New York. Sotheby's and Christie's auctions are located in New York. The auto auction companies, however, shy away from New York; some of the car auctions held in that city have been disasters, with very few bidders and indeed very few people in attendance just as an audience. For many car collectors and car buyers located in the East, car auctions are, to all intents and purposes, nonexistent.

A great collector car auction is held in Tulsa, Oklahoma, every summer, and this is the James C. Leake auction of an aggregation of a large number of the finest and most valuable classic and antique cars.

In this same class—enormous auctions of the finest and most valuable cars—is the Barrett-Jackson auction held in Phoenix in January of each year. The January 1983 auction gathered together a large number of some of the finest collector cars that exist, either in museums or privately owned.

On January 2, 1983, the Rick Cole auction was held. Ninety-nine cars were offered for sale, many of them fine cars and many rare classics.

The Rick Cole auction was followed a week later by the Barrett-Jackson auction, in which 540 cars crossed the auction platform.

Next came the one-time auction of the cars belonging to the Grand Old Cars Museum in Apache Junction, Arizona, near Scottsdale and Phoenix. About 160 cars were offered for sale, plus numerous car signs, classic car paintings, secondhand parts for cars (mainly for the Packards in which the museum seemed to specialize), and other car memorabilia. Everything offered for sale sold, as there were no reserves.

This sale was followed, still in the same month, by Scottsdale '83, the Twelfth Annual Southwestern United States International Collector Car Auction, held January 14–16, 1983. This too was a great car auction, with cars about up to the quality of the Barrett-Jackson cars, including a Mercedes-Benz 540K cabriolet and a beautiful 1934 Duesenberg phaeton.

No one could attend all the collector car auctions. There are just too many. *Hemmings Motor News*, among other publications, contains detailed advertisements, most with photos, of many upcoming auctions as well as swap meets in which one can both buy and sell cars. Sometimes the cars at swap meets are auctioned and sometimes they are simply offered for sale in special designated areas.

Auction Offerings and Prices

Rare cars and cars in demand are often offered at the collector car auctions, cars that are very hard to find at dealers' establishments and almost never located by scanning newspaper and magazine ads.

In the Rick Cole auction, the first collector car auction held in the Phoenix area in January 1983, an extremely rare car was offered for sale, a definite collector's item. This was a 1929 Windsor White Prince roadster in near-mint condition. I examined the car in detail, and its condition was class 1 as described. The car reached $17,000 but did not sell, as the seller was looking for more.

So then the Windsor was sent over to the Barrett-Jackson auction, where it did sell for $22,000—which tends to disprove the rule that if your car does not sell in one auction it is pegged at the high bid and its sale is jinxed for a long time, until the buying public forgets that it was offered for sale and did not sell.

In the same Rick Cole sale a 1933 Auburn boattail speedster was offered for sale, a car in class 2 condition but not mint. It reached $19,000, which was not enough for the seller. The seller then sent the car to the Barrett-Jackson auction, where it did sell—for $21,200. The car was rated class 2 at the Barrett-Jackson auction but class 1 at the Rick Cole auction. In any event it was a highly desirable car that I could have been talked into buying—not as desirable as my old 1935 Model 851 speedster, but fine nevertheless.

So if you wanted a fine 1929 Windsor White Prince roadster or a fine early Auburn speedster you would probably have to try to get such excellent rarities from the specialist car auctions. And the prices were by no means high. If anything they were under market.

The reserves on many outstanding cars were high and the estimated prices were high, hence most of these cars did not sell at the auction.

The reported sale rate at the 1983 Barrett-Jackson auction was 32%. In other words, 68% of the cars did not sell. Their reserves were too high for sales to be made. One dealer told us he bid on over a hundred cars and got practically nothing. Other dealers, knowing how high the reserve prices were, simply sat on their hands. There was no point in bidding $10,000 on a car that had a reserve on it of $15,000. In 1984 the sold percentage had risen to a healthy 80%, on the block and afterward.

When the auction is over the sale is not necessarily over. At the Barrett-

Jackson auction the car that fails to sell is driven off the auction platform and to the edge of the tent. There prospective buyers often wait to make an offer. They think they can do better buying a car that did not meet its auction reserve price and did not sell—and many times they are right. A sale is often consummated at the foot of the drive-off ramp.

If the car does not sell at the auction, and if it does not sell at the end of the drive-off ramp, then the buyer is in a particularly good position to make a buy. On the Monday following the Barrett-Jackson auction my wife and I stood outside the main gate of the auction, at the traffic light, and interviewed some of the new owners driving their cars away as well as some of the sellers who did not find buyers. There was a general willingness on the part of the unsuccessful sellers to make a final sale at a sacrifice price, and we could have made some good buys.

Condition of Cars Offered at Auctions

In the Barrett-Jackson auction in January 1983, I had never seen such an aggregation of collector cars. The cars I saw a few weeks in advance of the sale, those owned by Mr. Tom Barrett, were so rare, so fine, and in such good condition that I was determined to visit the actual auction in order to see how the cars sold. Only if one knows exactly what is being sold does the auction price have any meaning.

When my wife and I arrived at the car display immediately preceding the auction we were impressed by the cars owned by Messrs. Barrett and Jackson, but also by the other cars that were being offered. Most of these were apparently from private owners, but a number of them were offered by dealers, several of whom I interviewed, particularly to find out the condition of the cars they were offering. In general, the cars offered for sale were excellent, many of them being class 1 condition (out of five possible categories of condition).

Surprisingly enough, many, if not most, sellers, including dealers, are honest and forthright in disclosing the exact condition of a car. One dealer offered a Maserati Ghibli as well as a Jaguar XK140, a red roadster with an excellent paint job and chrome wire wheels. We asked this dealer the condition of both cars. He could and would state the condition of each car, up to a point. He had not taken apart the engines, apparently, and did not know the exact mechanical condition of each car. Since the Maserati Ghibli is a very tricky car and is often out of condition, this refusal to vouch for the interior of the engine was a "minus" for this car.

In the same sale there was a superb-looking 1952 Mercedes-Benz 300S cabriolet, painted yellow. The reserve on the car was $90,000. After the sale I talked to the owner, who began to tell me all the things that were wrong with the car. He stated that parts of the body still had to be replaced with metal. They had apparently rusted and had been filled in with fiberglass, the usual method of repairing bodies on standard transportation cars—but not on fine collector cars. He also stated that two of the dials on the dash were not working and that the steering wheel was set up wrong in relation to the front wheels, not a great problem.

The car did not sell and the owner then spent a day or two making various repairs. The car was in excellent condition and did not have enough drawbacks to prevent its sale at a high price. The owner, however, apparently scared off prospective buyers through his honesty in explaining the shortcomings of the car, and it didn't reach even $70,000, let alone the $90,000 original reserve.

In the next January 1983 sale, the Grand Old Cars Museum sale in Apache Junction, Arizona, a very rare and much-wanted car was offered, this one a 1937 Cord 812 supercharged phaeton. If any car in this auction was going to command a high price, we felt this was it. Just prior to the offering of this car the owner of the museum, Mr. Art Grandlich, stated that the fenders on the car were not metal but fiberglass—a value-diminishing replacement. Then someone in the audience stated that he had a set of original Cord 812 fenders that he would sell for $3,000 for the four. The Cord was sold for $40,000, under market.

All of the offerings at the collector car auctions are not, however, like the cars offered at the Barrett-Jackson auction and at the Grand Old Cars Museum auction. There are auctions in which dealers "dump" cars that they want to get rid of.

One New York dealer stated that unless I bought his car in which I had some interest he was going to put it into a New Jersey auction. This of course meant that the car was not in good enough condition for him to retail. In fact, both the radiator and the transmission leaked, and the upholstery needed attention. Selling it "as is" might pull down his reputation as a dealer in fine collector cars, but putting it into top condition might well cost him more than he could get out of it. The necessary restoration would place it in a price category above market.

Now suppose I had not bought the car directly from the dealer, but had seen it at the auction. The dealer could have put an additive in the transmission to stop the leak temporarily. He could certainly have put "stop-leak" in the radiator, which would have clogged the radiator at least a little, and the radiator on this make and model car is not known for its ability to cool the car, particularly on a hot summer day. He might have repaired the leather interior to match the superb paint job and I would have thought I was getting a near-mint condition car. I would have had some surprises when I got the car home and began a detailed examination of it.

In buying at auction there is no responsibility on the part of anyone for the condition of the car. If one buys from a dealer there is at least some responsibility. I returned my Italian car that the dealer was going to send to auction but sold me. I told the dealer that the brake pedal was low and that maybe the brakes needed adjustment. The dealer pulled off the wheels and told me that he had forgotten to put new brake pads on the front wheels when he first bought the car and brought it into his shop. I don't see how this failure was still his responsibility, but he felt it was and he replaced the pads and adjusted the brakes for me free of charge. No auction would have done this job for me and no dealer who had put his car in auction for sale. In fact, I don't think I would have been able to determine who sold the car in the particular auction and would thus have had no idea to whom to turn to get any adjustment made.

Buying a collector car at a collector car auction may be like buying a pig in a poke. There is no assurance on the part of anybody that the car is as described in the sale catalogue—if it is described at all. There is absolutely no one to go back to if the car is in worse condition than the buyer thought. A buyer can go back to a dealer, at least to some extent, and he most certainly can go back to a major dealer, who will not welcome a suit for misrepresentation and the attendant publicity.

I have known a dealer to go back to a private seller from whom he had bought a 300SE Mercedes-Benz and state that unless the seller took back the car he would cancel his check. Of course, the seller should have demanded cash or a cashier's check. The dealer is certainly a professional buyer.

It is, of course, possible that even a private seller will not know the condition of his car that he is selling. I once owned a Rolls-Royce Silver Cloud I James Young limousine that I had purchased from the biggest Rolls-Royce collector car dealer in London. When I had the paint removed for repainting I found body damage and the damage repaired with fiberglass, not with new pieces of aluminum.

On the other hand I once bought a Mercedes-Benz 300S roadster that required almost 1,000 hours of labor to piece in the body and smooth the piecing job for repainting. A Rolls-Royce that I bought seemed to have a bit of rust on the body, but otherwise the body and paint seemed reasonably good. The actual bodywork on this car required a year and three quarters! Still, the car was worth it.

What I would like to buy is a Barrett- or Jackson-restored car in Arizona, or a Lamborghini or Ferrari completely restored by Bob Wallace of Phoenix, or a car from a private collection I knew well. Or I would like to buy a car from a dealer known for *buying* for his inventory only the very best cars that he has examined in detail before buying.

Selling at Auctions

The first question to ask about the collector car auction *as a method of selling* is: "Is it likely that the car will sell at all?" The answer that comes to mind first is, "No. It is entirely possible that you will go to the trouble and expense of sending your car to an important collector car auction only to find that the car will not sell and you have to truck or drive it back to your home."

Almost no collector car auction in the United States has a high percentage of sales, no matter where the sale takes place or what the quality of cars offered is.

One collector car weekly newspaper had the headline in its January 1983 edition: "Barrett-Jackson Sale Steady."

The article went on, "... there were a total of 540 cars across the auction block on the three days of the sale. Originally a fourth sales day had been anticipated but perhaps not enough vehicles were available.

"Of this total number, 168 were announced as sold by the auctioneers, a sales figure of approximately 32%. This would be down from prior sales but hardly flat simply because of the really huge numbers associated with Barrett-Jackson auctions."

At this particular sale the highest-priced cars failed to find buyers. The great Mercedes-Benz 540K convertible had a reserve price on it of $400,000. At the auction it apparently received a top bid of $190,000. The other great 540K convertible offered reached only $110,000. It no doubt had a reserve on it of far more than this figure.

The customary way to figure percentage of sales and percentage of buy-ins is by dollar volume and not by the number of cars or other items offered for sale. This is standard procedure for the great auction houses of Christie's and Sotheby's for art, antiques, and whatever else they auction.

If we base the percentage sold and the percentage of buy-ins at the Barrett-Jackson sale on dollar value, then the percentage of cars sold was 24% and the buy-ins 76%—a pretty low percentage of sales.

On the other hand, twenty-three more cars were sold after the close of the auction, as is apt to happen in almost all auctions. The corrected percentage of the number of cars sold was 36%, not 32%. The buy-in rate was 64%. On a value basis, 34% were sold and 66% were bought in unsold. These figures are approximately correct, but not necessarily completely accurate. The auction house reported that the great Mdvani 540K Mercedes was bid up to $190,000, as I have indicated. I was present at the actual auctioning of this car in Phoenix. The car started off with a bid of $100,000. I recorded every bid from there—up to $360,000. How the newspapers got the $190,000 figure is unclear, except that there may have been "fictitious bidding" (auctioneer acknowledging nonexistent bids) from $190,000 to $360,000. On the other hand, at the actual auction the bidding on the car rose from $175,000 to $200,000 with no $190,000. Fictitious bidding is, of course, common at many art and antique auctions.

At the Rick Cole sale, there were ninety consigned cars, enough for only one day of sales. The second day of car sales did not materialize. The auction house had anticipated many more cars offered. Of these ninety, only thirty-three cars actually found buyers.

The obvious conclusion about auctioning one's car is that there is a limited chance that the car will actually find a buyer, and at the Arizona auctions there were many very disappointed sellers. I know because I talked to many of them on the Monday following the Barrett-Jackson sale.

One seller offered no fewer than seven cars in this auction. When he was removing his cars that were unsold we noted three splendid Mercedes-Benz cars in his offering—a 300S, a 300D four-door convertible, and a 220 convertible. Fortunately for this seller he lived in Phoenix and did not have to return his cars by van to Tacoma, Miami, or Connecticut! In any event, one of the seven cars did sell, a 220 Mercedes convertible.

Possible damage is a real fear for the collector car owner who sends his car to auction, particularly a faraway auction. A shipper recently sent two cars from White Plains, New York, to a buyer in Dallas. The cars were collector cars, a Ferrari Daytona and a Jaguar sedan. The carrier was a large car carrier, the kind used to ship new cars from Detroit and other factory locations. When the cars arrived there was fairly substantial damage to both cars (probably from banging into each other in the loading and unloading process), some structural damage and some paint and body damage. The extent of the damage was about $7,000 for each car. The buyer refused to accept the cars. The carrier had its own insurance on the cars it carried, but the limit for the kind of damage sustained was $5,000 per car, not the $7,000 actual damage to each car. The car buyer had to absorb the other $2,000 per car.

At the Barrett-Jackson auction there were very large vans—enclosed trucks. These are safer than open car carriers, but more expensive. The cost of shipping from White Plains to Dallas by car carrier was a little over $500 per car. An enclosed van for the same trip would have cost over $1,000 a car.

Now if the cars offered for sale by the owner were damaged en route, he might sustain a loss not entirely covered by insurance. In addition, the car would hardly be in condition to auction. So he would be faced with trucking cost down and back plus repairs plus an inability to auction the car.

There is a real risk at the auction itself. At the Barrett-Jackson auction a very fine Auburn boattail speedster had its fender scraped—inexpensive enough to repair, but it made the car look a little second-rate when it arrived at the auction block.

The troubles of the gentleman who offered seven cars for sale at the Barrett-Jackson auction did not end when he brought his cars safely to the auction and saw one of the seven sell. Someone put water in the gas tank of one of the cars. When he started the car to demonstrate its running ability at the display prior to the auction the engine started and then stopped. Fortunately the trouble was located and the tank and carburetors drained. I once got water leaking into the combustion chamber from the water jacket. The car blew off the head! Who would sabotage this man's magnificent Mercedes-Benz 300S? A competitor who had a similar car to auction? I doubt it. It may have been pure vandalism; but whatever the motive, the risk of such sabotage exists.

Then there is the cost of offering a car for sale at auction. The fee is generally less than the sales fees of the major auction houses dealing in art and antiques. The Atlantic City auction of February 1983 advertised a "consignment fee" of $125 for the first day of sale, Friday, February 18. For sale on Saturday the fee was $185, and for Sunday $125. This is the fee that must be paid by the consignor whether the car sells or not. The seller could establish a reserve or minimum price that he would accept for his car. If he established such a reserve and his car sold at the auction then he would have to pay 10% of the sales price but with a maximum of $1,000, regardless of how high the car went at auction.

The auction obviously would like to make sales, and to secure sales the commission was established at only 5% if no reserve price was set by the seller, and here too the maximum commission charged any seller, regardless of how high his car went at auction, was $1,000.

Registration fees of from $100 to $200 are common and are nonrefundable. This fee assures the auction house at least some compensation in case few cars actually sell and earn a commission.

One auction firm has a sliding scale which runs from 12% of sales price for a car selling for less than $500, a car on which the owner has placed a reserve price, down to 5% on a car selling for more than $20,000 on which the owner has not placed a reserve. The maximum commission charged on any sale is $8,000 if the seller has established a reserve on his car and $5,000 if he sells the car without any reserve. In addition, the seller may have to pay some commission based on the top price bid at the auction on his car—if the car did not sell.

The whole commission structure is not burdensome to any seller of a collector car, even if he doesn't sell his car. In the art and antique auctions there is now usually a 10% commission charged the seller and an additional 10% added to the hammer price at the auction, this 10% charged the buyer.

The car auctions have a bad record in regard to handling funds paid by the buyer for the car. Sometimes the seller of the car hasn't been paid. The attorney general of at least one state forbade one auction house from conducting any further sales in the state.

The procedure now is to require the buyer to pay the day he buys the car at auction—by cash, cashier's check, or bank draft. Funds are paid to the seller of the car directly and not via the auction house. So the buyer gets his car right away and the seller gets his funds—good money—right away.

What cars currently sell well at auctions? Hardly the finest, most expensive cars. In major art and antique auctions the finest things sell and at sky-high prices, even in poor times, and dealers always caution collectors to collect the very best, which usually sells at very high prices.

In the 1983 car auction market the lesser cars were the ones that sold well. The great cars owned by Tom Barrett did not rack up large sales at high prices, not even the superb Mercedes-Benz 540K convertibles estimated at $400,000 and $300,000 respectively and possibly more. On the other hand, a 1967 Maserati Ghibli brought $17,500, a very high figure. A seller refused a high bid of $10,500 on a 1964 Mustang convertible. A 1933 Ford Tudor sedan brought $9,600. A 1950 Olds convertible brought $10,000. Fine make and model cars in superb condition did well, like the Mercedes-Benz 300S coupe that brought the very high $76,000 and the 300S roadster that brought $100,000—a little under the owner's expectations. Two of Anthony Granatelli's turbine rarities sold for big sums—a jet-powered Corvette for $550,000 and an Indianapolis turbine-powered car for $450,000, both apparently bona fide sales and to the same Texas businessman.

There was a turnaround as the year progressed, and by 1984 the market showed great strength for the big heavy cars—the great classics in the over-$150,000 range. The market for the $20,000 to $60,000 cars was still slow, according to dealer/auctioneer Tom Barrett, but collectors were getting into the market again after a period of a little over two years. The 1984 Barrett-Jackson auction saw three great classics bring $400,000 or more. About 650 cars crossed the block and of these, 80% were sold on the block or immediately afterward. The dollar total: $7,400,000—a new high for the firm.

Maybe Christie's will return to auctioning automobiles in the United States. In early 1979 the firm shocked the automotive world by selling a Mercedes-Benz 500K roadster for $400,000 and a Mercedes-Benz SS for $320,000. Tom Barrett states that this 500K roadster was resold to a European buyer for about $620,000. I suppose for this reason he estimated his Mdvani 540K Mercedes was worth about $600,000.

These rules might be in order for sellers considering auctioning their collector cars:

1. Offer cars at auction that are in superb condition.

2. If the car is in superb condition it can be a "special-interest" car, almost any special-interest car.

3. The less expensive cars are doing well now at auction—those under $25,000 and especially under $15,000.

4. The buyers have not been pursuing the very best—the 540K Mercedes-

Benz cars, the Cadillac V-16 convertible coupes, the early-1930s Chrysler Imperials, the Duesenberg J and SJ convertibles—but in 1984 there was a resurgence of demand for top-quality top priced prewar classics.

5. The most complete coverage must be secured from a reliable insurance company when cars are sent to auction.

6. There is little doubt that Arizona is the center of the collector car auction business, and the January sales are the important ones.

7. Cars should not be sent long distances even to these highly important sales. The cost and the risk of damage are too great, the likelihood of a sale too small.

8. One might try a nearby auction if the cost of sending the car to auction and insuring it is not too great. Strange as it may seem, some high prices are achieved for fairly ordinary cars, but usually for cars in fine condition.

The collector car auctions have a lot of growing up to do, and they have to become far more professional. They may be on the brink of getting the attention of the general public, and if they do, their market may well broaden and the price level may rise a good deal. The general public is hardly aware of fine collector cars and their auctions, and, except for the very specialized collector car magazines and newspapers, the press is almost totally unaware of collector cars and their sales.

To start on an immediate program of making the collector car auctions of more significance to the sellers of cars, the auctions should not encourage unrealistically high reserves in order to get the owners to send in their cars for sale. Instead they should establish realistic reserves that are low enough to move the cars, or at least move most of them. If the owners do not agree on the reserves, then the cars should be refused. This is the exact policy of the major art and antique auctions worldwide, including Christie's and Sotheby's. Of course, not every car auction can expect to turn out as favorably as the 1983 Grand Old Cars Museum auction. The unique characteristic of this auction was that there were absolutely no reserves on any car or on anything else offered in this sale—parts, accessories, signs, mementoes, etc. The result was a rip-roaring success. The auction attracted buyers from all over. There were 1,166 registered bidders, so many that in a front-row seat I couldn't even see the cars as they were placed on the auction block. The bidders closed in on the cars for a last inspection before the cars sold. For everyone concerned, as far as we have been able to determine—the Grandlichs, who owned the collection, the dealers and others who bought the cars, and the auctioneers—the sale was a tremendous success, the only negative element being that some of the cars weren't in top-notch condition and were not quite used to running, since they had long been stored in the museum.

But I would not recommend to any collector car seller that he sell without a reserve. I would, however, advocate a realistic reserve, one likely to be low enough to secure a sale but not so low as to result in a giveaway.

Selling to Dealers

Newspaper advertisements of collector cars for sale not infrequently state, "No dealers, please."

The reason for this is that dealers too often in the past have tried to "steal" the collector's car. During World War II I went to visit a major collector car dealer in New York. I told the dealer that I had a Mercedes-Benz 540K coupe for sale, that it was in excellent mechanical condition, and that I had just had it painted. I asked the official of the company to whom I was speaking how much he would offer me for the car. His reply: $500. True, cars at that time were not worth by any means what they are worth today, but the car quickly sold via newspaper advertising for almost eight times this figure.

One such experience like that and a collector car owner will never even talk to a dealer about buying his car. Still, dealers will sometimes pay very well for a car they want and have a customer for. A dealer today should pay about $100,000 for a Ferrari Daytona Spyder. He should be able to turn around and sell this car for $125,000 without too much trouble. He should also pay at least $60,000 for a Lamborghini Miura SV of the last design. He should be able to sell this rather quickly for $75,000—or more.

These are the exceptions—cars that are very much wanted, fairly high-priced, and fairly rare. There is another kind of collector car in this category of cars that dealers will pay well for, and this is the mint-condition collector car. The car should be a collector car, not just a special-interest car, and certainly not just an ordinary car. For example, about a year ago, Nick Soprano, the White Plains dealer, answered an ad in the newspaper listing an early Jaguar XK120 roadster for sale. To say that the car was in mint condition would have been an understatement! Under the hood the car looked far better than when it was new. (I know what under the hood looked like in a new XK120, as I owned one of the first XK120's in this country.)

Nick made an offer on the car which was immediately turned down. So Nick walked away, but soon returned and bought the car for very near the owner's asking price.

This purchase represents the attitude of almost all dealers in all kinds of cars, not simply dealers in collector cars. For mint cars they will pay top dollar. They will pay super-top dollar for extremely low-mileage cars of earlier vintages. It is my opinion that many, if not most, car dealers love cars, and they particularly love collector cars that look as if they have just come off the showroom floor—or cars that look even better than that. A few years ago every Cadillac dealer seemed to be intent on buying the best 1976 Eldorado that he could find, and many Cadillac dealers set aside one of these last convertibles instead of offering it for sale, so it was brand-new and never delivered. Of course the car rose in value from a new price of about $13,000 to about $25,000. The Eldorado "ragtop" was discontinued with the 1976 model. Maybe the dealers saw an opportunity to make money on a new car by holding it for a few years until new and nearly new Eldorados were scarce and well worn. On the other hand, the way they stored and treated these cars indicated to me that the dealers loved them.

In general an individual seller of a collector car cannot, however, get top price for his collector car, unless it is a Ferrari Daytona Spyder or some similar great rarity. If a dealer doesn't buy such a car another dealer may well come along that same day and pay very near the asking price. Now that dealers know this situation of more demand for fewer important collector cars, the days of "stealing" cars may well be at an end, at least for most such cars offered for sale by owners.

On the other hand, the dealer has overhead, and many dealers have enormous overheads. If a dealer should buy a Daytona Spyder for $120,000 and sell it within a week for $125,000, that might seem like a good deal to anyone not in the business of dealing in collector cars. It is easy to make a quick calculation and determine that in a year the dealer might buy and sell ten such cars—for an income of $5,000 times 10, or $50,000.

Only it doesn't work that way. The dealer might have to wait months to sell the car. Interest at 15% per year on the $120,000 that the car cost the dealer amounts to $18,000 per year. Six cars bought and sold per year with a profit on each of $5,000 would cover this interest cost and some more— but not much more. Then, too, rent, heat, light, and all sales and shop costs have to be covered. A markup of $5,000 on each of six or ten cars would not do it!

All cars have to have something done to them. They may be near perfect when they are purchased from meticulous owners, but things go wrong even with mint cars, and there are some things that might be done to make the cars even more attractive to buyers—like chrome under the hood, chrome wire wheels, P7 Pirelli tires at $250 a tire.

The fact of the matter is that the price a dealer is usually willing to pay the owner of a car may well not suit the seller and not even remotely suit him. Dean Kruse in his *Official 1982 Price Guide to Collector Cars* has this to say about dealer buying prices:

"Naturally, no matter how exquisite a car you have, or how much in current demand, you cannot expect to get the full retail value from a dealer. Retail value is exactly that: the prices at which dealers sell to the public. Figured into the retail value are all their operating expenses plus their margin of profit. The retail price pays not only for the dealer's expense in buying the car, but his costs of repair or restoration, employee salaries, lot rent, utility bills, advertising, and so forth. On top of this he will add a profit margin of at least 10–15%. In general, dealers will pay a higher percentage of the retail value for *better cars*: collector cars in excellent condition, and major classics in heavy demand."

Kruse illustrates the dealer buying price of one of these important collector cars. A car that has a retail value of $85,000, a mint car in demand, the dealer might pay $45,000 for—a little over 50% of retail value.

If this same car is in "good" condition, but not mint, it might have a retail value of $45,000, not $85,000. For a car in this condition the dealer might pay $20,000—less than 50% of retail.

For the same car in "fair" condition the retail value might be $25,000, and for this car the dealer might pay $10,000.

As we indicated, the mint-condition car in big demand the dealer might sell right away, or at least soon after he purchased it. The poorer the car the longer he might have to own it, the more he will have to lower the price in order to "move it," and the more time and money he may have to spend on it before anyone will buy it.

Maybe Mr. Kruse's dealer buying prices are pessimistic as far as the car seller goes, but they're not so unrealistic. At the major auctions, including the Kruse auctions, the main buyers are dealers, not collectors or investors. These dealers often pay prices not very far from retail. Maybe they can get markups like the Kruse estimates. Maybe not. In any event many collectors who want to sell their cars are not extremely pleased with their offers from dealers. Of course, it may be that the only real offers backed by cash come from dealers. Dealers do have the cash to buy, and many would-be purchasers, collectors or investors, sometimes do not have cash or at least take time to gather together their cash and sometimes give bad checks.

Consignments

Very often the price a dealer will pay the owner of a car is not acceptable to the owner, and sometimes nowhere near acceptable. In such cases it is sometimes possible to consign the car to the dealer. Here the car must be covered by insurance taken out by the owner of the car, and the dealer must agree in writing as to the condition of the car mechanically and in appearance. I once consigned a show car to a dealer to sell. After some months, when no offers had been received, I went to look at my car. No one would have bought the car in the condition the dealer had let it fall into. The car stood under a leaking pipe, and when it was not under the pipe it was "driven to death." To get it back in condition cost me thousands of dollars.

Consignment may work well if the car is a very important collectible like a mint Bugatti convertible or a Packard 734 speedster or a Ferrari Daytona Spyder. If the car sells quickly, well and good. If it does not, watch out! It may go progressively downhill in condition and appearance until a sale at a good price is impossible. Dealers are not known for the care they give consigned cars. Nor are they known for pushing consigned cars. Why not push their own cars and get the full sales price out of their cars, then use the sales price to buy another car for inventory? If they sell your car all they get is a sales commission of perhaps 15%.

But the dealer can finance the purchase of the car, while you probably can't and he can take a trade-in if necessary, while you in all probability don't want a trade-in. Recently I answered an ad for a Rolls-Royce Phantom III convertible coupe for sale. The price was certainly not low, but the seller's ad stated that he would take a car in part payment. When I asked him what he would take in trade he said, "Only a classic Packard. That's all I want in trade." Since I didn't have a Packard that was that!

Selling Privately Via Advertisements

Theoretically, the best way to sell a collector car is to locate a collector through advertising—either in the *New York Times* or in another local newspaper or in the collector car press. Also theoretically, the potential buyer has been shopping around at various dealers in classics and antiques and knows retail prices. Perhaps, too, he has been following the car auctions and is aware of the fact that one such car as he would like to buy recently sold for the "very high price" of $50,000. A number of people know that a Mustang convertible, 1964½, sold for over $20,000. The Mustangs that sell for $4,000 do not make the news.

My own experience in selling via advertising to collectors has been good—not extraordinarily good but reasonably good. In most cases, I did not get a retail price, but I did get more than a dealer's buying price.

In the first place, I would caution that not all cars can be sold to individuals via advertising. For almost a year Binder of New York, the auto body company, advertised my prizewinning Italmeccanica with special Cadillac engine. In the end Binder returned the car to me, unable to sell it. Neither could a firm in Greenwich, Connecticut. My own advertisements finally paid off, though I got a low price for the car, not even the restoration cost. At the time, and now too, few collectors wanted a special based on American components, except big-name specials like the Avanti II or Duesenberg II.

If I had a standard classic in fine-to-mint condition for not too much money I would expect to sell it via advertisements—an XK120 Jaguar, a fine-condition MG TC or TD, a mint Lamborghini Miura P-400. The more unusual the car and the higher the price, the harder it is to sell via advertising. The Lamborghini Countach is one of the greats of automotive history. Still, these cars are pretty regularly advertised for sale at $75,000 to $100,000 and over; and they do not seem to sell very well, not even a special Countach that is reported to go over 205 mph. Nor do classic racing cars sell very well via advertising. A car that a number of people can use as a collector item or as transportation can be advertised, like a Rolls-Royce Silver Cloud III sedan or a Cadillac Eldorado 1976 convertible.

A number of retail buyers—collectors—simply do not have a spare $75,000 floating around with which to buy a car; and some buyers find it hard to raise $15,000.

Then there are buyers who don't have much trouble paying. In the New York area there was a Chase Manhattan Bank cashier's check that was "printed several times" and used for car purchases. Of course, the Chase bank never saw the check or had anything to do with it. It was a strict forgery and was finally uncovered because several such checks were passed, each one having the same number. My own bank, Putnam Trust Company in Greenwich, Connecticut, was notified of these forgeries and notified me of them.

For one of my cars the buyer, a retail buyer, a Rolls-Royce collector, gave me a certified check. I had my bank call the buyer's bank and find out whether the check was good and whether the signature seemed to be his signature. My bank described what his signature looked like—not a very accurate way to determine whether or not the signature was authentic, but the buyer checked out in all other ways. The check was good and so was the buyer.

Some time ago the word went out to car sellers to be very careful about offering a Rolls-Royce for sale, since there were a number of Rolls-Royce thieves on the lookout for Rolls-Royce cars advertised. The potential buyer who answered the ad would arrive and ask to drive the car around the block. After he drove off and around the corner he was not seen again.

A variation of this scam was to locate a Rolls-Royce by answering an advertisement. The "buyer" would "case the joint" and later on, in the night, steal the Rolls-Royce. One seller of a Rolls-Royce whose ad I answered stated that he did not keep the Rolls-Royce at his home and I could not see it unless I came to his home in person and looked honest. If I passed the honesty test then he would drive me to where the Rolls-Royce was. A number of sellers do the same thing, and they have their cars in guarded public garages with extremely tight security. It was in one of these secure garages that I first saw the Lamborghini I finally bought from illustrator Stan Zagorski. Stan drove me from midtown Manhattan down almost to the Battery to the garage in which he kept the Miura.

When I sell privately right now I demand cash, not even a cashier's check, unless I know the buyer or know his reputation. This is where dealers come in. They are prepared to pay in cash, and the typical container for this cash is often a small brown paper shopping bag. This was the way I sold a car to Nick Soprano of Motor Classic Corporation. Nick is now so well established in business that if I sold him a car today I would ask him to mail me a check for the purchase price at his convenience!

One of the big troubles with selling privately through ads is that it is very hard and time-consuming to secure any legitimate offer. There are many window shoppers who have little intention of buying or ability to buy.

Then there are those who have the ability but "not right now." They may be able to put down a deposit or even a down payment, but they find it hard to locate the rest of the money. After a while, the seller feels it would make life much easier to forget about selling the car and keep it.

It is sometimes possible to finance the car, but it is still hard to finance many collector cars, particularly the more expensive ones. Banks are still not used to this type of financing. The seller may finance the sale himself and give the buyer a monthly payment book. I financed two of my cars this way as I have recounted elsewhere. The buyer of my Cadillac convertible didn't make the first payment. The buyer of my Buick convertible paid about 50% of the car off in down payment and time payments. When I repossessed the car it had lost at least 50% of its value; it was nearly a wreck. I lost money on this deal.

So the auctions do have a function in sales, and so do the dealers. When you sell your car today at auction you are almost always paid the day of sale with cash, cashier's check, or bank draft—made payable directly to you, the seller of the car. The dealer-buyer pays, and right on time, but even he should not be allowed to give you a check. He might cancel it.

A Summary for Sellers and Buyers

There is no absolutely satisfactory way of selling a collector car. In fact, it is difficult to find even a reasonably satisfactory way. Auctioning is expensive and risky, and the chance of actually finding a buyer is not very great, at least for the majority of would-be collector car sellers. They find themselves with their car still on their hands after the auction, and also after they have spent a good deal of money entering the car in the auction, trucking it to and from the auction, and paying for insurance, which is an absolute must.

Many car sellers are not willing to recognize that a dealer must mark up the car he buys to cover his overhead. Most dealers must buy from individuals and sell to individuals. Maybe they make something on their repair shops—if they have one. In any event they do not have a new-car business with fairly fixed prices from the factory to the dealer and sticker prices on the cars they are selling. Consignment sales through dealers are not the best of all possible ways to sell, and the condition of the car may go down fast.

The other main way of selling the car is by advertising in a newspaper or magazine specializing in collector cars. This process may work out and may not. There are pitfalls, and the process is very time-consuming.

Over a period of time a workable method of marketing collector cars will be developed—by the auction houses and by dealers. It will have to be worked out as the collector car market develops and cars become a major collectible.

Caution is advised, but maybe I have urged too much caution on both buyer and seller. If the buyer or seller is familiar with the car he wants to buy or the car he is selling, if he knows the market and price trend, and if he exercises caution, he can both buy right and sell right. I have been collecting cars for a long time. For some I may have paid too much. Others I bought were in worse condition than I anticipated and my restoration costs ran very high. Still, the cars on which I lost money are few. I took plenty of time to buy, and usually it took me time to locate a buyer when I was ready to sell, but overall I did well both buying and selling. In summary, today I would not hesitate to buy at auction or from a dealer or individual. I would not hesitate to sell (when the time seemed right to sell), but I would be prepared to spend a good deal of time locating a buyer who I would be sure would pay me a suitable price—and with a good, not a bad, check.

17

Restoration and Repair

IF A BUYER can find almost *any* kind of prewar classic car in original condition, one that does not require restoration, he has a collector car and probably an investment. The original-condition car hardly needs to be a classic. It can sometimes even be an ordinary car. The 1940 Buick sedan that sold in 1982 for the enormous sum of $11,750 is hardly a classic car. It is certainly not a prime collector car; although it is a good car (and I drove one a good many miles during the war) there is no great market demand for it in average or even good condition. What distinguished this car and made the price skyrocket was the fact that it was "near new." It had been driven only 21,000 miles, and the paint, chrome, and interior were about equal to new.

This is an example of original condition and what original condition does to value, even for a fairly common car. Nothing had to be done to this car and nothing should be done to eliminate any part of its original condition. This is the ultimate, the old car in original flawless condition. (Had the car been a late-model prewar Mercedes-Benz, like the 540K roadster in this same original condition and with 21,000 miles on the odometer, who knows the price it might have brought! At auction it probably would have passed the $500,000 mark.) However, this is more the exception than the rule. I can count on one hand the number of prewar cars that I have seen in the same condition as the 1940 Buick sedan.

The Object of Restoration

Original-condition cars are as scarce as hen's teeth, and there is hardly any point in trying to locate a prewar classic investment car in this original condition.

It is hard enough to locate a *postwar* classic in this original condition. In recent years, however, automobiles have come into their own as investments and more and more of these original-condition cars are coming to light—cars that were bought and kept as investments and driven very few miles. Some of these collector cars have been stored very carefully away from the elements, from humidity, and from any possible tamperers.

As for the antique automobiles, unless these have been in museums or private collections there is almost no chance of locating an original-condition car for sale.

A major object of restoration is to get a purchased car back to condition as near to original as possible. Let's take two cars, a Ford Mustang convertible and a Rolls-Royce Silver Cloud III, and compare what restoration amounts to. The two cars can be 1965 models, so we don't get back to prewar classic car and antique restoration, a procedure that can be difficult, time-consuming, costly, and sometimes next to impossible.

I have gone through a complete restoration of a Ford Mustang convertible (though mine is a 1966), so I know something about the restoration job that has to be done and its cost. The object in the restoration of this car is to get the car into its original condition, which is probably not as good condition as the condition of the 1965 Rolls-Royce, for instance, the latter being an elegant automobile with finish almost flawless when original.

The body on the Mustang must be in good condition. It may be rusted in places, and the rusted places must be cut out and metal pieces welded in. The welds must be smoothed, filler applied, and paint put on. This paint can be enamel, since the original Mustang paint was enamel. In fact, a good case can be made for painting the Mustang only in enamel, since the car is more original with the type of paint it came with new.

The body on my car was "rough." It had rusted-out places, and much work had to be done on it. All in all, bodywork and paint came to about $750. Currently, a good enamel paint job can cost $400.

The paint on the other hypothetical car, the Rolls-Royce 1965 Silver Cloud III, is quite a different proposition from the paint on the Mustang. The Rolls-Royce came new with a multicoat lacquer most carefully hand-rubbed. The Rolls-Royce, more than any other car, must be in almost flawless condition to be a significant investment. Rolls-Royce collectors demand the very finest in all aspects of the car they buy, and they know what the best is. I wish I had known how demanding Rolls-Royce collectors are before I bought my first Silver Cloud ten years ago. I never would have touched the car I ended up buying! The car had an aluminum body by James Young, and it takes a paint shop highly skilled at painting aluminum to do a Rolls-Royce quality job. Too often the paint does not stick to the aluminum of the body and lifts in "bubbles."

A suitable paint job on a Rolls-Royce will cost *at least* $2,500, and this is about what the paint job on my Rolls-Royce Silver Cloud II cost—just the paint, not bodywork or chrome. Such multicoat lacquer jobs (and all Rolls-Royce cars must be painted with several rubbed coats of lacquer) will cost $2,500 and up, and $5,000 is by no means an unusual price to pay.

The Mustang came with a very attractive interior of imitation leather, a material that lasts almost forever, even on a convertible. It seems best to redo in this same material.

The cost of seat coverings for all seats in the Mustang, front and back, is $189.95 from one Mustang parts supplier, and most Mustang parts firms are competitive in price. For this price one gets coverings complete for the two front bucket seats and for the back seat. The door panels cost $99.50 the pair. Dash covering costs $135. Carpets for front and back cost $135. The cost of *installing* these parts should not be over $250, at most.

Since I have recently finished the interior of my Rolls-Royce I know what that job cost. The job I did was better than what came on the car new. The headliner was upholstered in leather, as was the slide in the roof. Even the rear deck was padded and trimmed with leather on the underside. The leather— twenty hides—was the best I could buy. I did not use Connolly English leather, although that is pretty much standard Rolls-Royce leather. The leather cost me about $1,200; the installation cost $5,350. The upholstering job was the very best obtainable, but I think the price was about double what I should have paid. I know that I could have secured such a job from National Auto Top Company in Washington, D.C., a firm that has done bodywork, painting, and upholstery for me for decades, at a cost of about $1,500 for labor.

The Rolls-Royce has much bigger surfaces than the Mustang, of course, but aside from that the quality of materials and the amount of labor must be far greater for the Rolls-Royce than for the Mustang.

It is more than difficult to sell a Rolls-Royce that lacks perfect wood trim. If the wood trim is ragged the car will hardly appeal to any Rolls-Royce collector. To convert average wood trim into perfect wood trim on a Rolls-Royce can easily cost $1,000 or more. On the Mustang there is no wood trim and hardly any other kind of trim.

The object of restoration is to put the car back into its original showroom condition (as far as possible). The original showroom condition of the Mustang is one thing, and the original showroom condition of the Rolls-Royce is another.

There is a new theory in the restoration of cars, and that is to restore any car "to Rolls-Royce standards." Even if you have a Mustang, restore it so that Rolls-Royce would be happy to turn out such a car. The body should be perfect and pieces welded in, if necessary. There should be no fiberglass filler.

The paint should be multicoat lacquer, hand-rubbed. The interior should be the finest leather, possibly even the Connolly English hides used on Rolls-Royce. The interior leather might even be an exotic color like white that never came on a new Mustang. Everything should be rechromed. Fine high-pile carpets should be installed and a top of the finest material, possibly even fiberglass. The result might look like either a special Rolls-Royce or a "super California custom job."

Don't laugh! These cars are real eye-stoppers. Sometimes they are parked at filling stations, and cars stop while people get out to inspect the car. The price of a Mustang convertible restored along these lines can easily be $10,000. Sometimes such cars are designated "overrestored."

So restoration standards may be changing. They certainly are for Italian exotics like Maserati and Lamborghini, and it is not at all unusual to see one of these Italian sports cars with finish and interior of the quality of a Rolls-Royce. In fact, my own Lamborghini Miura was painted by Sal Marinello of Brooklyn, who, at the time, had several Rolls-Royces in his shop to paint for the Carriage House, leading New York Rolls-Royce dealers. The Miura also had Connolly English leather installed. It was fully up to Rolls-Royce standards of finish and interior.

Some Italian car owners and dealers are going beyond both Italian and Rolls-Royce car standards. Mr. Nick Soprano, the Ferrari dealer and owner, continually takes apart his Ferrari 275GTB-4 to have parts on the engine chrome-plated. He even removed the engine so that he could do a fine paint job on the engine compartment. Had an ordinary car owner had this engine-compartment paint job done the cost might well have been $1,000.

Two years ago a classic car dealer had a DeTomaso Mangusta for sale. I saw this Italian-bodied "Ford product" many times when I visited the dealer's showroom. The car was of beautiful design and in excellent condition. If anything had to be done to the car before delivery the dealer would have done it. The car was near perfect and priced at $18,000.

In December 1982, I saw this car again in the same dealer's establishment, only this time it was in the repair shop. A rather extensive "transformation" had taken place in the car. The dealer had sold the car to a collector. The collector apparently found no fault with the car, but he simply wanted to make it a more powerful, more beautiful, and better-handling car. The Ford engine turned out 230 horsepower. The new owner had the engine rebuilt and the horsepower upped to 300. Some of the original Mangustas had 300 horsepower instead of the usual 230.

The new owner had the suspension elaborately worked over so that the car handled more like a Ferrari 275GTB-4 than a Mangusta, and the suspension of the 275GTB-4 comes pretty close to being the ultimate in suspension.

The paint was very nearly perfect when I first saw the car back in 1980, but it wasn't what the new owner wanted. So he imported Italian lacquer of exactly the shade he desired and had the car completely repainted.

The cost of all of this "upgrading"? From $12,000 to $15,000. So now the owner has not $18,000 in the car, but $18,000 plus $12,000 at least—probably $31,000 to $32,000 in all.

Now what does he come out with? What does he have that he didn't have before? Certainly a better performer. The car apparently acts as though 100 horsepower had been added, not 70. The paint is more nearly perfect, but how much more? The suspension is better—but though a racing driver can probably tell the difference, the ordinary classic car buyer may well not be able to.

The market price on the Mangusta (in the condition it was in when the buyer purchased it in 1980 for about $18,000) would currently be about $21,000 to $22,000.

What is the rebuilt and upgraded car worth? Is it worth $32,000? It is not original. Maybe it is better than original, but how much has the value gone up, if any? An absolutely top price for this car would be $31,000 to $32,000, and I think a purchaser would rather pay $10,000 less for a mint-original condition car. Maybe because of the upgrading the buyer would stretch his offer to $26,000 or $28,000.

There is most certainly a limit past which one cannot go in "improving" any car. In 1950 a man bought a Cisitalia, one of the great sports cars of all time, and proceeded to turn it into a competition 1500-cubic-centimeter car for class racing. An experimental Offenhauser racing engine was built for a token price of $2,500. This engine he had installed in the Cisitalia in place of the original four-cylinder engine. The installation cost was $5,000—in 1950! He also had to buy a Ford transmission, have a special flywheel made, put in a special cooling system, etc.

Then I bought the car for about $3,000. His upgrading had not paid off. I had the Borg-Warner Corporation Pesco Products Division supercharge the car, but supercharging entailed lowering the compression ratio, putting in new pistons, and designing a steel belt drive system for the supercharger. I had to find a new set of carburetors, and a trip to England to buy these carburetors was necessary. The cluster gear in the transmission had to be changed. A De Dion differential was installed over a period of six months. My total cost? About $15,700.

When I finally sold the car I received less than $5,000 for it. The lesson is: "Don't overrestore." There is a point at which restoration becomes simply changes and attempts at upgrading, upgrading which may well not add much to the value of the car and may well destroy its originality, at least to a degree.

If I had to predict the future I would guess that more and more restoration jobs on all cars, from 1966 Mustang convertibles to Ferrari Daytona Spyders, will be in the nature of superb restorations, jobs that make the cars better than they were when new, cosmetic restoration jobs that make the Mustang something of the quality of a Rolls-Royce as it was originally. But I would guess that restoration will not often go beyond this point—that original specifications and original equipment will not be changed.

One of the standouts that I have owned was the famous Rust Heinz Phantom Corsair built on the Cord 810 chassis. I sold this car to my very good friend the comedian Herb Shriner. The doors were opened by solenoids, and when the main door opened outward, a small door in the top on each side opened upward so that you didn't bump your head getting into and out of the car. The doors were linked to each other—the main door and the door in the roof.

Herb Shriner did not like this "gearing" arrangement, so he eliminated it. He had the little door in the top fit in like the top of a kettle. You took the little top door off completely when you wanted to and put it in the back seat or in the storage compartment.

The front of the hood covered the radiator too much, so in hot weather the car sometimes overheated. He cut slits in the front of the hood to let in more air.

Later the car was sold to the Harrah Collection, and here Mr. Harrah saw as his objective returning the car exactly to its original condition, with the "geared doors" and the original solid front of the hood. The car is now in its original condition, the condition it was in when I owned it. The Harrah program of restoration was, I feel, correct, and the value of the car is raised by this restoration.

Restoration Cost Variations

One still hears the so-called maxim "You get what you pay for." I feel this statement is true only in a limited sense. In almost all departments of life you sometimes pay far more for far less—starting with fancy restaurants. I know of few areas, however, in which what you get for your money varies as much as in automobile restoration costs. I had a superb upholstering job done on my Mercedes-Benz 300S convertible for $350 for the labor. I supplied the hides to the upholsterer. The next car I brought to the same shop to have upholstered was bigger, the Rolls-Royce Silver Cloud II I have discussed earlier in this chapter. I expected to pay $1,000 to $1,200, because the car was bigger and several years had passed since the Mercedes upholstery job for $350 had been done. I did not expect a bill for $5,350—for the labor alone.

In Connecticut, where I live, I got an estimate of $900 for making the enamel paint on my Mustang convertible perfect. I took the car to Bostian's Garage in Union Bridge, Maryland. Rodney Bostian did a superb job for $125. Quite a price difference!

One estimate on repainting my Mercedes-Benz 300S was $2,500. I know the paint job would have been very good. I do know that Sal Marinello, who does the paint jobs on the Rolls-Royces brought in by the Carriage House of New York, quoted me a firm price on my Mercedes of $1,600—and his paint job would have been superb. I went back to the shop that had painted the car originally, Bostian's, and pointed out that the paint was not the best and that many years ago he had painted the car for me. He repainted it over a period of months and did a splendid job, maybe not quite the equal of Sal Marinello's, but splendid, nevertheless—for $600.

Labor cost variations are tremendous. The restoration shop that I have used for over thirty years is Bostian's, where labor is $15 an hour. I can send any and all cars to this shop for mechanical and body restoration, and I have done so over the years—such cars as Bentley, Ferrari, Italmeccanica, Fiat 8V, Mercedes-Benz 300S, Rolls-Royce Silver Cloud II, and all kinds of American cars, including the 1966 Mustang convertible that Mr. Bostian sold me originally.

In the area in which I live I use Paul Longo of Texaco of Greenwich, Connecticut. The labor rate in this shop as of early 1984 is $30 an hour. Paul Longo is probably the best Rolls-Royce mechanic in Fairfield County. He also works on my Mercedes 300S and on my Italian cars.

The specialist firm that I use on Italian cars is Motor Classic Corporation of North White Plains, New York. Italian cars, all aspects of them, are Motor Classic's specialty. The chief mechanic understands all aspects of sports and competition cars from suspension to wiring to engine overhaul. The rate is $35 an hour.

A new firm has opened up specializing in Ferrari repair. In its advertising this firm uses the phrase "Keep your horses prancing"—the Ferrari horses. It advertises a labor rate of $65 an hour—quite a jump from the $15 an hour charged by Bostian's in Union Bridge, Maryland. Certainly Bostian's does not advertise that it will "keep your horses prancing," but the clutch J. P. Bostian installed in my Ferrari 250GT in 1967 is still operating!

The Repair of Collector Cars

One often has the idea that once the collector car is restored—restored correctly and completely by competent people—that's it! Maintaining the car in restored condition is thought to be relatively simple.

How wrong! Maintaining a collector car in restored condition is difficult and often enormously expensive. Let's take as an example two Italian cars—both mine. The first is one of the fairly rare and very exotic Lamborghini Miuras. This car I bought in early 1980 from another car collector, an extremely knowledgeable man. Two years before I bought the car from him he had purchased it from a Ford dealer. Over the two-year period he had done all the things I would have thought necessary on the car, and he certainly did not spare the expense. He took out the engine and rebuilt everything that needed to be rebuilt in the engine interior, and he had one of the best Lamborghini mechanics in New York do the job.

Next he upholstered in the finest black leather—Connolly. He then removed all the paint from the body and Sal Marinello put on a superb paint job—in Italian red. All worn chrome was replaced. Brakes were worked on.

I inspected the car carefully before I bought it. The seller had put about $13,000 into restoration, but I did not get the car at a bargain price, and I thought he should put in what more was necessary in order to get the car in as fine condition as I felt it should be. As a matter of fact, I agreed to spend $600 of my own money to do a few more things that he felt were unnecessary. So everything was done and the car was delivered to me.

On the way home from New York to Connecticut, I stopped at a toll booth to pay the toll. The brake pedal went to the floor and stayed there, and the battery wouldn't start the car after it stalled while I was paying the toll.

My first job, after taking delivery on this restored car, was to rewire almost the whole car, at a cost of $478.19. I also bought an alternator for $120.

When I bought the car I intended to buy new Pirelli tires, and these I did buy for $410. Then I really went to work. I found the brake master cylinder was coming off the firewall and the metal was weak. The brakes had to be worked on. The chassis was somewhat twisted, and I could not see this twisting at the time I inspected the car originally. The carburetors leaked, and I had to have all of them rebuilt. All in all my bill for this work (and the work required over a year) was $4,572.02, including painting necessary after the repair people who straightened the chassis apparently left the car out in the elements for an extended period. Perhaps if I had looked harder before I bought the car I could have estimated these necessary repairs, but I doubt it.

The other Italian car I bought at about the same time was a Maserati Ghibli coupe. The price was very satisfactory for 1980—$10,900—and the selling dealer agreed to repair many things that I felt were wrong. This car was not in perfect condition when I bought it and I knew it; but the price was under the going price for a fine-condition Ghibli. When I got through paying the dealer for extra work I wanted done, but work he was not responsible for, my total outlay on the car was $15,882.40, not $10,900. My repairs on the car came to almost $5,000—about half of the purchase price of the car. Whether this sum represented repairs or restoration is debatable. As the car was being delivered the water pump began to leak badly, and it had to be rebuilt at considerable cost. The transmission had to be repaired at least three times. The radiator and cooling system had to be reworked several times, as the car continually overheated. The engine had to be taken apart and the valves ground, and four valves had to be replaced.

The point in all of this detailing of expenditures for repairs is that though I am no novice, I had little idea that as soon as I took delivery on these cars I would be faced with these expenses. When I bought the cars I paid figures which would allow me to make some unanticipated repairs, and I certainly had to make unanticipated repairs, and very expensive ones—almost $10,000 on two cars that I had driven practically not at all.

Parts Problems

Anyone writing about repair and restoration of automobiles should make a very serious and continuing effort to achieve objectivity. He should see both sides of the repair and restoration problem—or problems. He should see both the car owner's side and the repair and restoration shop's side. After careful consideration of both of these sides it is hard to arrive at any other conclusion than that replacement parts are a disaster area. I live about 20 miles from the garage I use in my home area. I had a bad carburetor, so bad that I had to have the car towed the 20 miles. My mechanic determined that the carburetor had to be replaced. For my particular car a new carburetor was hard to find and the mechanic bought a rebuilt one. I drove the car home and the car had the same trouble.

In any event, this time I could get the car going, and I drove it back to the repair shop. The replacement carburetor was defective, so the garage sent back the replacement carburetor and got me replacement carburetor number two.

I drove the car home with replacement carburetor number two. The next morning the same trouble! In fact, the car almost stalled on the road, and when I parked it I had a great deal of trouble starting it again.

So back the car went to the shop. Carburetor again! So replacement carburetor number three was installed. And now, for the first time, it is right. When I visited the garage I saw the two defective replacement carburetors in their boxes ready to be returned to the jobber from whom the garage bought them. Had I not seen these two carburetors in their boxes I might have found it hard to believe that two replacements were bad.

Replacement parts are perennially defective—far too many of them—and for this deplorable state of affairs I blame inept labor at the rebuilding plant or at the factory where the new parts are made in the first place. Quality control and final testing are poor, to put it mildly.

Who stands the cost of replacing the defective part—replacing it again and again? If the garage charges the customer, that customer may well not come back. It was not the customer's fault that the replacment parts were defective and had to be replaced. The garage should try to get the supplier of the defective parts to pay for the labor of putting in the defective parts. The garage may try, but it will not get far!

For some cars entire defective engines seem to be the norm. For one make and model car I have seen at least two dozen advertisements of the cars on the secondhand market that announce, "Fresh engine." The owner of one of these cars might be wise always to have on hand at least one spare engine, and these engines can sometimes be bought rebuilt for about $3,500. When these engines are advertised for sale it is a good guess that they have been replaced by an American engine, in this particular car probably a Chevrolet or Ford engine, usually Chevrolet.

Some parts are staggeringly expensive. An advertisement sometimes appears in one of the car magazines for oil pumps for the Rolls-Royce Silver Ghost— at $700. This is a rebuilt oil pump. This price compares with about $50 for an oil pump for an American production car.

It is very difficult to find certain new or rebuilt parts. Many years ago I bought a three-pointed-star radiator cap for my Mercedes-Benz 300S. This cap with star is a large and imposing one, not like the cap on the 300 sedan, which is much smaller. I recall having paid $7.50 for this cap in the 1950s.

Today the cap can hardly be secured at all. I anticipated having this cap stolen, so when I bought the replacement cap in the 1950s I bought another to use as a spare for another $7.50. Today I feel certain I can advertise one of these caps for $500 and get an immediate buyer. One of these two caps that I own I keep on the car as long as I am driving it. Otherwise I remove it and lock it in the trunk or in the house. The other cap is locked in the safe deposit.

There is in Phoenix, Arizona, a large supplier of parts for Italian cars. It has a lot of Ferrari and Lamborghini parts. It does not carry Maserati parts. When I asked why not, I was told that they were too hard to get.

I would like to buy a new chassis for my Lamborghini Miura. Where I will be able ultimately to find one I do not know. I have had no luck yet at any price.

On the other hand, I have just purchased a replacement engine for my 1966 Ford Mustang. It cost me $619 plus $150 for installation. It runs fine and will probably keep on running fine for the next 60,000 miles at least.

Had I shopped more closely I would have bought a Ford Mustang engine from Parisi's Mustang Parts in Bridgeport, Connecticut, an engine with 2,000 miles on it since overhaul, for $150. To this figure I would have had to add $100 for installation.

Securing Skilled Mechanical Work

The owner of a car that needs repair is looking for (1) competent work and (2) reasonable prices. In these times one must expect to pay $35 to $45 an hour for highly competent work on a Ferrari or other Italian car of sophisticated design or on a luxury car like a Rolls-Royce. More one should not have to pay, but by shopping around a rate of $25 should be possible once in a while.

In the very expensive town of Greenwich, Connecticut, the most expert labor on my Rolls-Royce, done by a highly experienced Rolls-Royce mechanic, costs $30 an hour. He charges the same rate for work on my classic Mercedes-Benz 300S, my Lamborghini Miura, and my Maserati Ghibli. In this shop an overhaul job on the carburetors of my Ghibli plus a valve-grinding job cost $500, well under the price of the nearest Maserati repair shop. The Maserati shop would no doubt do the work competently and possibly faster.

It is often the task of the classic car owner today to visit various repair shops and to ask about the qualifications of the mechanics who will be put on one's car.

The charge of the mechanic's time on your job—on your car—can be a matter of some flexibility. When I visit the shop of Paul Longo in Greenwich he and his son are always working on some car or else working on billings or on the books. When I visit another shop the chief mechanic often seems to be leaning on the workbench thinking things over. When I asked how the mechanic's time was apportioned to the jobs in the shop, I was told that his eight-hour day at work was apportioned to the jobs he worked on—all of the eight hours to one or another job. But what about those minutes or hours when he leans against the workbench and thinks things over? Are those minutes or hours charged to my car? I hope not!

Performing Major Restoration

The standards of classic and antique cars are getting higher and higher. Buyers demand the very finest cars and will pay the very finest prices, particularly for the great classics and antiques in mint condition.

In the Barrett-Jackson auction of 1983 an absolutely mint 300S Mercedes-Benz cabriolet brought $100,000. Another similar car reached a bid of about $65,000 in the auction—$35,000 less than the car that sold. Was the condition of the $65,000 car very much poorer than that of the $100,000 car? By no means! I examined both cars several times and talked to the owner of the $65,000 car. Unless the prospective buyer was a real expert the difference in the two cars did not seem like $35,000. Actually the steering wheel of the $65,000 car wasn't set quite right in relation to the front wheels when straight— a most minor fault that could have been easily corrected at little cost. A few of the dashboard dials on the $65,000 car didn't work, and they could have been repaired. The paint jobs looked comparable. Actually I believe the same shop did both jobs. The condition of the body of the $65,000 car (under the paint) was not as good as that of the $100,000 car. All rusted parts had been replaced with metal in the $100,000 car. In the $65,000 car some rusted parts had been replaced by metal, and I believe fiberglass fill had been used where some holes had been. The refilling of these holes with metal would have cost something, possibly as much as several thousand dollars, and the paint would have had to be repaired most carefully and at a cost of at least $1,000, possibly more. There were a few other "inferiorities" in the $65,000 car.

Did the $35,000 difference in price reflect $35,000 that needed to be spent on the $65,000 car to make it the equal of the $100,000 car? Hardly!

This example is used to indicate that a mint car is worth a disproportionate amount more than the "almost-mint" car. It is believed that the restoration job on the $65,000 car amounted to $24,000. It is also believed that the $100,000 car had originally cost its owner a little over $25,000; so the difference between his purchase price (within a year of resale) and the $100,000 selling price was ample to cover all restoration *and* give him a profit. The lesson? It probably pays to restore to mint condition absolutely top cars—cars selling in the six-figure price range or close to it. Either one of these cars in average condition would probably have sold for $40,000. I feel I know this car and its values, since I have owned four 300S Mercedes cars over the past three decades and own one now.

Total Restoration

Before any work on any antique or classic car is contracted for, some inquiry should be made of the quality and cost of the work of any shop. If one is thinking of having a paint job done, the paint shop should be asked to show the prospective customer a paint job that it recently completed. This is a reasonable request with which any good shop should be willing to comply. In addition, the price of the paint job should be determined. No job of restoration of any kind should be contracted for without a clear idea of the cost. When an upholsterer charges $350 for a job on my Mercedes-Benz 300S convertible, and then charges $5,350 for my Rolls-Royce, a lawsuit would seem to be indicated. This is exactly the experience I had. What I should have done was to contract for the job at a specific price, or a maximum price should have been agreed to. One should not buy a pig in a poke.

Total restoration can cost a great deal. One of the finest restoration jobs I have ever seen, a ground-up restoration job, cost a fair $38,000, a staggering sum perhaps, but a fair one for a Lamborghini Miura restoration of engine and drive train, chassis and suspension, body, paint, chrome, leather, carpets, exhaust system, and a complete updating of the early Miura to make it at least the equivalent of the latest and best Miura. The car was converted from a $25,000 car to an $80,000-plus car.

Another fantastic ground-up restoration I had the privilege to witness was accomplished by my old friend Philip Haslewood Blake of Canterbury, England, the man who got me started in collector cars. For years he owned a Bentley Speed Six coupe of the late 1920s, a car that was run down and not much admired when I rode in it in 1959. I believe he paid about $600 for it in the early 1950s.

In 1964 Phil undertook the restoration at the world's leading Bentley repair and overhaul shop, Hoffman and Mountfort of England. The car was rebuilt from the chassis up, and while the body was completely standard Bentley in design, it was new—a four-passenger open car, a dream to look at and drive. It was sold in 1967 for about $17,000. Today it would sell for more than $100,000.

There are certain shops specializing in restoration of all kinds and degrees from a paint job to ground-up restoration. White Post Restorations of White Post, Virginia, is often in the news in connection with its restoration jobs.

It is believed that Russ Jackson's Classic Carriage House of Phoenix, Arizona, restored the magnificent Delahaye 135MS with van den Plas body that was offered at auction in January 1983. A restoration job of this quality is hard to come by regardless of the shop that did it.

Hemmings Motor News carries many ads of restoration shops specializing in classic and antique cars, and there is no trouble in finding such a shop in almost any section of the country.

There is another way to do total (or ground-up) restoration, and that is to contract with a repair shop to handle the total job. The shop would do, say, all mechanical work, but it would also handle contracting for paint, upholstery, chrome, radiator overhaul, etc. Thus the owner of the car has to deal with only one shop and one man. The main shop can often get a very favorable rate from other shops because it contracts out many paint jobs, brake jobs, etc. over the period of a year.

There is still another way to carry out total restoration, and that is to handle all contacts oneself. You, the owner, must know enough about restoration to secure all parts and services yourself. If you do, then the cost saving can be great. Hyde Ballard was twice president of the very large and important Antique Automobile Club of America. I recall visiting his barn during World War II and looking at his Thomas Flyer, which he was overhauling completely. He would even take small pieces to be chromed. This is a long, drawn-out and tedious process for an expert or at least a semi-expert, but it often results in getting each job done extremely well and at a minimum of expense. My Rolls-Royce Silver Cloud II restoration was a combination of this direct kind of contracting by me personally and the use of a competent repair shop to contract out chrome work, carpeting, upholstering, etc.

Specialist Firms

A chrome-plated exterior part of a car that is broken, worn, or cracked is difficult to repair. The part probably has to be welded, then chrome-plated. Such welding and rechroming jobs seldom work out. The chrome is not as smooth as it was originally. One firm, Qual Krom in Poughkeepsie, New York, can weld and rechrome so that the weld and rechroming job cannot be seen—so Qual Krom claims, anyway. This quality of work can rarely be secured.

Earl Reynolds of Tulsa, Oklahoma, repairs broken castings, even engine blocks that are broken in many pieces at the top of the cylinders. Again, such work is almost impossible to secure.

West Coast Porcelain of El Monte, California, even puts new porcelain on antique license plates so the plates look original.

Everett Wheel Service of Everett, Washington, rebuilds and restores antique and classic car wheels and claims it can supply custom-made spokes for any wheel.

International Speedometer and Clock Company of Chicago, Illinois, rebuilds car speedometers and clocks. One has no idea of the difficulty of having an old clock from a Mercedes-Benz 300S repaired unless he tries to find a firm specializing in this work!

Pot Metal Restorations of Tallahassee, Florida, restores pitted pot metal that was once smooth and chrome-plated.

Rolls-Royce Motors, Inc., of Nyack, New York, specializes in the restoration of wood in Rolls-Royce cars.

One firm sells rebuilt Rolls-Royce oil pumps for $700, and heads for Phantom I and II Rolls-Royces for $2,000 a head.

Securing Bargain Parts

The last Rolls-Royce oil pump I bought for my Silver Cloud II was supplied as a used part to me by Bob's Auto Parts of Kingston, New York—for $125, not $700. The Rolls-Royce windshield is very expensive, but Bob's supplied me with two such windshields for $250 each. These windshields are now made in New York at a reasonable price for the Rolls-Royce. Usually the Rolls-Royce radiator emblem lady costs $350 for the Silver Cloud and $450 for the Silver Shadow. I secured one of the $350 ladies for $150 by answering an ad put in one of the car magazines by a California firm. The part was an original, not a later copy, and there are many such copies for sale today.

The collector car clubs are of considerable use in locating repair shops and parts suppliers. The Lamborghini Miura uses some lights from the Fiat 850, a cheap little car whose parts are in keeping pricewise with the original price of the car, and the car originally sold for about $1,400 in Italy. The lights are the same, but the Fiat price is much less than the Miura price.

If you buy a compressor for a Ghibli air-conditioning system from the Maserati shop, the price is one thing. But the compressor is American and it can be bought from an American parts supplier—the exact same compressor—for far less money.

For unusual and hard-to-find parts and services one should start out by consulting *Hemmings Motor News*, and then next the car club specializing in the kind of car you have—like the Maserati Information Exchange of Mercer Island, Washington.

Restoration can cost a fortune, particularly if one falls into the hands of an unscrupulous restoration shop. It can cost a fortune sometimes even if the job is done by an honest and competent shop, and I do not consider the total restoration and updating of a Lamborghini Miura by Bob Wallace's shop in Phoenix to be in any way excessive at $38,000. If you handle the job yourself, and shop around for services and bargain parts, you will not come out with as competent a job, in all probability, but you might save money—while adding immensely to the time you personally spend on the restoration.

In a way it is best to go to a low-priced area for repairs and restoration. New York City is not one of these low-priced areas, I have looked at some of the bills charged by Rolls-Royce firms for repairs—and they are incredible. I can get the same quality of work done in Greenwich, Connecticut, for $30 an hour or in Union Bridge, Maryland, for $15 an hour.

So maybe the best advice in the end is to buy a car in at least *near*-mint condition and preserve it carefully, running it only on occasion and watching it for rust and other deterioration, which should be caught at the earliest possible moment.

18

Buying and Building a Collection

STRANGE AS IT may seem, it is probably easier to buy collector cars today and to build a collection than, say, ten, fifteen, or twenty years ago. True, prices are very much higher today than they were, but now there is a definite price trend—up—and there wasn't such a clear uptrend a decade or two ago.

It was not until after 1970 that the price trend of collector cars seemed clear. A few years before 1970 I could have picked up a very good 300SL Mercedes-Benz roadster for $2,500, and one in under-par condition from the Greenwich, Connecticut, Mercedes dealer for $1,500, a car the dealer had always maintained. I could have bought a fine 1909 Maxwell two-cylinder for an asking price of $1,200. I did pick up a 1960 Ferrari 250GT convertible for $2,500, a car in excellent mechanical condition but in need of chrome and paint. These are some of the most-wanted cars on today's market, but a decade and a half ago there was little interest in them as collector items or investments.

Today there is definite collector interest. There are collector car dealers and there are collector car auctions, many of which have sprung up in the last decade. There is also a definite rising price trend for these cars and for other collector cars, almost all of them, so that when one buys (or invests) today he can be, at least to a certain extent, secure in the knowledge that the uptrend will continue.

On the other side of the coin, the demand for collector cars is today not quite as great as it was in 1981. The recession dampened the demand of collectors and investors. These buyers have pulled in their horns, and even the great collector cars like the Mercedes-Benz 540K and Duesenberg J and SJ did not find a ready market. By 1984 there were indications of an upturn.

Collecting the Best

At the four collector car auctions in Arizona in 1983 there were definite investment cars, cars with a history of important collector interest and a rising price trend, but the vast majority did not sell. One day we will probably look back at the great collector and investment cars that were offered in these auctions and wish those sales could be brought back so that buyers could have a "second chance." By the 1984 auction the "second chance" was gone!

At or near the top of the collector-investment pyramid come the mid-1930s Mercedes-Benz 500K and 540K roadsters. This may well be the highest-priced collector car with the exception of certain rarities that virtually never appear on the market, like the Bugatti Royale.

If I were investing I would start with the 500K and 540K roadsters. I would try to get a roadster, but I would probably not succeed in locating one. Then I would turn to the special-bodied convertible coupes that seat two—not four. The two convertibles at the Barrett-Jackson auction are what I have in mind. To my way of thinking, and as a former owner of both a 540K and 500K, I would pick the convertible with body by Graber. This body is far more beautiful than the English Corsica body on my 500K. I know the quality of the Graber body, since I owned a Bentley with Graber body, but again, although by Graber, it was far less beautiful than the body on the Barrett Mercedes-Benz 540K.

If I could not find a convertible two-seater then I would go for a four-seater cabriolet, which is far less rare than the two-seater convertibles. There were many of these cars made with Sindelfingen bodies, beautiful cars but less beautiful than the roadsters and two-passenger convertibles.

For a roadster one might have to pay as much as $500,000, perhaps even more. For the Graber convertible belonging to Tom Barrett one might have to go to $400,000. For a cabriolet the price might be $250,000, possibly a little less.

After the Barrett-Jackson sale apparently someone brought in an SSK Mercedes-Benz of the late 1920s. This great car might have sold after the close of the auction for $250,000, and this is a very fair price for this much-in-demand "great." The SSK is my second Mercedes choice.

Next I would certainly recommend a Duesenberg J or SJ, preferably an SJ, although there is not much difference in the values of the two cars. The model to buy is the open car, either roadster, speedster, convertible coupe, tourer, or convertible sedan, the big open cars that have dual cowls being the most desirable. For $250,000 one of the best of these cars should be located.

The next car to select in this group of prime cars would be the Cadillac V-16 roadster of 1931 or 1932, the later cars being less desirable and less valuable. For this car a top price of $200,000 to $250,000 would have to be paid.

Next we move on to the Chrysler Imperial of the early 1930s, preferably the large touring car, although the roadsters and convertibles are also desir-

Among the attractive collector cars is this 1933 Packard convertible coupe which reached $75,000 at auction in 1983. It might have brought only $10,000 in 1970. (Julia Rush)

able. This car might be purchased for a maximum of $175,000.

From this era I would move back to antiques, and here I would purchase one of two cars—or both. The preferred car is the Mercer Raceabout of 1911–1913. Next is the Stutz Bearcat of 1914–1916. The two cars are comparable in quality and in price—about $150,000.

In this prime collector car group I would certainly want a Packard, and the Packard I would select would be a Model 734 speedster. Two of these cars, both apparently mint, were offered for sale in recent years at about $125,000 each, a price I consider very low. One might get an important early-1930s tourer, a V-12, for $200,000, possibly more. A convertible coupe V-12 of this era might be bought for as low as $100,000, up to perhaps $150,000.

To this group of American collector cars I would add a pre–World War I Rolls-Royce Silver Ghost tourer or roadster, for which I would expect to pay $150,000, possibly as much as $200,000.

There are other fine cars that could be added to this list, but these were the criteria we used in setting up this "model collection":

1. I am thinking primarily of American collectors rather than foreign collectors.

2. The cars are to be sold in the United States eventually, and they are marketable here in the United States. The market for all of these cars is good in this country.

3. The cars can easily be collected in this country. They can be bought at auction, from dealers, and sometimes from private sources.

4. The cars can fairly easily be maintained, and replacement parts are available.

5. The cars are appreciated by the "American audience." They easily give the owners any prestige they may be looking for.

6. All of the cars on the list of top collector cars are fine cars, and certainly all are beautiful cars if judged along classic and antique car lines—by classic and antique car standards.

7. For one wanting to invest a sum in six or low seven figures the number of cars in the collection is not so great as to be unmanageable or tremendously expensive.

8. Prices of all of these cars have risen rather steadily. They have not dropped, at least significantly, and prices are likely to resume their upward march in the future.

Collector Cars in the Medium-High Price Range

The person who pays $320,000 for a Mercedes-Benz SS roadster (as happened at Christie's Los Angeles auction of early 1979) runs some risk. That was a new high for this make and model car. In the 1983 Barrett-Jackson auction there was a comparable Mercedes-Benz SS, this one a tourer. I looked it over carefully and remarked to the owner that it looked like my old car that I bought in 1939. I asked the owner what he felt he should get for the car and he replied, "At least $300,000"—less than the comparable SS sold for four years earlier in the Christie's auction. But in the actual Barrett-Jackson auction the top bid was nowhere near $300,000. In 1984 Barrett-Jackson auctioned a 1927 Mercedes-Benz S tourer for an incredible $410,000.

In some ways it might be wise to buy less expensive cars than the great cars I have discussed above. The downside risk is less, although I have limited the high-priced cars to the finest and most desirable of all collector cars in the United States. In any event, the following are my selections for a collection of somewhat less expensive collector cars.

In this less-than-top-price category the first car I would pick would be a Mercedes-Benz 300S roadster or cabriolet or the early to middle 1950s, one in absolutely mint condition. The market has been tested for such a car twice, and in a somewhat down general car market. The Barrett-Jackson auction in early 1982 sold one such car for $100,000. One year later the same auction sold the same make and model car in the same mint condition for the same price—$100,000. Ten years earlier the car would not have sold for over $10,000, if that.

The next car I would select for a collection of cars in the medium-high price category would be a Mercedes-Benz 300SL Gullwing in good-to-mint condition. This car might well be bought for under $100,000 and possibly as low as $75,000.

My next selection would be the most copied car in the world—the Auburn 851 and 852 boattail speedster of 1935 and 1936. These cars in mint condition should be purchased for around $75,000, in average condition for $65,000.

The next car selected is a related car, the Cord 810 and 812 of the mid-1930s, either a convertible sedan or a convertible coupe. These cars do appear in the $40,000 range, but top-condition cars are about in the $75,000 range.

There is another Cord that I prefer because of its unique qualities and its scarcity—the L-29 that first appeared in 1929. This is a straight-eight with front-wheel drive. The 810 and 812 models were V-8 cars with front-wheel drive. The L-29 is a car with verve, perhaps not so universally in demand as the 810 and 812 but very much wanted nevertheless. The price would be around $100,000 to $125,000.

I'd pick an Isotta Fraschini Type 8A of about 1930, the open car or convertible model. This is a car in great demand, particularly in Europe, and it can be bought for around $100,000. It is a great collector car and a great prestige car. In 1984 one brought the huge price of $410,000.

I'd like a Hispano-Suiza Model H6 32CV, the 46CV, or the V-12, called

1930 Cord L-29 sedan that commanded $50,000 at the Leake sale conducted by Christie's in May 1974. The car would have brought less than $15,000 in 1970 and would be valued at $125,000 today. (photograph by A. C. Cooper Ltd., courtesy Chisties's)

1930 Hispano-Suiza touring car with specially built body, designed for Rudolph Valentino, was sold by Kruse auctioneers for $176,000 in 1978. (Kruse International)

the Type 68. These cars are all in demand, particularly in Europe, and the price of the V-12 can be very high. The other cars can be purchased in the $100,000 range or a little up, and the cars on which to concentrate are the open models. The Hisso has a reputation so high that it is likely always to be in demand.

Rolls-Royce should be included in this price category, and here I would also pick an open car, a Phantom I or Phantom II roadster or touring car (or convertible) or a late-model Silver Ghost tourer or roadster—not that a later Ghost is more desirable than an early Ghost, but the later Ghosts are the only ones that can be purchased for, say, $100,000 or a little less. A mint Phantom I or Phantom II convertible sedan can cost well into six figures, but slightly lesser models can still be bought for somewhere around $100,000.

Collector Cars in the Medium Price Range

By "medium price" I mean cars selling for $50,000 or $60,000, perhaps a little more or a little less.

At the Grand Old Cars Museum auction in Arizona in January 1983, a superb collector car in this price category was sold. It was a 1937 Packard V-12 convertible coupe in excellent condition and with a chromed radiator. It was listed as in class 2 condition but it certainly missed class 1 very narrowly. It brought $58,000. Of all of the cars auctioned in the sale this would have been my first selection, regardless of price.

From this prewar classic Packard I would move to the postwar classic Ferrari Super America of 1960–1964, a car that in Italy seems almost worth its weight in gold. The car is old enough to have earned the designation "classic." It should not go down in value over the years—only up. It should easily be bought in the United States for $50,000 in mint condition.

Next I would select a Rolls-Royce, this one a Silver Cloud III convertible with Park Ward body, 1963–1965. It should be in excellent condition and should be purchased for $60,000.

If a Cloud III cannot be located then I would take a Cloud I. If no suitable convertible can be located I would take a sports coupe or a Rolls-Royce Flying Spur four-door sedan, few of these cars having been built. All cars should have left-hand drive.

1981 Ferrari Berlinetta Boxer which sold for $62,5000 in 1983 at Motor Classic Corporation. (Julia Rush)

My next selection would be a Lamborghini Miura SV, the most perfected car, the one put out as the last series of 1972, with separate transmission and crankcase. I believe I would send it right away to Bob Wallace of Phoenix, one of the designers of this car and its test driver, to have it modernized and updated to SV plus! I would expect to have invested $60,000 to $70,000 in the car when I was finished modernizing and restoring it.

Now I would return to Ferrari, to the great road car, the 275GTB-4 of the late 1960s. This car is a superb performer; there are probably no production cars produced even today that will outperform this model Ferrari on the open road and on hilly, twisty courses.

Right behind the 275GTB-4 (if behind it at all) would be the Ferrari Daytona coupe. This car is a powerhouse and has as good acceleration as the later and more sophisticated Ferrari 512 Berlinetta Boxer. The 275GTB-4 and the Daytona should be bought for $60,000 to $65,000. The Daytona Spyder costs twice this figure and is very hard to find, and the "conversions" of the coupe to the Spyder are worth much less than the true Spyder.

In the same price category is the Cobra 427, probably America's highest-performance car ever, a simple roadster but a road-holding powerhouse.

Collector Cars in the Lower Price Range

Very near the bottom of this last category, at least near the bottom in cost, is the Ford Mustang of 1964½ to 1966, the convertible model—in mint condition. Top-condition cars of this make, model and body style can be bought for $10,000 or a little more, and they are not hard to find. At the Grand Old Cars sale a very fine 1966 Mustang convertible that looked to me to be in at least class 2 condition or better went for $6,750. This would have been one of my selections had I been buying at this sale of about 150 cars in all.

My next selection in this lower-priced category would be a 1963–1967 Chevrolet Corvette. This car has a very classic, and not out-of-date, line, and it is not like the later-to-latest Sting Rays. It is a fine-performing car and in great demand by young and older collectors. It can be bought for somewhere around $15,000 in mint condition. The roadster is probably the preferred model, but the split-rear-window coupe sells for about the same price and is certainly sought-after. The models earlier than 1963 are most certainly collector Corvettes, but they are now getting somewhat scarce and high in price, and they are not the refined cars that those of the mid-1960s are.

The Ford Thunderbird of 1955–1957 is certainly a classic and has been for some time. It is not only an excellent-running car but it is always in demand and in a generally rising price trend. At almost any collector car auction a Thunderbird of 1955–1957 will be in demand, and today can be bought for $15,000 to $17,000. In 1984 one auctioned for $32,500.

We move now to another Ford, this one the V-8 roadster of the 1930s, and the car should be in mint or near-mint condition. In the right market the car can sell for $30,000, but it can frequently be bought for much less. Perhaps the most-wanted year, and at the highest price, is the 1934 model. The 1932 models, though, are also in demand, as are all roadsters, touring cars, convertible coupes, and convertible sedans up to the war. The target price should be $15,000 for a car in mint or near-mint condition.

In about the same price category is the four-cylinder Model A Ford roadster made from 1928 to 1932, and a fine-condition car should be bought from $14,000 to $16,000.

It might seem the wrong place to place the car, but the Mercedes-Benz 220 and 220S should be included in this list of lower-priced collector cars. The car on which to concentrate is the 220 convertible of the early to middle 1950s. The later cars of essentially the same model are the 220S convertibles, and these are as popular as the 220 models of earlier years. The 220 in mint condition is a "near-great classic," and there are fewer of these cars than of the later 220S. On the present market a price of $15,000 to $20,000 for these cars should be a target, although many of the cars are rising in price out of this price level.

The 230SL is the later sports car, the six-cylinder car of the 1960s. It can sometimes be bought in the $15,000 range, especially at auction. So can the 190SL, and sometimes at auction this car even goes for under $10,000. It is not a scarce car but it is sporty and very popular.

One final car I would include in this price category is the Maserati Ghibli, possibly the most beautiful sports coupe ever made anywhere in the world. The body is magnificent. The interior is luxurious. The car comes with power steering, power brakes, power windows, air conditioning, and automatic transmission if such a transmission is wanted. The engine is a powerhouse, and the car may well move along at 170 mph. The main trouble is that it is very temperamental, and unless care is taken on a regular basis, expensive engine troubles can develop.

The car seems to be a big bargain on the present market. For $15,000 or a little more one can get a mint-condition Ghibli, and for $18,000 a late-model Ghibli SS with larger engine and with many of the bugs of the earlier car worked out. This car did not move up in price from 1981 to 1984, and there are many such cars available for purchase. The convertible is a collector's car but it sells for $10,000 to $25,000 more than the coupe, and it may have the distinction of being the most beautiful convertible ever made.

Outlook by Price Class

The cars in the highest price category are comparable to the Dow Jones blue-chip stocks. They have, in the past at least, been the market leaders; but like the blue-chip stocks they have been subject to both surges and slackening in demand. They rose in price enormously, far more than the blue-chip stocks, but they developed a price plateau around 1981, and, unlike the blue-chip stocks, they did not emerge into a bull market in August 1982. The great Duesenberg went up to 1981 and then prices stuck and even went down a bit.

Still, these cars are the cream of the collector car market. They are the most-sought-after cars in the United States and they bring by far the highest prices. They also have the ultimate quality—in artistic design, in mechanical design (at least in most cases), and in construction. To invest in these cars is a conservative course to follow. Maybe other cars will go up faster in price, at least in the short run, but these cars are like bank loans that banks make to their soundest customers. A loss is unlikely, but so are speculative profits unlikely.

All of the cars in the top price category are mature, fine investment automobiles, and I have no hesitation about including any of them.

In the next category down in price, the cars that might just make six figures or a little more are still pretty much on safe, conservative ground as far as investment is concerned. If any cars move up in price these cars probably will—all of them that I have included, from the Auburn boattail speedster to the Mercedes-Benz 300S open car. They are, of course, not the market leaders as much as the more expensive cars are.

When we get to the next group of cars, more questions can be raised about cars to include and where the group is going pricewise. I placed the Lamborghini Miura in this group. This is a very specialized car, a car of very advanced mechanical and artistic design, a car far in advance of its time, a car that set the mechanical and body trend for all high-performance cars of the late 1960s. How will this car endure, particularly if we get even higher-performance cars and of the basic design of the Italian cars of this era, cars manufactured now according to this basic design? Will a new Ferrari model very much outdate the Miura? What about the more advanced and "space-age-looking" Lamborghini Countach? Will this car outdate the Miura? Is the Miura a phenomenon of the 1980s, in a sense a car that will pass by at least a little as a collector automobile?

Is the Ferrari 275GTB-4 in something of the same category? This car will outperform almost anything on the road, even though it ended in production in the late 1970s. But what if Ferrari puts out a transverse-rear-engine 5-liter car that outperforms its biggest and fastest car, the 512BB, and also the 275GTB-4? Isn't much of the demand for the 275GTB-4 dependent on its performance on the road right today? Will there be obsolescence in this prime car?

In this category it is somewhat harder to find true classics, timeless classics, than in the two higher price categories.

When we come down to the lowest price category the question about how the cars will endure the passing of the years is not so important, simply because the cars are not that expensive. If a mistake in a $15,000 car is made its consequences are far less than if a mistake in a $250,000 car is made.

The ubiquitous Mustang of 1964½–1966, the convertible, has been in a price uptrend for at least three years. These cars always appear at major auctions in force, and they never go cheap, but the rise has slackened.

The Maserati Ghibli coupe seems underpriced to me, and it should not long be underpriced.

On the other hand, the prewar Ford V-8 convertibles seem in some ways to be nearly fully priced, when a mint-condition 1934 roadster goes for $30,000 in the Grand Old Cars Museum auction in January 1983. Still, this make and model car is in tremendous demand and it can sometimes be bought for $15,000 or thereabouts. So I have included it in this bottom price category, but I am less sure of this car's price future than of the price future of, say, the Mercedes-Benz 540K convertible coupe and roadster.

Selecting Collector Cars

A beginning collector might collect just one car, either a 540K Mercedes-Benz roadster or convertible coupe or a six-cylinder Mustang convertible of 1966—according to the collector-investor's pocketbook. The first he might possibly be able to buy for $250,000 to $300,000. The second should easily be bought for $7,500 and possibly $5,000.

The fewer cars one has in his stable the fewer headaches and the lower the expense; and one must face the fact that the ownership of a collection of cars is far from easy, simple, and inexpensive.

If one wants to build a collection and not have simply one collector car he most certainly does not have to select a single price category and buy only cars in that price category. In fact, a person might well follow a foolish investment policy by buying cars only in one price category. During my car-collecting life, which began when I was twenty-three years old, I have collected cars of all kinds and price categories, from 500K and 540K Mercedes-Benzes to a six-cylinder Mustang. All of the cars gave me satisfaction and all rose in value over a relatively short period of time.

If I were to put my own investment capital into a collection of cars right now, I would choose the following automobiles, remembering that I have only a certain amount of money which I could invest in collector cars. I also have definite preferences, and while investment is important, so is pride of ownership in this entire area of collector cars.

Starting with the most expensive car and moving down the price scale, my first purchase would be a 540K convertible coupe or an SSK roadster, if available. These are my two favorite collector cars. I would look until I found one of these cars for a maximum of $250,000, a car in very fine, but not necessarily mint, condition. The body would have to be beautiful, like the Graber-bodied 540K convertible coupe owned by Tom Barrett and offered in his January 1983 auction.

My next car would come from the next category down pricewise, and this car would be a Mercedes-Benz 300S cabriolet or roadster, and right now I own one of these cars, a 1955 roadster that I bought in 1966. Over the years I have owned four of them, most of which I used for everyday transportation. If I could not get a 300S open car I would want a Gullwing. I would like to pay $90,000 top for such a car in near-mint condition—either the 300S or the 300SL Gullwing.

For a little less money I might buy an Auburn boattail speedster of 1935 or 1936, having owned such a car in the past. This car is top in popularity and is an easy seller. I would pay $65,000.

In the next category I would definitely pick the Lamborghini Miura, the last model, the SV, and if I could not get this last model then I would get an earlier model, which I would immediately send to Bob Wallace, the Lamborghini engineer in Phoenix, for overhaul and updating mechanically. I would expect to have $60,000 to $65,000 in the finished car.

In this same price category I would pick a Rolls-Royce Silver Cloud III convertible with Park Ward body and left-hand drive, for which I would expect to pay $60,000, possibly a little more. It should be mint. If I could not get a convertible I would take the coupe or the Flying Spur four-door sedan.

In the bottom category I would pick the same car I have now, the Mustang convertible. I would prefer the 1964½ model to my present 1966 and the 289-cubic-inch V-8 to my six-cylinder car. The car should be mint and I would expect to pay $8,000 for it.

It is easy to see that one has preferences. In this "era of the Ferrari" everyone seems to want this make of car. I think the Daytona is a beautiful and excellent car, as is the 275GTB-4, but I have my own preferences. I have owned two Ferraris and the last one I owned was one of the finest cars I have ever owned or driven.

Personally I have had enough of the Model A Ford of the late 1920s and early 1930s. This is the car in which I drove to high school in the Depression and I don't want anything that reminds me of those days! As a matter of fact, for the $15,000 that a Model A Ford would cost me I would rather have a Ferrari 250GT twelve-cylinder coupe, but again, this is a matter of personal preference. Anyway, I think the price outlook for the Model A Ford is more positive than for the 250GT coupe.

So this is how the automobiles in this theoretical collection stack up and add up in investment requirements:

Mercedes-Benz 540K convertible coupe	$250,000
Mercedes-Benz 300S roadster	90,000
Lamborghini Miura SV	65,000
Rolls-Royce Silver Cloud III convertible	60,000
Ford Mustang convertible 1964½	7,000
	$472,000

There are all sorts of combinations of quality collector-investment cars that can be made. This combination cuts across all price classes and comes up with a workable number of desirable automobiles, desirable from the standpoint of investment and desirable from the standpoint of pride of ownership. As a matter of fact, I have in my own collection a Mercedes-Benz 300S roadster, a Lamborghini Miura, a Rolls-Royce Silver Cloud II sedan, and a 1966 Mustang convertible, a collection not far from my own choices for an optimum collection. The Mercedes-Benz 540K never seems quite to come within my reach, particularly in view of the fact that my own 540K bought many years ago cost me $1,500.

I would not hesitate to add these cars to an optimum collection:

Mercedes-Benz 300SL Gullwing	$65,000
Auburn 851 boattail speedster	65,000
Rolls-Royce Silver Cloud III coupe	50,000
Ferrari Daytona coupe	60,000
	$240,000

If I had very little money to invest in a classic car and felt I could handle *only one car*, that would be a Ford Mustang convertible, the 1966 model, which is a little less expensive than the 1964 or 1965. I would shop around until I found a very good one for about $5,000 to $6,000.

This Mustang would cost me very little for upkeep and I could use it occasionally. In no way would this car be a headache or cost a lot for maintenance.

If I had a little more money I would select a car not on this "collection" list. It would be the Maserati Ghibli coupe of 1972, and if I could not get the last model put out in 1972 then I would take an earlier model. For this car I would have a target price of $15,000. Of course, if I had another $20,000 or $25,000 then I would buy the Ghibli Spyder, the convertible. These are two magnificent-appearing cars and, I think, are underpriced.

With more money I would definitely pick the Lamborghini Miura, a "statement car" if there ever was one, and an excellent piece of performance machinery. I could get an earlier-model car for about $30,000, possibly a few thousand dollars less, the model P-400 rather than the later S and the most-wanted SV of 1972 that would cost at least $60,000.

With a bit more money to invest in just one car I would pick the Rolls-Royce Silver Cloud III with Park Ward convertible body and left-hand drive, a car I would expect to buy for $60,000, possibly even a little less.

My next choice would be a Mercedes-Benz 300S roadster, 1952–1957, a fine-condition car, for which I would have to pay $90,000 if full retail and possibly as low as $65,000 to $70,000 if I were lucky. I would not expect for this price range to get anything like the 300S that sold in the Barrett-Jackson auction in January 1983 for $100,000.

Moving up in the price scale to the top, and still trying to buy *just one car* rather than a collection, my top choice would be a Mercedes-Benz 540K convertible coupe, a two-seater, and I would want to buy this car for a maximum of $250,000 if at all possible. Should I fail to get this make and model car I would move on to Duesenberg and attempt to buy a tourer or convertible coupe, Model SJ, for $200,000 to $250,000 on the present market.

There are, of course, endless possibilities to buy just one fine collector car. As I have mentioned, in the Grand Old Cars auction there was a 1937 Packard V-12 convertible coupe that sold for $58,000. In the Barrett Jackson sale a 1933 V-12 phaeton sold for $92,500. The cars were certainly in comparable condition. In the Grand Old Cars auction there was simply no one present willing to bid the car up and there were no reserves placed on any car—so the car sold for essentially a bargain price.

In the same Grand Old Cars auction a 1933 Chrysler Imperial sold for $40,000—not the most-wanted Imperial and not with as fine a body as on the 1931 Imperial phaeton that was bid up to $125,000, a fair price. The Custom Imperial is the six-figure car, the standard Imperial the five-figure car. Still, there is quite a difference between $40,000 and $125,000.

In the Grand Old Cars auction a mint Duesenberg speedster, but the Duesenberg II, not the original car, sold for the reasonable price of $56,000. It should have brought $20,000 more to arrive at a normal auction price for this replica.

In the Barrett-Jackson auction a 1933 Auburn boattail speedster was reported to have been sold for $21,200. This was a car in class 2 condition, "excellent," and I would agree, having inspected the car at least twice before the sale. True, the car is not the 1935 or 1936 boattail speedster, but these latter cars in similar condition sell for a minimum at auction of $50,000 or thereabouts, and a class 1 car of this make and model retails for about $75,000. The 1933 that brought $21,200 was certainly underpriced by about $20,000.

What the Mercedes-Benz 540K convertible two-passenger coupe with body by Graber would have sold for we do not know, but we did learn from Tom Barrett that since the auction he did sell the car privately for $325,000.

Criteria for Buying

I have pointed out at some length the criteria to use in buying a collector car. In today's market, certain criteria are perhaps of paramount importance and other criteria of lesser importance. The following seem to be the criteria to stress now in buying one of several cars to form a collection that has investment potential.

1. The time to buy is the slack time, just as the time to get into the bull market in stocks was August 1982, when volume on the stock exchanges began to soar, when the institutions stepped in to buy, and when prices began to jump.

It is difficult to say, "Now is the time to buy, because prices are going to rise and volume climb." All that we can say is that at present there has been something of a long lull in the collector car market and prices have not been climbing noticeably. Many cars are for sale at auctions and through dealers, and sellers are willing to make some concessions. One cannot buy at the bottom of the market, any market, just before the onset of a boom—in stocks or in collector cars. One can only use his best judgment as to when to buy, and now might be a good time, with stocks of good cars on hand, top-notch cars being offered at auction, and prices certainly not on the high side.

2. One might buy cars after comparing the alternative investments. The stock market of 1983 was still in the rising phase. On the other hand, interest rates are not at astronomic levels, and one can hardly find a safe fixed-income deposit earning 15%—or anything like the 15% to 20% that could be found in 1981. By early 1984 stocks were dropping but cars rising.

The lower the interest rate, the less money invested at interest earns. In consequence, equity investments (and cars certainly are an equity investment and not a fixed-interest investment) look good. If a car rises 30% in two years in value, that 15% per year growth (increase in equity) does not look so bad today. Two years ago it wouldn't have looked so good.

3. Restoration can be accomplished now. Materials are not too high in price compared with what they have been in the past. Labor can be secured to do quality work, and scarce parts may be more available than in a bull market in collector cars, when everyone is trying to buy a car and restore it.

4. As time goes on it is more and more possible to secure bank financing on collector cars. Ten years ago such bank loans were anathema to bank officials.

5. The strict investor cars are available, those cars wanted by collector-investors—starting with the top cars. Few auctions have ever taken place like the Barrett-Jackson auction of January 1983, in which two 540K cars were offered, the most sought-after Mercedes-Benz classics and with the most beautiful bodies—and in at least near-mint condition. Never before has a better Delahaye convertible been offered for sale than the Jackson car that brought $110,000. In North White Plains, New York, a dealer has a Ferrari 275GTB-4 with about 5,700 miles on it, a "museum piece" restored in every fine detail, and the car might be bought for under $75,000—maybe not for the $65,000 market price, but the car is a standout.

At the other end of the scale, in the Barrett-Jackson sale a 1929 mint-condition Windsor White Prince roadster sold for $22,000. The car is a rarity, and $22,000 would hardly restore a Windsor White Prince in average condition to class 1 condition. This car was in class 1 condition. One might have to hold this car for a time to find a Windsor White Prince collector, but he could afford to wait at a purchase price of only $22,000.

6. Right now, buy a car in the very best condition. More and more emphasis is being placed on condition by buyers, and the class 1 cars bring disproportionately higher prices. An average car may take years and cost way over estimate to get in class 1 condition. Right now too, a disproportionate number of class 1 cars are available at dealers and certainly at the big auctions.

7. Great rarities in great demand are available right now, like the Mercedes-Benz SSK that was reportedly sold by the Barrett-Jackson auction *after* the auction had finished. Where does one go to buy such a $250,000 car at all? I passed up an SSK in 1952 and I have been regretting it ever since.

8. You can work with auction houses now and you can work with dealers now. They have time to help you with your collecting, and they have time to discuss your investment plans and program with you. They can hardly do this when they are moving cars fast and must deliver every day and buy as fast as cars can be located.

9. Fine-condition collector cars are being offered by private owners—with no takers. Dealers inform me right now of offerings, the latest being a mint Mercedes-Benz 300SL Gullwing at $55,000, certainly no high price for this important collector car. The dealers pass on this information because right

now they are stocked up on cars and do not have the space or the wherewithal to buy more cars. If they can locate a private buyer they may be able to make a "finder's fee" from the seller, not a great fee but at least something in slack times.

10. Right now the lesser-priced cars seem to be selling much better than the high-priced greats that are on the market, and we repeat that more greats are being offered for sale now than in the recent past. The policy right now might be to buy the greats or the near-greats, the Duesenberg J and SJ, the Mercedes-Benz 500K and 540K open cars, the Chrysler Imperial open cars of the early 1930s, the Cadillac V-16 roadsters of 1931 and 1932, and so on. In a real bull market in times of prosperity these finest cars should be the movers.

11. One must get used to high prices. For most of the finest collectibles, low prices are highly unlikely to return. It is highly unlikely that any Duesenberg J or SJ will sell for under six figures in the future. Maybe in a world war they would. Maybe in an all-out depression they would—but I doubt it. The same for the great Mercedes-Benz cars and many other such collector cars.

12. Right now it is wise to think about one or a few very fine cars as investments rather than a large collection of low-priced cars. The fewer the cars the less space required to store them, and the lower the insurance, tax, and registration, and certainly the maintenance costs. Right now, it would seem that the great cars selling at higher prices will always be there to buy. They will not be. Yet they will always be in demand by real investors and connoisseurs.

19

A Look to the Future

IT IS ALWAYS difficult to see the future with any degree of clarity. When the Dow Jones Industrial Average hit 1,100 in early 1983, scores of professional forecasters, including some chief economists of the largest brokerage houses, firmly and publicly announced that there would be a correction of somewhere between 10% and 15%. Only there wasn't, and the Dow Jones continued up for quite some time. It was also difficult to forecast minimal inflation in the United States for early 1983. Few professional forecasters came up with a low rate.

In some ways it is easier to forecast market trends in particular areas—demand for investment art, the price level of investment art, demand and price for antique furniture. While the very short run may be hard to forecast in art and antiques and in most other things, the long-term trend is somewhat easier, although by no means certain. These trends seem likely in the future:

1. The demand for investment automobiles will increase. The market is an undeveloped market and is bound to spread. A decade ago, vintage wines were an undeveloped market. Now vintage wines are the "in thing" and the market is developing extremely rapidly. A decade ago, investment automobiles were still very much of an enigma. Where were they going? Would demand for them increase? Would prices rise? By about how much?

By the 1980s the concept of "investment automobiles" had arrived—definitely. Still, that demand has not peaked—by any means.

2. The collectors who were collecting as of the early 1980s will not drop off—at least not drop off in total. As prices rise, the wisdom of their investment in automobiles will very likely be demonstrated, and so they will continue to invest in automobiles.

3. These collectors are likely to get more and more used to the idea that collector cars cost money, and the price of such cars is not likely to come down. A decade ago a Ferrari Daytona might have been bought for $15,000.

367

It could have been bought new in 1969 when it first appeared for under $15,000 in Italy and for $19,000 in the United States. As of 1982 the price of a good late-model used Daytona was $65,000. Today the same car could well be priced at $75,000.

The idea is spreading that the Mercedes-Benz 540K of the mid-1930s is one of the choicest collector cars anyone can buy anywhere at any time. The idea of paying $300,000 for a roadster or convertible two-seater still shocks many people, but it is being accepted by enough car investors that this price level will certainly stick—and rise higher. Naturally the best costs a great deal of money, but at the same time spending top dollar may be a sound investment policy. The best seems almost always in demand and at escalating prices.

4. The collector car "motif" will continue to spread and probably spread rapidly. More and more we see collector cars as background elements in advertising. The more the collector car motif is used in advertising the more the idea will spread that a collector car is something like a yacht. It is the badge of distinction, the badge of success, the badge of a high net worth.

Collector cars are likely to be used more and more in TV series and motion pictures. The Ferrari 308 of *Magnum P.I.* has no doubt done a great deal for the sale of this car. The use of collector cars in this way will inculcate into the minds of many people, if not almost everyone, the importance of owning such a car as the badge of success. Hence sales are almost certainly bound to follow.

5. The market for these cars is thus likely to broaden, not to the present owners of such cars, who will buy better collector cars or more cars or both, but to people who never before have owned a collector car. This is where the real growth in collector car sales is likely to take place in the future, and this is the segment of the market which may well cause further substantial rises in prices.

6. The collector car dealer organization is likely to improve. It will have to if sales of collector cars are to increase. Currently, collector car dealers are very few and very far between. The dealers have, in general, inadequate inventories of collector cars. They are not adequately staffed. They do not know enough about handling the public. And a number of collector car dealers closed up shop in the recession of 1981–1982.

As demand for collector cars increases, more dealerships are likely to open up, and for this reason alone the market for collector cars will broaden.

7. Repairs are likely to become more affordable. In New York City the repair rate on Rolls-Royce cars is enormous. Sometimes the rate is flat, sometimes it is stated as so much per hour; but whatever basis is used the cost is far above the cost of repairing an American car. It will have to decline, at least some.

Parts are far too high, and they will likely decline in price. Reconditioned parts will increase in availability and in sales. Radiator firms will be able to supply new radiators made up to the exact specifications of rare collector cars. Muffler companies now advertise exhaust systems for most foreign cars, and they can make them up for almost any car. The same for transmission-overhaul firms. Some advertise now that they will overhaul foreign transmissions. This move to do work on exotic cars by American repair shops will continue.

8. Retail financing should develop for classic cars. This is likely to be a slow process, as it has been a slow process in the art and antique field. It may be some time before one can find a bank or finance company that is willing to finance $200,000 on a Mercedes-Benz 540K that sells for a bona fide $300,000. It may be difficult to secure a loan of $3,000 on a 1966 Mustang convertible that sells for $6,000.

9. The big risers should be the well-established prewar classics, even though these cars have already risen very well in the past. The cars are recognized as the ultimate in collector-investment automobiles. The list will include the Duesenberg J and SJ, the Cadillac V-16 convertible of the early 1930s, the Packard convertible of the same period, particularly the V-12, the Chrysler Imperial of the same era, the Mercedes-Benz S, SS, SSK, 500K, and 540K— among many other cars. These cars should develop into standard investments whose prices will be fairly well established and fairly well known.

The 1984 Barrett-Jackson sale saw "breakthrough prices" for the time. A 1927 Mercedes Benz S brought $410,000, a 1935 Hispano-Suiza V-12 sold for $400,000, and a 1935 Isotta Fraschini was sold for $410,000.

10. The prices of these cars may seem high, but are they high? For a top price of around $300,000 one could get a fine Mercedes-Benz 540K two-passenger cabriolet, a Cadillac V-16, a Duesenberg SJ dual-cowl convertible sedan, and some other top cars.

How high is $300,000? It is the price of a second or third-string painting by Renoir. A fine Renoir will sell for $1,500,000.

Is this analogy realistic? Does it imply that if one buys a Duesenberg Dietrich-bodied tourer for $300,000 it will someday be worth $1,500,000? Who knows? Maybe it will. The same car in 1960 could have been bought for $10,000. I had one of these Duesenbergs offered to me in 1940 for $600. The rise from $600 to $300,000 is a long way. From $300,000 to $1,500,000 is less distance in percent.

Is there any intrinsic reason for a limitation of $300,000 on the price of the finest collector car? The answer is, of course, no. How high prices will rise is anybody's guess. There is no guesswork, however, about the fact that the present high prices of the prewar classics will rise in the future, and probably in the very near future.

11. Another important rise should take place in the postwar classics, though it is not quite clear which cars will emerge as the important postwar classics. We do know that the Mercedes-Benz 300S of 1951 to 1957 is a definitely established prime classic whose price touched $100,000 at a January 1982 auction and again in January 1983.

The Mercedes-Benz 300SL is in the same well-established investment category. The Mercedes-Benz 220 and 220S convertibles are lower-priced, but they are investment cars nevertheless. The Lamborghini Miura is in the same investment class. The Ferrari second series Super America (and probably the first series as well) is an investment automobile, as is the Superfast.

The rest of the Ferraris are not yet sorted out—the 275GTB-4, the Daytona coupe, the Daytona Spyder. While they are all top-performance cars, they are not yet "pieces of automotive history." They will probably be, and they are rising in price, but the whole postwar classic car category has still to be sorted out in order to see which cars emerge as gold-plated investments like the great prewar classics.

12. Antique cars are in general underpriced and overlooked. Their top prices are in the neighborhood of $150,000, even for the early Rolls-Royce of four cylinders, the Mercer Raceabouts, the Stutz Bearcats, and the one- and two-cylinder pioneering classics. Still, the buying public, the collector car buyers, have yet to become educated about antique cars.

13. The special-interest cars are developing rapidly but still have to be sorted out. It would appear that the 1955 and 1957 Chevrolet Bel Air convertibles and hardtops have emerged as prime investments in the category of special-interest cars. These cars can now sell in mint condition for $20,000. Is the future price level of these cars $25,000, or $30,000, or more? Maybe, but the price level of these cars may to a degree represent a fad. Maybe the fad will emerge into a true investment. Maybe demand will shift away from these cars to others.

14. The special-interest cars and the less expensive classic cars will find their market in the younger buyer. It is this group of cars that will demand repairs and restoration, including a supply of parts. Cars will move from the special-interest and lower-priced postwar classic category into clear-cut classic cars that will show an overall appreciation over a fairly short period of time.

These special-interest cars will continue to provide most business for the auto auctions, including the important Kruse auctions and the Barrett-Jackson yearly auction in Phoenix.

15. The auto auctions will become more professional and less bedlams. They will have to become more professional in order to attract the type of buyer in the future that the general auctions have attracted—Christie's and Sotheby's. These major auctions are orderly, and one can rely on them far more than he can rely on the present collector car auctions. The dishonesty in the auto auctions may be a thing of the past—the recent past—and it is expected that sellers of cars will now get their money, and quickly, rather than having the money disappear somewhere. In the past, state officials have taken action to bar auto auctions by some firms because of dishonesty. It is hoped that most dishonesty has disappeared.

The auto auctions seem to appeal to a certain type of buyer—the dealer in collector cars and a relatively few collectors and some occasional buyers. These auctions are far from being a generally accepted business participated in by the affluent buyers who might be induced to buy a collector car or two.

16. The media will be brought into the collector car business, mainly the auction business. In Phoenix, Arizona, in January 1983 more than 1,000 cars crossed the auction block. In the Barrett-Jackson auction alone over 500 cars crossed the auction block, some cars selling for $100,000 and more. It might be expected that the news media would cover these sales, but in general they do not. Not even the Phoenix newspapers covered the sales. In the week I spent attending these auctions I saw not one newspaper item about the auctions or their cars.

The auctions do not realize the importance of the news media and do not know how to cultivate them. They have no press departments. In fact, at one of the big auctions a press representative was told to stop talking to one of the car consignors. This official apparently thought the press representative wanted to make a side deal to buy a car after the auction had concluded, in order to cheat the auction house of its commission. The press representative was not interested in buying; and when the discourse was finished he was not interested in giving any publicity to the auction either.

Unless the general media become aware of the sales and auction business in the collector car field the market for these collector cars cannot develop importantly.

17. The important cars, the postwar and prewar classics and the antiques, will be objects to display only. They will be run little or not at all. It is simply too expensive to keep these cars running, even though they are used a minimum amount of time. A Lamborghini Miura P-400 coupe was overhauled in early 1983. The car before restoration had a maximum value of about $30,000. The overhaul job cost $38,000, so the car represented a total investment of $68,000. The last time I had my own Miura in the shop, after it had been restored at a cost of $13,000 and had never been run, my cost was $4,500—just to fix a few things that weren't taken care of in the original restoration of a month earlier. When I got the car out of the shop and paid the $4,500 it was shoved into storage, where it remained for over three years. It was never licensed.

One response to the delicacy of collector cars and the extremely high cost of restoring and repairing them is to convert one's garage into a display museum, placing the car or cars artistically for display. In any event, costs of restoration and repairs are now an almost insuperable obstacle to running a collector car on the highway. For that reason we rarely see any collector car on the roads or parked on the street.

18. Collector cars will probably be divided like the stocks traded publicly. In stocks there is the New York Stock Exchange, the American Stock Exchange, and the over-the-counter market—plus some regional stock exchanges. The important, well-established, generally large companies have their stock listed on the New York Stock Exchange. The lesser companies, in general, are listed on the Amex (American Stock Exchange). The least important stocks do not have an exchange with a trading floor but are bought and sold by brokerage houses directly.

In the New York Stock Exchange the really important stocks are in the Dow Jones average of thirty stocks—IBM, General Motors, etc. In a way, collector cars are like the stocks traded in these three markets. The important cars are like the stocks traded on the New York Stock Exchange. The really important collector cars are like the stocks that compose the Dow Jones Industrial Average—Duesenberg, Cadillac V-16 convertible, etc.

Down the scale come the lesser classics and antique cars—the "Amex cars" like the Mercedes-Benz 220S, the 1963 Chevrolet Corvette, etc.

In the "over-the-counter car market" are the cars like the Chrysler 300 convertibles, the Chevrolet Corvairs, and many many others.

The stocks on the New York Stock Exchange tend to rise the least in an up market. Even IBM tends to be one of the constant, but not spectacular, risers, although it about doubled in the bull market of 1982–1983.

The further down we go in stock trading and in car dealing the bigger the possible appreciation. In the bull market the lesser stocks traded in the lesser markets tended to rise the most—in general. This is a general rule, of course, and a stock like Brown Group on the New York Stock Exchange almost quadrupled, but this was a special situation due to the genius of its chief executive, Hadley Griffin.

In the over-the-counter market several stocks tripled and quadrupled. Thus some portfolio managers, like the Hall Group of Shearson American Express, tended to invest clients' money almost solely in Amex stocks and in the over-the-counter market, and the group chief proudly compared a curve showing the growth in price of the stocks he bought for his clients with the Dow Jones stocks—much to the advantage of his stocks.

Currently, the Chevrolet Corvair convertible might be considered an "over-the-counter car." It can be bought in good condition for under $5,000, sometimes under $2,500. But there were (and are) collectors of this car, and more and more of these cars are being restored to mint condition. It is expected that this make and model car will gradually move upward from its present low price and general lack of prestige as a collector car.

In the future more and more "over-the-counter cars" will become sorted out as collectibles and will tend to move upward. In 1970 the Mercedes-Benz 300S convertible coupe and cabriolet could be bought for $2,000 and less, cars in good condition. They were being sorted out. From this more or less bottom-of-the-barrel position these cars rose to be what is probably the number-one prestige car in the entire postwar classic car category—and possibly the highest-priced car. Only the Ferrari Daytona Spyder is higher in price, and the Daytona Spyder is a rather rare car and does not often come onto the market.

In the future there will be a good deal of "speculation" in the cars of the over-the-counter category and the cars of the level of the American Stock Exchange, and there will be a constant movement upward of cars from the bottom of the category to the top and on up to higher categories. In this way the Bugatti Royale Weinberger cabriolet moved from more or less scrap which sold to engineer Charlie Chayne during the war for about $250 to a present value of well over $2,000,000. This is a "Dow Jones car" if there ever was one!

Today there is an enormous restoration business in Ford Mustang convertibles of 1964½–1966. These are often bought for a low four-figure price and elaborately restored, most of them restored by young buyers who do a good deal of the work themselves. When the cars are done their owner-restorers often sell them, and at constantly increasing prices. A mint 1964½ Mustang convertible now brings over $10,000, sometimes well over. The man who buys and restores a Chevrolet Corvair convertible to mint condition will likely see his total investment of, say, $5,000 to $6,000 move up as the car becomes more and more recognized as a postwar classic rather than simply a rather unimportant special-interest car. This sorting out and restoration process at the bottom of the collector car market will go on in the future and will almost certainly intensify as more and more collector cars are "discovered" at the bottom of the market and are restored and move upward in the market.

19. Collector cars will gradually develop into prestige collectibles and prestige investments. In the future one may not have to secure prestige simply through the ownership of a fine home, a yacht, a Renoir, but he may secure equal prestige through the ownership of a 540K Mercedes roadster. Of course, the ownership of collector cars might develop into a status contest something like this:

We visit a middle-level business executive who asks us after dinner at his home whether we would like to see his new collector car. We are very

pleased to see that our friend Dick has a 1955 Mercedes-Benz 300S roadster, and he informs us that he was very much in luck in this purchase
since all he had to pay was $80,000.

A few weeks later we visit someone else in Dick's company, this man
a senior executive. We tell Bob, the senior executive, that Dick took us
to his garage and showed us his latest acquisition, a 300S Mercedes that
Dick got at the bargain price of $80,000. The senior executive then says,
"That's certainly very nice. A 300S Mercedes is certainly a fine car. But
I'd like to have you see my latest car, a 1938 Mercedes-Benz roadster, a
540K. Now, I will admit that I didn't get any buy—I had to pay $540,000
for the car. But look at it!"

This entire view of cars as collectible investments in the future may
seem farfetched; but maybe not. I do recall talking with an owner of a
fleet of New York taxicabs who said he had great trouble getting people
to attend parties that he gave in his apartment—until he began to collect
contemporary American art. As soon as he had a fine collection, he said,
he couldn't keep people away! His art had developed into a social asset.
Cars may occupy that same position in the future—in addition to working
out as a good investment.

20. The trend of the collector car market is up, especially the longer-
term trend. The movement of prices will not, however, always be up. Nor
has the movement of short-run prices always been up in the past since the
upward thrust in collector car prices began in earnest in the 1970s. Sometimes the trend has been down, and sometimes prices have simply been
more or less flat. It is anticipated, however, that the *immediate* price trend
will be up. The long-term price trend will almost certainly be up. What
takes place between the immediate upward thrust and the longer-term
uptrend will not always be favorable. As in the past, prices at times will
be flat and at times down.

In 1982, Tom Barrett sold about $8,000,000 worth of cars. In 1983,
his sales reached $11,800,000—and we are talking about his sales outside
the auction. In 1983 the Barrett-Jackson auction sold 32% of the cars
offered, but in 1984 about 80% of the cars offered were sold in the greatest
sale of the firm's 13-year history. This was an enormous "sold" percentage
for any classic car auction, and most were sold over the block although
some, as always, were sold after they appeared on stage.

Through 1983, Dean Kruse reports a 12 to 15% rise in classic car
prices—about 1% to 1½% every month.

21. Collector car prices are expected to behave something like art prices.
Sometimes Impressionist prices forged ahead while at the same time some
other school of art, like American Old Master portraits, actually went down

in price. In 1981 the skyrocketing prices of Duesenbergs came to an end, and prices remained on a plateau through 1982. Ferrari roared ahead in 1981, on the other hand.

While general categories of cars will have different price movements, the price movement will vary even as between or among different models of the same car or as between or among different year cars of the same make.

Like securities traded on the stock exchanges or in the over-the-counter market, different groups of cars move up and down, some with the general market trend, some more than the trend—either up more or down more. Subgroups of stocks and collector cars vary from trends in general and vary from the larger groups. Fortunately, prices of collector cars do not move as fast as stock prices—or as *definitely* as stock prices.

22. One is tempted at times to draw an analogy between collector cars and the great group of art, antiques, and collectibles. Collector cars are a Johnny-come-lately addition to the broad category of collectible investments. They came into their own only a little over a decade ago. Art was a viable investment soon after the close of World War II, and perhaps even earlier.

So why won't car prices move as have the prices of the important Old Master paintings or Impressionists? Because there are definite limitations to the market for collector cars. The ownership of collector cars is not a simple activity. The cars are big and bulky. They must be adequately stored, insured, and repaired periodically. They take up a good deal of space—somewhere. They are not the easiest things to dispose of and are thus unlike Impressionists and American furniture of the eighteenth century. They are certainly far less liquid than collector postage stamps and rare coins, among many other collectibles.

As collector car prices rise, the market at the top will become more limited, at least for the finest cars. They cost a good deal of money right now, many of them well into six figures. These cars in the top categories can be owned only by the very well-to-do investor-collectors.

How many six-figure cars will be owned by any one collector? The cost of even one is great, and the ownership of just one car is expensive and somewhat troublesome. It may, in fact, be that the ownership of collector cars is something like the ownership of fine sculpture. A fine piece of modern or early sculpture costs a good deal—as a collector car costs a good deal. The ownership of a piece of sculpture is not an easy thing. Where do you put it? Where do you display it? How many pieces of sculpture can you own and be able to display? The market for fine sculpture, because of its "ownership" problems, is limited and is likely to be limited in the future. The same limitation may very well apply to collector cars—perhaps more so, since the cars are bigger and require a good deal more care than a piece of sculpture.

Even at the bottom of the price level the ownership of cars is not easy and will not be easy in the future. The ownership of one relatively inexpensive collector car may not be difficult, particularly if it can be used for transportation—at least at times. The ownership of a second such car is vastly more difficult, and the ownership of ten automobiles, even though relatively inexpensive, that can be used for occasional transportation is difficult indeed. The collector tends to become a slave to too many cars and seems always to be taking one or another car to the repair shop for one thing or another.

So the collector car market is certainly not limitless, and it is not likely that a well-heeled collector-investor will own anything like as many collector cars as he owns Impressionists or pieces of Louis XV furniture. But when everything is considered, the collector car market has a good deal of developing to do, and prices seem to have a long way to rise yet before any substantial cutback in the rising price trend is felt.

Collector Car Clubs and Dealers

CLUBS—GENERAL

Antique Automobile Club of America, Hershey, Pa. One of the largest car clubs specializing in old cars in the world, with about 48,000 members and a head office and staff and a top-notch automobile library of books and periodicals for the use of members. The club issues the very important publication *Antique Automobile*.

Classic Car Club of America, Madison, N.J. A club for owners of cars dating from 1925 to 1948 and with a membership of over 4,400.

Contemporary Historical Vehicle Association, Antioch, Tenn. Over 2,000 members interested in all vehicles made at least twenty-five years ago and back as far as 1928.

Horseless Carriage Club of America, Downey, Cal. This club, which has a membership of over 6,000, puts out the important publication *Horseless Carriage Gazette*.

Midwestern Council of Sports Car Clubs, Arlington Heights, Ill. Milestone Car Society, Indianapolis, Ind. This organization compiles a list of the highest-quality cars built between 1945 and 1967. If a car is on this master list it is a definite plus for the quality of the car and its value.

Sports Car Club of America, Denver, Colo. Perhaps the oldest and certainly the largest automobile club in America and probably in the world in the sports car area.

Southeast Vintage Racing Association, Inc., Sebring, Fla. For vintage, historic, and prewar racing car enthusiasts.

Veteran Motor Car Club of America, Andover, Mass. Specializing in antique automobiles, this is a very important club of about 4,000 members which puts out a significant publication, *The Bulb Horn*.

CLUBS—SPECIFIC

Aston Martin Owners Club, USA Centre, 195 Mt. Paran Road, N.W., Atlanta, Ga.

Auburn-Cord-Duesenberg Club, 963 West Hathaway Road, Harbor Springs, Mich.

Austin Healey Club of America, Inc., 603 E. Euclid Ave., Arlington Hts., Ill.

Austin-Healey Sports and Touring Club, P.O. Box 3539, York, Pa.
Bentley Drivers Club, Ltd, Bentley Mem. Bldg, 16 Chearsley Rd., Long Crendon, Aylesbury, Bucks, England
BMW Car Club of America, Inc., 345 Harvard Street, Cambridge, Mass.
BMW Vintage Club of America, Inc., 148 Linden Street, Wellesley, Mass.
Bricklin International Owners Club, 20 Bradford St., New Providence, N.J.
American Bugatti Club, 8 Church Street, Rockport, Me.
Buick Club of America, P.O. Box 898, Garden Grove, Cal.
Buick Club of America, 36 Massasoit St., Northampton, Mass.
Cadillac Club International, Box 1, Palm Springs, Cal.
Cadillac Convertible Owners of America, P.O. Box 920, Thiells, N.Y.
Cadillac La Salle Club, Inc., 3340 Poplar Drive, Warren, Mich.
Camaro Owners of America, 701 N. Keyser Ave., Scranton, Pa.
Classic Chevy Club, International, P.O. Box 17188, Orlando, Fla.
Late Great Chevys, P.O. Box 17824, Orlando, Fla.
Corvair Society of America, P.O. Box 2488, Pensacola, Fla.
National Corvette Owners Assn., P.O. Box 77A, Falls Church, Va.
Imperial Owners Club, 1926–1975, P.O. Box 991, Scranton, Pa.
Continental Mark II Owners Assn., 17230 Oldenberg Rd., Apple Valley, Cal.
Ass. les Amis de Delage, 4 Blvd Gabriel Guist'hau, Nantes, France
Club Delahaye, Marco-Polo Galion C, Mandelieu, France
De Lorean Club International, P.O. Box 93, Mercer Island, Wash; also Box 23040-RT, Seattle, Wash.
Edsel Owners Club, Inc., W. Liberty, Ill.
International Edsel Club, P.O. Box 86, Polo, Ill.
Ferrari Owners Club, 15910 Ventura Blvd, Encino, Cal.
Fiat Club of America, Inc., Box 192, Somerville, Mass.
Fiat Drivers International, P.O. Box 33370, San Antonio, Tex.
Model A Ford Club of America, 250 S. Cypress St., La Habra, Cal.
The Model T Ford Club of America, Box 7400, Burbank, Cal.
Model T Ford Club International, P.O. Box 915, Elgin, Ill.
Mustang Club of America, Inc., P.O. Box 447, Lithonia, Ga.
Shelby American Automobile Club, 22 Olmstead Rd., W. Reading, Conn.
Classic Thunderbird Assn, P.O. Box 6171, Broadview, Ill.
Vintage Thunderbird Club of America, P.O. Box 2250, Dearborn, Mich.
The H. H. Franklin Club, Cazenovia College, Cazenovia, N.Y. (club dedicated to the Franklin air cooled car)
Hispano Suiza Society, P.O. Box 688, Haywood, Cal.
Jaguar Clubs of North America, Inc., 600 Willow Tree Rd., Leonia, N.J.
The Lagonda Club, 68 Savill Rd., Lindfield, Haywards Heath, Sussex, England
Lagonda Club, U.S. Section, Ten Crestwood Trail, Sparta, N.J.
Lincoln Continental Owners Club, P.O. Box 549, Nogales, Ariz.
Lincoln Owners Club, P.O. Box 189, Algonquin, Ill.
Lincoln Zephyr Owners Club, 2107 Steinruck Road, Elizabethtown, Pa.

Marmon Club, 3044 Gainsborough Dr., Pasadena, Cal.
Maserati Information Exchange, P.O. Box 772, Mercer Isl., Wash.
Mercedes-Benz Club of America, P.O. Box 9985, Colorado Springs, Colo.
Mercer Associates, 842 East Ave., Bay Head, N.J.
The MG Car Club Ltd., 67 Wide Bargate, Boston, Lincolnshire, England
New England MG T Register, Ltd., P.O. Drawer 220, Oneonta, N.Y.
The Packard Club, P.O. Box 2808, Oakland, Cal.
Packards International Motor Car Club, 302 French Street, Santa Ana, Cal.
Pantera International Car Club, 5540 Farralone Ave., Woodland Hills, Cal.
Pierce-Arrow Society, Inc., 135 Edgerton St., Rochester, N.Y.
Plymouth 4 and 6 Cylinder Owners Club, 203 Main St. E, Cavalier, N.D.
Pontiac-Oakland Club, Inc., P.O. Box 5108, Salem, Ore.
Porsche Owners Club, P.O. Box 54910, Terminal Annex, Los Angeles, Cal.
United Renault Club of America, P.O. Box 2277, Cypress, Cal.
Phantom III Technical Society, P.O. Box 25, Mechanicsburg, Pa. (specializing
   in the Rolls-Royce Phantom III V-12)
Studebaker Automobile Club of America, P.O. Box 5036, Hemet, Cal.
Studebaker Drivers Club, Box 3044, South Bend, Ind.

A more comprehensive list is included in Hemmings' *Vintage Auto Almanac*
and the *Official Price Guide to Collector Cars* put out by Kruse International.
Road and Track magazine also lists clubs in every issue.

DEALERS IN CLASSIC AND ANTIQUE CARS

United States

Auto Locators, Suite 10, 3939 N. 48 St., Lincoln, Neb.
Barrie Imports, Upper Saddle River, N.J.
Carriage House Motor Cars, Ltd., 520 E. 73 St., New York, N.Y.
Collector Cars, Inc., 56 West Merrick Rd., Freeport, N.Y.
Continental Motors, Hinsdale, Ill.
Dream Machines, Inc., 18627 S.W. 107 Ave. Miami, Fla.
Ferrari West, 851 Del Monte Ave., Monterey, Cal.
Foreign Cars Italia, 4100 West Wendover Ave., Greensboro, N.C.
Grand Touring Cars, 7652 E. Acoma St., Scottsdale, Ariz.
George Haug, Inc., 517 E. 73 St., New York, N.Y.
Steven Kessler Motor Cars, Inc., 317 E. 34 St., New York, N.Y.
Joe Marchetti's International Auto, 825 W. Erie, Chicago, Ill.
Motor Classic Corp., 868 N. Broadway, White Plans, N.Y.
North American Motor Imports, 4700 San Pedro, San Antonio, Tex.
Nostalgia Cars, 2602 S. Dixie Highway, West Palm Beach, Fla.
Rallye Motors, Inc., 20 Cedar Swamp Road, Glen Cove, N.Y.
Charles Schmitt & Company, 3500 S. Kings Highway, St. Louis, Mo.
Thorobred Motorcars, Inc., 3200 N. Washington Blvd., Arlington, Va.

Ron Tonkin Gran Turismo, 203 N.E. 122 St., Portland, Ore.
Volo Museum, 27640 West Highway 120, Volo, Ill.

Great Britain

W.T. Aked & Co. Ltd., St. George's Rd., Lytham St. Annex, Lancashire
Coys of Kensington, 2–4 Queensgate Mews, London
Frank Dale and Stepsons, 101 Farm Lane, Fulham, London
Duncan Hamilton & Co., Ltd., Hamilton House, The Square, Bagshot, Surrey
C. A. R. Howard Ltd., 16 Queens Gate Place Mews, London
Laurence Kayne, 18 Bruton Place, Berkeley Square, London
Stanley Mann, Edgeware, Middlesex
Dan Margulies, 12 Queen's Gate Place Mews, London
Nigel Dawes, Birtsmorton Court, Near Malvern, Worcestershire
Nostalgia, Briar Forge, Vicarage Causeway, Hertford Heath, Herts.
Paradise Garage, Heathmans Rd., Parsons Green, Fulham, London
Performance Cars Ltd., Great West Rd., Brentford, Middlesex
Royle Hepworth, Pool Rd., Pool in Wharfedale, Otley West, Yorkshire
Straight Eight, 158–160 Goldhawk Rd., Shepherds Bush, London

APPENDIX **B**

Price Trends of Investment Cars

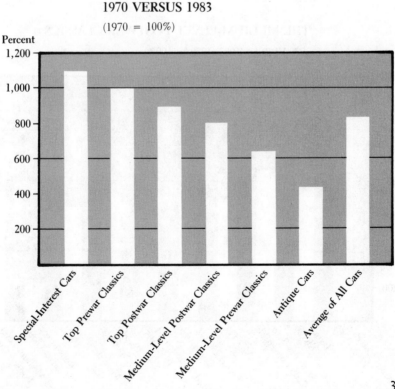

1970 VERSUS 1983

(1970 = 100%)

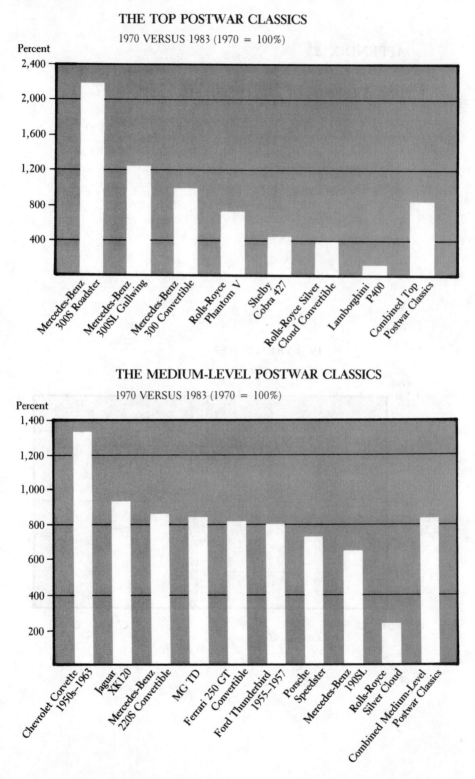

THE TOP POSTWAR CLASSICS

1970 VERSUS 1983 (1970 = 100%)

THE MEDIUM-LEVEL POSTWAR CLASSICS

1970 VERSUS 1983 (1970 = 100%)

THE MEDIUM-LEVEL POSTWAR CLASSICS

1975 VERSUS 1983 (1975 = 100%)

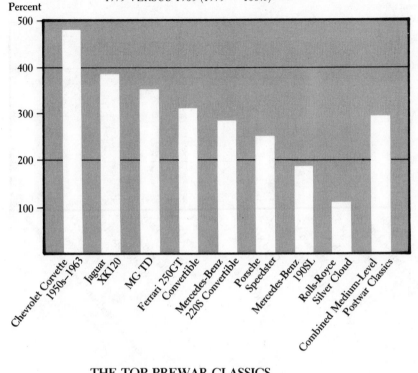

THE TOP PREWAR CLASSICS

1975 VERSUS 1983 (1975 = 100%)

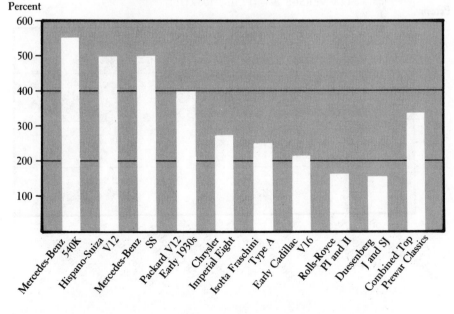

THE MEDIUM-LEVEL PREWAR CLASSICS

1975 VERSUS 1983 (1975 = 100%)

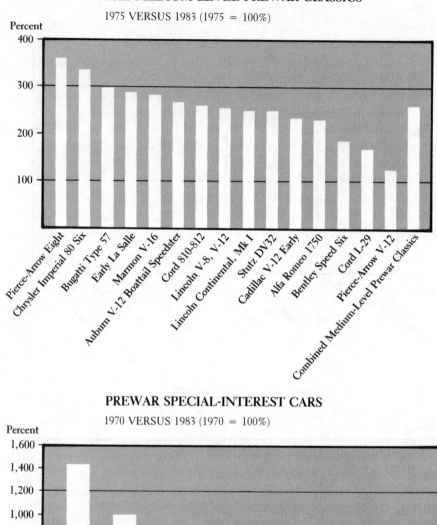

PREWAR SPECIAL-INTEREST CARS

1970 VERSUS 1983 (1970 = 100%)

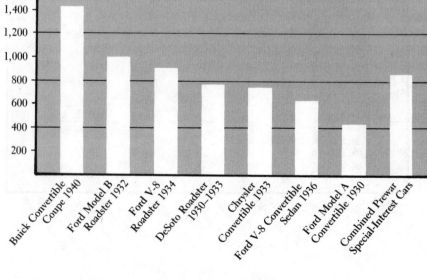

THE MEDIUM-LEVEL PREWAR CLASSICS

1970 VERSUS 1983 (1970 = 100%)

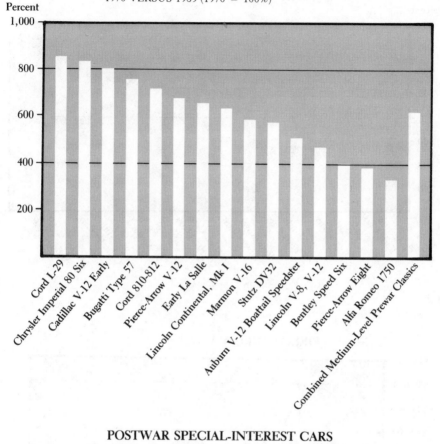

POSTWAR SPECIAL-INTEREST CARS

1970 VERSUS 1983 (1970 = 100%)

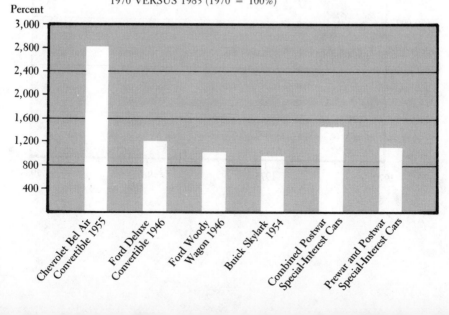

ANTIQUE CARS

1970 VERSUS 1983 (1970 = 100%)

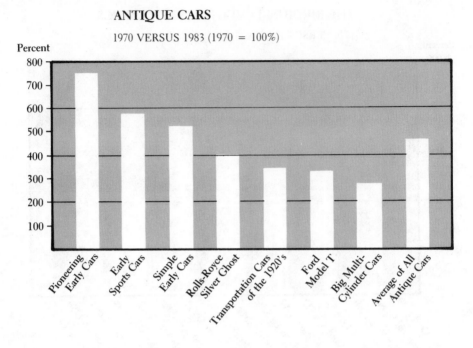

PIERCE-ARROW V-12

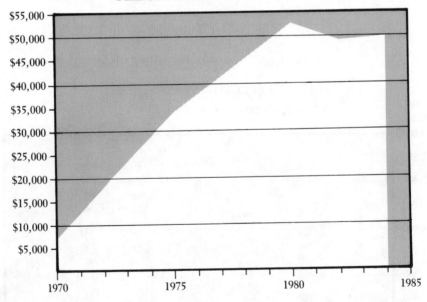

STUTZ BEARCAT 1914

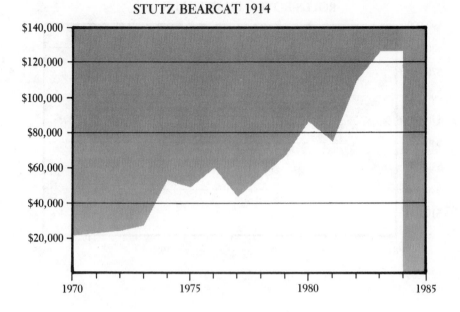

CORD L-29

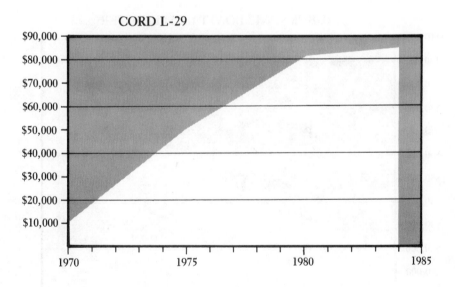

ROLLS-ROYCE PHANTOM II

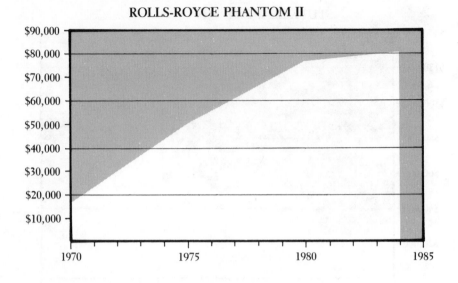

AUBURN V-12 BOATTAIL SPEEDSTER

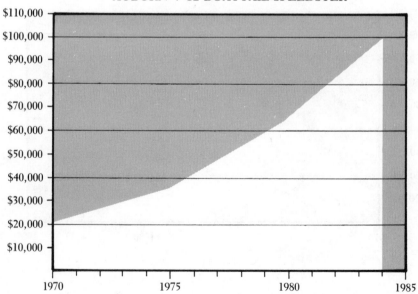

MERCEDES-BENZ 500K/540K AND S/SS

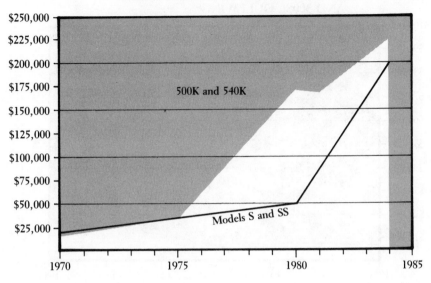

500K and 540K

Models S and SS

DUESENBERG J AND SJ

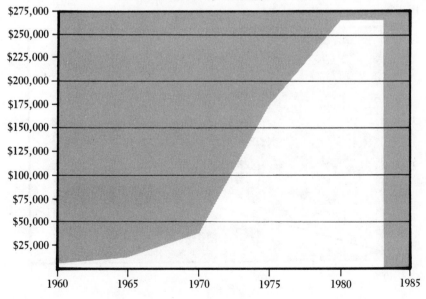

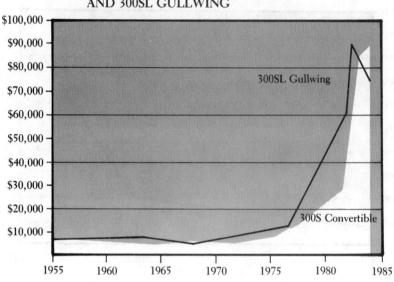

MERCEDES-BENZ 300S CONVERTIBLE AND 300SL GULLWING

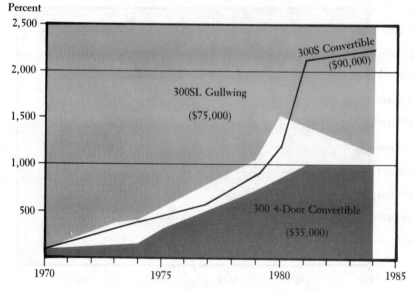

MERCEDES-BENZ 300 SERIES

LINCOLN CONTINENTAL MARK I (FIRST SERIES)

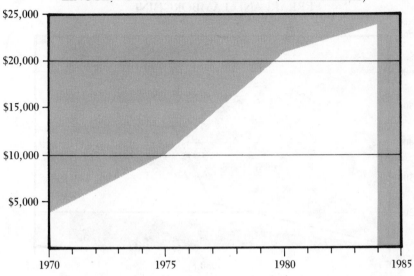

CHEVROLET BEL AIR CONVERTIBLE 1955

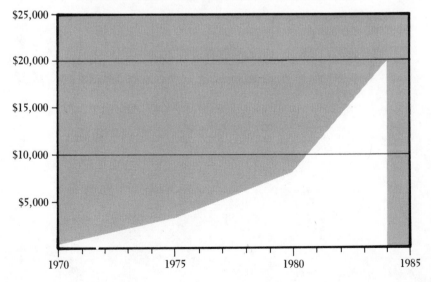

TOP POSTWAR CLASSICS
FERRARI AND LAMBORGHINI

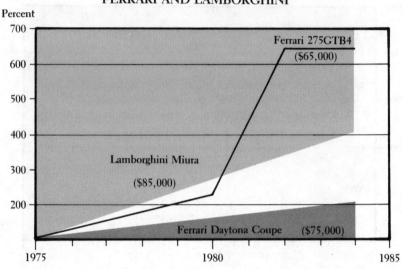

Percent

Ferrari 275GTB4
($65,000)

Lamborghini Miura

($85,000)

Ferrari Daytona Coupe   ($75,000)

1975   1980   1985

Bibliography

BOOKS

Bell, Roger. *Mercedes-Benz (Great Marques)*. London: Octopus, 1980.

Bennett, Martin. *Rolls-Royce: The History of the Car*. New York: Arco, 1974.

Bishop, George. *The Age of the Automobile*. London: Hamlyn, 1977.

———. *Classic Cars*. New York: Crescent, 1979.

Boschen, Lothar, and Jurgen Barth. *The Porsche Book: A Definitive Illustrated History*. New York: Patrick Stephens, Cambridge Publ., 1978.

Bowler, Michael. *Track Tests, Sports Cars*. London: Hamlyn, 1981.

Brazendale, Kevin (ed.). *Great Cars of the Golden Age*. New York: Crescent, 1976.

Car Spotter's Encyclopedia: 1940–1980. New York: Beekman House, 1982.

Columbia House World of Automobiles, An Illustrated Encyclopedia of the Motor Car. London: Orbis Publishing Limited, distributed by Columbia House, N.Y. 1974.

Consumer Guide (eds.). *The American Sports Car*. Skokie, Ill.: Publications International, 1979.

———.*Cars of the 30s; Cars of the 40s; Cars of the 50s; Cars of the 60s*. New York: Beekman House, 1980.

———. *Elite Cars*. Skokie, Ill: Publications International, 1979.

———. *Grease Machines*. Skokie, Ill.: Publications International, 1978.

———. *Mustang*. Skokie, Ill: Publications International, 1979.

Cosucci, Piero. *Guida Alle Automobili d'Oro* ("Guide to All Golden Automobiles"). Milan, Italy: Arnoldo Mondadori Editore, 1978.

Dumont, Pierre. *Bugatti*. Minneapolis: Motorbooks International, 1975.

Eaton, Godfrey. *Ferrari (Great Marques)*. London: Octopus, 1980.

Frostick, Michael. *The Mighty Mercedes*. London: Dalton Watson, 1977.

Garnier, Peter, and Warren Allport (comp). *Rolls-Royce*. Secaucus, N.J.: Chartwell, 1977.

Harvey, Chris. *Haynes' Guide to Postwar Collectors' Cars and Their Values*. Newbury Park, Cal.: Haynes, 1980.

———. *Porsche (Great Marques)*. London: Octopus, 1980.

Kestler, Paul. *Bugatti: Evolution of a Style*. Lausanne, Switzerland: Edita, 1977.

Kimes, Beverly Rae (ed.). *Great Cars and Grand Marques of Automobile Quarterly*. New York: Bonanza, 1976.

Langworth, Richard, Graham Robson, and the Editors of Consumer Guide. *The Complete Book of Collectible Cars: 1940–1980*. Skokie, Ill.: Publications International, 1982.

Lewis, Albert L., and Walter A. Musciano. *Automobiles of the World*. New York: Simon & Schuster, 1977.

Ludvigsen, Karl. *Porsche: Excellence Was Expected—A Complete History of the Sports and Racing Cars*. New York: Dutton, 1977.

Matteucci, Marco. *History of the Motor Car*. New York: Crown, 1970.

Nitske, W. Robert. *Mercedes-Benz: Production Models, 1946–1975*. Osceola, Wis.: Motorbooks International, 1977.

Olyslager, Piet. *Illustrated Motor Cars of the World*. New York: Grosset & Dunlap, 1967.

Roberts, Peter. *Collector's History of the Automobile*. New York: Bonanza, 1978.

Roediger, Wolfgang, and Siegfried Herrmann. *Veterans of the Road*. New York: Hart, 1978.

Rogliatti, Gianni. *Great Collectors Cars*. New York: Grosset & Dunlap, 1973.

Scott-Moncrieff, David. *Three-Pointed Star: The Story of Mercedes-Benz*. London: Gentry, 1979.

Taylor, Rich. *Modern Classics: The Great Cars of the Postwar Era*. New York: Charles Scribner's Sons, 1978.

Wieder, Robert, and George Hall. *The Great American Convertible*. Garden City, N.Y.: Doubleday, 1977.

Wise, David Burgess. *Classic American Automobiles*. New York: Galahad, 1980.

The World of Automobiles: An Illustrated Encyclopedia of the Motor Car. 22 volumes. New York: Columbia House, 1974.

PERIODICALS

Antique Automobile—the official publication of the Antique Automobile Club of America, Hershey, Pa. This is one of the oldest and most valuable periodicals in the entire area of collector cars. Includes a section on cars for sale—antiques, prewar classics, and postwar classics—and many of the cars are illustrated and with prices.

Auto Week—published in Detroit, Mich. There is a cars for sale section, and the emphasis is on older competition cars, some of them classics. A major emphasis of the weekly newspaper is on racing.

The Bulb Horn—the official publication of the Veteran Motor Car Club of America, Andover, Mass. Most cars listed in the for-sale section are true antiques. Many of the cars are illustrated, and their condition is described in some detail. This publication is a must for those interested in learning about the market for antique cars and the availability of antiques.

Car and Driver—published by Ziff-Davis Publishing Company, New York, N.Y. A very popular and readable magazine. The "Car and Driver Marketplace" section lists a few cars for sale each month, some illustrated. Available at newsstands as well as by subscription.

Car Collector and Car Classics—published monthly by Classic Publishing, Inc., Atlanta, Ga. Contains beautiful illustrations of fine collector cars in each issue and has a for-sale section with some of the cars illustrated.

Car Exchange—published monthly by Krause Publications, Inc., Iola, Wis. Has a for-sale section and includes cars from early antiques to special-interest cars.

Hemmings Motor News—published in Bennington, Vt. Has the largest number of automotive items for sale of any car publication, and probably ten times the cars for sale of any other publication.

Horseless Carriage Gazette—the official publication of the Horseless Carriage Club, Downey, Cal. Another extremely valuable publication with a large section on antique and classic cars for sale, but mostly true antiques. Many of the cars for sale are illustrated and described in detail.

Motor Trend—published by Peterson Publishing Company, Los Angeles. The magazine, in addition to its regular features, has a few listings of cars for sale in its "MT Marketplace" section.

Old Cars Weekly—published in Iola, Wis. To the collector car world this is what the *Wall Street Journal* is to the world of stocks and bonds. It is a good way to keep abreast of activities in car collecting and is probably one of the periodicals which the active collector and buyer should have on hand. It covers the major car auctions and many of the minor ones as well and gives auction prices on cars sold in these auctions, in some cases all of the cars sold in the auctions as well as the top prices bid. Upcoming auctions are listed, and the for-sale section is large.

Road and Track—published by CBS publications, New York, N.Y. Has a very good section on cars for sale, and many of the cars are illustrated and described in some detail.

The Robb Report—published in Atlanta, Ga. A monthly magazine for car connoisseurs. Has a very fine section on Rolls-Royce and Bentley cars for sale. The cars are illustrated in color and described in detail. In the "Connoisseur Motorcars" section, makes other than Rolls-Royce and Bentley are offered for sale, and these are also illustrated in color and described in detail.

The Vintage Auto Almanac—a publication of *Hemmings Motor News*, Bennington, Vt. Dealers are listed in specific makes of cars and car parts. Clubs are listed as well as car museums, salvage yards, and publications.

PRICE GUIDES

Antiques and Their Values: Veteran and Vintage Cars— compiled by Tony Curtis, published in 1979 by Lyle Publications, Glenmayne, Galashiels, Selkirkshire, Scotland. Cars are listed alphabetically, and under each make are the outstanding collector years and models and their prices in pounds sterling and dollars.

Auto Capital—an Italian bimonthly magazine published in Milan, Italy. There is a section on many cars made in past years, including collector cars, with present minimum and maximum and sometimes median prices indicated. There is a section giving minimum and maximum prices of cars made from 1975 to the present. There is also a section on used cars for sale, mainly collector

396 **Bibliography**

cars. The magazine is priced on the newsstands in Italy at about $3.50. The address of the publisher is Concorso Alfa Romeo, Via Scarsellini 17, Milan, Italy.

Classic and Sportscar—issued monthly by Haymarket Publishing, Ltd., 38–42 Hampton Road, Teddington, Middlesex, England. There is a very good section on cars for sale, including many collector cars. Subscription is about $45 a year.

Collector Cars—Official Price Guide—by Kruse Auctioneers, Inc., published annually by the House of Collectibles, Inc., Orlando, Fla. Cars are listed by make from A to Z all through the book, each make listed from the earliest car on which a value has been established, through the latest. Prices for three grades of each car priced are presented. Auctions and private sales, when known, are presented. The compilation is by major collector car auctioneer Dean V. Kruse.

The Collector's Guide to Car Values—by Brian Nelson Jones, published annually by Collector-Car Auction Reporter, Inc., Bloomington, Ind. Cars are listed from A to Z and by year from the earliest sold in the year covered to the most recent. The condition is listed and the high bid on the car as well as the reserve placed on the car by the seller and the auction which handled the sale.

Gente Motori—an Italian monthly magazine which is priced at less than $2 on the newsstands in Italy. The address is Via Vitruvio 43, Milan, Italy. Most makes and models of cars are priced according to year of manufacture on the present used-car market—1974 to the present—with minimum and maximum market prices today. There is one price guide or list for the north of Italy, one for the south, one for central Italy and one for the Italian islands—four different sets of market prices.

The Gold Book—published semiannually by Quentin Craft Publications, Inc., El Paso, Tex. This is a value guide for all American cars built from 1950 through 1973 as well as imported cars and light trucks. Cars are listed from A to Z with prices for three grades of each car.

Motorists New and Used Car Price Guide—published monthly by Blackfriars Press Periodicals Limited, Leicester, England. Lists many prices (17,000 prices advertised in a recent issue on the cover). The date a particular make and model car was introduced is given, and the price new. Used-car prices listed according to the condition of the car (three prices for three grades.)

Old Cars Price Guide—published quarterly by Krause Publications, Iola, Wis.

Old Car Value Guide—published annually by Quentin Craft, El Paso, Tex. A comprehensive price guide put out since 1968. A recent issue is 168 pages long and classifies cars as follows: (1) antique, (2) classic, (3) modern classic and special-interest, (4) antique trucks, and (5) antique fire engines. Cars are listed by make and model, body style, and price and according to five grades of condition.

Quattroruote ("Four Wheels")—published monthly at Via Grandi 5/7, Rozzano, Milan, Italy. In every issue there is listed every important make and model of car, both Italian and from other countries, together with maximum and minimum market prices for every year of manufacture from 1970 to 1978. As the years pass, more years are added, so later issues will, no doubt, quote prices on later models as they become more collectible. This is an excellent price guide for the Italian car market. There is also a section on used cars for sale which includes many collector cars.

Ray's A Record of Cars That Sold in Auctions Nationwide—published periodically by John Ray Utter, Shawnee, Okla. A small but comprehensive listing of prices. Cars are listed by make under the auction that sold the car. There is also one issue that combines cars by make, model, and condition sold in major auctions.

Sport Auto—published monthly at 41 Boulevard Barbes, Paris, France, priced in Paris on the newsstands at about $2. Lists present market prices for a number of makes and models of cars built from 1978 to the latest year. Some collector cars are included.

Motor Sport—published monthly at Standard House, Bonville Street, London, England; available in England on the newsstands at about $1 an issue. A subscription mailed to the United States is about $37 a year. This is a leading car price and market magazine—probably the leading one—with hundreds of cars for sale, illustrated. Following prices in *Motor Sport*, issue by issue, gives a good idea of market trend.

Standard Catalogue of American Cars, 1946–1975—issued by the Editors of Old Cars Publications, Iola, Wis. This is an enormous publication containing 736 pages of all models and body styles of American cars made between 1946 and 1975, not just strict collector cars. It even contains specifications and prices on cars that almost no one ever heard of, but still made in the postwar period in America. Present (1982) prices are listed for each make and model, by years, for five grades of cars from mint to "poor."

ACKNOWLEDGMENTS

My very old friend Smith Hempstone Oliver, former Curator of Land Transportation of the Smithsonian Institution, has, over a period of forty years, supplied me with a wealth of material and advice on sports cars and antique cars. He was one of the earliest "spark plugs" of the Sports Car Club of America and the one who developed its publication into a major automobile journal. When I have been really stumped on a collector car problem I knew pretty well that if anyone had the answer, Hemp Oliver would. I knew he could tell me the exact date of the Vanderbilt Trophy Race of 1915 as well as exactly how long the course was.

One of the most energetic and dynamic individuals I have ever known was Frederic Moskovics, former president of the Stutz Motor Car Company of America. It was Frederic Moskovics who developed the prizewinning Stutz Black Hawks of 1927 and 1928. He had been a racing driver in his early days and once told me that he had driven more miles over the highway at over 100 mph than anybody else ever had—and this way back in 1948 when 100 mph on the highway was quite a high speed.

Bob Minshall, president, and Bud Middendorf, chief engineer, of the Pesco Products Division of the Borg-Warner Corporation supercharged the Offenhauser engine installed in my Italian Cisitalia, one of the epoch-making early postwar sports and competition cars. In working out the problems of supercharging I learned an immense amount about boosting torque and horsepower and I came up with a magnificent competition automobile.

I never worked directly with Comm. Enzo Ferrari, but I did work on a plan with him, by phone and mail, to establish a Ferrari plant in the United States in the late 1940s. Actually three of us worked fairly closely together— Count Giorgio Geddes da Filicaia of Florence, Italy, Enzo Ferrari, and myself, with Count Geddes the contact man with Enzo Ferrari and his plant. It was quite clear to me, even back then, that I was dealing with one of the all-time greats of automobile design and automobile racing.

I knew the American Ferrari representative, Luigi Chinetti, when he was a racing driver right after the war, and I was certainly influenced by his knowledge of racing and sports cars and by his ability to drive in competition.

George Felton, my old boss in the National Security Resources Board in Washington, where I was director of the Aircraft Division, was an inspiration to me in the restoration of automobiles. As I recall, his collection consisted of eighteen Rolls-Royces, including the rare four-cylinder model, and I rode many miles to and from races in his Phantom II Rolls-Royce as well as in his Vauxhall 30–98, one of the great sports-competition cars.

Once in a while a person needs a push to get him started in a hobby or new interest. Philip Hazlewood Blake of Northern Ireland gave me that push. I had a passive interest in supercharged Mercedes-Benz cars in my high school days, and when I finished at the Tuck School of Business Adminstration of Dartmouth and got my first job, I was in a position to buy my first classic automobile. Phil Blake continually talked up the Mercedes-Benz S, SS, and SSK, the big supercharged sports-racing cars. What he told me about the performance of these cars, from his actual driving experience, pushed me over the edge, and I bought my first real sports car—a 1927 Mercedes-Benz S with cabriolet body.

This car led to my second purchase. Now I fell under the influence of former Indianapolis driver Ray Gilhooly, who sold me a Mercedes-Benz SS, so I owned an S and an SS at the same time. I spent many hours with Ray getting educated on competition and sports cars. It was Ray who was responsible for the phrase "He pulled a Gilhooly." Ray was racing at Indianapolis when he hit the wall and spun. He not only spun, but he mounted the wall and spun off that. Then he bounced down off the wall and spun again. In all I think he spun five times—and emerged unhurt. That performance was called a Gilhooly, and now the term is applied to any real boner.

Ed Priest and his garage in Chester, Connecticut, started me on auto mechanics and auto repair, and I would spend an entire day, whenever Ed Priest would permit, examining the cars in for repair and watching how he would repair them, back when I was ten years old.

In 1952 I found another quality garage that could do work on any of my cars, no matter how exotic—the garage of J. P. Bostian and his son, Rodney, in Middleburg, Maryland. J. P. Bostian could repair literally anything, and he did—from my Ferrari to my Italmeccanica special to my Ghia-bodied Fiat 8V to my four Mercedes-Benz 300S roadsters and cabriolets to my Rolls-Royce Silver Cloud to my Bentley—besides working on a number of lesser American cars. I will never forget my first bill from this firm in 1952. The labor charge for the mechanical work was $1.10 an hour and for the body and paint shop $2 an hour. The thing about the Bostians, father and son, is that they could improvise, even if they could not find scarce parts. They could fix the car as well as the Ferrari or Rolls-Royce specialists, sometimes fix the cars far better, and at about one-fifth the cost.

To move from the very simple but ingenious shop to the top engineering firm, I had the privilege of knowing Bob Wallace of Phoenix, Arizona, engineer on the Lamborghini and test driver for Lamborghini's great 190-mph Countach. When he finished overhauling a Lamborghini or a Ferrari I would have faith that the job was done at least as well as the factory would have done it.

Stan Zagorski, the magazine and newspaper illustrator, probably knows more about the Lamborghini Miura than anybody else around. He has owned seven of them, many of which he has restored from the ground up. No "layman" is better informed on this great car than Stan, and he has been a major source of information on Lamborghini as well as Maserati.

I have made at least two dozen phone calls to Tom Barrett, in Scottsdale, Arizona, probably the leading collector car dealer in the country, the man who has handled (and handles) the finest classic cars, particularly the great prewar classics. He is dealer, auctioneer, and collector extraordinaire. He tells what he paid for a car and what he sold it for. He is very savvy in the collector car sales and auction business, and if he has not bought or sold a car himself he has often known the purchase or sales price—and he has passed this information along to me, along with such information as whether the car reported as sold at an auction really did sell or was bought in, whether the car was really in the fine condition stated in the catalogue, and whether a car described as original really had a replaced body on it.

Tom Barrett's partner in the auction business, Russ Jackson, has been equally helpful in supplying me with information on the market and the trend of the market and on restoration of collector cars, a specialty of his.

Austin Clark, who for years had the large and superb collection of antiques and classics in his Long Island Automotive Museum, has been helpful in determining exactly what museums were operating and what ones were not operating, despite the fact that many current publications listed them as still in busines. Austin knows collections, what is in them, and where particular cars have gone—into what museum or what collection.

Kenneth Fahnestock, executive administrator of the Classic Car Club of America, has given me a number of extremely useful leads as to who the big collectors are. Probably most big car collectors are members of the Classic Car Club. One member has no fewer than ten Duesenbergs. One member collects just one make of car but has any number of year models of the one make. One member collects just one year and one make of car but has every body style manufactured by the firm in that one year. One member apparently has no fewer than twenty-two garages to house his collection.

Some highly interesting and valuable information was given me by Howard Snyder, president of the Maryland Chapter of the Model T Ford Club International. Mr. Snyder stated that there are at least 50,000 owners of Model T

Fords in the country. He added that there are more Model T Fords of the year 1915 on the road than there should be. Model T's of other years are faked to look like the great and much-wanted 1915 model, near the end of the brass-radiator era. Mr. Snyder's club sells a "judging book" to help owners and buyers determine whether their cars are authentic cars of a specific year of manufacture or are, to a degree at least, fakes.

The greatest mechanic I have had the pleasure of knowing in the past fifteen years is Paul Longo of Texaco of Greenwich, Connecticut. He is something of a combination of Bob Wallace and the Bostian family. He keeps at the problem until it is solved, and many automotive problems require infinite work plus knowledge to solve. He did particularly fine work on my Rolls-Royce and on my Italian competition cars.

Sometimes I think the staff of Motor Classic Corporation of White Plains, New York, are of the opinion that they are simply a department of my publishing company. Again and again they have taken out their cars so that I could see how they drove and rode. Time and time again I have had Nick Soprano, the proprietor, take out a car and drive it somewhere for me to photograph—perhaps a dozen times, perhaps two dozen times, until the photos were ready for publication. It has always been quite an experience to ride with Nick driving, as his style is very reminiscent of that of Juan Manuel Fangio, the Grand Prix driver.

Quite a big acknowledgment must be given to Motor Classic Corporation. Nancy Roth of that organization spent a tremendous amount of time securing facts for me for inclusion in the book. Her knowledge of the very numerous models of Ferrari and other Italian cars is vast. In addition there have been many times I have called her to verify some obscure fact for me or a date a particular race was run, or how the Lamborghini Countach rides and drives. She was always willing to give me the benefit of her knowledge and experience—no matter how busy she was conducting the business of Motor Classic Corporation.

I want to thank Robert Brooks, director of Christie's Motor Car Department, as well as Michael Sedgewick, technical adviser, for their generosity with their time and their frankness in informing me about the collector car market in England and the car market in the United States.

Jeffrey Pattinson and Douglas Jamison of Coys of Kensington spent quite a time with me explaining the market for the higher-priced (and highest-priced) collector cars, the kind of cars they handle.

For at least ten years I have relied heavily on the information on the market for Rolls-Royce cars supplied by Laurence Kayne, Rolls-Royce dealer, Berkeley Square, London. Laurence is probably the largest dealer in secondhand Rolls-Royce and Bentley automobiles in the world, and he has supplied invaluable information on values, which my wife and I have regularly passed along in our column and newsletter.

I could not have written one word of this book without Bernard Skydell, senior editor of the Linden Press, Simon & Schuster. He looked at another automobile book I had written and then asked me to write a very much more comprehensive one. A good editor is harder and harder to find, an editor who will take time to read every word of a manuscript and work to improve it. Collector cars are rather technical, and too many editors know little or nothing about the subject and seem unwilling to learn. Buddy Skydell has learned, and he has worked on the manuscript about as hard as if he himself were writing the book.

There is a serious doubt in my mind that I would have written a book on automobiles without the assistance and encouragement of my wife, Julie. Even more important, she was directly responsible for my ownership of many classic cars. She on her own bought me my first Mercedes-Benz 300S cabriolet as a wedding present. She bought me my second 300S as well. She was determined that I should buy the absolutely beautiful Ghia Fiat 8V coupe that took many prizes in the custom car shows. On a milestone birthday she bought me *two* cars—a Maserati Ghibli and a Lamborghini Miura. She loves the Ferrari Berlinetta Boxer 512 and seems determined either to get me to buy one or to buy one for me. Quite a wife! Besides, she works on every book of mine and has coauthored several hundred of my articles.

INDEX

About the Author

RICHARD H. RUSH has owned fine cars since 1938—eighty-eight automobiles, including great classics and show winners. A Summa Cum Laude graduate of Dartmouth College, he has two master's degrees in Business Administration: an M.B.A. and an M.C.S. His doctorate is from the Harvard Business School. Dr. Rush is a well-known authority on investing in art, antiques, and other collectibles. He is the author of eleven books and more than six-hundred articles in this specialized area of nonstock investment, which outperformed the stock market in the 1970s. A full professor and Department Chairman at the American University, Washington, D.C., he was Contributing Editor of The Wall Street Transcript and wrote the biweekly Art/Antiques Investment Report. He has lectured throughout the U.S. and was invited to give sixteen lectures at the Smithsonian Institution. His interest in cars has been a lifelong love affair; his wife, Julie, shares this interest and took many of the photographs used in this book.